Fragile
Victory

Fragile Victory

The Making and Unmaking of Liberal Order

JAMES E. CRONIN

Yale UNIVERSITY PRESS/NEW HAVEN & LONDON

Published with assistance from the foundation established in memory of Philip Hamilton McMillan of the Class of 1894, Yale College.

Yale University Press books may be purchased in quantity for educational, business, or promotional use. For information, please e-mail sales.press@yale.edu (U.S. office) or sales@yaleup.co.uk (U.K. office).

Set in Minion Pro type by IDS Infotech, Ltd.
Printed in the United States of America.

Library of Congress Control Number: 2022934310
ISBN 978-0-300-24785-5 (hardcover : alk. paper)

A catalogue record for this book is available from the British Library.

This paper meets the requirements of ANSI/NISO Z39.48-1992 (Permanence of Paper).

10 9 8 7 6 5 4 3 2 1

To my grandchildren—
Charlotte Clementine (CC) Shelby,
August Ford Shelby, and
Colin James Cronin

Contents

Note to Readers

The Invasion of Ukraine and Liberal Order

ragile Victory is a history of the creation of a liberal international order in the 1940s, its stabilization and maintenance throughout the postwar era, its dramatic but flawed expansion after the end of the Cold War, and its weakening after 2000. The book argues that the progress of liberal order was always fraught and never entirely secure. Its establishment required inspiration, diligence, and resources and was in no way inevitable. So, too, the related history of liberal democracy, which was nurtured by the existence of a liberal international order and which in turn helped to sustain it. Both have been under threat since the turn of the millennium. Now, Russia's brutal invasion of Ukraine, its targeting of civilian populations, and wanton destruction have made that threat a reality, painted in deep red. Although the solidarity of Western democracies and of NATO in the face of these events has shown the potential resilience of the sort of liberal democratic internationalism that kept the peace in Europe for almost 80 years, the prospects of liberal order and democracy have nevertheless become more uncertain.

Russia invaded Ukraine on February 24, 2022. For months, American and British intelligence had reported that Russian troops were deploying on Ukraine's border and likely to cross it, while Putin, his spokespeople, and compliant Russian media had denied it. The invaders

advanced on multiple fronts: the Donbas region in the east, where supporters and surrogates of Russia had been fighting since 2014; the south,
particularly against ports like Mariupol; and the capital, Kyiv, from the
east and the north. The Russians moved in large numbers of tanks and
artillery, which they used to pound their opponents. Many Ukrainians
died, property destruction was enormous, and millions were forced to
flee. Since the invasion had been predicted for months, it was not a complete surprise. Still, it shocked the world and left experts second-guessing
themselves. Nothing on this scale had occurred in Europe since 1945,
and nothing like this was supposed to happen in the post–Cold War era.

The response brought more surprises. Ukrainians fought back effectively, slowing the advance toward Kyiv. Russian troops began to
withdraw from the area in early April, leaving behind destroyed towns
and dead, apparently executed, inhabitants—clear evidence of war
crimes.[1] Elsewhere, Ukrainians harassed Russian forces using their own
rather basic, and sometimes improvised, weapons and arms supplied by
western countries. Ukraine's success was genuinely heroic. Its leadership,
particularly that of President Volodymyr Zelenskiy, acquitted itself mas-
terfully, demonstrating courage, defiance, and tactical savvy.

Ukraine was aided by the ineptitude of the Russian military, which
was unprepared for resistance and had no plan for overcoming it other
than brutal bombing. It turned out that Russia's armed forces, though
reputed to be highly trained and armed with sophisticated weaponry,
performed poorly. Logistics were botched, and Russia's vast superiority
in numbers and in equipment was largely nullified. It was widely reported that morale was low to begin with and got worse as fighting continued. Though it will be some time before the details and dimensions of
the failures are known, over the first two months of the war, the Russians
were embarrassed, and Putin's boasts were revealed as hollow.

The response of NATO and other allies was the second thing Putin
miscalculated. The United States and its NATO allies worked effectively
together to send supplies to Ukraine and, even more surprisingly, united
behind several rounds of increasingly drastic sanctions that severely
curtailed Russia's ability to participate in the global economy. Gas and
oil were still sent to Europe, and payments flowed back, but serious efforts were at least begun to find alternative energy sources and to lessen

dependence on Russia. Europeans, especially the Germans, counted on Russian imports to heat their homes, drive their cars, and power their industries. Putin counted on this to prevent an effective collective response to his move in Ukraine. It seems he also overestimated the damage that Donald Trump had done to NATO.[2]

Whatever the outcome of Russia's invasion of Ukraine, it has caused a rupture in the international system that will not easily or quickly be repaired. The liberal order was under duress well before Putin's reckless move: Russia's revanchism and China's desire to acquire geopolitical influence to match its economic clout had already made the world more multipolar and less liberal. The war in Ukraine was a more decisive break. Russia, because of Putin's actions, has become something of a pariah. It is difficult to imagine just how it could rejoin the international community whose norms it has so recently and so brazenly violated. When the war ends, on whatever terms, Putin and Russia will want to escape their isolation, but it is not very likely that the nations and institutions that imposed sanctions will be willing to lift them and welcome Russia back without painful concessions on the part of Russia.

Given the drastic consequences of the invasion, it seems important to try to understand why Putin made the choice he did. The simplest approach would be to take him at his word. Unfortunately, the rhetoric and reasoning he offered cannot be taken seriously. Ukraine, with its Jewish president, was not run by neo-Nazis; Ukraine was not committing genocide in the Donbas; and NATO was not directly threatening Russia.[3] Still worse, Putin and his allies have made it clear that they do not regard Ukraine as a legitimate nation but rather as a wayward child of Mother Russia. The logic is to eliminate it as an independent state.

It is tempting to try to locate a kernel of rationality in Putin's thinking and Russian moves, if only because figuring that out might reveal the path to a resolution of the conflict. What appears most plausible is the argument about NATO expansion. Russia long objected to NATO's move to the east, and in the early 1990s American and German leaders did hint to Gorbachev and Yeltsin that NATO, or at least NATO forces, would not encroach on Russia and its interests. There was never a formal agreement, however, and one major party to the discussions—the Soviet Union—ceased even to exist in 1991. The United States and NATO nevertheless made serious efforts to work with Russia to make expansion less threatening. The Clinton administration proposed the "Partnership for Peace" in 1993 as a mechanism for managing the security needs of the countries of Central and Eastern Europe. Russia formally joined in 1994. Clinton and his advisors walked a fine line between the pleas of nations in the east for NATO membership and Russia's opposition to it, making sure to delay the admission of new members until after Yeltsin's reelection in 1996. Accession talks between NATO and Poland, Hungary, and the Czech Republic began in earnest in the fall of 1997, but the process was preceded by the signing of the NATO-Russia Founding Act in May, another effort to assuage Russian concerns. The three countries would formally join in March 1999. At that moment, Russian leaders seemed more upset about the bombing of Belgrade and the fate of the war criminal, Slobodan Milošević, than about NATO enlargement per se.

NATO would expand further, and Russian leaders would continue to object, but the disagreements were managed without crisis. It is reasonable to argue that US and NATO leaders could have done better at reassuring Russia. The declaration at the Bucharest meeting in 2007 stating that the Ukraine and Georgia would become members—pushed by the outgoing Bush administration over the objections of France and Germany—was clearly a mistake. Even so, the statement was not accompanied by a plan for membership and no further efforts would be undertaken to make it happen. While the question of NATO was being debated in the 1990s, Russia had at least twice promised to respect Ukraine's sovereignty. In the 1994 Budapest Memorandum, Ukraine agreed to give up its nuclear missiles, and in response, both Russia and the United States pledged to respect Ukraine's borders and independence. Russia made a similar commitment in 1997 when it reached an agreement with Ukraine on leasing the naval base at Sevastopol on the Black Sea. What was it about the process of NATO enlargement that could have pushed Russia to violate its promises and invade Ukraine? The answer, it would seem, is everything and nothing. NATO's action may have been an irritant to successive Russian leaders, but it would be naïve to think it would cause or provoke Putin's decision to go to war.[4]

If NATO expansion cannot explain the choice for war, what might? The answer is likely extremely complicated, but the fundamental issue would seem to be the divergent histories of Russia and Ukraine since 1991. Chronology is important here. Ukraine's independence referendum in December 1991 precipitated the end of the Soviet Union. Since then, it has been eager to unwind its ties to Russia and has moved, hesitantly and inconsistently, toward becoming a stable democracy. The new nation contained many whose first language was Russian, but that did not prevent them from identifying as Ukrainian as well. Most importantly, the Ukrainians have twice rebelled to rid themselves of a leader who was too close and too beholden to Russia. The first occasion was the so-called Orange Revolution that began in late 2004. In the run-off election of November 21, independent polling agencies announced that Viktor Yushchenko had defeated the pro-Russian candidate Viktor Yanukovich. The next day, however, the official election commission claimed otherwise. Opposition erupted and after massive and sustained protests and violent repression, the election was run again. In January, Yushchenko prevailed and took office.

Politics remained unstable in Ukraine, and corruption undermined faith in political leaders on all sides. Public opinion, meanwhile, moved steadily behind a vision of Ukraine's future as aligned with the West and as a member of the European Union. There were also movements toward "decommunization": more open debate about the reality of the Holodomor, the mass starvation of 1932–33; beheadings of statues of Stalin; and the removal of monuments to Lenin.[5] Yanukovich nevertheless managed to get himself elected president in 2010, but in office he was pressured to acquiesce to an association agreement with the EU. On the eve of signing the agreement in November 2013, he came under intense pressure from Vladimir Putin. Yanukovich reneged and agreed instead to a Russian loan and to joining with Russia in a Eurasian economic organization.

His caving in to Putin provoked the second uprising against the pro-Russian president. It began on November 21, 2013, and brought thousands into the streets and, more specifically, into Independence Square (the Maidan) in Kyiv, which gave the movement its name: Euromaidan. Protests continued to build through November and December and were met with increasing violence and repression. "Anti-protest" laws proposed in mid-January further inflamed opponents, and when talks failed in late February, Yanukovich fled to the east, ending up in Moscow on February 26. The Verkhovna Rada (Ukraine's parliament) declared that he had abandoned his duties and thus forfeited office—while demonstrators entered his massive estate, Mezhyhirya, revealing a zoo, golf course, a fleet of cars, and a boat. An interim president was appointed, and in May elections Petra Poroshenko was elected president.

Russia and Putin were not happy: they responded by sending troops into Crimea at the beginning of March 2014. They seized control with little opposition and quickly organized a referendum on whether Crimea should secede from Ukraine and become part of Russia. A frankly unbelievable majority agreed and the region was incorporated into Russia on March 18. Russia also began to encourage and to assist local pro-Russian forces in the Donbas in their efforts to take control of the region. Russia's allies and supporters advanced, then were pushed back, at which point actual Russian forces fought back. The result was a local stalemate that dragged on into 2022 and in which thousands lost their lives. The invasion of February 2022 initiated a new round of conflict in the eastern part of the country. While Putin's intention was obviously to turn Ukraine away from the Europe and back toward Russia, his tactics backfired. After 2014 Ukrainians became more determined to move toward the West, mainly toward the EU but increasingly also toward NATO. It was this resolve that underpinned their surprisingly strong and effective resistance to the attack by Russian forces in 2022.

The political trajectory of Russia after 1991 ran in the opposite direction. Gorbachev was genuinely interested in moving the country toward the values and practices common in the West. Yeltsin was also inclined in that direction, but his rule was regularly contested by the enduring strength of extreme nationalists and former communists. Liberal political leaders and parties consistently failed to attract voters. Perhaps most important, Russians of all persuasions were deeply traumatized by the economic and political collapse of the early and mid-1990s. It was not just the former KGB officer Putin who regarded the break-up of the Soviet Union as a "geopolitical catastrophe." Well before Putin rendered his judgement, Vladimir Zhirinovsky, the ultranationalist leader, claimed that "the Russian people have become the most humiliated nation on the planet."[6] The implication was that once Russia regained its strength, it would be justified in reasserting its domination within and even beyond its sphere of influence.

The Russian economy stabilized in the late 1990s and began to grow under Putin from 2000. Russia has huge reserves of oil and gas, and rising prices and demand made the country more prosperous. Putin launched a second war against Chechnya and brutally suppressed rebellion there. He also made minor economic reforms in his first years in office and spoke as if he wanted to be a good European. That began to change after 2003: he criticized the United States over the war in Iraq; and he was deeply shaken by the "color revolutions" in Georgia (2003–4), Ukraine (2004–5), and Kyrgystan (2005). These made it clear that regimes in the post-Soviet space were fragile structures and presumably caused Putin to worry that Russians might want their own color revolution. Putin more or less officially announced his turn against the liberal order, and the United States especially, in his speech to the Munich Security Conference in 2007, in which he made a point of denouncing America's global role and institutions like the Organization for Security and Co-operation in Europe (OSCE), which had helped to legitimize the color revolutions. In August 2008, he demonstrated his turn to hostility with a brief military campaign on behalf of separatist regions in Georgia. Putin had handed over the presidency to his close ally Dmitry Medvedev, and in May he became prime minister. When Putin maneuvered to become president again, protests broke out against supposedly rigged elections in early December 2011. These and subsequent demonstrations of discontent were easily enough suppressed, but Putin's fears of a color revolution in Russia were confirmed. Putin blamed the United States, NGOs with western connections, and Hillary Clinton. It was in this context that Russia responded to the Euromaidan revolution with an obvious violation of Ukraine's sovereignty accompanied by real violence.

What was and is Putin's goal? Where will he stop in his drive to restore Russian pride and reverse its supposed humiliation? Geopolitically, the aim seems to be to bring together Great Russia, White Russia (Belarus), and Little Russia (Ukraine) on the model of the Russian empire before 1917. This goal is now, however, being described in messianic and civilizational terms. The Putin government has developed close ties to the Russian Orthodox Church, whose Patriarch Kirill labeled

Putin's rule "a miracle of God" and twice supported invasions of Ukraine. The church helps justify Putin's aggression by claiming that Russia is battling for Christianity and morality against a secular, decadent, and consumerist West that destroys the family and pushes for LGBTQ rights. The link between the Orthodox leadership and the Russian state was perhaps best symbolized by the building of the Cathedral of the Russian Armed Forces, consecrated in June 2020.

Putin has surrounded himself with advisors who echo these views and the reactionary arguments of writers and philosophers like the "white Russian" thinker and avowed fascist Ivan Ilyin; the extreme nationalist writer and editor Aleksandr Prokhanov, advocate for a Russian "fifth empire"; and Aleksandr Dugin, critic of the Euro-Atlantic world. Putin helped to arrange, for example, the removal of Ilyin's remains from Switzerland to a monastery in Moscow in 2005. He also presided over the construction in Moscow of statues of Ivan the Terrible and St. Vladimir, the tenth-century ruler of Kievan Rus who converted to Orthodoxy. The Putin regime has actively worked to promote this odd and toxic ideological brew, appointing a proponent, Vladimir Medinsky, as Minister of Culture from 2012–20. Medinsky was later tasked with leading the Russian team negotiating with Ukraine after the invasion, surely an indication the Putin was not interested in bargaining toward a peace settlement.

Is this alliance of church and state and mixing of apocalyptic religion and government policy merely opportunistic? on one or both sides? Or is it a sign that Putin himself sees his actions as part of a world-historic struggle? Whichever it is—and it could be an amalgam—it makes it hard to envision Russia's role in the world after the invasion of Ukraine. If this is Holy War, how and on what terms are peace and its inevitable compromises possible? Russia has already broken the norms on which the liberal world order was premised: respect for self-determination and sovereignty. How can that breach be repaired?

If Putin's venture were thwarted, and widely perceived to have been, the rift in the international order could begin to heal. That seems unlikely, however, and absent a Russian defeat and a new leadership, Russia will be regarded for a long time as a disruptive force internationally, and the global order will remain fractured. The world economy will also likely be reshaped in important ways. Russia will become more self-reliant, but considerably poorer as a result. It will also reorient its exports away from the West, though its new customers will have less to sell back to Russia. Russia will probably become closer to, perhaps even dependent on, China, but China will be the dominant partner in that arrangement. Countries that have opposed the Russian invasion will also reorient their economies. Even before Russia's move, there was a growing awareness of the need to reshape supply chains and to encourage the domestic production of strategic goods, and the list of those will undoubtedly grow. The Europeans will need to wean themselves from their reliance on Soviet energy sources by speeding up the transition from fossil fuels and, in the meantime, by diversifying the sources of essential goods. These processes will not happen overnight, but they would seem almost inevitable, and the effect will be a reconfigured global economy.

None of this means that the institutions through which the international system functions will all collapse. They will stand, but they will function less well, and there will likely be more violations of norms, more conflicts, and more violence. It will be difficult if not impossible to describe the international system as liberal or even rules-based. Russia and Putin will not be completely ostracized, for they have critical resources and, however poorly it has performed of late, a powerful and nuclear-armed military. Even though much of the world recoiled in horror at Russia's action in Ukraine, countries like China, India, and Indonesia did not impose sanctions or cut ties.[7] But the more prosperous West did, and given its economic clout and its central role in international finance and the fact that Russia's exports mostly flow in that direction, Putin's continued isolation will have major costs. There will be pain all around, and fear of what the resort to the politics of force portends. The promise of liberal order will endure, but realizing it will take longer and face more obstacles than it had before the invasion of Ukraine.

Notes

1. On the Russian military's mixed record since 2014, see Lawrence Freedman, *Ukraine and the Art of Strategy* (New York: Oxford University Press, 2019), and his posts on the 2022 invasion on *Comment is Freed: Sam and Lawrence Freedman*, samf@substack.com.

2. Very big questions about NATO's future nevertheless remain, even if they have been momentarily eclipsed. See, for example, Adam Tooze, "The Second Coming of

Nato: The Alliance Has Been Revived –But It Can't Save the West," *New Statesman*, May 18, 2022.

3. There are extreme nationalists in Ukraine with links to a sordid if complicated past, but they do not run the state. In recent elections, they have received very few votes.

4. Much has been written on the issue of NATO and Russia. For the most recent and reliable assessment, see M. E. Sarotte, *Not One Inch: America, Russia, and the Making of Post-Cold War Stalemate* (New Haven: Yale University Press, 2021); and also Serhii Plokhy and Mary Sarotte, "The Shoals of Ukraine: Where American Illusions and Great-Power Politics Collide," *Foreign Affairs* 99, No. 1 (January/February 2020), 85–91.

5. See especially Serhii Plokhy, *The Frontline: Essays on Ukraine's Past and Present* (Cambridge, MA: Harvard University Press, Harvard Series in Ukrainian Studies, 2021); Larry Wolff, "Governed in Slavery: the troubled rebirth of Ukraine," *TLS (Times Literary Supplement)*, May 27, 2022; and Tim Snyder, "The War in Ukraine Is a Colonial War," *New Yorker*, April 28, 2022.

6. *New York Times*, January 11, 1996.

7. See Angela Stent, "The West vs. the Rest," *Foreign Policy*, May 2, 2022; and, more generally, Anne Applebaum, "There Is No Liberal World Order," *The Atlantic*, May 2022.

Introduction

Liberal Order and Its Troubled History

The results of two elections in 2016—the "yes" vote in the Brexit referendum in Britain and the election of Donald Trump in America—shocked observers and participants in equal measure. The most prominent supporters of Brexit were clue- less and without a plan on the morning after, and by all accounts Trump did not expect to win either. Opponents of Brexit and Trump had diffi- culty believing what had happened and kept thinking and hoping that the results did not mean what in fact they did mean. Brexit seemed so inexplicably wrong that many thought it would be reversed outright or somehow fudged. Trump was so outrageous as a candidate that people could not help but hope that a different person would emerge once he assumed office. Such hopes were soon disappointed in both the UK and the US. What remained were two overriding questions: how did these largely unpredicted results come about; and what did the choices portend?

The questions were closely related, for both votes were essentially negative, rejections of what had been assumed by many to be stable and worthy features of the political and economic landscape at home and abroad. While the roots of these rejections may well have been domestic, as voters do not regularly make decisions based on foreign policy, what was explicitly rejected in each case was the nation's status in and engage- ment with the world outside. Internal and external were inextricably linked. Brexit, by definition, was a campaign about whether the United Kingdom should break its association with its closest neighbors and largest trading partner and withdraw from the organization through which it effectively managed its relationships with the global economy.

Trump's pitch was, as he put it at his inauguration, about "American carnage," which had come about because foreigners had systematically taken advantage of the US. In Trump's telling America had been disadvantaged by trade, most obviously by China but also by its NATO allies. The United States was also supposedly inundated by waves of unwanted and possibly criminal immigrants, legal and illegal, and by refugees whose claims were spurious. The appropriate response, according to Trump, was a policy of "America First" that would entail restrictions on immigrants and refugees, demands that allies pay more for the security the United States provided, the repudiation and renegotiation of trade deals like NAFTA (the North American Free Trade Agreement), and the imposition of tariffs to redress trade imbalances. Trump's domestic program was minimal and frankly contradictory—tax cuts, the Republican staple, plus increased spending on infrastructure and no cuts to, even possibly increases in, entitlements. He meant little of what he said, or so it would seem by his behavior in office, and he achieved very little beyond a massive tax cut skewed to benefit the well-to-do. On matters of foreign policy, including trade, presidents have more discretion; and Trump moved, fitfully and often ineffectively, to make things happen in that sphere. Much the same could be said of British Conservatives since 2016: they gestured toward a move away from their signature policy of austerity, but did very little to reverse it; instead, they spent virtually all of their energy trying to sort out Brexit and eventually make it happen. The emphasis on the international, and on external threats, was almost a substitute for the lack of a domestic program, serving to anchor a campaign whose mass appeal was grounded in a sense of grievance and powered by an aggrieved national identity.

The import of the international in Brexit and with Trump has not unreasonably been seen as a "crisis of the liberal international order."[1] This formulation is useful in identifying something quite distinctive in the two elections, but it needs to be clarified and qualified. It is necessary, above all, to determine just what is meant by liberal order. The phrase is commonly used to describe the principles underlying the set of institutions created near and at the end of the Second World War that largely governed the postwar relations of states and the workings of the international economy. The ideas that animated those responsible for designing and putting these in place had deeper roots, of course, but their realization was a direct consequence of the effort to bring order out of the chaos of the 1930s and the disaster of the war.[2]

Characterizing the postwar order as liberal nevertheless demands a series of qualifications. How liberal was this order; and was it in any sense a world order? Classical liberalism meant free markets, laissez-faire in internal economic policy and free trade with the world. Though the postwar international order aimed to free up trade after the turn to protectionism in the 1930s, for some time it was more an aspiration than a reality for many states and key economic sectors. The political dimension of liberalism was commonly and plausibly understood to imply democracy and free elections. Those who designed the postwar order sought to promote democracy in general, but the exceptions were so egregious as to raise doubts about the design itself. The biggest exception was empire. The country that did the most to bring the new order into existence was the United States, which chose to regard itself as anti-imperial but whose practice often belied that claim. Not only was America large enough to be an empire or imperial state, it got that way by acting much like a marauding empire, conquering and subjugating the previous inhabitants of the territories it came to rule. The United States also had several small colonies of its own but, unlike the European empires with which the nation so often contrasted itself, had no real interest in obtaining or administering a substantial overseas empire. On the other hand, the United States would build a postwar order in alliance with those older empires run by the British, the French, the Dutch, the Belgians, and the Portuguese. Until decolonization stripped those countries of their imperial possessions, the liberal international order was complicit in the denial of political independence and self-government to huge numbers of colonized people. It may well be that ending colonialism was implicit in the project of creating and extending liberal order, but it took a long time—and much struggle and pain—for it to be achieved.[3]

A liberal international order is almost by definition to be built on liberal politics within states and commitments to foster democratic norms within and across states. This connection, too, must be qualified, if only because of the obvious democratic deficits of the dominant power in the liberal order, the United States. Democracy and voting and representation for white men came early in America, quite a bit later for white women. For Black Americans it took a civil war and two different reconstructions for democracy to become a reality. Even then, it was far less secure and complete than for whites. Again, the promise of liberal order, particularly in the context of the Cold War, may well have encouraged the adoption of more democratic norms and practices in America, but promise and aspiration are not descriptions of what actually is.

The fact that the setting up of a liberal international order coincided with the moment of American global leadership requires that the concept be qualified still further. It is obvious that the institutions and structures of the postwar order reinforced the dominance of the United States as a hegemonic power. Understandably, the invocation of liberalism and liberal order could and did serve as cover and justification for policies that were in the interests of the United States. Whether that is sufficient reason to regard the entire structure as a vehicle to secure US global domination is rather more questionable, for it implies a standard of behavior that no great power has ever lived up to. Clearly, in bargaining out the terms of the postwar order, the United States and its allies and rivals sought to protect and advance their national interests, but they chose to do so in a manner that involved compromise and collaboration as well as self-interest and competition.

That choice was significant. For states to have risen completely above self-interest would have been unimaginable. To imagine specifically that the United States, having spent blood and treasure to defeat the Nazis and Japan, would have decided after the war to cede authority to the defeated or to states that had failed to prevent the coming of war and could not on their own stand up to the aggressors in that war, comes close to fantasy. It was in any case not a fantasy widely shared in the United States; and absolutely no one could voice such a hope or plan in the other country that could reasonably be said to have won the war, the Soviet Union. What the United States did choose was to work with allies to set up an order that involved a degree of shared decision making and that put distinct limits on America's freedom of maneuver.[4] It should come as no surprise that the United States and its allies continued to calculate and seek to advance their separate national interests while constructing an international order that was multilateral and largely rules-based, that mostly promoted democracy, and whose economic institutions helped fashion a more open world economy. What was notable was that the most powerful country in the world decided to pursue its national interest by creating such a liberal order. To label this behavior imperial is also ahistorical, for it ignores what was historically distinctive in an order defined by the bargained and brokered dominance of the United States.

Limits then, and qualifications, must be attached to any notion of liberal order. The most severe limit to the postwar order was, of course, geographic. The existence of the Soviet Union and its control over Eastern Europe meant that nothing like liberal order or liberalism was possible there. The Chinese Revolution removed another huge area and a giant share of the world's population from the order that was being constructed in the West and Japan. The exclusion of these lands and peoples in the East meant that the writ of liberal order and democratic rule would not prevail in large parts of the world. Liberal order, in other words, obtained on only one side of the Cold War divide and was embedded within a much broader Cold War order.[5] This limitation, however, may well have been useful, perhaps even a precondition for its relative success. By confining its workings in geographic space, the Cold War allowed liberal order to be established and stabilized. Could anything like it have taken root and functioned effectively on a grander scale?

Clarifying the meaning of liberal order, qualifying how liberal it was, and taking note of its limits are essential to understanding its history as well. Telling that history is in turn critical to assessing its present crisis and prospects. It will become clear that recent challenges to liberal order were not simply the product of external shocks. They emerged from the combined effects of actions and processes occurring outside the sphere of liberal order *and* from its internal development *and* from choices and adaptations made to the system in the past. The history of liberal order was extremely complicated and in no way a linear or logical progression.

Its creation was not easy or automatic but required unique conditions; its maintenance was not assured, but very much depended on prosperity and on political systems whose effective functioning was by no means guaranteed. The economic formula that was adopted at its founding and followed for the quarter century after 1945 largely ceased to work in the 1970s and was replaced with market-friendly policies that altered the meaning of liberal order. The order's ability to prevail in the Cold War owed as much to the failures of the Soviet Union as to its inherent superiority. The massive extension of liberal order after the Cold War was based partly on its attractions but also on the absence of viable alternatives. The stalled progress of that expansion, and in some cases its reversal, after the turn of the century was predictable. And finally, the weakening of support for liberal order within the United States, Britain, and elsewhere had its origins in the evolution of domestic political systems and in the consequences of economic policies decided upon through those systems.

Making the history of liberal order understandable means putting its development in context, deciding what the changing context allowed and precluded, and how context and prior choices combined to produce the outcomes they did. The illiberal policies and politics of the 1930s were the realities that the construction of a liberal order was meant to avoid. Understandings of that dismal decade informed the details of postwar planning. So, too, did the hard realities of war: the early success of Germany and Japan meant that much of the world would have to be reshaped, political institutions recast, and economies thoroughly rebuilt. The enormity of the tasks more or less demanded a global response and presaged the need for a world order of some sort. What sort of order would be possible and whose interests would be privileged were also largely determined by the war. The emergence of the United States and the Soviet Union as the dominant military powers, and of the US as the most productive economy would mean that however much the rhetoric of war promised democracy and political independence, those two states would make sure to secure their interests in the peace. More specifically, it meant that the defense needs of the USSR would decide the fate of Eastern Europe, the part of the world that probably suffered the most during the war, first under Nazi conquest and occupation and then during and after its "liberation" by the Soviets.

The Cold War that ensued forced the architects of postwar order to adapt their plans in unanticipated ways, developing new policies like the Marshall Plan and institutions like NATO and the Warsaw Pact. The effect was to create a global division in which liberal order was operative and democracy the norm in one part of a now bipolar world while a more authoritarian and repressive order would be the model elsewhere. Both sides sought stability, but achieving it was quite straightforward for the Soviets, who outlawed opposition and enforced conformity through secret police, party-dominated political systems and, on occasion, military force. Engineering political stability in the West and among allies elsewhere was much trickier, for it required more or less voluntary consent, participation, and ultimately elections. That meant reestablishing democratic political systems in Germany, Japan, and Italy, where democracy had perished in the 1930s, and reviving viable systems in other parts of Europe where they had been put in abeyance, compromised, or violently crushed by the Nazis.

In practice, the key would be putting in place and making legitimate politics and parties that converged near the political center and avoided extremes of right and left. Parties of the right had been largely discredited by their association with the ideas of the Nazis or Fascists. For political systems to work, more moderate center-right parties were essential. The most successful new ventures would be linked to churches and inspired by Christian social thought and values. The problem of creating a stable center-left was equally hard, for liberals and social democrats had been persecuted by the extreme right before and during the war, then later eclipsed by the Communists in the resistance in places like Italy and France. The Soviet occupation of East Germany ironically helped to revive the fortunes of the Social Democratic Party in West Germany, where the German Communist Party would be outlawed. In France and Italy, by contrast, throughout the postwar years Communists continued to receive the votes of a good section of the working class. So long as they did, those parties were excluded from power at the national level by centrist coalitions that frequently included socialists or social democrats but that were seldom led by the center-left.

Ensuring political stability required less innovation in the United States and Britain, for center-left and center-right parties emerged in strong positions from the war and early postwar reconstruction. Even in these countries, stability would be enhanced by moves toward the center encouraged by the exigencies of the Cold War. Bipartisan agreement on the need to fight the Cold War provided at least one issue on which Republicans and Democrats could work together. The belief that the US needed to stay involved globally, to spend the money necessary for that involvement and for the maintenance of the alliances and multinational commitments through which the Cold War would be fought came naturally to Democrats and liberal Republicans, but some Republicans resisted. The issue would not be resolved until the party rejected Robert Taft and nominated Dwight Eisenhower in 1952. Eisenhower's election and presidency also marked the moment when Republicans effectively came to accept the New Deal, although hopes of reversing it continued to animate the party's right wing and certain business interests. In Britain, the Cold War also had a centering effect: Churchill's Iron Curtain speech, for example, was regarded by the Attlee government as consistent with its policies; and Bevin's efforts to take the lead in organizing on behalf of the Marshall Plan and then NATO were supported by top Tories. It was in the shadow of the deepening Cold War that British Conservatives reconciled themselves to the achievements of the Labour governments of 1945–51.

The unprecedented economic boom of the first three decades after the war contributed massively to political stability in the West. Prosperity seemed to confirm the wisdom of the choices and compromises made in the early postwar years and reinforced the legitimacy of political leaders and party systems. Economic growth was made possible by a deep structural shift in demand. Depression, the war, and postwar reforms, plus the newfound strength of trade unions, brought a redistribution of income from elites to ordinary workers and consumers. The shift made it possible for ordinary people to consume more than mere necessities, which in turn encouraged businesses to invest in the technologies of mass production. The effect was not merely sustained but relatively equitable growth unique to the history of capitalism. The political effects could not be anything but beneficial.

Politics was not unruffled. Four issues could have, and to some extent did, more than ruffle the surface of politics in the first quarter cen-

tury after 1945. These were trade and immigration, which were to prove
so destabilizing in subsequent decades, along with decolonization and
the question of race, particularly in the United States. The politics of
trade were clear enough after the war: the United States wanted a more
or less open system of exchange and strongly encouraged others to eliminate protections on domestic industries. There was resistance, and those
resisting could easily cite contradictions and inconsistency in the American position, with its protections for agriculture and other industries.
What made it possible to move toward more open arrangements was
economic growth and increasing world trade, which eased the pain for
industries and regions that lost protection. For the most part the issue
was not debated in the US domestic sphere but displaced outward to
negotiations between states and international organizations and upward
from Congress to the president. The effect was that the issue was not
particularly salient until at least the 1980s.

The politics of immigration were also less troublesome and less
salient than they had been or would later become. In the United States,
the relative absence of debate was due primarily to the fact that immigration was already severely restricted by legislation passed in 1924. The
postwar boom would require more workers, but this was achieved by
migration from north to south and from the countryside to the city. The
movement of African Americans from the depressed South to the more
prosperous North would have major effects on those who made the
transition, on the areas affected, and on parties and politics. The effects
were not about immigration per se but rather race, and it seems likely
that if they had been about both at the same time, the consequences
would have been more explosive. In Europe and Japan, immigration did
not become a major source of political conflict because it was mostly
through internal migration that the demand for more labor was satisfied. None of this meant that Americans or Europeans had become liberal and tolerant on questions of immigration. It required, after all, only
a modest flow of immigrants from the former colonies to trigger race
riots in Britain. The point, rather, is that for largely accidental reasons
the issues were less important politically than they would later become.

Decolonization was the third issue that could have fueled partisan
divides, divided parties, and disrupted democratic politics. It largely

did not, though the two major exceptions—Algeria and Indochina—demonstrated the potential for the battle over colonies to rattle domestic politics. The French had been determined to restore control over their empire after 1945 and fought bitterly to do so. They failed to achieve their goal in Indochina and bequeathed that conflict to the United States in 1954. The United States would continue to fight in Vietnam and the effort would elicit mass protests at home that forced Lyndon Johnson from the White House and came close to tearing the country apart. By the time the French left Indochina, efforts to win independence for Algeria were underway and the French fought a nasty war to thwart the movement. Algeria was closer to France and had a more intimate relationship with the colonial power, and the French presence there was anchored by a substantial population of settlers and backed by supporters in the military. The political fallout from the insurgency and efforts to suppress it toppled the Fourth Republic in 1958, bringing De Gaulle back to power; and when the general decided that the struggle was lost, it almost got him killed.

Elsewhere, however, decolonization was less destabilizing than it might have been. For Britain, the key was that almost everyone understood the strategic impossibility of holding onto the empire. The decisions to grant independence to India and to withdraw from Palestine in 1947 prompted few regrets, even from Tory supporters of empire. Britain was not eager to abandon the rest of its empire so quickly, however, and conducted brutal counter-insurgency operations in Malaysia and Kenya. These could well have provoked more controversy, but did not attract the attention necessary to spark large-scale protests. Britain and France did join together for one last effort to hold the line against decolonization at Suez in 1956. The venture failed utterly and caused the resignation of the British prime minister, Anthony Eden. That failure became the signal for a broad retreat. Well before the British and French had reconciled themselves to loss of empire, Belgium and the Netherlands had already been forced to do so. Decolonization was undoubtedly the most significant geopolitical transformation between 1945 and 1989—and it produced organizational innovations, like the Bandung Conference, the Non-Aligned Movement and, within the United Nations, the founding of the UN Conference on Trade and Development

(UNCTAD) and the increasing importance of the General Assembly—but its effects on postwar politics within liberal states were modest.

Race mattered much more, but the political consequences were mostly confined to the United States. The battle for civil rights for African Americans was the most important social and political movement of its time and its success added up to a second Reconstruction. It led to a broad-based, if still incomplete, desegregation of American society, as its workforce, its schools and public institutions, and its culture became much more integrated. Its crowning legislative achievements were the Civil Rights Act of 1964 and the Voting Rights Act of 1965. Every step along the way was controversial and provoked a predictable backlash from white Americans. The political effects reshaped the party system and the nation's political geography. What they did not do, ironically, was to bestow a more or less permanent advantage on either of the two main parties. The continuing battle over race led many whites in the South to side with the Republicans while encouraging Black voters to favor Democrats across the country. With more African Americans migrating from the South to cities in the Northeast, the Midwest, and the West Coast, the Democratic Party retained or gained strength in these regions. Overall, the electoral balance remained broadly similar, while the most notable effect was to make Republicans the party of white Americans. With this new identity, they effectively chose to recast their appeal and their program to favor white voters and to disfavor African Americans and other racial minorities. This was a serious shift that would become more toxic over time, but not something that threatened political stability even during the height of the agitation for equal rights.

If the first task of the book is to chart the creation of liberal order and the second is to investigate the conditions and choices that made it more or less stable, the final task is to examine and explain what happened to weaken liberal order. The process began with the economic crisis of the 1970s. The faltering of the economy was due in large part to the external shocks of the oil crises, but also to the inability of the policies pursued in the early postwar era to deliver growth at the same level after the early 1970s. There was also a geopolitical dimension to the disruption: the inability of Western countries to compel oil producers to sell in sufficient quantity and at the accustomed price was widely understood as a sign of political weakness. Even more important, the difficulty that governments had in controlling inflation and regenerating growth seemed to demonstrate that the political and economic formulas that had shaped policy since 1945 no longer worked. Existing policies seemed refuted by events, and the parties and leaders that attempted to make them work also became discredited.

In response, Thatcher and Reagan pioneered a turn to the right, specifically a turn away from what had worked for a quarter century and toward a policy framework that relied more exclusively on markets. This "neoliberal" turn was pushed furthest in Britain and the United States but affected other countries as well. By 1989, the resulting "Washington Consensus" affected not only domestic economic policy making but had been accepted as the set of rules by which the international economy operated. The new paradigm had mixed success. It had been put into place in an effort to tame inflation, and on that measure it succeeded: inflation was effectively defeated by the mid-1980s. How much the policies of Thatcher and Reagan contributed is difficult to say, for the early 1980s witnessed the steepest recession since the Great Depression. When the economy did recover, moreover, it never again approached the rates of growth of the postwar boom. What did happen was that the postwar settlement—in terms of the balance between capital and labor, the rich and the poor—was redefined. Social protections were weakened and the gap between rich and poor began to widen. The liberal order would become less generous as it became more market-oriented, and what it could offer ordinary people was less attractive. The move benefited parties of the center-right, which dominated the politics of the 1980s and early 1990s. It also confronted parties of the center-left with difficult choices: already weakened by structural changes that were eroding their bases of support, should they embrace or resist the policies implemented by their opponents?

The turn to markets in the West was not of great consequence for the East and probably had little effect on the outcome of the Cold War. The 1980s had begun with a heightening of Cold War tensions and rhetoric, but the decade ended with the collapse of "actually existing socialism" in Eastern Europe and the disintegration of the Soviet Union itself in 1991. Socialism failed in these countries largely due to its own flaws. It could not generate consistent growth in output or living standards, and its draconian policies to compel compliance could not disguise the illegitimacy of its rule in Eastern Europe or the futility of Soviet efforts to make the system work. The problems were not accidental or of recent origin, but built into these systems. When Mikhail Gorbachev opted to reform the economy and politics of the USSR, and made it clear that the Soviets would not intervene to prop up the regimes of Eastern Europe, the end came very quickly.

When the collapse came, it created an opportunity for liberal order, for capitalism, and for political democracy to extend their reach. The eastern part of Europe, including the republics of the former Soviet Union, were all to undergo rapid transitions from command economies to market economies and from undemocratic to democratic rule. They were encouraged to do so by the United States and its allies. They were given some financial support to ease the pain, but the prevalence of market-oriented policies in the West and in international financial institutions meant that support was very limited. The result was that progress toward market economies and political democracy was modest and accompanied by considerable economic pain and political instability; and in consequence "democratic backsliding" remained a possibility throughout the region.

The extension of liberal order was also limited by the unwillingness of voters in countries like the United States and Britain to support policies to organize a more stable global order. There was great reluctance, for example, to get involved in sorting out the bloody conflicts that attended the breakup of Yugoslavia. Over time a rather weak consensus emerged that the United States and its allies, possibly working through the United Nations or at least through NATO, should be willing to undertake "humanitarian intervention" in places where local rulers threatened the lives and rights of citizens. This consensus evaporated quickly, as its consequences became clearer and as other powers objected to interference in what they regarded as their spheres of influence. What had appeared as a great opportunity for liberal order to expand and put in place a more liberal world of states had become, by the late 1990s and early 2000s, a controversial undertaking with uncertain results.

The end of the Cold War also had unforeseen results in domestic politics as well as in the level of public support for the spread and maintenance of liberal order. It became clear that in retrospect the Cold War had served as a glue that kept political parties, particularly on the right, attached to the center. Without the Cold War, center-right parties in numerous countries moved further to the right and certain parties that had been dominant for much of the postwar era, like the Christian Democrats in Italy and the Liberal Democrats in Japan, fell apart. Politics became less predictable and less solidly grounded, including in the United States and Britain. At the same time, the appeal of what has been labeled market fundamentalism began to fade as memories of the 1970s became dimmer. By the 1990s, the crusade to liberate animal spirits and unleash rapid growth had been replaced, it seemed, by a more mean-spirited refusal to raise taxes and by blunt efforts to rein in entitlements. With the attractions of market-based policies waning, parties and leaders on the right began to flirt with other issues—extreme nationalism, anti-immigrant sentiment, and the various causes summed up by the phrase "culture wars"—to win votes. It was a dangerous move, and it would only get worse after 2000.

The weakened foundations of liberal order and democratic stability would be fully on display after the turn of the millennium, when novel challenges arose and enduring problems became more formidable. There were external challenges: the increasing resistance to and declining appetite for humanitarian intervention; the attacks of 9/11 and America's blundering and destructive response; Russia's turn to authoritarianism and toward a more revanchist foreign policy, especially in its "near abroad"; and the rise of China economically and politically. The Great Recession, which began in 2008 and persisted for several years, was not exclusively an external shock or challenge, but it was global in scope and represented a setback for the economic policies pursued in the West, especially the United States, and reinforced the external challenges to liberal order.

These were accompanied by internal challenges, although the fact that they happened in many countries more or less simultaneously suggests connections across borders, at least in terms of causes. The starting point here were the asymmetrical shifts in the politics of left and right. The center-left had for decades been confronted with an erosion of support from its previously solid bases of support: the working class and trade unions. Structural changes in the economy and in technology were more important causes of this than the actual behavior or policies of particular parties, but policy was not always responsive. What center-left parties did do, and fairly effectively, was to try to attract voters from other social groups—professionals, minorities, and working women— by incorporating the issues they cared about into party programs and policies. Overall, this meant an effort to enlarge their appeal while remaining attached to the political center. Parties on the right, by contrast, chose explicitly to abandon the center, and the ending of the Cold War facilitated that choice. A commitment to market-oriented politics was common to most (though not all) parties and movements of the right, but to that would now be added more unsavory appeals to nationalism, traditional values, and antipathy to immigrants, especially Muslims and, by a curious extension, to the European Union in certain parts of Europe. The result was a surge of populist, and frequently authoritarian, parties across Europe.

The move toward populism, and its antipathies and grievances, also occurred in Britain and the United States. In Britain, it took the form of Euroscepticism, which meant not so much skepticism toward Europe as open hostility. It would take almost three decades for this stance to take over the Conservative Party, and it required the formation of a separate party, UKIP (the United Kingdom Independence Party), with its own charismatic leader, Nigel Farage, to make it a reality. The decisive moment came with the Brexit referendum of 2016, which was won by the "Leave" supporters. Republicans in America had been moving to the right since the election of Ronald Reagan, if not earlier. They were aided from the 1990s by the growth of a uniquely effective right-wing media environment. Though they faced the same problem crafting a convincing appeal to voters as other right-wing parties committed to market fundamentalism and austerity, they were more willing to invoke the culture wars to attract support. Their efforts would get a major boost with the election of Barack Obama. The reality of a Black president provoked immediate hostility from whites, who were told, or understood already, that demographic trends were loosening their grip on the levers of power and threatening their privileges. Donald Trump's first serious foray into national politics in 2011 built on and played to this hostility by questioning Obama's citizenship.

In his run for the presidency, Trump would give prominence to two further divisive issues: immigration and trade. Republicans had been ambivalent about both before Trump, but Trump was not inhibited by any commitment to ideological principles. He had no difficulty denouncing Mexican immigrants as rapists and murderers and proposed to build a wall to keep them out; and he promised a trade war, or a series of trade wars—they were "easy to win," he claimed—to get not only China but also America's allies to agree to measures to erase America's trade deficit. What Trump managed to do was to combine the negative partisanship of most Republicans with more populist appeals to racial animosity, anti-immigrant sentiment, resentment of foreigners, and fears of foreign competition. It took a political newcomer, an outsider, to make it work, for more "mainstream" Republicans had past commitments that made it impossible fully to embrace Trump's message. Also, they could not claim his outsider status and were unwilling or unable to puncture the myths he wove about his career as a successful businessman. Nor could they match the hours of free publicity Trump got from his outrageous pronouncements. All these factors produced Trump's limited, but in the end decisive, success in the 2016 election. He would not win the support of a majority of Americans, losing the popular vote to Hillary Clinton by close to 3 million, but he scored enough victories in closely contested states to prevail in the Electoral College.

The 2016 votes represented dramatic turns, proving that liberal order was never inevitable, only superficially stable, always a matter of choice and political will. The study ends with a very quick look at politics after 2016, partly to determine whether what seemed ominous at the time has proved to be as bad as feared—or even worse—and partly to assess the state of liberal order and democracy and the threats to both after Trump, after Brexit, and after the invasion of Ukraine.

An Illiberal World of Rival "Orders"

The order that came into being in and around 1945 was liberal in inspiration but compromised in detail. Deep inspiration may have come from the vision of Woodrow Wilson, but the details of the postwar arrangements were crafted in response to more recent experiences and understandings. The most important were the Great Depression, the rise and temporary triumph of fascism, and the horrors of the Second World War. Memories of the interwar era, revised and reinforced by the war itself, told the victors what must be avoided and what must be ensured in any new world.

Understanding the resulting liberal order requires, then, a brief look both at the realities of the years 1929–39 and how people came to make sense of these during the war. It seems clear that what made the 1930s a uniquely illiberal decade was the simultaneous retreat of democracy, the abandonment of economic liberalism, and the failure of the international system to prevent another major war. All three were products largely of the Great Depression and, more specifically, of the failure of governments to find the means to end the slump. Without the depression, the relations of states might have been managed without a great conflict and, without the criticism and popular disaffection that the economic crisis invited, democracy may have prevailed. It was not to be. The entire interwar period was bedeviled by economic issues. A full decade after the "great crash" of 1929, Western economies had not yet recovered or, as in the United States, had partially revived and then slipped back into recession. Only rearmament decisively ended the slump. Equally troubling, as of 1939 the world economy had divided into rival blocs that typically overlapped with empire or with plans for empire, and these blocs would shape the alliances that confronted each other in wartime.

Before war broke out and made things worse, democratic governments were largely on the defensive, unable to generate solid support for the moderate reforms that appeared necessary to make democracy stable. By contrast, authoritarian regimes and rulers were ascendant in most countries in Europe and the norm across much of the world. Italian Fascists had pioneered the repudiation of liberal democracy, but the Nazis surpassed in repression and brutality anything that Mussolini had done, and they were committed to spreading their system and conquering those who resisted or did not fit into their racial ordering of society. Authoritarians were in power in Eastern and southern Europe from the Baltics to Greece and across to Spain and Portugal. Further east, the Soviet Union under Stalin was a brutal regime that brooked no dissent. Beyond Europe, empires governed much of the world; and although they sought increasingly to portray themselves as benign, they, too, were all variations on authoritarianism and invariably based upon racial hierarchies.

The international system itself was threatened by the turn toward nationalism in economics and in geopolitics and the movement away from democracy. The settlement reached at the end of the First World War was fraught and always fragile: the war had destroyed four longstanding empires in Central and Eastern Europe and replaced them with new states in which democracy had great difficulty taking root and which would prove unable to withstand the challenges they would face. Most important, the settlement did not resolve the great imbalance destabilizing European geopolitics ever since 1871—the role of Germany. Rather, it made it worse. German grievances dating from its defeat, the settlement, and the imposition of reparations were central to the country's ensuing political instability and to the triumph in 1933 of Hitler and the Nazis.[1] In power, the Nazis set about rejecting the outcome of the Great War, the Versailles settlement, and the institutions that had

arisen from the peacemaking and enforced its terms. The European victors of 1918 had no consistent or effective response: first they resisted
German, or Italian, demands, then chose to appease both, and then belatedly decided to resist again. As war threatened in the 1930s, they were
unwilling or unable to bring the newest great power, the Soviet Union,
into an alliance against Hitler and Mussolini. The United States remained aloof. In the end, only the actions of Germany and Japan brought
together the coalition that ultimately defeated them.[2]

    These three interlaced crises and the fact that none could or would
be solved short of war served to discredit all matter of conventional wisdom in politics, economics, and international relations and ensured that
the postwar world would be constructed on different principles and institutions and with new people in charge. Of course, no new order is
completely new, no practice utterly without precedent, but what most
distinguished the postwar order was how it was designed to ensure that
the past, especially the recent past, would not be repeated.

Economic Failure

The world economy never truly recovered from the First World War.
Leaders spent the decade after its end trying to re-create the prosperity
that they remembered from before 1914. Those memories were not always accurate and the nostalgia for the earlier time was in part based on
fantasy. Still, the memory was powerful and the quest for a return real. It
mattered especially to businessmen and bankers, who were deeply unhappy about the effects of the war. War brought mobilization, which
meant much higher levels of taxation on elites—who else, after all, could
pay?—and frequently also controls on prices and profits. It also gave significantly greater clout to workers and unions, and bosses did not like to
cede even partial control over what went on in their factories. The state
had also expanded massively to meet the needs of war, and elites feared
that the precedent would be used to prolong state controls into the postwar years so as to provide benefits to those disgruntled and empowered
workers and to returning veterans insisting on their fair share. When the
war ended, newly organized unions and their members were quick to
demand that the sacrifices of wartime be paid back with a better life.

Huge waves of strikes, occasionally verging on insurrections, greeted the end of hostilities in both the states that had prevailed in the war and in those that had lost. At least some of these movements took inspiration from the Bolshevik revolution—and there is no doubt that the authorities were gripped by the fear of Bolshevism.

A most visible symptom of economic dislocation was inflation. Currencies ceased to be convertible as states realized that they needed to hoard whatever reserves they had to buy goods needed for war production and to feed their people. Absent the link to gold, the value of currencies dropped and prices rose everywhere, though more in some countries than others, and the disparities would be accentuated after the end of hostilities. British prices were 225 percent of their 1913 level in 1918 and rose to 283 percent by 1920; American prices were 203 percent higher by war's end, but then stabilized before dropping to just 23 percent higher in 1921. The pattern was still worse in Germany and France: German prices stood at 217 percent of the prewar value in 1918 but soared to 1,486 percent in 1920; and in France, 1918 prices were 340 percent of prewar in 1918 but a staggering 510 percent in 1920. Restarting trade after the war would require currencies to be exchanged, but it was not clear at what rates: bankers and policy makers were desperate to re-create the prewar gold standard, but at what level should national currencies be pegged, relative to gold and to one another? The elite consensus was that inflation needed to be wrung out of the economy at almost any cost, and the result was the imposition of policies of high interest rates, continued high taxes, and austerity aimed at lowering wages. Inevitably, economies contracted and unemployment increased.[3] Such "stabilization" might work for bankers and businessmen, but at an enormous cost to others and to the economy as a whole.

Each country stabilized in its own way, but Great Britain's approach was classic and something of a model. As the postwar strike wave began to recede, the Bank of England raised interest rates and government felt that it could cut the budget. Depression followed and workers were told to accept wage reductions. As government turned control of the mines back over to the owners in March 1921, the miners faced reductions in wages. They threatened to strike and expected the backing of their Triple Alliance allies—the unions representing workers on the railways and the docks. On Black Friday (April 15), these unions decided not to strike. Resistance collapsed across British industry and in 1922 even the highly skilled and well-organized "engineers," elite metal workers, faced a lockout and lost the contest. Wages did decline, slowly and painfully, enough so that in 1925 the chancellor of the exchequer, Winston Churchill, could announce the "return to gold" at a rate of $4.86 (or its gold equivalent) to the pound. The decision was meant to mark the restoration of sanity and fiscal responsibility. In truth, it pleased the financial sector, whose assets and those of their clients were denominated in pounds, and it also meant that British products were overpriced by roughly 10 percent in world markets.[4] This meant that exports remained uncompetitive through the 1920s and they never recovered before the Great Depression set in. Unemployment continued at near 10 percent until, with the depression, it rose still higher—to 25 percent or 2.5 million in 1933. What was dubbed "the Norman Conquest of $4.86," which Churchill came to regard as "the biggest blunder of my life," was achieved on the backs of the industrial working class.[5]

The quixotic effort to return to the world before 1914 dominated the making of economic policy everywhere in Europe. The idea, and the practice, guided the economic efforts of the League of Nations, which helped to enforce orthodoxy in the successor states in Eastern Europe and also underpinned policy in Western Europe and the United States.[6] Austerity was put in place by late 1919 or early 1920 in Japan, the United States, Britain, and beyond. In the US Presidents Harding, Coolidge, and Hoover repeatedly cut taxes. Growth there was reasonably robust, mainly because of a growing population and the technologies of the "second industrial revolution." Globally, however, the policies of the 1920s produced misery and failed to restart growth, and they also created a climate that prevented any reasonable solution to the major international problem of the moment: war reparations. The payment of reparations on the scale demanded of Germany and its allies was barely possible economically, literally impossible politically. Not only were Germans unwilling to pay, but many outside Germany were in sympathy with their plight. After the runaway inflation of 1923 and the occupation of the Ruhr the economy stabilized and, helped by two American initiatives—the Dawes Plan of 1924 and the Young Plan of 1930—grew with the aid of loans from the

United States. Recovery did not last long: the depression put a stop to it and, in 1931–32, to the payment of reparations.

The depression that began in 1929 differed from previous downturns in its breadth—virtually the entire capitalist world was affected—its depth, and its duration. Unemployment, though hard to measure, rose to nearly a third in the United States and higher in Germany. No country was exempt. Agriculture suffered terribly, as did commodity producers in the colonies and less developed countries. International trade collapsed, and all that effort to get back to the gold standard and currency convertibility came to nothing.

The duration of the slump was a consequence and a symbol of the failure of policies adopted to counter it. The experience of prolonged depression scarred a generation and produced a popular resolve to prevent it from ever happening again. Before that was possible, of course, the world had to endure a decade of economic crisis and the much worse suffering caused by its political ramifications and then by war.

Predictably, there was disagreement then, and now, about causes and possible remedies, but in 1929 the conventional wisdom among economists—and the bankers, businessmen, and conservative politicians with whom they were largely in accord—was to continue the orthodox policies that had been put in place after the war. Having for the most part achieved a general return to gold—Japan did not do so until 1930—they were reluctant to disturb the order they had only just created.[7] The initial government response was more austerity, making matters worse. The typical business response was also to cut. As Andrew Mellon, the treasury secretary, explained to President Hoover, the thing to do was to "liquidate labor, liquidate stocks, liquidate the farmers, liquidate real estate." "It will purge the rottenness out of the system," he explained.[8] In truth, Hoover's economic policies were not as austere as Mellon advocated or as prevailing doctrine would have dictated, but were still limited by the constraints exerted by America's adherence to the gold standard and the president's aversion to the expansion of the state.[9]

There were also, inevitably, frantic efforts to maintain the gold-based global financial system, all destined to fail. A major reason was the persistent and corrosive politics of war debts and reparations. As early as

1918 it was obvious that Britain and France would demand that Germany pay huge reparations so long as they were expected to repay inter-allied war debts, mostly to the United States. The US administration resisted the linkage at the time and demanded that war debts be repaid. As the depression ravaged the global financial system, the United States came to accept that Germany was unable to keep paying, but at the same time insisted that Britain and France keep paying war debts. Cooperation, even among erstwhile allies, evaporated as countries abandoned gold, devalued their currencies, and increased tariffs. America, with tariffs high enough already to make it difficult for European exporters, raised them further with the Smoot-Hawley Act of 1930.[10] The American Economic Association got over a thousand members to oppose the bill's passage, but to no avail.[11]

The rippling consequences of the depression and of the now long-standing issue of debt and reparations produced an international financial crisis in 1931. The Germans imposed exchange controls, but it was the British response that had the widest effects. The British abandoned gold in 1931 and let the pound float, and with the Ottawa agreements of 1932 its historic attachment to free trade came to an end as well. A top treasury official conceded, "No country ever administered a more severe shock to international trade than we did when we both (1) depreciated the £ and (2) almost simultaneously turned from free trade to protection."[12]

Efforts to restore the system of international finance and the gold standard would continue, but without success. The most public international effort to develop a cooperative effort to rescue global finance and the world economy, or to prevent its further deterioration, was the World Economic Conference, held in London in June and July 1933. Different countries brought different priorities to the meeting: for many, it was monetary and currency stability and the desire to put an end to devaluation; for others, it was debt and reparations. The position of the United States was schizophrenic: its delegation, led by Cordell Hull, left New York with ideas for opening up trade, but learned while traveling that the president was not willing to submit the necessary legislation on reciprocal trade agreements to Congress. Hull was left without an agenda. In reality, the US administration wanted more time and the freedom to shape its own policies and did not want to be lured into arrangements for exchange stability that would benefit France or the UK and simultaneously restrain America's actions. That was the reason behind Roosevelt's July 3rd "bombshell" message to the conference explaining that the US would not agree to any proposal that would prevent further adjustments to the value of the dollar. The president went on to criticize the "old fetishes of so-called international bankers."[13] The US had only recently abandoned the gold standard and its refusal to stem the slide of the dollar before it reached the level desired by Washington was critical to the failure of the meeting. No state, in fact, was willing to make the necessary compromises, and the conference petered out, having accomplished very little.[14] Currencies continued to depreciate, trade remained blocked, and nations embarked on policies developed primarily in relation to domestic politics and conditions. Hull believed, at least in retrospect, that the failure of the conference allowed the "dictator nations"—Germany, Japan, and Italy—to proceed with their plans "on the military side, to rearm in comparative safety; on the economic side, to build their self-sufficiency walls in preparation for war."[15]

Success in combating the slump was elusive. In Britain, continued austerity, protection, devaluation, and low interest rates allowed for a gradual if selective revival that was later enhanced by rearmament. In the United States, the Roosevelt administration managed to stimulate demand, raise prices, and engineer a modest recovery by 1935–36. The New Deal would also bring major social and labor reforms with long-term consequences, but fewer short-term results. More significantly, the administration's adherence to an orthodox fiscal stance led to retrenchment and the return of high unemployment in 1937. It was rearmament that finally brought the country out of the depression. The slump was less dramatic, and came a bit later, in France, but recovery came later as well. France had its own version of the New Deal with the Popular Front government in 1936. The reforms it brought would last, or at least set precedents for reform that would be taken up by the Resistance and enacted after the war. The Popular Front did not last long, however. It disintegrated, and soon the nation confronted disaster in the Second World War.[16] Sweden, by most accounts, adopted the most enlightened package of policies and was rewarded with a steady recovery, but its distinctive characteristics made it less of a model than it might otherwise have been. In general, the democratic countries did not acquit themselves well in their responses to the economic crisis.

Nations that dispensed with democracy did better. The Soviet Union proclaimed itself to be a higher form of democracy that could dispense with such bourgeois freedoms as elections. The Russian economy had suffered horribly in the war and the ensuing civil war, but the USSR recovered substantially under the New Economic Policy (NEP) adopted in 1922. Fearing that the NEP would lead to a restoration of capitalism, the party leadership under Stalin lurched in 1928 to the policy of Socialism in One Country, to be implemented through planning and state control. That produced the first Five-Year Plan, which combined rapid industrialization with the collectivization of the rural economy and "dekulakization," the elimination of the kulaks (or richer peasants) as a class. The effects were brutal, but people were nevertheless at work.

Japan's descent into authoritarianism was gradual and took place in tandem with aggressively nationalist economic policies and aggression toward its neighbors in East Asia. Japan left the gold standard in December 1932 and devalued the yen by over half in the next year. The move gave a boost to exports and the economy began to recover. Japan's economy turned increasingly to the East and there was talk of creating a New Order in Asia and, later, of a Greater East Asia Co-prosperity Sphere.[17] It was an imperial and frankly racial vision, cloaked in a rhetoric of anti-imperialism.

Democracy had died earlier in Italy at the hands of Mussolini. The new Fascist order had from the beginning a distinctive economic vision. It would be based on a corporatist state underpinned by organizations designed to bring together both workers and owners in different industries. The idea was to overcome the horizontal division of society into classes and replace it with a system that was vertically organized and could unite those who toiled with those who owned, directed, and profited. The various corporate groups, cartels in effect, would be brought together at the higher reaches and ultimately form a fascist council to plan the economy. The effect would be to limit competition and control production and prices so as to match supply and demand. The system would be powered by government spending, at first on public works and then on the military and defense, and was intended to keep unemployment low. In practice, policy lagged behind theory and Italy was hit hard by the depression. The response involved massive government bailouts and continued public spending. Because Italy remained a largely agricultural economy, the unemployed were not always as visible as elsewhere and soon the preparation for war provided yet further stimulus, so the results gave at least the impression of success.

The depression hit Germany especially hard and was a major factor in the rise of the Nazis. The Nazis also benefited from the failure of governments to develop an effective response to the crisis. As chancellor, Heinrich Brüning had little choice but to follow the orthodox script closely and so met the slump with austerity. Conditions worsened, with unemployment rising, and unrest grew. Even before Hitler's appointment as chancellor in January 1933, the conservative governments that had succeeded Brüning's had initiated plans for a large program of public works. These the Nazis pushed forward as part of a mobilization they labeled The Battle for Work (*Arbeitsschlacht*). The projects were financed by the state but kept "off budget" for accounting purposes. Initially, the focus was on civilian tasks like road building, urban redevelopment, and agricultural improvements, but rearmament was always Hitler's top priority. Just days after his appointment as chancellor, he told a Cabinet committee, "The future of Germany depends exclusively and only on the reconstruction of the Wehrmacht. All other tasks must cede precedence to the task of rearmament." At first this had to be done in secret, but it did not take long for the reality to become clear.[18]

Germany's path to rearmament, and to recovery, required imports. Imports were needed for virtually every industry, but especially for those that would add to the country's military might. The problem was that by repudiating its debts Germany had cut itself off from imports from Western countries and those nations that traded in, and wanted payment in, their currencies. The response, largely engineered by Hjalmar Schacht as president of the Reichsbank, was a set of tight controls on currency exchange that allocated scarce funds for approved imports and efforts to strike bilateral agreements with countries whose goods Germany needed. These and other barter-like agreements, primarily with countries in

Central and Eastern Europe, became the centerpiece of German international economic policy, and they established or enhanced links between its economy and the economies of nations to the east.

Germany's policies aimed at a regional autarky. So, too, did Japan's. These developing patterns and structures sat alongside not dissimilar relations that existed between the Western powers and their economic partners. There was, by the mid-1930s, a dollar bloc, the sterling area, and a gold bloc. The sterling area was roughly defined by membership in the British Empire or, in certain cases, what had been its "informal empire"; and the gold bloc brought together France, Belgium, Holland, their imperial possessions, and certain smaller European countries. During the 1930s Britain and France had both begun to trade more with their colonies and to speak in terms of colonial development. Empire, unfashionable since 1918, had made a comeback, and with Italy, Japan, and Germany adopting economic policies inspired by imperial visions, a set of rival imperial orders was emerging as the alternative to a liberal world order. And who in 1939 would bet on the triumph of liberal order?

Democracy at Bay

If the First World War left material life in Europe, and beyond, damaged and distorted, its political effects were even more dire. The empires that had ruled most of Central, Eastern, and southern Europe had fallen. The Ottoman Empire had ended and splintered; the empires of the Romanovs, the Hapsburgs, and the Hohenzollerns had been overthrown or abandoned. The leaders of the victorious countries also faced massive discontent at home and the imperative not only to design a new international system but also to determine the states that would populate it.[19] There was much talk of self-determination, but it was not clear who would get that right. There was also an assumption that the peoples who got themselves a state would choose to exercise their new autonomy through democratic methods, though there was no guarantee of that and no mechanism to make it happen. The word *democracy* did not make an appearance in President Wilson's "Fourteen Points" speech, and that was surely not an accident.

The most straightforward task was to make whole the countries that had been invaded and occupied by Germany and its allies. To the extent that this restoration would require reparations from the defeated powers, it was far from simple. In determining who would pay whom, and how much, those who met at Versailles would not merely be adjudicating claims of damage but also setting the conditions within which postwar politics would develop. Outside of Russia, now the Soviet Union and left out of the peacemaking, France had the strongest moral claim and no doubt had suffered the greatest damage. Other occupied countries pressed claims that were equally difficult to dismiss. Britain had not suffered occupation or serious physical damage, but the human costs were enormous. It had also provided finance to its allies, suffered substantial losses in capital, and incurred huge liabilities. The negotiations between allies bid up the demands to be placed on Germany. The disagreements were so intense that the precise determination of reparations and the means by which they would be paid were put off for two years after the peace agreement. The issue would not go away, however, and would burden the German economy and, indirectly, the world economy through the following decade.

The nature of the peace settlement also burdened German politics. The leaders of the new Weimar Republic had no choice but to acquiesce to the terms of the treaty, and that meant accepting Germany's responsibility for starting the war and for compensating its victims. They were mercilessly attacked by right-wing nationalist forces for selling out the nation's interests. The German military never acknowledged its defeat and encouraged the myth that it had been "stabbed in the back" by politicians. The result was that the democratic parties and leaders who would try to make a success of Weimar were never trusted, always suspected of being disloyal Germans. Democracy itself was suspect.

Germany had known democracy from before the war, but it was an imperfect democracy. The new nations that emerged from the fallen empires in Eastern and southern Europe had little or no such experience, and so typically lacked the political traditions and the institutions of civil society that nurture and sustain democratic politics. The social structures in the East were also not conducive to the implantation of political democracy. They were still largely agricultural societies and in certain regions large landowners were dominant. Almost everywhere, nationalism was more important than liberalism and democracy. The so-called successor states all adopted formally democratic political arrangements, but these were seldom able to withstand the tough tests of the interwar years.

Beyond Europe, large swathes of territory were still ruled as empires. Despite the collapse of imperial rule during the war and the belief that empire did not have a future, it expanded its reach just after the war and became more important economically during the depression. The British and the French moved in to take over from the Ottomans in the Middle East and from the Germans in Africa. The Mandates System of the League of Nations was meant to make imperial rule less harsh and more responsible, and it did expose abuses, but it was not meant to end empire and it did not.[20] By the mid-1930s, countries without empires, such as Germany, or with modest empires, like Italy and Japan, launched bids to build serious and more expansive empires that would compete with those of the British, the French, the Dutch, the Belgians, and the Portuguese. The prospects for expanding democracy outside Europe were not at all favorable prior to 1939.

The fate of democracy in Europe was deeply connected to the workings of capitalism and the social fissures it generated. Creating and sustaining democracy was especially hard in a context of intense class conflict. The war and postwar had unleashed a wave of strikes and working-class protest suppressed through the efforts of the police, joined by the military and employers. In Italy, bands of Fascist thugs helped keep order. Across Europe deflation soon cut the ground out from under unions and workers by creating unemployment. The fear of labor unrest and what it portended remained. It was intensified by the example of the Bolshevik revolution, which boasted of being the first step in a universal project and whose leaders called for workers to revolt around the world, but especially in Europe. The founding of the Comintern (Communist International) in 1919 had the effect of dividing and effectively weakening the left in every European country, but it also delivered a frightening message to elites.

The specter of Communism was a vague dream and a rhetorical stroke of genius for Marx and Engels back in 1848, but something like it really did linger over the politics of the postwar era. Behind the specter, moreover, was the powerful, horrible but, to some, alluring reality of Soviet power. Capitalism, by contrast, had few defenders in the lean years after 1918 and fewer still during the depression. Both Mussolini and Hitler proudly proclaimed their anti-capitalist sentiments. Intellectuals across the political spectrum came to doubt the compatibility of capitalism and democracy and took to criticizing the inequities and dysfunction of capitalism and the ineffectiveness and corruption of democracy in roughly equal measure.

The interwar crisis of capitalism would not bring socialism anywhere, but it did lead conservative political elites to make alliances with demagogues and thugs against the left and its working-class supporters. In Italy, it was the hope that Mussolini would bring political stability that led right-wing sections of the establishment to allow him to seize power. Equally clear was the complicity of conservative and nationalist parties, and the generals, judges, and bureaucrats allied with them, in facilitating Hitler's accession to power. A succession of extreme right governments in Germany could not command the necessary support from the country or the Reichstag to govern effectively, and so Hitler was brought in to provide the necessary popular support. In both cases, but especially in Germany, these traditional elites believed that they would control the fascists. Franz von Papen, Hitler's predecessor but one, remarked, "We've hired him."[21] Papen and others like him were spectacularly wrong: like the Italian Fascists, but even more so, the Nazis came very much to dominate their sponsors and accomplices.

The ruthless domination that the Nazis and Fascists exercised over allies, enemies, and society as a whole was unprecedented. The empires that had fallen at the end of the Great War had been undemocratic and repressive, but the new dictators were different: they were backed by mass movements and claimed to speak on behalf of the people—indeed, the nation, the *Volk,* and the race—and treated dissent as treason; they disdained the norms of liberal society and recognized no safe spaces beyond the control of the state or the party; and they were driven by ideologies of hate and aggression. The Nazis' racial thinking was central to their outlook and demonology and they moved quickly to apply it to the nation they now controlled. Both regimes were also frankly revisionist toward the existing international order, and they moved decisively to alter it when they could. Of course, the Nazis ruled a larger and more powerful country, so their actions were inevitably more consequential.

Italy and Germany were not the only countries to move toward authoritarian rule. By the late 1930s the only genuinely democratic polity in Eastern and Central Europe was that of Czechoslovakia. Elsewhere, local despots were in power. Some were nationalists who found it easy to dispense with democracy when convenient; others were military men; and some were traditional monarchs around whom elites rallied when the citizens became unruly. Most were inspired by the Fascists or Nazis and aped their policies, though some were eventually conquered by them. It was not unreasonable, then, to fret over the long-term viability of democracy in Central and Eastern Europe.

Nor were the liberal democracies immune to such movements. France saw right-wing, largely Catholic reactionaries organizing against the Third Republic and faced a major crisis in 1934. The British Union of Fascists remained marginal but made trouble all the same. In the United States, populists secured large followings. Huey Long of Louisiana launched a Share the Wealth campaign in 1934. After he was assassinated in 1935, the movement continued under the more right-wing and racist leadership of Gerald L. K. Smith. Before his death Long began to coordinate his efforts with a Dr. Townsend, author of the Townsend Plan for "rotating" pensions, and with Father Coughlin, the "radio priest" broadcasting an anti-Semitic message from Dearborn, Michigan, that was heard, mainly by Catholics, all across the country. The followers of Long and Smith and Townsend were typically rural and southern or midwestern, but they had support more broadly. And Coughlin had strong support among urban Catholics who listened in every week. There was also Henry Ford, who chose to publish and disseminate the *Protocols of the Elders of Zion*, also from a base in Dearborn. Roosevelt and the Democrats, deeply worried about these populist threats, responded with reforms like the Social Security Act. Roosevelt and his allies well understood the racism, nativism, and anti-Semitism behind these movements. They were constrained in their opposition, however, by their own fragile coalition with southern Democrats, which put limits on their advocacy of liberal values and measures. Race seriously retarded the elaboration of a truly liberal culture in America. The

demagogues of the 1930s never got close to power in the US, but they
were a sign at least that the antipathies and resentments tapped so effectively and frighteningly by Hitler and Mussolini had resonance even
in the countries with the deepest and presumably strongest democratic
traditions. Clearly, the depression was not good for liberal sentiments
and democratic commitments.

International Disorder

International relations between the wars were shaped overwhelmingly
by the legacies of the Great War. The depression would later alter domestic political balances, with major consequences for relations between
states, but the starting point was the aftermath of the earlier global conflict. The post–World War I settlement sharply divided winners and losers. For the states that had prevailed in 1914–18, that meant finding ways
to enforce the peace and a determination to avoid another war. Three
imperial states—Russia, Austria-Hungary, and the Ottoman Empire—
did not survive the war. The new states that succeeded them had varied
agendas: the Soviet Union promoted its own vision for a socialist world
order but was mainly consumed by internal matters; Turkey began the
process of turning itself into a modern nation-state within reduced borders; Austria was but a rump of the former empire, as was Hungary, and
they were left to jostle with successor states ruled by former subjects.
Germany was weakened, punished, and isolated, but remained a potential threat to its neighbors and took a fundamentally "revisionist" stance
toward the Versailles settlement. Italy, not defeated but disappointed that
it did not gain more from the war, would also look to revising the international settlement, though in a less menacing way than Germany.

Despite these divergent interests and objectives, the discourse and
diplomacy of the 1920s was largely about peace and arms reductions.
Though its institutional foundations were weak, the League of Nations
enjoyed wide support and spoke in exactly this language. Appropriately,
the international landmarks of the decade included the Washington
Naval Conference of 1921–22, the Locarno Treaties of 1925, and the
Kellogg-Briand Pact of 1928. The Washington conference brought
together the United States, Britain, Japan, and six other countries and

produced agreements to limit the building of battleships. The United Kingdom, long the dominant naval power, acquiesced to co-equal status with the United States and to a bigger and more powerful Japanese navy. The agreement was modified at the London conference of 1930, and Japan was allowed to build more. Still, the deal did limit naval armaments and it largely held, at least into the mid-1930s. The Locarno Treaties effectively ratified Germany's western borders and the demilitarization of the Rhineland. The Germans were unwilling to commit themselves to the country's borders to the east and the British were unwilling to commit to their defense, though the Germans agreed to arbitration with key neighbors. In 1928, the Kellogg-Briand Pact, which in theory outlawed war, was signed in Paris.[22] Together, these agreements demonstrated the desire of much of the world to ensure continued peace.

Preparations began in earnest for the World Disarmament Conference, which was convened under the auspices of the League of Nations in Geneva in 1932. Like the World Economic Conference, it would fail. Germany insisted that it be allowed equal arms and military forces with France and Britain. The French were unwilling to acquiesce without a firm security guarantee that Britain would not provide. That led to an impasse and adjournment. By the time the conference reconvened in 1933, Hitler had come to power: Germany withdrew from the meeting, and from the League, on October 14, 1933. The conference adjourned again, then reconvened in the spring and wound down in desultory fashion, as Germany began to rearm and to renounce provisions of the Versailles Treaty. As the leading historian of interwar diplomacy explained:

> While the German rearmament programme was put into high gear, Hitler could watch from the sidelines as other countries fell to quarrelling over the proper response to Germany's new course. All the participants in the disarmament talks knew that Germany was rearming. The League's efforts at disarmament failed in the most public way and to its singular discredit.... Talks continued, outside of Geneva, because popular disapproval and budgetary considerations ruled out the alternative. They went on, too, because the Great War cast a large shadow and few wanted to think of a new war.[23]

The desire to avoid another war remained strong well into the 1930s and was undoubtedly a major factor leading Britain and France to make concessions to Germany. Opposition to war was also strong in the United States, with popular opinion very suspicious of the designs of European countries that, it was thought, had brought America into the First World War. The Nye Committee of the US Senate, set up in 1934 to investigate the munitions industry, laid out the argument that it was "merchants of death"—financiers and arms manufacturers—who had pushed the country into war. The implication was that the US had been tricked into entering the war and that while soldiers died, others profited. The committee's work was wrapped up in 1936, but the belief that the war was the work of bankers, arms merchants, and wily Europeans persisted.[24]

In Britain, the Oxford Union debated war and peace in February 1933, and a solid majority backed the resolution that "this House will in no circumstances fight for its King and Country." Hitler, it was reported, was impressed. In 1934 the League of Nations Union organized a massive "peace ballot" in which 11.5 million voted. The results, tallied and released the next summer, showed that those voting massively supported the League, disarmament, and deterring aggression through sanctions. Far fewer would support the use of force. This aversion to military action was bipartisan. It would take, for example, the reality of Italian aggression against Ethiopia and a dramatic debate at the Labour Party conference of October 1935 before the party reversed its position. The trade union leader Ernest Bevin famously attacked the party's leader, George Lansbury, for "hawking your conscience round from body to body asking to be told what to do with it." The Tories in government were equally reluctant to rearm, fearing the expense and unwilling to raise taxes or take on debt. Similar sentiments were common in the United States. In April 1935, some sixty thousand American students signed on to the Oxford Oath; in 1936, roughly half a million students demonstrated against war. If war was to be avoided, moreover, rearmament was also to be avoided, for it simply brought war closer.

It is difficult to know why the commitment to peace, noble as it is, lasted as long as it did. How could one hold onto it when confronted with the repeated acts of aggression by Japan, Italy, and Germany? It is worth recalling how frequent and obvious these acts were. Japan actually took the lead in 1931 when its forces staged the so-called Mukden Incident and used it as an excuse to invade all of Manchuria. The invasion succeeded quickly and in March 1932 the puppet state of Manchukuo was established. International condemnation was swift, but had no tangible results. Japan withdrew from the League in 1933 and served notice that it would withdraw from agreements limiting naval rearmament. There could be little doubt that Japan was determined on a course to advance its interests by military force.

Italian policy under Mussolini was more erratic, but clear enough overall. Italy had aims to expand its influence in the Mediterranean, most specifically in Albania, but its grander ambition was to expand its empire in Africa. It already controlled Eritrea, had a foothold in Libya, and moved consistently to crush resistance in Libya during the 1920s and 1930s. It had succeeded by the early 1930s and turned its sights on Ethiopia. All this was visible to Britain, France, and the United States, but with the rise of Hitler the French and British were eager to find a way to separate Rome and Berlin. France in particular sought to woo the Italians. In early 1935, therefore, the French foreign minister (and soon to be prime minister) Pierre Laval met with Mussolini and effectively gave the Italians "a free hand" in Ethiopia. Using troops and weapons taken to Eritrea and Somaliland through the Suez Canal, Italy invaded in early October 1935 and by May 1936 had captured Addis Ababa. The League of Nations condemned the move and ordered sanctions, but they were not effectively enforced. In December 1935 word leaked of a pact between UK foreign secretary Samuel Hoare and Laval that would have recognized most of the Italian gains. It was never formalized, and Hoare was compelled to resign, but the very notion of the Hoare-Laval Pact signaled the futility of League efforts to confront aggression.

The Germans had already proclaimed their decision to rearm and to disregard provisions of the Versailles Treaty in 1933–34 and in 1935 made clear the seriousness of the campaign against the Jews with the passing of the Nuremberg Laws. It was becoming extremely difficult to ignore the nature of the regime and its intentions. Hitler would take a further and critical step by remilitarizing the Rhineland in early March 1936. Britain, France, and much of the rest of Europe were deeply unhappy, indeed close to panic, but refrained from taking action. The

French would not act without British support, and the British did not think it worth the risk of all-out war. The German move gave an impetus to rearmament in both Britain and France, but the moves were late and less extensive than what the Germans were doing. It also led the two Western European democracies to intensify their efforts to conciliate the Germans, not only with continued meetings but also with the prospect of deals on economic and financial matters and with colonial concessions.

As the Germans began constructing their fortifications in the Rhineland, with Krupp turning out concrete sections in round-the-clock shifts, attention turned to Spain.[25] A "popular front" government was elected in February. The idea of a popular front uniting the center and various parties of the left was first and most prominently proposed by the Comintern at its Seventh Congress in 1935. It was a repudiation of the "class against class" policy of the so-called Third Period. After Hitler's accession to power, the Soviets came to realize that it had been a mistake to encourage the Communist parties across the world to attack moderate socialists and social democrats as "social fascists." Instead, they would push for a "united front against fascism" globally and try to create "popular front" coalitions domestically wherever possible. In Britain, the Labour Party rejected the call for a popular front; in Spain and in France, it met with a more favorable reaction and led to electoral victories in Spain in February and in France in May 1936. The Popular Front government in France succeeded in bringing about numerous reforms before it collapsed; in Spain, the Popular Front was more radical than in France, with an added edge of anti-clericalism. There, it provoked a rebellion by conservatives and the military, with critical support from the Catholic Church. A cabal of generals, led ultimately by Francisco Franco, began the uprising in Morocco in July and in short order controlled about a third of the country. But the defenders of the Republic rallied and stopped the rebel advance very quickly. A civil war that would last well into 1939 ensued, producing enormous military and civilian casualties.

The Spanish Civil War came to engulf all of Europe, whatever side one took. The rebels had control of the army and its weapons. Soon they would seek and receive support from Italy and Germany, further enhancing their advantage. The Republic also sought foreign support, but with mixed and ultimately fatal results. Leon Blum, leader of the Popular Front government in France, at first promised support, but he soon learned that the French were deeply split on the issue. More critically, the British wanted to stay out of the conflict; and once again, without British assistance, the French backed off. Rather than supply weapons and other aid, the British and French declared an arms embargo. It was a deeply hypocritical move, for while Franco's forces were well supplied by their fascist allies, the Republic was starved of the weapons it needed to fight and survive. In August the United States proclaimed a "moral embargo." The government of the Spanish Republic was thus forced to rely upon Stalin and the Soviets, whose help began to arrive in October. It came with political strings, however, and unintended and unhappy consequences. The Republic could also count on help from volunteers from France, Britain, and even the United States. Support for Spain was to become a great cause for the left in the late 1930s and attracted writers and artists along with militants, but they were no match for Italian and German bombs.

The Spanish Civil War would produce important works of art and literature, but also death and suffering. It also served as a kind of testing ground for German and Italian planes and weapons and made their cooperation closer and more effective. It was interpreted on the right, not only in Germany and Italy but also in France, Britain, and the United States, as a desperate clash with Bolshevism. Maurice Hankey, the Cabinet secretary, went so far as to speculate in July 1936 that "with France and Spain menaced by Bolshevism, it is not inconceivable that before long it may pay us to throw in our lot with Germany and Italy, and the greater our detachment from European entanglements the better."[26] Hitler, understanding the appeal of the notion, would sign the Anti-Comintern Pact with Japan in November 1936. Italy would join the next year, and Franco would celebrate victory by joining in March 1939.

Hitler, by all accounts, moved closer to war during 1937, but the reality of war itself came first in China. A local incident at Marco Polo Bridge in July led to a full-scale invasion by Japan. The war was "undeclared," but real enough to those who were in it and suffered from its brutality. The Japanese took Beijing and its environs quickly and seemed, for a time, content with that, but the Chinese under Kuomintang leadership chose to counterattack. They failed, and the Japanese responded with offensives further into the interior and with "the rape of Nanking." The two sides became bogged down by 1939, and in 1941, with Japan's attack on Pearl Harbor and its offensives in South and East Asia, the conflict merged into the broader struggle of World War II.

The Germans, rearming at a rapid pace, became more outwardly aggressive in 1938. On March 12, Germany moved to annex Austria in what was called the *Anschluss*. The move had been contemplated for some time and was the subject of much diplomatic maneuvering, but nonetheless it was shocking when it happened. It was defended by Germany as a response to the wishes of the Austrians, who did vote to approve it, and as a step in fulfilling a more fundamental goal: reuniting the Volk, wherever they might be found. The same argument would be used later when Hitler spoke of the supposed plight of the Sudeten Germans and began pressuring the government of Czechoslovakia to cede that slice of territory. It would also be the ruse that Hitler and the Germans used to pressure, and later invade and carve up, Poland.

It was during the crisis over Czechoslovakia that the reality behind the Nazi rhetoric became clear. And it was during and after that confrontation that the folly of appeasing Hitler became visible for those with eyes to see. The story of Munich is well known. The Germans threatened to invade Czechoslovakia over the fate of the Sudetenland and in September 1938 the British and French caved in, allowing Germany to begin the process of carving up its neighbor. The person most eager to placate Hitler so as to secure, as he hoped, "peace for our time," was the British prime minister, Neville Chamberlain. He met Hitler at Berchtesgaden, his retreat outside Munich, in mid-September and agreed to the substance of Hitler's demands. Negotiations over details ensued, but they came to nothing. Chamberlain flew to meet Hitler twice more, including another trip to Munich on September 29, when he also met with Mussolini and the French prime minister. Chamberlain capitulated utterly, and the four signed the infamous agreement giving the stamp of international approval to Hitler's conquest. Chamberlain returned to London and was greeted with praise. He seems to have actually bought into Hitler's argument about German minorities trapped in hostile environments, claiming that "the object of his [Hitler's] policy was racial unity and not the domination of Europe."[27] Soon enough, the praise and the hopes for peace faded, replaced by a growing sense that seeking to conciliate Hitler was a mistake.

Hitler himself helped to make that case, first with Krystallnacht on November 9–10, 1938, and then with the invasion and dismemberment of Czechoslovakia on March 15, 1939. (Poland and Hungary also got bits of the now-defunct state.) The ratcheting up of the persecution of the Jews provided evidence that Hitler's efforts to reunite Germans was not some romantic fantasy but a policy that boded ill for non-Germans as well as for German Jews. The continued pressure on Czechoslovakia convinced more sober analysts that the Nazi vision was focused on conquest, not on the redress of plausible grievances. These actions led to urgent efforts in Britain and France to rearm and, as rearmament was progressing, to put together alliances to block Germany's path. The first step was the extension of guarantees to Poland at the end of March.

After that, attention turned to the question of where to get help against what seemed a likely German move on Poland. The obvious option was the Soviet Union. German antipathy to the Soviets was obvious, as was the Germans' ultimate objective of moving to the east in search of *Lebensraum*. But reaching a deal would prove difficult. The Poles, who desperately needed Soviet intervention against Hitler, were as distrustful of the Soviets as they were of the Nazis, and so were unwilling to allow Soviet troops to cross into Polish territory. A more basic problem was the long-term distrust of the Soviets by the French and, especially, the British. Chamberlain in particular detested Bolshevism and also doubted Soviet military strength. Recent purges of both the foreign policy apparatus and the military fed into these doubts. Distrust was reciprocated on the Soviet side; Soviet leaders feared that the British and French might themselves make a deal with Germany. There was a flurry of diplomatic activity in the summer of 1939, but there was no deal. Instead, Germany and the Soviet Union signed a Nonaggression Pact in Moscow on August 23, 1939. The Nazi-Soviet pact cleared the way for Germany to invade Poland on September 1, 1939. Negotiations continued in the week before and even after the German choice for war. On August 25, for example, Hitler made a final offer to the British ambassador: when he had resolved the issue with Poland, he would rest content. If allowed to move east, Hitler and the Germans would agree on the border to the west and offer a guarantee to Britain and its empire. Nothing came of this or other efforts, and by early September Europe was at war.

America: No Exception

It had taken quite a lot of aggression on the part of Germany, Japan, and Italy to convince leaders in Britain and France that they could not be conciliated and that their demands were not about legitimate wrongs but a pretext for regional or even global domination. It would take still longer for the United States, or many in the country, to come to the same conclusion—it would require the attack on Pearl Harbor in December 1941 and Hitler's subsequent declaration of war on America. As for the Soviet Union, whose own illusions about Hitler and Germany persisted until the launch of Operation Barbarossa, it was not until June 1941 that the country was forced to go to war with the Nazis. These delays meant that it was not until January 1942 that the alliance against Hitler, Japan, and Italy truly came into being. That lag, which extended even further into 1942 as America mobilized for war, would allow the Germans, the Italians, and the Japanese to overrun and occupy most of Europe, a vast chunk of the Soviet Union, large sections of North Africa, and a great swathe of East and Southeast Asia. It meant millions of people were forced to live under brutal regimes in these conquered territories, and it would make the business of defeating the Axis powers more tortured and protracted.

The reason it took so long for the alliance against Hitler and his allies to come together has been much debated. The issue matters not because of a need to assign blame—that is too easy to do and it is decades too late for that—but to determine what it was about the politics and economics of the era that made "appeasement," as the phenomenon appeared in Britain and France, or "isolationism," as the American analogue was labeled, so attractive. For Britain and France, the most important factor was surely the legacy of the First World War, which was seared into the consciousness of its survivors and whose lasting consequences were so pervasive and visible. In both nations there was a sense that they would not survive another war. The response to the depression, especially the turn toward autarky and empire, also encouraged the belief that if Germany and Italy could be tempted to turn east and south to create their own empires or spheres of influence, they would not threaten the countries of Western Europe and their colonial possessions. As a further incentive to look east, not west, and to leave the French and British alone with their empires, the colonies taken from Germany after 1918 could be given back. In theory, the same logic might apply to the challenge of Japan, though compromise in Asia might be harder because it was British and French colonies that might be coveted by the Japanese. To many in Britain and France, it was reasonable to contemplate German domination in Central and Eastern Europe and to accept the possibility that the Germans might just move on and dismantle the Soviet Union. Indeed, a recurring if secondary theme in strategic thinking was the idea that war between Germany and the Soviet Union could weaken both and rebound to the benefit of their rivals and enemies.

The mix of motives and beliefs varied a bit in the United States. Thousands of miles from Europe and from Asia, separated by oceans, the country was much less vulnerable to attack. Europeans lived close by one another, and the continent's borders were often drawn not by nature but by whoever won the last war, and they were far more permeable. It was thus not entirely delusional that America's best strategic option was to stay out of world affairs. From its beginnings the country has been enmeshed in the world economy, but the United States had done well by remaining aloof politically. Its vision of its destiny and proper sphere of influence was more continental or hemispheric than global, and many Americans felt that it should generally avoid entanglement with the affairs of the Old World. The major deviation from that pattern had come during the Great War, and many Americans believed that venture had been folly. This critique mixed nativist and conspiratorial sentiments into a determined effort to remain detached after the First World War and into the 1930s.[28]

America's professed opposition to empire also worked against the idea of cooperating with European countries on collective defense. Depending on one's definition, the United States may or may not have been an empire, but Americans routinely thought of themselves as anti-imperialist.[29] The nation's expansion across the continent, for example, was widely considered an almost natural phenomenon, the replacement of lesser peoples by their betters. When the United States got involved in the last act of the late-nineteenth-century scramble for empire, it did so under the banner of maintaining an "open door" to China. Whatever the nation's own imperial or quasi-imperial behavior, not least toward its neighbors to the south, Americans had long resented the pretensions and ambitions of the European imperial powers and were loath to form alliances with them. This did not prevent the United States from playing an active role in international relations and in the economic diplomacy of the 1920s, but it did place limits upon its commitments. It was also the case that Britain and France, in searching for ways to alleviate German or Italian grievances, thought as empires, reaching for compromises that treated their rivals as aspiring empires and seeking to appease them in ways that empires understood.[30] That was less appealing to the United States, whose aspirations were in theory anti-colonial but, in key respects, even grander, for America was less likely to concede the validity of rival empires or hegemons. Its reach would be global and brook no deals with established or newly aspiring empires.

There had also been an upsurge in antipathy to foreigners, and especially to immigrants, after 1918.[31] The wave of strikes and labor unrest after 1918 was blamed on radicals from elsewhere. Domestic unrest was also linked to fears of the spread of Bolshevism, prompting the "Red Scare" that produced numerous arrests and occasional deportations. Simultaneously, the politics of immigration restriction became more widespread and intense, linked as it was to the pervasive eugenics discourse mouthed by more than one American president and otherwise worthy politicians, and endorsed by supposed men of science, Protestant bishops, and college presidents.[32] The result had been the 1924 Immigration Act, which sharply reduced immigration overall and placed tight quotas on immigrants from the countries of eastern and southern Europe and from Asia. The restrictions fell particularly hard on Jews, Italians, and various Slavic peoples, as intended by those who pushed the new law. The fundamentals of the law remained in place throughout the 1930s and 1940s, effectively barring large numbers of Jews from seeking refuge from the Nazis. The law was finally revised only in 1965.

The refusal of the United States to intervene in Europe, or Asia, during the crises of the late 1930s was possibly more deeply rooted in the nation's past and its political culture than was the case with the appeasers in Britain and France. The most ardent advocates of nonintervention came typically from the Midwest and the West. Many were conservative Republicans, though some of the most prominent were "progressives" or "populists" who had supported the New Deal. They were joined, too, by ethnic minorities in the cities of the Midwest and even the East. Italian Americans were reluctant to censure Italian aggression, and German Americans were often predisposed to support Germany. Irish Americans, for their part, were deeply antipathetic to Great Britain and unwilling to see the United States rally to the defense of the British Empire. To this extent, "isolationism" and antiwar sentiment were more genuinely popular in America than the equivalent views were in Britain, where appeasement was more of an elite phenomenon. In fact, an opinion poll in February 1937 found that 95 percent of Americans opposed any participation in a future war.

Of course, those called isolationists in America shared the anti-Communism of their British and French counterparts, and the fear of the destruction that another war would bring was real as well. Still, the United States had come out of the Great War stronger than when it entered—indeed, potentially the dominant world power. Its losses were far less than those suffered by Britain and France, whose status as great powers was put in doubt by the effects of the war. Despite emerging from the war relatively unscathed and despite the ambitious plans of Woodrow Wilson, the United States continued to see itself as at some remove from the concerns of Europe and from the responsibility that others felt its enhanced position required of it.[33] It would take the experience of the Second World War and, at its end, the confrontation with the Soviet Union for the United States to accept its "international responsibilities."[34] Even then, it would do so with considerable ambivalence.

Meanwhile, Americans of a more interventionist disposition would labor mightily but with evident futility to move the United States into opposing and resisting German, Japanese, and Italian aggression. The contest between the Roosevelt administration and a variety of more or less "isolationist" opponents was waged in the press, in Congress, and in the minds of Americans. Roosevelt confronted not merely vague antiwar sentiment but laws passed explicitly to restrict his ability to respond to armed aggression. Congress passed three separate Neutrality Acts, in 1935, 1936, and 1937, requiring that the US place embargoes on trade in arms and war-related products with both sides in international conflicts. They effectively prohibited the administration from coming to the aid of Britain and France and the defenders of the Spanish Republic battling Franco. Roosevelt secured a revised Neutrality Act after the outbreak of war in Europe in 1939, but the new law only allowed threatened countries to purchase what they could on a "cash and carry" basis, and that meant that purchases had to be transported on foreign ships as well. Finally, in 1941, the administration convinced Congress to approve the so-called Lend-Lease Act, which finally allowed the United States to export significant amounts of arms to Britain (and later to the Soviet Union).

Still, the resistance to getting more involved was remarkable, even after Hitler invaded Poland in September 1939.[35] Roosevelt immediately convened a special session of Congress to revise the neutrality laws, and his opponents sprang into action. There was the usual cast of characters—politicians like William Borah, Burton Wheeler, Gerald Nye, Hiram Johnson, and Hamilton Fish; businessmen such as Henry Ford and Robert McCormick, publisher of the *Chicago Tribune*; and more than a few military men—but they were now joined by the famed flyer Charles Lindbergh. Lindbergh entered the fray with a radio address on September 15, 1939, insisting, "We should never enter a war unless it is absolutely essential to the welfare of our nation." The present war was not. Rather, the fault lay with the victors in the last war. As Lindbergh explained, "The Treaty of Versailles either had to be revised as time passed, or England and France, to be successful, had to keep Germany weak by force. Neither course was followed." Lindbergh proceeded to proclaim his commitment to a strong defense, especially in the air, and outlined the circumstances in which he would support going to war. The United States should fight when and only when "our civilization is defending itself against some Asiatic intruder." The current war "was not a question of banding together to defend the White race against foreign invasion," but "simply one more of those age-old quarrels" among like peoples and races. He ended by warning of propaganda pushing America to war and urged his listeners to be wary of its origins: "We must learn to look behind every article we read and every speech we hear. We must not only inquire about the writer and the speaker—about his personal interests and his nationality, but we must ask who owns and who influences the newspaper, the news picture, and the radio station."[36] Lindbergh's easy move from antiwar sentiments to defense of the white race as the bearers of civilization, and the subsequent slippage from a commonsense skepticism toward propaganda to the standard anti-Semitic trope about Jews owning the media conjures well the set of assumptions prevalent in the wider political discourse in the country.

Roosevelt would win the battle to loosen the restrictions of the Neutrality Acts in November 1939, and over the next two years he edged the American people toward opposition to the dictators and support for their victims and enemies. Still, the case against intervention continued to be made, and forcefully. The last major flare-up of such sentiment came in 1940, after the fall of France had occurred and as the bombs began to fall on Britain. The lead was taken by students at Ivy League universities who founded and supported the America First Committee. Students had expressed opposition to war throughout the 1930s. By 1940, with the prospect of war that much closer, they became more organized. Harvard's commencement that year was rancorous, pitting alumni who had fought in the Great War against those about to graduate and perhaps be sent off to fight another war. In September, the editors of the *Yale Daily News* and the *Harvard Crimson*, Kingman Brewster and Spencer Klaw, wrote a piece for the *Atlantic Monthly* denouncing the case for joining in the war on the side of Britain and France. Brewster and his friends proceeded that same month to found the America First Committee. In October, the group invited Lindbergh to New Haven, where he delivered his antiwar message to three thousand students. Though it began in the East, the organization set up headquarters in Chicago, where it joined forces with other stalwarts of the anti-interventionist persuasion. The movement would ultimately attract close to a million supporters, but what was most notable was their elite status: Potter Stewart, who would become a respected Supreme Court justice,

Joseph Kennedy Jr., who took a lead in the Harvard branch of the committee; Gerald Ford, future president; Sargent Shriver, later to run the Peace Corps; Gore Vidal, still in high school at Philips Exeter; and two of Teddy Roosevelt's children.[37]

Despite initial success and its distinguished pedigree, the America First Committee would gradually lose momentum and, as it did, it became more associated with the extreme right wing and with notorious anti-Semites like Henry Ford and Avery Brundage. Lindbergh, though a formal member of the movement for only a brief period, remained a supporter, and his personal trajectory was similar. As late as September 11, 1941, he gave a major speech in Des Moines, Iowa, that reiterated his opposition to war but went further in attacking "the subterfuge and propaganda" of "the major war agitators." These consisted of three groups: "the British, the Jewish and the Roosevelt administration." He claimed "to understand why Jewish people desire the overthrow of Nazi Germany," but warned Jews that war would breed intolerance and they would in turn "be among the first to feel its [the war's] consequences."[38] Whether meant as friendly advice or threat, the speech echoed a speech Hitler himself had given in January 1939.[39] Lindbergh's address was understood as anti-Semitic and widely denounced. By this time, it seems, the public had been weaned off of its opposition to intervening in the widening conflict.

Still, it would take the bombing of Pearl Harbor and the German declaration of war against the United States for the country to become fully involved in the war in both Europe and the Pacific. Only after that did the America First Committee formally dissolve and urge its members to support the war effort. The country's best-known and most influential advocates of isolation finally rallied to Roosevelt's side and pledged to pitch in to win the war. The Roosevelt administration, eschewing retribution, appointed many former opponents to positions of responsibility during the war. At the time, it seemed the right thing to do. Perhaps it was—but perhaps it was not. A more thorough reckoning with the forces of illiberalism might well have been called for. Beyond that, there was an obvious need to design a new world order that would replace the competing orders that had brought on the Second World War. But at the moment there was a war to be fought and won.

Defining the Enemy, Crafting Strategy, Imagining a New World

Dilemmas

The alliance that would defeat Hitler and his Japanese and Italian allies took a long time to come together. When it did finally form at the end of 1941, the military balance shifted dramatically.[1] Adding the military and industrial might of the United States to that of the Soviet Union and Great Britain meant that the Axis powers were outmanned and outgunned and that, over the long term, they could not prevail. Making war was from the beginning a complicated matter: it required managing alliances while deciding strategy, mobilizing troops and material resources, and fighting actual battles.

The inevitability of Axis defeat was, of course, not at all obvious in December 1941. As of that moment Germany and Japan had advanced on three wide fronts: Germany was dominant in Western Europe, and its weaker partner, Italy, added strength to the south and southeast; Germany, with aid from the armed forces of like-minded and/or dominated states in Central and Eastern Europe, had tight control there and had moved east, reaching the gates of Moscow and Leningrad. Japan was paramount in Northeast Asia, waging a successful war of conquest in China and achieving a series of quick victories in Southeast Asia and the western Pacific.[2] In addition, there was as yet no guarantee that the new allies would collaborate effectively or that their disagreements might not work to the advantage of the aggressors.

The first task, then, was to tend to the alliance, but that was not so simple. Building the alliance meant defining the enemy and understanding its strengths, weaknesses, and goals. It then required that the new allies define appropriate strategy, but strategy had to be based not only on a reasonable grasp of the enemy but also on the different capacities and objectives of those fighting against them. Objectives would necessarily be both short-term and long-term, and they would shift—expanding or contracting as the war progressed. It is possible to separate these tasks analytically, but they were pursued simultaneously in the frantic early days of the alliance and need to be seen in all their messy connectedness.

Logically, the question of how to fight and defeat the Axis powers ought to have been the top priority, but strategy depended also on capacity. The entry of the United States into the conflict vastly augmented the resources available to the allies, but it would take time for America to raise, train, and equip its forces and to rebuild the navy after Pearl Harbor. In the meantime, the US would continue its role as the "arsenal of democracy," but the fighting would be done by others. The Soviets had no choice but to dig in and resist the Nazi onslaught on their own territory. They desperately wanted the United States and Britain to open a second front in the west. The US and the UK did undertake a serious and damaging bombing campaign, but an amphibious landing against well-fortified coastal positions was judged too risky until May/June 1944. By that time the Soviets had stopped the Germans, first at Stalingrad and then more broadly, and begun a long campaign to push them back across Eastern Europe. The British, for their part, preferred a focus on the Mediterranean, where the Germans and Italians were less deeply entrenched. Fighting there also served to protect British interests in the region and the link to India. In the United States, there was considerable sentiment for going after Japan first. They had, after all, attacked the US directly. Roosevelt disagreed and gave priority to the battle for Europe, though in practice the administration devoted serious attention to both Europe and the Pacific.[3]

With strategy constrained, decisive and direct action was often delayed and directed toward goals with less clear and obvious impact on

Berlin or Tokyo. While logistics slowly improved and capacities grew, debate over strategy was nevertheless constant; and by the time certain moves became possible, visions of the future had come into play. In addition, over time the United States and its British ally developed a deeper understanding of the nature of the regimes in place in Germany, Japan, and Italy as their wartime actions could be seen and documented and their propaganda refuted and undermined. This affected strategy. What the Nazis and their allies did in practice spoke more forcefully and truthfully about what kind of future they envisioned for themselves and their victims than their prewar rhetoric of grievance.[4] Their actions were not only brutal, even genocidal, but they manifested a grand ambition to dominate other peoples and vast stretches of territory. The Germans, Italians, and Japanese aimed to establish new regional orders that would merge into a global order. The scale of their objectives demanded that the allies counter with visions and programs that could match up. It was, in fact, in direct response to the German proposal for a new order in conquered Europe that the British began serious talk of a "British-American world order."[5] In the context, the arguments of isolationists or noninterventionists in the US appeared as relics of an earlier, simpler time: it was now obvious that America's physical isolation provided no guarantee against rival powers and that the choice was either to shape a more attractive (and liberal) order or to live within, or acquiesce to, someone else's illiberal world.[6] The immediate need to counter the Nazi vision for a new order meant that United States and Britain would begin early and then continue to work on their evolving visions. That would be done by planners in government but also by a wide network of organizations and individuals outside government eager to determine the principles of postwar order and to shape its institutions.

War Aims, Rhetoric, and Strategy

The powers that came together to defeat the Axis brought to the struggle distinct interests and objectives that jostled and clashed and had to be bridged. Part of that bridging happened at the level of rhetoric. Words used in wartime to rally the support of the public and inspire the sacrifices of so many are not always to be taken seriously or literally, but they are not without effect. They contain at least implicit promises that might well have to be redeemed in some fashion; and political actors can take slogans and push them in different directions than originally intended. So, rhetoric matters.

The Nazis and their allies provided their opponents with the simplest and most effective slogan: their undisguised acts of aggression made the achievement of peace the first plank in what the British, the Americans, and the Soviets offered to their own people and to the world. It was almost inevitable, then, that they would also propose the establishment of an international organization, like the League of Nations but presumably more effective, to guarantee the peace and prevent a recurrence of war.[7] Opposing aggression was a powerful motivation, but it was basically negative. Ensuring peace was a genuinely positive goal, but necessarily distant and difficult to guarantee. More was needed, and it would have to speak to the kind of world one was fighting for both internationally and at home. The leaders of Britain and the United States began to define that in the Atlantic Charter, signed by Churchill and Roosevelt in August 1941. The document built on Roosevelt's State of the Union address of January 6, in which he spoke of the "Four Freedoms"—freedom of speech and expression, freedom of religion, freedom from want, and freedom from fear. The charter swore off "aggrandizement" and territorial changes made without consent and embraced "the right of all peoples to choose the form of government under which they will live." It promised also an effort to provide to all states "access, on equal terms, to the trade and raw materials of the world" and "the fullest cooperation between all nations in the economic field." It held out the prospect, "after the final destruction of the Nazi tyranny," of "a peace" that would assure that "all the men in all the lands may live out their lives in freedom from fear and want" and that would "enable all men to traverse the high seas and oceans without hindrance." Lastly, the two leaders agreed to work toward the "abandonment of the use of force" in international relations and, to that end, toward disarmament.[8]

Three features of the statement stand out. First, freedom from want and fear were explicitly contrasted with Nazi tyranny. Although the document did not say how these new freedoms would be secured, it was clear that any effort would necessarily involve proposals for social and economic programs that would be expensive and controversial. This was, pretty much by definition, a matter of domestic reform and reconstruction, but it was now cast as a goal to be shared across nations. Second, freer trade and self-determination all around would mean the end of policies like "imperial preference," formally adopted by Britain in 1932, and ultimately the end of empire. The implication would be made still clearer in Article VII of Lend-Lease, in which Britain, as a "consideration" for aid, would be committed "to the elimination of all forms of discriminatory treatment in international commerce, and to the reduction of tariffs and other trade barriers." The United Kingdom was, of course, committed to the preservation of the empire and the argument over the meaning of the Atlantic Charter and the implementation of Article VII would bedevil US/UK relations throughout the war. France's would-be leaders were equally uninterested in getting rid of France's empire. Having fallen to the Germans, the French were not parties to the charter or subsequent agreements until after the liberation in 1944. Still, previous French governments and the governments of France from 1944 on were keen to hold onto the French empire; in May 1945, as representatives from many nations were meeting in San Francisco to decide on and agree to the Charter of the United Nations, the French invaded Syria and Lebanon.[9]

Perhaps the most obviously odd feature of the charter and its principles was what it did not say about the Soviet Union. The idea that all peoples should have the right to choose the form of government under which they would live would seem to imply that states ought to be democratic in order to be legitimate. Could anyone in 1941 say that that principle applied to the Soviet Union? Could anyone say that the people of the Soviet Union, still subject to Stalinist terror so visibly on display in the 1930s, were able to enjoy freedom "from fear" in any meaningful sense? Clearly not, but such awkward facts did not prevent the adherence of the USSR to the allied cause and its participation in a theoretically anti-fascist crusade. Nor did it preclude the United States from offering Lend-Lease aid to the Soviets.

Nonetheless, the principles of the Atlantic Charter would serve as the basis for the alliance between the United States, the UK, and the Soviet Union. Shortly after Pearl Harbor, Churchill came to the United

States to meet with Roosevelt at what was known as the Arcadia Confer-
ence, which lasted into January.[10] There the two decided on the priority
of defeating the Nazis and established the Combined Chiefs of Staff
Committee, which would coordinate the war effort of the two countries.
At the same meeting it was decided to label the new alliance the United
Nations and the United Nations Declaration, announced on New Year's
Day in 1942 by the US, the UK, China, and the Soviet Union, made explicit reference to the Atlantic Charter.[11] Support for the charter was also
incorporated into the Anglo-Soviet Treaty agreed on May 26, 1942. Every country that joined in the alliance, now the United Nations, was required to sign up to these objectives as well.[12] Contradictions between
reality and the meaning and application of these principles would be left
unaddressed for most of the war. There was no disguising them, however, and as the war dragged on and plans for after the war began to be
formulated, the implications of the formal commitment to the charter
and the contrast between rhetoric and practice would become more
evident and consequential.

The ambiguities within the principles of the Atlantic Charter and
the discrepancies between the ideals it embraced and the realities it obscured guaranteed that there would be continued debate not only about
the nature of the Axis enemy but also about the purposes of those who
resisted and made war against it. Debate in fact accompanied the signing of the charter, for its terms could easily be read as a plan for a world
run by the United States and Britain and that was, almost by definition,
an imperial project. The charter was not, in fact, widely popular in the
countries that would be the subjects of Anglo-American domination;
nor was it widely applauded in the United States. American and British
leaders and postwar planners quickly grasped the problem and began to
connect the principles of the declaration with proposals for a world organization that would lead to the creation of the United Nations.[13]

The debate about the Atlantic Charter and what it meant for the
postwar world is a reminder that politics did not cease because a war
was on, and public opinion shifted both because of the war and despite
it. The effort to understand the Nazi dictatorship and its allies occurred
simultaneously with plans and decisions about what to tell the public
about the enemy. There was therefore an interaction between intelli-

gence gathering, research analysis, and propaganda in both the United States and Britain. The occupied or exiled French, skilled at research and argumentation, were in no position to undertake these tasks, and there was no need or political space in the Soviet Union. In the US and the UK, however, governments enlisted the skills of specialists to discern the peculiarities of the enemy.

The effort in the US engaged both American scholars and émigrés from Europe. It was also closely linked to British intelligence. In May 1940 William Stephenson, who worked for the Secret Intelligence Service (MI6), was made British security coordinator in New York. He was there to promote British interests in whatever way necessary—by warning Americans of the dangers of Nazi aggression, spreading word about a supposed pro-Nazi fifth column, and undertaking harassment of German interests in both the US and Latin America. The main aim at this point was convincing the United States to assist Britain in its desperate and lonely struggle against the Nazis. Stephenson managed to get close to officials in the Roosevelt administration and worked directly with William (Wild Bill) Donovan, a longtime Republican eager to support the British cause. Donovan led one of several missions to the UK meant to assess the ability of Britain to resist the Germans. Once convinced that it could stand up to Hitler's forces with help from the US, he would return and organize on behalf of greater US involvement. Donovan would eventually become the leader of the Office of Strategic Services (OSS), the predecessor of the Central Intelligence Agency.

The army, navy, War Department, State Department, and FBI also had intelligence capabilities, which they were each keen to maintain, and in February 1941 Roosevelt set up a group that reported directly to him.[14] A critical part of the effort involved the Research and Analysis Branch (R&A), which undertook more academic and "objective" work on a variety of topics. Led for most of its existence by the Harvard historian William Langer, it employed an eminent roster of young American-trained scholars who would go on to distinguished scholarly careers after the war. These included, among many others, Arthur Schlesinger Jr., Carl Schorske, H. Stuart Hughes, Leonard Krieger, and Wassily Leontief. They worked alongside, and often under, more senior scholars like Felix Gilbert and Hajo Holborn. In addition, R&A also relied upon the work of European émigrés, most notably refugee scholars from the Institute for Social Research in Frankfurt such as Herbert Marcuse, Franz Neumann, and Otto Kirchheimer. In theory, research and analysis were supposed to inform the more practical work of influencing the public, that is, propaganda. Responsibility for that task was lodged formally, at least for a time, in the Office of War Information led by Archibald MacLeish, but efforts to educate Americans and encourage support for the war were widely dispersed. They were aided—indeed, often guided—by the results of opinion polls conducted directly by the government or by private polling firms.[15]

In Britain, the Ministry of Information played a major role, but the Foreign Office, the military, and other agencies also undertook key tasks. Some analysts worked alongside the code breakers at Bletchley Park; others were attached to the Special Operations Executive (SOE), MI6, or the Political Warfare Executive. Two leading historians, A. J. P. Taylor and Geoffrey Barraclough, would produce influential books on German history from their wartime researches; a third, Hugh Trevor-Roper, would begin a lengthy career editing and writing about Hitler and other Nazis.[16] As in the US, however, lots of people and groups were engaged in intelligence work, propaganda, and analysis. Crane Brinton, an American academic responsible for the Research and Analysis Branch office in London, pointedly referred to "the 57 varieties of M.I. [military intelligence]" he encountered there and from which he had to extract information.[17]

This extensive activity meant that fighting the war, for both the US and the UK, was an intellectual and educational exercise as well as a military one. The overlap of agencies and actors meant an array of agendas were brought to the task and coordination was always difficult. Nevertheless, the cumulative effect was dramatic. Before the war, public opinion in the United States, Britain, and France was split between those who wished to resist fascism and those who wanted to compromise with or appease it. A few were actually sympathetic to the Nazis and many more shared some of their ideas. During the war, a genuine and popular anti-fascism became the norm: fascist ideas lost their attraction as their consequences were revealed; and fascist sympathizers were disabused about the objects of their affection, or at least persuaded to be quiet about them. The growing aversion to fascism and to the fascist powers also brought into disrepute ideas about racial hierarchy and various justifications for imperialism.

A measure of the extent of this transformation can be seen in the treatment of anti-Semitism in allied propaganda and education efforts, especially in the United States.[18] Early in the war the Roosevelt administration was happy enough to focus on how the Axis powers mistreated those they defeated, but they often played down the specific targeting of Jews for fear that Americans would think that the country was going to war mainly to help the Jews. This, it was assumed, would diminish the resolve to fight; and the assumption was backed up by opinion polls. The same polls also showed that Americans held reasonably favorable beliefs about ordinary Germans. They were, after all, white and Christian. No such sympathy was felt toward the Japanese, of course, because they were neither white nor Christian. Over the course of the war these attitudes changed significantly as the public became more aware of the politics and ideas that tied together the dictators. It also became possible to talk explicitly about the fate of the Jews. None of this meant that anti-Semitism or racism toward people of color, at home or abroad, was eliminated by the educational and propaganda efforts that accompanied the war. Such sentiments became more marginal, however, and they would stay marginal and unspoken for years to come.

To what extent this shift was due to the efforts of governments and their supporters is difficult to say with precision, but they surely contributed. It was also, and just as surely, a product of domestic politics, which moved decisively to the left in the US, Britain, and France.[19] The wartime shift to the left was due to conscious efforts to change minds, but also to the discrediting of old elites and the policies they had pursued during the 1930s as well as to a strengthening of unions and other organizations that underpinned left-wing politics. The organizational basis of the shift was essential. The depression had initially served to weaken trade unions in most places, including the United States. It is difficult for the unemployed to organize or to go on strike. Over time, however, the balance of advantage shifted as massive discontent produced election victories for the center-left and more pro-labor policies from the government. The Roosevelt administration had taken steps to make unionization easier in 1933 through the National Recovery Act, and then more decisively with the National Labor Relations Act of 1935. Organization surged from the mid-1930s. The Congress of Industrial Organizations (CIO), which leaned left, took the lead and enrolled millions. The trend continued as the nation rearmed and during the war due to a tight labor market and continued government support. The Ford Motor Company would sign its first contract with the United Auto Workers (UAW) in June 1941. The dynamism of the unions, notably those in the CIO, was critical to the sustained support that urban workers gave to the New Deal and later to Harry Truman and the "Fair Deal." As the strength of labor increased, the respect accorded to business and the wealthy, and their political supporters, declined.

The grounding of politics also altered in Great Britain. Trade unions were traditionally stronger in Britain, where membership expanded during both world wars. Over 8 million had belonged to unions in 1920, better than 45 percent of the labor force. The unions nevertheless spent much of the interwar era on the defensive, and membership was halved by 1933. Rearmament and war led to steady growth after that, and by 1943 over 43 percent of workers were organized.[20] As in the US, the growing strength of trade unions served to underpin the strength of center-left politics and the revival in the fortunes of the Labour Party that culminated in its massive election victory in 1945. The seeds of Labour's victory were planted earlier, as the Tories had presided over years of depression and the diplomatic failures of the late 1930s, finishing in appeasement and Chamberlain's ineffective leadership early in the war. A popular pamphlet of 1940, *Guilty Men*, brought these themes together and cemented the identification of Conservatism with failure bordering on treason.[21] Churchill's soaring rhetoric and the UK's eventual military success appeared to obscure this connection, and the Tories approached the 1945 election confident of victory. They were wrong. In retrospect, the indictment of Tory elites in 1939–40 had been decisive and lasting, and the Tories reminded voters of their fundamental lack of sympathy by the underwhelming reception they gave to the publication of the Beveridge Report on social security and its de facto promise of major social reform after the war. The 1945 reckoning was transformative.

In France, union membership was historically lower than in Britain, and both the unions and the left were more fractured. Union strength did increase massively with the election of the Popular Front govern-ment in 1936. The huge strike wave in June of that year simultaneously marked and encouraged this great leap, and it also produced the famous Matignon Agreements, which granted a forty-hour work week, substan-tial wage increases, two-week paid vacations, and new rights for unions. Not all the gains lasted, but many did. Employers, momentarily on the defensive in 1936, pushed back against the gains of the Popular Front over the next four years, but those efforts were nothing compared to the impact of war and defeat.

With the fall of France in May 1940, the unions and the left were effectively routed. But occupation and collaboration eventually led to resistance, and the trade unions and left parties managed to regroup, paper over their deep divisions, and play a huge role. After Hitler's inva-sion of the Soviet Union, Communists would join the resistance in large numbers, and their superior organization and dedication gave them even greater influence. The Common Program of the National Council of Resistance (CNR), adopted in March 1944, reflected the waxing strength of the left. It called for punishing traitors and purging collabo-rators and for convening a constituent assembly at war's end to create "a veritable economic and social democracy" and to enlist the state to guarantee "a rational organization of the economy." The program prom-ised as well a "complete plan of social security."[22]

Because winning the war was inevitably the top priority of the British and American governments, as liberation from Nazi tyranny was for the French Resistance, the leftward drift of opinion was often missed, fully registered only at the end of the war.[23] Even then, it was merged with patriotism in an unprecedented fashion. Indeed, it might well be argued that the signal achievement of the left or center-left in the allied countries in the course of the war was that they managed to identify themselves and the interests they represented with those of the nation at large. With the notable exception of the Communists between the Hit-ler-Stalin Pact and the Nazi invasion of June 1941, it was the left that had warned most fulsomely against fascism and, with exceptions, had fought hardest against it. By contrast much, though not all, of the traditional right had been neutral before the advance of the fascist right, frequently willing to deal with it and slow to resist and mobilize against it. The left was far less ambivalent. The left, or at least the center-left, was also by the 1940s armed with an economic program that sought to link the interests of the less well-off with those of the nation as a whole and with the health of the national economy. That link was largely the result of the widespread adoption of Keynesian economics, whose focus on demand implied that providing work and welfare to the poor and the working class would also benefit the economy overall.[24]

The changed political landscape after the war would mean that politics would be conducted on different terms and with different policies and coalitions than before 1939. Old discredited parties could not be restored, old hierarchies were permanently gone, and political authority would have to be rethought and reestablished over large parts of the world. Logically, there would be less need for restructuring in countries that had prevailed in the war than in those that had experienced defeat, but nowhere would it be possible to return to the patterns that had held, or rather not held, before 1939.

Just what new arrangements and which parties and policies would prove viable would depend on local conditions but also on the state of the world after the war. Deciding the contours of the new international system was the task taken on by the leaders of the winning side. They did this conscious of their long-standing and likely future differences, although often without any clear sense of the shifting political allegiances within their own countries and with even less knowledge of internal politics elsewhere. Still, they bargained hard and made grand efforts to restructure the international order. In this effort they were guided not merely by self-interest, but also by their views on what had failed after the First World War and what went wrong in the 1930s. Clearly, there were more precedents to be avoided than models to be emulated.

There was also an understandable hesitancy among wartime leaders to make commitments they would later regret. The Soviets, for example, were determined to keep the territories they had gained, or regained, while they were allied with the Nazis. They had no intention of giving independence to Latvia, Lithuania, or Estonia. Stalin was also intent on creating a buffer zone of friendly—and ultimately Soviet-dominated—states in Eastern Europe more broadly. During the war Soviet intentions remained vague, and discussions of postwar arrangements reflected that. The main reason was that until June 1944, when the western allies finally invaded France and opened the "second front" so long demanded by the Soviet Union, the Soviets were eager to keep on good terms with Britain and the United States. By that moment, of course, Soviet tanks and troops were pushing the Nazis back along a lengthy front in the East, creating power on the ground that limited the options available to the US and Britain and to the peoples and states in the East. The United States, and also Britain, had equally good reasons to postpone confrontation with the Soviets: they were eager to get Soviet help in the battle against Japan. So, while much bargaining occurred at a series of high-level and by now famous conferences, much was left unsaid or undecided. Strategic decisions taken during the war nevertheless very much shaped the possibilities for postwar political choices.

Hesitancy and deferral were balanced by ambition. The global character of the war ensured that there could be no small, modest visions for the shape of postwar. The fact that at the peak of their success the Nazis and their allies controlled such wide swathes of territory meant that the US, the UK, and the USSR had to develop plans for the world, not just for themselves and their narrow, or not so narrow, possessions and interests. The Nazis, of course, also thought globally and envisioned an order, or a set of huge regional orders, stratified by race. Hitler's personal outlook was marked by hatreds, weird quirks, delusions, and a consistent underestimation of his opponents, but his ambition was grand and brutal.[25] A thorough opposition to that sort of ambition would need to be democratic and liberal, and potentially as far-reaching as the visions of the dictators.

The most effective responses would, of necessity, come from allied leaders with the power to turn plans into practical measures. Alongside their efforts, and occasionally inspiring them, were ideas about global order. By one measure, attention to "world order" and "the global" became widespread during the war, peaking in 1945.[26] Scholars and writers—scientists, social scientists, even philosophers—had much to say, turning out a huge volume of work on how to reorganize the world after the cataclysms of the previous three decades. Nazism and the atomic bomb often gave the discourse on postwar an apocalyptic cast. Some demanded a new morality, others new social orders, and others offered schemes for world government. To take the most elaborate and serious effort, the Chicago Committee to Frame a World Constitution convened in 1945 and elicited input from a dazzling array of intellectuals from across the country and abroad. Committee members published a draft constitution in 1948: it covered forms of government and representation, the question of decolonization, and human rights.[27] The plan's scope inevitably rendered its application impossible, and this "staggeringly implausible document" had little, if any, effect.[28] It emerged, after all, only when the key decisions had already been taken and the institutions that would carry out those decisions already established. The same fate overtook other visions of world order and global governance. Such utopian visions had an obvious appeal in light of the disasters of the past three decades and potential horrors of the coming atomic age, but the confrontation with Nazism in particular had actually underlined the importance of sovereignty and the power to defend it. Ceding that sovereignty—only recently defended and in cases reclaimed—to a higher power representing the interests of the entire world was simply not about to happen. Still, the aspirations these debates reflected were an indication of how far-reaching the choices made in the mid- to late 1940s would be.

However grand and noble the competing visions of the postwar world, actual plans and decisions were also informed by traditional interests of state. Stalin, in theory committed to world revolution, had dissolved the Communist International in 1943 to demonstrate the modesty of Soviet aims and the Soviets' reliability as an ally. Toward the end of the war, his goal was mainly defensive. He hoped to succeed by continuing the wartime alliance, but the Soviets insisted on a free hand in what they regarded as their proper sphere of influence. Britain was also committed to maintaining a working relationship with the Soviets, but its main goal was to protect the empire and a set of interests in the Mediterranean and the Middle East that were based on a sense of what was best for the empire. Just how to do that was unclear, though it would be necessary to work with and through the Americans. France lacked the military or political strength to have a major impact on the decisions reached at the end of the war, but it did manage, by default almost, to get a seat on the UN Security Council and a share of the occupation.

De Gaulle's "une certaine idée de la France," which was not identical to or fully compatible with the politics of the resistance but was grudgingly acknowledged by the allies, was mainly a matter of restoring the nation's traditional interests and grandeur. That required the rebuilding of the French state and the reassertion of control over France's empire.[29]

If there was a state with a bolder vision of postwar possibilities, it was the United States. The Roosevelt and Truman administrations were by no means "revolutionary," and they were careful to work within established traditions in the making of American foreign policy, but if they succeeded in their objectives, the resulting global order would indeed be very different. Roosevelt was especially attuned to the hesitations of the US public and to the potential criticisms of his opponents. He was nevertheless determined to see the nation adopt a new and more forceful role in ordering the world. He and his administration were proposing, in effect, a "New Deal" for the world, though it would necessarily occur within a geopolitical order defined by US dominance. The vision would involve a push for democracy and self-determination and the implanting where possible of a type of capitalism that was less enamored of laissez-faire and more restrained by government involvement and greater social protections than before the war. The US under Roosevelt and then under Truman became committed as well to the creation of a new international organization to keep the peace and oversee the global order, but one more effective than the League of Nations. The United States was also a fundamentally post-imperial, if not always anti-imperialist, power. It would not force its allies to give up their colonial possessions immediately upon the end of the war, but there was little doubt that its vision did not include colonies permanently run by the European powers. Put simply, the US outlook was more forward-looking than that of Britain and France and less defensive than that of the USSR. That was only fitting from a country that was still on the rise economically and politically and that had suffered far less from the war than its allies. This did not make its rivals feel any less threatened or overwhelmed, and for many it confirmed long-term predictions and fears of American hegemony. Working out the meaning of this new status would have enormous consequences.

The implications of the altered balance of power after the war would become obvious very soon after victory, a product of underlying strengths amplified during wartime and of strategic choices made during the conflict. The British and Americans coordinated closely during the conflict, while the Soviets mainly fought their own desperate war. Decisions on overall strategy, however, of necessity involved the Soviet Union, and they would typically be taken in trilateral or bilateral meetings of the top leaders—Roosevelt, Churchill, and Stalin (and later on Truman and Attlee)—or of their foreign ministers. The first critical meeting had been that between Churchill and Roosevelt in August 1941 to draft the Atlantic Charter. What Churchill and Britain got from the meeting was a de facto commitment of American support in the war even before its formal entry; what the US got was language embodying the commitment to the "Four Freedoms," and that presaged an end to empire and the opening up of world trade. The Soviet Union was not represented, but it formally agreed on the terms of the charter in a bilateral agreement with Britain the following summer. Clearly, the Soviets did not fret much over the commitments to democracy and self-determination to which they were signing up. The signing of the Atlantic Charter definitively ended any doubt about whose side the United States would take. That had been no secret after the passage of Lend-Lease the previous March, but the charter provided the rationale for that choice.

The question that mainly dominated negotiations between the top leaders was when and where to open the second front in the war against Hitler. The British and the Americans agreed in principle that the Soviet Union needed relief, but the British consistently pushed for a peripheral strategy, focusing on North Africa and the Mediterranean as their top priority. The Soviets wanted a second front in Western Europe, and the United States basically agreed, but the Americans and the British were also in agreement that invading northern France required overwhelming force and that meant winning the battle of the Atlantic and freeing up shipping to allow the transport of troops and armaments. In practice, therefore, the US acquiesced to the British insistence on delay and agreed to undertake military action in North Africa in 1942. That would be followed by the Italian campaign beginning in 1943. These strategic decisions made the Soviets doubt the commitment of their new allies who, in truth, continued to harbor suspicions that Stalin would do another deal with Hitler. To reassure the Soviets, the US and UK announced the policy of "unconditional surrender," applied to both Germany and Japan, at the meeting in Casablanca in January 1943. Stalin did not attend, but he later agreed to the formulation in the Moscow Declaration of October 30, 1943, which also committed the "Big Three" and China to the postwar creation of an organization to keep the peace. A simultaneous "Statement on Atrocities" promised to punish Germans guilty of war crimes, while specific policies on the future of Germany were referred to a European Advisory Commission.[30] The three top leaders would meet soon after in Tehran, where the final details of the invasion of France would be settled and the Soviets agreed that they would join the fight against Japan after the defeat of the Germans. Roosevelt elicited an explicit statement of support for creation of the United Nations and secured an agreement for the meeting at Dumbarton Oaks to draft a constitution for the new organization. Stalin, in turn, got the US and UK to acquiesce on the new Polish border, which would be pushed further west into what had been German territory.

As of late 1943, the allies were mainly bargaining over strategy for winning the war, with little attention to what would happen afterward. There were two exceptions to this relative silence: the question of the United Nations, a major preoccupation of Roosevelt, and the Polish border, a top priority for Stalin. The effect of this sequencing was that by the time the allies got around to the specifics of postwar conditions, key issues had been settled by earlier decisions or by military action. Most important, stunning advances by the Red Army meant that the Soviets were in control across much of Eastern Europe by the time leaders began to discuss postwar arrangements explicitly. Both Roosevelt and Churchill understood this and could do little more than acquiesce. The most embarrassing example was Churchill's "percentages agreement" with Stalin in Moscow in October 1944. Churchill wrote a note to the effect that the Soviet influence would be 90 percent in Romania and 75 percent in Bulgaria; in Hungary and Yugoslavia Anglo-American and Soviet influence would be 50 percent each; while in Greece UK influence would be 90 percent. Stalin amended the note to give the Soviets 100 percent influence in Romania and 80 percent in Hungary. Churchill later protested that the note was simply a set of vague guidelines, agreed on to avoid conflict and disruption in the Balkans. He did not, however, immediately share the details with Roosevelt. The exchange did not specify the share of influence in Poland or Czechoslovakia. The existence of the agreement nonetheless confirmed that the Soviets would have the predominant say in what happened in Eastern and southern Europe and that Churchill (and inevitably Roosevelt) understood that there was little that could be done about it.

Soviet domination in the East was effectively reaffirmed at Yalta the following February. Roosevelt and Churchill pushed for assurances that democratic elections would be held in Poland and in other recently "liberated" countries, and the Soviets made verbal commitments to that effect. The *Declaration on Liberated Europe* promised that the newly freed peoples of Europe would be allowed "to create democratic institutions of their own choice," but there was no mechanism to enforce that promise.[31] The Soviets also agreed to let representatives of the London Poles, who had constituted themselves as a government-in-exile, return and participate in politics alongside the pro-Soviet "Lublin" group. The meeting also agreed on the date of the San Francisco conference to found the United Nations, and the Soviets came to accept the functions of the UN Security Council as proposed by the United States. Much time was also spent in trying to work out the details of the occupation of Germany and how it would be treated after the war. The discussion produced agreement on the four occupation zones, the policy of demilitarization and denazification, and that the Soviet Union would receive half the reparations the Germans would be forced to pay. More fundamental decisions about the shape of Germany and its future role were put off.

In a sense, then, the most immediately consequential decisions concerned Eastern Europe. The reality was that the fate of the peoples of Eastern Europe would be decided by the Soviet Union and their local allies and agents. Within weeks of the Yalta meeting, on February 27, a coup installed a Communist regime in Romania. The Soviet-controlled regime in Poland allowed the London Poles into the country, but would then arrest members of the Polish underground who had worked with them. Free and open elections did not happen in Poland until 1989. The US, which had already communicated its decision to withdraw troops from Europe within two years, and the UK were helpless to intervene. The UN was successfully established and the Soviets did agree more precisely on participation in the war against Japan three months after Germany's surrender. Still, the military balance meant that Europe would be divided between East and West for a long time to come. Almost inevitably, the Yalta meeting and decisions became controversial and provided fodder for conservatives wishing to attack Roosevelt for being soft on the USSR and having sold out Poland and other countries in the East. The fact was that there was no viable alternative.

When the leaders came to meet again at Potsdam from July 17 to August 2, 1945, much had changed. Roosevelt had died on April 12 and was succeeded by Harry Truman. Germany had surrendered on May 7 and was already occupied. Churchill went into the meeting as prime minister, but was replaced in the middle by Clement Attlee after Labour's victory in the general election. Policy toward Germany was again the priority, and the allies reaffirmed their commitment to "the complete disarmament and demilitarization of Germany and the elimination or control of all German industry that could be used for military production."[32] There would be serious efforts to denazify the schools and the judiciary and to purge Nazi officials from the bureaucracy and the top ranks of industry. It was also decided that the occupying powers could extract reparations only from their own zone. Further decisions, it was agreed, would be put off until further meetings of the Big Three, which never happened, or of their foreign ministers, which would soon end in acrimony.

It would seem that Truman was more forceful in his dealings with Stalin than Roosevelt had been, but the context was different as well. The US had successfully tested the atom bomb just before the meeting, and Truman now knew he had leverage that FDR, faced with the need for Soviet support in the war against Japan, had lacked. By July there was also clear evidence that the Soviets were not going to live up to the agreements made at Yalta. Knowing that, Roosevelt would likely have taken a harder line as well. Still, the American and British positions had hardened marginally, and tensions with the Soviets had increased. A toughened stance was also manifest in the Potsdam Declaration of July 26 addressed to Japan. Issued by the US, Britain, and China (the Soviet Union had still not declared war on Japan), it called for "unconditional surrender" and threatened "prompt and utter destruction" if Japan resisted. The declaration also promised that Japan would be occupied and forced to undergo the sort of demilitarization already occurring in Germany; and specific mention was made of efforts to encourage a genuine democracy. In response to the threat, Japan's leaders argued and chose delay, and then they reaped the destruction wrought by the bombings of Hiroshima and Nagasaki. On August 9, the day Nagasaki was bombed, the Soviets declared war on Japan and invaded Manchuria.

The results of the wartime conferences largely reflected the priorities of the US, UK, and USSR and closely tracked their relative military and economic strength. The Soviets achieved their objectives in Eastern Europe, if at great cost to the local populations; and the United States was effective in advancing its claims to global leadership. It managed to secure acquiescence to the establishment of the United Nations and imposed its vision of how that organization should operate. The United States also ended up in a dominant position in the Pacific after the defeat of Japan. The British were in alignment with the US on key issues, and prevailed to the extent their ally did. The British were also reasonably successful in their efforts to keep fighting in the Mediterranean and, to the extent possible, maintained their profile and influence there and in the Middle East. The achievement was evanescent, of course, as British weakness soon forced the country to cede its role in Greece and Iran and to retreat from Palestine and India. More generally, Britain would see its global position eclipsed by the rise of the two new superpowers. These relative strengths and weaknesses, and the achievements that resulted from them, were further reflected in the arrangements for governing the world economy and in the character of the United Nations.

The principles and institutions that would structure the world economy were worked out at the Bretton Woods conference in the summer of 1944. The decisions reached at the meeting had been hammered out by the United States and Britain since the two became allies. The British were represented by John Maynard Keynes, whose brilliance no one disputed and whose theories had finally won over the majority of his fellow economists and his antagonists at the UK Treasury. A key turning point had been the publication of Keynes's book *The General Theory of Employment, Interest and Money* in 1936, but his new status was officially recognized only with his appointment to the treasury early in the war and then as a director of the Bank of England. He was in effect charged with overseeing war finance and economic planning for after the war. His US counterpart, in terms of negotiating at Bretton Woods, was Harry Dexter White, a relatively undistinguished economist who worked for Henry Morgenthau at the US Treasury. Keynes would proceed to win all the rhetorical debates, but the outcome was basically the set of arrangements that White designed to serve American interests.[33]

What the United States and Britain wanted largely overlapped, but their differences also mattered. Both sides wanted to open up the closed world of the 1930s, where the retreat behind tariffs, controlled and inconvertible currencies, and quasi-imperial autarchy impeded trade and growth. The United Kingdom wanted, however, to preserve the protections provided by the system of imperial preferences. The UK also wanted to protect its reserves of currency by holding on to the "sterling balances" it had built up during the war. That would mean resisting pressure to repay them to those within the empire and Commonwealth to whom they belonged and allowing them instead to be converted into gold or dollars. To that end, Keynes offered a plan for an "International Clearing Bank" that would have its own noncirculating currency, the proposed "bancor," allocated to countries based on their share of world trade. The initial amounts would increase with exports or be depleted with imports and nations could purchase more with gold. The goal was to allow international trade to expand while limiting the effects of imbalances that, under a classic gold standard, would require debtor countries to adjust through austerity or depreciation. Under Keynes's plan, in fact, creditor nations would be forced to adjust by adopting policies designed to increase imports, further expanding trade and in the process putting money in the hands, or accounts, of debtors. It was a system quite compatible with British interests, of course, for "Britain had little gold but needed to conduct lots of trade."[34]

The United States, by contrast, was by this point the world's main creditor nation, with the largest gold reserves. In the context, it was unlikely to agree to an arrangement that created a rival to gold and the dollar and diminished its clout. The US plan accordingly called for a "Stabilization Fund" and a "Bank for Reconstruction and Development." The fund would replace the gold standard with the dollar, backed up by gold, although in later iterations the US plan would involve the creation of a unit of account called the "unitas" which, despite looking like the bancor, would actually be based on the dollar. The American proposal would be rather less favorable to debtors, but it was assumed that it would nevertheless serve to produce a more open trading system.

Variations of these plans emerged early in the war. Keynes got to work in August 1941 and had a draft ready in September; White was tasked by Morgenthau with developing a plan in December 1941 and had a proposal ready in March 1942. Over the next two years representatives of the two countries would argue over details. The result, agreed at Bretton Woods, was the creation of a set of institutions that would undertake the functions envisioned in the rival plans. These were the International Monetary Fund and the World Bank. A third institution, an International Trade Organization, was also planned, but agreement on its precise structure was elusive and bargaining would continue after the war. Even then, what was created was not the robust organization envisioned at Bretton Woods but the General Agreement on Tariffs and Trade, which came into being in 1948. The principles and practices embodied in the new framework came closest to the American vision, but Britain won important concessions. Again, this outcome was a fairly accurate reflection of the underlying strengths—economic, financial, military—of Britain and the United States.

What is easily missed in seeing Bretton Woods as an instance in the larger process through which the United States replaced Britain as global economic hegemon is the scope of the ambition behind American plans.[35] The plan to redesign the world financial system was of a piece with Roosevelt's Four Freedoms, especially freedom from want, which inspired the Atlantic Charter. It was linked, too, to his advocacy of an economic bill of rights.[36] The Beveridge Report of 1942 spoke a similar language, styling itself as "a necessary measure to translate the words of the Atlantic Charter into deeds."[37] When Morgenthau sent Roosevelt White's draft plan, he referred to it as aiming to create a "New Deal in international economics." Recent research has in fact shown that American proposals, modeled largely on the Good Neighbor policy toward Latin America, involved greater interest and commitment to development than what Keynes proposed.[38] The centerpiece of the effort would be the International Bank for Reconstruction and Development, later the World Bank, which would help to provide the "large investment sums that will be needed to raise the very low productive level of countries in the Far East, South America, in the Balkans, and the Near East," as White explained in September 1943.[39] There was even talk of mechanisms to compensate for the fluctuations in commodity prices that wreaked havoc on underdeveloped countries' accounts and of the potential value of capital controls. Not every suggestion along these lines prevailed in the bargaining at Bretton Woods, and the emphasis on development would be scaled back in the early years of the Cold War. Still, US objectives were grand and in key respects "progressive," rooted in the belief that a world that was more prosperous and equal would also be more peaceful. This was rather naïve, but not the worst assumption, and it was timely and appropriate to the moment when anti-fascist powers sought to build a set of institutions to secure the future.

The other major institutional innovation to come out of the war and postwar planning was the United Nations. The imperative to create an organization to maintain the peace was obvious to American leaders well before Pearl Harbor. Cordell Hull, the secretary of state, had set up committees on postwar plans in September 1939. A top State Department official, Leo Pasvolsky, was set to work on what would become the United Nations in early 1941, well before US entry into the conflict. Roosevelt was to prove a consistent supporter and worked hard from 1943 to get the Soviet Union to cooperate. Britain went along, though without the same enthusiasm, and through 1942 American and British officials worked separately. More active collaboration began the next year.

Roosevelt proceeded cautiously, for he was haunted by memories of what had happened to Wilson's plans after 1918 and the sorry fate of the League of Nations. He worried also about the potential opposition of critics who, though no longer explicitly against, were nevertheless skeptical of foreign entanglements, the compromises they would entail, and the costs of international commitments. In consequence, his strategy was to gradually win over possible opponents by involving them early and at least appearing to take their views seriously and, at the same time, moving things along quickly to take advantage of the politics of wartime and get a new organization in place before the end of hostilities.

Though he did not live to see it, Roosevelt achieved success on both counts. The United Nations (the alliance, not the organization, which did not yet exist) Conference on Food and Agriculture, convened in Hot Springs, Virginia, in May 1943, led to plans for a permanent organization linked to the future United Nations Organization; in November 1943 the United Nations Relief and Rehabilitation Administration was founded and began distributing aid to victims of Axis aggression.[40] In addition, the Bretton Woods meeting in July–August 1944 was officially a United Nations operation.

Plans for the new organization were developed primarily by the Americans and the British. The Soviets were initially fairly indifferent to the idea—later, they would be fearful of its implications and begin to make trouble—but went along as part of the price for the opening of the second front. The Soviet Union was also initially committed to maintaining cooperation with the US and Britain after the war. After the D-Day invasion, all sides became more interested in details. A key meeting was held at Dumbarton Oaks in Washington in the summer of 1944. Much was agreed there: the new organization would deal not just with security but have a wider mission, including social and economic matters; in terms of structure, it would have a general assembly, an executive council (later the Security Council) with seats reserved for the four great powers (the United States, the United Kingdom, the Soviet Union, and China) and several rotating seats, a court of justice, and a permanent secretariat. Roosevelt envisioned the great powers as "Four Policemen" who would oversee their respective regions of the world. The US, the UK, and the USSR were largely in agreement at Dumbarton Oaks; seasoned diplomats were taken aback at how relaxed and friendly the Soviet representative, Andrei Gromyko, was throughout the meeting.[41] However, some disagreements remained, particularly over membership and the nature of the veto power to be wielded by the permanent members of the executive.

Between the meetings at Dumbarton Oaks and the conference that crafted and approved the United Nations Charter in San Francisco in late spring 1945, some disagreements were worked out at Yalta, although others were not resolved until the San Francisco meeting.[42] Membership was critical: the Soviets wanted all sixteen republics to be members, arguing that members of the Commonwealth and India would be members and fearing that otherwise they would be outnumbered and outvoted. The Soviets also wanted to include Poland, despite the undemocratic nature of the Soviet-controlled regime. The Latin American states, key allies of the US, insisted on membership for Argentina, despite its dubious democratic credentials. After much haggling, Belarus and Ukraine became members, as did Argentina. Equally critical was the question of whether the new organization would have a military force of its own. It would, all agreed, be capable of military action against aggressors, but whose troops would undertake it? The US administration was deeply worried that its domestic critics would jump on any plan for an armed superstate and decided against the proposal. Rather, troops would be supplied on an ad hoc basis.

The final major question was the role of the Security Council. Would the permanent members, expanded now to include France, have veto power and, if they did, how far would it reach? It was the Soviets who had been most insistent on the veto at Dumbarton Oaks.[43] The US and Britain wanted to prevent the big powers from being able to use the veto if directly involved in a dispute. For the Soviets, that was rather the point. The US and Britain came to see the value of such a broad veto power, especially in selling the UN to domestic audiences. The outlines of a deal were reached at Yalta, in which it was agreed that the permanent members of the Security Council could have a veto on matters of substance but not over procedures. The deal would also allow each of the big powers to veto enforcement actions that might threaten their interests. Ambiguities remained, for the distinction between procedural and substantive issues was unclear. The Soviets again took a hard line, arguing that since debating and investigating issues and conflicts could be the prelude to enforcement actions, even scheduling discussions and investigations was a matter of substance. The United States and Britain disagreed, realizing that smaller nations would regard such a broad veto as making it impossible for them even to raise issues. During the meeting at San Francisco, delegates from a number of smaller nations pressed this objection and went so far as to draft a list of "twenty-three questions" that the five permanent members should answer about the limits of the veto. Proceedings came to an impasse as the conference was nearing its end in early June. The US and Britain, with support from France and China, held out against the Soviet position. To reach a deal the US administration asked Roosevelt advisor Harry Hopkins, then in Moscow, to intercede with Stalin. Stalin acquiesced, and the issue was resolved along the lines agreed at Yalta as interpreted by the US and UK. The price was that the US essentially agreed to accept Soviet domination of Poland. By that moment, there was no genuine alternative, but it was nonetheless a blunt recognition of the power of the Soviet Union on the ground in Eastern Europe.[44]

The signing of the UN Charter on June 26 was followed quickly by its ratification by the US Senate. Though the process went smoothly, it was something that the administration under Roosevelt and Truman had worried deeply over. It was in the US Senate that the Treaty of Versailles had been rejected in November 1919. To avoid such a debacle, the administration chose to work closely with Republican opponents in preparing and negotiating the charter. The two key senators were Arthur Vandenberg, Republican from Michigan and a leading anti-interventionist before the war, and Tom Connally, Democrat from Texas and chair of the Foreign Relations Committee. Vandenberg had expressed concern over the terms being negotiated at Dumbarton Oaks, but chose not to obstruct. For its part, the administration closely involved both senators, and others, in the preparations for San Francisco and in the actual meeting. An indication of likely success had come in January 1945, when Vandenberg gave what became a famous Senate speech announcing his conversion to the cause of internationalism. As he told his colleagues, "We not only have two wars to win, we also have yet to achieve such a peace as will justify this appalling cost." Securing such a peace would, he explained, require an international organization. And, he concluded, "I am prepared, by effective international cooperation, to do our full part in charting happier and safer tomorrows."[45]

After that, Roosevelt and Truman continued a fundamentally bipartisan approach to the development of the United Nations, and the few remaining opponents themselves became more and more isolated in their opposition. Equally important, public opinion—often skeptical about foreign engagement, suspicious of foreigners, and worried over being manipulated by the British—came around to supporting Roosevelt's plans for after the war and for the involvement of the United States in the new organization. A Gallup poll conducted in late March 1945 found that nine in ten Americans believed the US should join "a world organization to maintain peace" and fully 89 percent believed that the organization should have "police power."[46] Such sentiments were not entirely spontaneous. They had been elicited by broad public relations campaigns undertaken by the government, civic groups, and other supporters of the UN. Nevertheless, they were decisive enough and persisted into the summer and fall of 1945, helping to secure ratification of the UN Charter and passage of legislation making US participation a reality. The United Nations formally came into existence on October 24, 1945, when France, China, the USSR, Britain, the United States, and a majority of others who had signed the charter ratified it. The first meeting of the General Assembly took place in London on January 10, 1946.

A Framework for a Liberal Order

By 1945, then, key features of the postwar order had been determined and put in place. The precondition, of course, was the complete defeat of Germany and Japan. It had also been necessary for leaders and publics in the allied countries to come to understand the nature of the Nazi regime, its ideological roots and goals, and those of its ally, Japan. Put simply, that growing understanding had made the war into an anti-fascist crusade whose logic guaranteed that the two aggressors would be occupied and their institutions and cultures remade. It also created a powerful urge to create institutions that would prevent a recurrence of war both by guaranteeing security and by redesigning the world economic order to ensure that the conditions that had produced war would be eliminated. The security guarantee would, it was assumed, be realized through the United Nations; the effort to relieve economic distress and prevent a relapse into the competitive economic nationalisms of the 1930s would be carried out through the institutions and agreements reached at Bretton Woods.

What was notable about these new frameworks for peace and prosperity was that they were agreed upon before war ended and began to function soon after. It would take some time for them to be fully operational, but the rough shape of the postwar system was set. The system was by necessity a product of the collaboration between the United States, Britain, and the Soviet Union and inevitably reflected their interests and objectives. Those interests were by no means identical. All three wanted cooperation to continue after the war, but beyond that, objectives diverged. The Soviets brought to the negotiations over the postwar order a limited and largely defensive set of priorities. They were determined to protect their interests in Eastern Europe by installing friendly regimes there. American and British leaders were willing to concede to Soviet demands, but they harbored hopes, or perhaps delusions, that the Soviet Union would be satisfied with governments that were geopolitically aligned but otherwise moderately democratic. The British also brought to the task of designing a new world order a defensive mentality: they wanted to preserve Britain's global influence and maintain the empire. UK leaders also understood that the country was in desperate shape economically, and would need continued aid from the United States. The UK also shared with the United States an ideological preference for a more open international order, economically and politically, so long as Britain retained a global role, its empire, and imperial preference. Their goals were to this extent contradictory, but British leaders had long ago convinced themselves that the British Empire was consistent with liberalism and liberal internationalism.

The United States brought to postwar planning a vision that, in intention at least, was much more radical. Its commitment to economic openness was more intense and it had the means to press its case on others. America had responded to depression by retreating from the global economy, but the Reciprocal Trade Agreements Act of 1934 reversed that stand and gave the president the authority to negotiate deals on his own and to seek to open up trade opportunities for American industry and US farmers. Cordell Hull, Roosevelt's secretary of state from 1933 to 1944, was an avid free trader and fought for that policy during the planning for postwar. The strength of the US economy in 1945 meant that its producers had little to fear from foreign competitors and much to gain from freer trade. Under Roosevelt, moreover, the United States maintained a more robust commitment to democracy and to reform than either of its key allies. The administration saw its role as creating a global New Deal, with real commitments to economic and social rights—

what Roosevelt would call a Second Bill of Rights. It had brought that commitment to the negotiations that led to Bretton Woods and to the United Nations. Whether the results were up to the aspiration would not be known for many years, decades perhaps, but it was an aspiration grander than those that animated Britain or the Soviet Union.

The arrangements for postwar therefore tended to be more or less liberal in three senses: they were aimed at creating a more open world economy; they were deliberately framed and argued for as the means for making a reality of the Four Freedoms and the Atlantic Charter and therefore eliminating, or drastically mitigating, "freedom from want"; and they explicitly favored democracy and self-determination. Together, they constituted a framework for a liberal order. Of course, there was the contradiction between the hard fact of empire and these pronouncements; and there was the more glaring contradiction between the promise of democracy and the practice of the Soviet Union, both at home and within its newly enlarged sphere of influence. The contradictions would endure and the tensions they produced had consequences: making it more difficult for those who still clung to empire to persist and exposing the Soviet Union to sustained criticism. Grasping the importance of these tensions requires that the postwar order be recognized as incompletely liberal, or as liberal in theory but not always in practice, but the fact of contradiction does not invalidate the use of the term *liberal* to describe the emerging world order.[47]

Just how liberal the postwar order would be in practice would, of course, be determined by how well it survived the tests of the years after 1945. The major test was the Cold War, which led to policy responses that were not always possible to regard as liberal and that reshaped the context in which the framework and its institutions would operate. The questions are complicated and the answers elusive. Did the Cold War, by dividing the globe into opposing spheres, limit the effective reach of liberal politics and liberal institutions? Did the expedients with which the United States and its allies waged the Cold War render the new order less liberal? More interestingly, did the geographic limitations that circumscribed the workings of liberalism actually make its functioning more effective and, over time, more liberal?

Toward a Cold War World Order

Reality regularly confounds expectations, most notably in war. It can also do so in peacetime. The last years of the Second World War were rich in plans and in efforts to construct the institutions to carry out those plans, but these were to be seriously complicated by the realities of 1945 and beyond. The devastation that greeted the victorious armies in Europe and the East was shocking, vastly greater than imagined. Coping with the devastation would require cooperation between the victors, but rivalries, suspicion, and ideological antipathy erupted in a series of sharp disagreements and conflicts that persisted, recurred, and became the Cold War. Inevitably, the framework for a liberal international order would be altered. The result was a new, Cold War world order. It would be liberal in crucial respects, as intended by its founders, but liberal only with qualifications and within a restricted space.

There were anticipations of both these possibilities during the war. Reports coming out of Europe gave strong hints of the destruction being wrought by the Nazis. Reports from Asia were equally dire and chilling. And the allies did respond. The founding of the United Nations Relief and Rehabilitation Agency (UNRRA) in November 1943 was proof of this; so, too, was the UN Conference on Food and Agriculture held the previous May at Hot Springs, Virginia. The extent of hunger and physical devastation revealed in 1945 nevertheless surpassed what allied planners had envisioned.

Likewise, the possibility of tensions and hostility emerging between the Big Three was never far from the minds of any of their leaders. The Soviets, after all, had entered into a pact with Hitler in 1939, going to war only when the Nazis attacked them in 1941. While the Nazi-Soviet Pact held, the Soviets gave material support to the Third Reich and divided up the spoils in the East. Britain and the United States never forgot this brief alliance and worried throughout the war that Stalin would make another deal with Hitler. For his part, Stalin feared that the US and UK could do a deal that would leave the Soviet Union alone in the battle with Germany. In addition, there was the ideological conflict between the Soviets and their temporary allies. Though in practice the Soviet Union and its avatars further west did not always pursue revolution and disruption, they believed in the fundamental incompatibility between Communism and capitalism and that Communism would in the long run prevail over its rival system. Stalin made this clear when talking with comrades from Yugoslavia and Bulgaria in January 1945. It was a mistake, he explained, to believe that Communism and capitalism could continue to collaborate as they had during the war. "The crisis of capitalism," he went on, "has manifest itself in the division of the capitalists into two factions—one fascist, the other democratic. . . . The alliance between ourselves and the democratic faction of capitalists came about because the latter had a stake in preventing Hitler's domination, for that brutal state would have driven the working class to extremes and to the overthrow of capitalism itself. We are currently allied with the one faction against the other, but in the future we will be against the first faction of capitalists, too."[1]

The ease with which Stalin could revert to Marxist orthodoxy did not mean that he was tactically inflexible and impatient. It is clear that he wanted to continue the alliance with the US and UK into the postwar period, at least long enough for the Soviet Union to rebuild and to extract the maximum in reparations from the Germans. The Soviets did not want another war, and after 1945 they disarmed to an extent comparable to what the United States and Britain did. The British and the Americans also hoped to prolong the alliance. Despite these shared objectives, in the two years after the defeat of Germany the former allies were at odds and beginning what would become a siege that lasted four decades. How and why did this happen?

To some extent, the falling-out among the powers was highly likely, perhaps even inevitable, for at least three reasons. The first was the great gap that existed between the US and the USSR and everyone else. There were no serious competitors for regional, let alone global, influence, and the vast reach of the superpowers guaranteed that they would butt up against one another in Europe, Asia, and elsewhere. Second, there was the essential incompatibility of the social and political systems in the Soviet Union and in the US and Britain. Stalin was not wrong about that.

The third underlying cause was the great political vacuum that existed at the end of the war. States in Eastern Europe had either collaborated with the Nazis or been overrun by them. When the Soviets pushed the Germans back, in most places there were no legitimate rulers to take over. Conservative parties and leaders had disgraced themselves by their complicity or passivity, while social democratic leaders and parties had largely been destroyed by the Nazis and their allies. A few liberals and social democrats managed to flee and tried to set themselves up as part of governments-in-exile, but their claims were not always recognized and their return after the war was not always welcome by those who had stayed or by the occupation authorities. Local Communists suffered different fates and had different prospects. Many had been eliminated by the wartime right-wing regimes. Some had fled or been brought to Moscow. They did not all fare very well in the home of socialism, for it was all too easy to run afoul of the changing party line or to find oneself linked to the wrong faction. Those who did survive would return just behind the Red Army and become the loyalists upon whom the Soviets would depend, but they had very weak local roots. There was less of a vacuum in Western Europe, but putting together legitimate and stable regimes would prove to be no simple matter in France or in Italy.

Much of Asia also lacked stable governments and credible political leaders. The Japanese had defeated imperial administrations in Hong Kong, Singapore, Malaysia, Indochina, Indonesia, and Burma, proclaiming themselves as liberators. The British, French, and Dutch sought to restore imperial control, but their competence and claim to rule had been severely damaged. Japan had long ruled Korea, but that ended in 1945. Most important, the Japanese had conquered much of China, weakening the Nationalist government militarily and politically. It hung on in 1945 and was even given a seat on the UN Security Council, but its grip on the country was not solid and it would be overthrown by the Communists in 1949. There was unrest in imperial possessions in Africa and the Middle East as well, though the threat to colonial control was less immediate.

Overall, therefore, the most distinctive geopolitical feature of the early postwar years was the fluidity and precariousness of rule. That openness was a standing invitation for the emerging superpowers to get involved, to cultivate client parties and governments, and to recruit allies. And, of course, the fear that the rival superpower might do so led the other to intervene to prevent it. The context virtually ensured that cooperation would give way sooner or later to confrontation.

What precipitated the actual coming of the Cold War was the unsettled situation in Europe or, more precisely, the effect of the consolidation of Soviet domination in the East on the lack of a settlement in the West.[2] The determination of the Soviets to control Poland was the first indication of how firmly they would seek to dominate the region. Roosevelt and Churchill understood that with the Red Army firmly in charge, there was little that could be done, but they tried at Yalta to get the Soviets to agree to broaden the character of the regime they were in process of installing and to hold elections. It did not happen, and by the time of the Potsdam meeting hope for a more independent Poland had given way to recriminations that anticipated the rancor that was to characterize the early Cold War.

The focus then turned to Germany, where the Four Powers (Britain, France, the USSR, and the US) each controlled occupation zones. The Soviets wanted to keep Germany down and weak and fragmented and intended to extract large reparations, including the transfer of entire factories to the Soviet Union and forced labor from Germans. The other three powers were less clear about what to do. The United States and Britain were committed to denazification and demilitarization, but came soon to the view that European political stability and economic recovery required that a reformed Germany resume a major role. The French, by

contrast, reprising their position at the end of the First World War, wanted to see Germany punished—disarmed and dismantled economically,
with valuable industrial regions broken off and subject to French control. The French were also irritated that decisions were being made without their input. It would take until the spring of 1947 for the French to
acquiesce to the policies of the US and UK, which had long ceased to
allow the Soviets to extract reparations from their zones and had by this
time merged their two occupation zones into what became the Bizone.

Pushing the US and UK, and eventually and grudgingly the French,
toward the decision to rehabilitate Germany was the carnage that greeted the occupying powers and the cost of relief. The British worried that
the expense of feeding the Germans meant that they, though victors,
were effectively paying reparations to the former aggressors. It was also
becoming clear that recovery across Europe required a healthy German
economy. Policy needed to be changed. This realization was accompanied by the growing sense that the Soviets were not going to cooperate
in rebuilding Europe and were not going to lessen their grip in the East.

It is generally understood that the Soviet Union was not interested
in war or military conquest during the late 1940s and that Stalin's foreign
policy was opportunistic, flexible, and cautious.[3] On the other hand, the
Soviet posture was resolute and confident. In February 1946 Stalin gave
a bold, triumphalist speech at the Bolshoi Theater in Moscow, claiming
that the war had been a fundamental test of the Soviet system and of its
priorities and conduct both before and in the course of the war. The
country, he asserted, was far better prepared for war than it had been in
1914 and this was the result of the Soviet drive to industrialize through
the succession of Five-Year Plans and the parallel collectivization of agriculture. After the retreats and devastation of 1941, the country proceeded to outdo itself in producing for war and winning it. He chose not
to mention the massive amounts of aid that came from the West and
attributed victory mainly to the exertions of the Soviet Union itself. Victory, then, "proved that the Soviet social system is a . . . fully viable and
stable form of organization of society. More than that," Stalin went on,
"now the issue is that the Soviet social system has proved to be more viable and stable than the non-Soviet social system, that the Soviet social
system is a better form of organization of society than any non-Soviet

social system."[4] Convinced by recent history, or by a particular reading of it, Stalin was not about to let the spoils of victory be bargained away to maintain friendly relations with the United States or other capitalist countries that, as he claimed, were likely to relapse into economic crisis and imperialist rivalry anyway.

Stalin's speech got noticed: Supreme Court justice William Douglas regarded it as "the Declaration of World War III."[5] A response of sorts came in the form of George Kennan's famous "long telegram" sent thirteen days later.[6] Kennan, number two in the Moscow embassy, had strong and well-developed views on the nature of the Soviet Union.[7] He understood the Soviet position as deeply rooted in Russian history: "At bottom of Kremlin's neurotic view of world affairs is traditional and instinctive Russian sense of insecurity. . . . To this was added, as Russia came into contact with economically advanced West, fear of more competent, more powerful, more highly organized societies in that area." "It was no coincidence," Kennan argued, "that Marxism, which had smoldered ineffectively for half a century in Western Europe, caught hold and blazed for first time in Russia." Fittingly, the Soviets saw the "outside world as evil, hostile and menacing." To counter this hostile environment, Soviet leaders had decided that "everything must be done to advance relative strength of USSR as factor in international society."[8]

The Soviet analysis of the capitalist enemy predicted recurring crises and conflicts. An attack on the Soviet Union was possible, but more likely were battles between rival capitalists. In the perspective of the Soviets, as Kennan explained, these "conflicts between capitalist states, though likewise fraught with danger for USSR, nevertheless hold out great possibilities for advancement of socialist cause, particularly if USSR remains militarily powerful, ideologically monolithic and faithful to its present brilliant leadership." The Soviets and their supporters should therefore seek to exacerbate and exploit these divisions; "If these eventually deepen into an 'imperialist' war, this war must be turned into revolutionary upheavals within the various capitalist countries." As Kennan saw it, the Soviet Union would be relentless in its efforts to weaken and divide the West internally and would also work to encourage unrest in the colonial world.

Despite this dire analysis of the Communist foe, Kennan ended his message on a more hopeful note. The West was stronger, possessed a vision of a better society and a more attractive future and could, if its citizens were properly educated and led, resist the challenge posed by the Soviet Union. Equally important, "Soviet power, unlike that of Hitlerite Germany, is neither schematic nor adventuristic. It does not work by fixed plans. It does not take unnecessary risks. Impervious to logic of reason, and it is highly sensitive to logic of force." It could for that reason be contained. Although in his telegram Kennan did not use that word, the idea of "containment" was critical to his understanding and would become the key phrase embodying US strategic thinking for much of the Cold War.

The Soviets were not adventurist, they were not likely to overrun Western Europe or undertake risky adventures elsewhere. They were nevertheless determined to hold onto their sphere of influence in Eastern Europe. That translated at war's end into a series of governments in the East that were in theory, and to some extent in practice, coalitions friendly to Moscow but not fully dominated by parties and leaders loyal to the Soviet Union. Communists, socialists, liberals, and agrarian parties all participated. These governments were understood as popular fronts that excluded fascists and the remnants of the old parties guilty of complicity with fascism, and the party line emanating from Moscow assumed that proletarian revolution was not yet in the cards. Throughout Eastern Europe, however, Communists or close allies controlled the ministries of the interior and hence the police and the justice systems; and quickly on the heels of the Red Army came the secret police, often trained in the Soviet Union.[9] These coalitions, or popular fronts, proved not to be stable, long-term solutions for two obvious reasons. First, the Communists and non-Communists would eventually, and usually much sooner than anticipated, come to disagree over policy; and when that occurred, Communist control over the police and security services and the nearby presence of the Red Army ensured that disputes would be resolved on the terms of the Communists. Second, in most countries the Communists were not popular, receiving only modest support in elections. In the Berlin election of October 1946, for example, the Communists—competing as the Socialist Unity Party (SED)—received only 20 percent of the vote, while the Social Democrats won 49 percent. In some places, like Czechoslovakia, they did better; in other places, like

Poland, they would have fared even less well if proper elections had been held.[10] For the Soviets, lack of popular support meant that squeezing out opposing parties and concentrating control increasingly seemed the most attractive strategy.

The process was especially rapid and complete in Bulgaria and Romania. In Bulgaria, former Comintern leader Georgi Dimitrov took over the small Communist Party, which assumed control as part of a broader coalition. As was often the case in the region, the most popular party was based in the countryside, but it was easily outmaneuvered. The Communists soon fell out with the agrarians and by October 1945 had gained near total control. The leader of the Peasants' Party, Nicola Petkov, was arrested, and two years later he was executed. A similar fate befell neighboring Romania, where a million Red Army troops looked on as the takeover proceeded.[11]

The Polish case was most closely watched by outside observers, but the outcome was adumbrated early on. Communists trained in Moscow began arriving with the Red Army and by mid-1944 had helped to set up a Polish Committee of National Liberation based in Lublin. The committee became the provisional government in early 1945 and soon the "Lublin Poles" were recognized as the legitimate government instead of the "London Poles" in exile. The allies insisted at Yalta that the provisional government be broadened, but only token efforts were made. The Communists came to dominate the new regime and, with the aid of what by the fall of 1945 were nearly twenty-four thousand security forces, began to repress their political opponents and those resistance forces, mainly the Polish Home Army, that were not loyal to the Soviets.[12] The Communists still did not enjoy much popular support: the party had just a tenth of the membership of the Polish Peasant Party in late 1945, but their control of the police and security apparatus allowed them to gradually weaken their rivals. In obviously engineered elections in January 1947 the so-called Democratic bloc, dominated by the Communists, would win eight in ten votes and the Peasant Party just 10 percent.

In Hungary, Communists were also very weak to start: they numbered only four thousand in 1945, and in the November election the Smallholders Party won a clear majority. But as in Poland, a provisional government set up in December 1944 afforded the Communists effective control of the apparatus of repression. From these positions, they waged a campaign of harassment and had deputies and members of the Small-holders Party arrested for conspiracy and espionage in February 1947. Despite this intimidation and a blatantly rigged election, in August 1947 the Communists received only 22 percent of the vote. Continued repression of the opposition nevertheless allowed the Communist-dominated "People's Front" to claim over 95 percent of the vote by May 1949.

The most notorious case was the "coup" in Czechoslovakia in 1948. There, by contrast with Poland and Hungary, the Communists began with some support. Czechoslovakia was a more developed country than most in Eastern Europe and agrarian parties were weaker. In elections in May 1946 Communists won 38 percent of the vote nationally, over 40 percent in Czech districts, and 31 percent in the more rural Slovakia. In addition, the Red Army had withdrawn from the country at the end of the war. The Czechs were nonetheless loyal to the Soviet Union, partly because of the memory of their abandonment by the West in 1938–39. For Stalin, however, the most loyal supporters were not always loyal enough, and the Czech leaders had committed the mistake of initially responding favorably to the prospect of participation in the Marshall Plan. As the Cold War division deepened, moreover, popular front–style coalitions and democratic paths to socialism became less viable and less attractive to the Soviets. In February 1948 the Communists in Czecho-slovakia forced the president, Edvard Beneš, to dismiss the existing government and install a regime, controlled fully by the Communists, that promptly began purging and repressing its opponents.

The installation of Communist regimes in Eastern Europe would not be completed until the transformation of the Soviet occupation zone into the German Democratic Republic (DDR) on October 7, 1949. It was clear well before then that the Soviets were not going to permit the foundation and functioning of anything resembling democratic political systems anywhere. Most Western leaders had drawn that conclusion by early 1947; for others, the decisive moment was probably the coup in Czechoslovakia early the next year. People living in Eastern Europe, especially those in parties and movements opposed to the Soviets and their local allies, recognized what was happening much earlier. It would be hard to maintain, though some still do, that the outcomes in the East were a response to the coming of the Cold War. Rather, they were part of its first act and to some extent a cause of the onset of the global confrontation. Appropriately, it would be the cracking up of those regimes four decades later that marked the beginning of the end of the Cold War.

If Europe, particularly its central and eastern portions, was the site of the Cold War's origins and most visible impact, it was not the only locus of conflict. In fact, the dramatic escalation of Cold War tensions in 1947 was provoked by events on Europe's periphery. The key was a decision by Britain that it lacked the resources to maintain its positions in Greece and Turkey, and effectively the entire eastern Mediterranean and Middle East, and that the United States should take its place. There was a civil war in Greece between the government and left-wing insurgents aided mainly by Yugoslavia, and Turkey was faced with insistent pressure from the Soviet Union over the Straits. The British ambassador delivered a dire message to the US State Department on February 21: British aid would end in six weeks and, as Dean Acheson later explained, "His Majesty's Government devoutly hoped that we could assume the burden in both Greece and Turkey."[13]

Truman and his advisors were not surprised. Since he had assumed the presidency, Truman's views on the Soviet Union had hardened considerably. As early as late April 1945 Truman pushed the Soviet foreign minister Molotov hard on the Soviets' refusal to live up to their promises on Poland. In a note to himself on May 23 he was even more blunt about not trusting the Soviets: "I've no faith in any Totalitarian state be it Russian, German, Spanish, Argentinian, Dago or Japanese."[14] Truman's rather loose use of "totalitarian" was surely not analytically precise, but his point was clear enough. He delivered his message to his secretary of state, James Byrnes, in January 1946, explaining his frustration with Soviet behavior and Moscow's refusal, as he saw it, to carry out agreements. "I do not think we should play compromise any longer. . . . I'm tired of babying the Soviets."[15] Truman's was obviously not the nuanced understanding that Kennan displayed in his "Long Telegram," but the president and his circle fundamentally agreed with its assessment of Soviet behavior.

It was only logical, therefore, that Truman himself would be directly involved in arranging, and even helping to formulate, Churchill's famous "Iron Curtain" speech in Fulton, Missouri, in March 1946. He subsequently commissioned a review of the situation from his close advisor Clark Clifford. "American Relations with the Soviet Union" was ready by September 1946 and was, if anything, more critical of the Soviet Union than Kennan had been. While Kennan diagnosed the problem of Soviet behavior in terms of psychology, the Clifford memo focused on ideology, arguing that the Soviet leadership was "blinded by its adherence to Marxist doctrine." That doctrine foresaw the "ultimate destruction of capitalist states by communist states" and demanded, as that conflict matured, efforts "to strengthen and prepare the Soviet Union for its clash with the western democracies."[16] To counter this, the memo urged that the US work closely with Britain and other allies to encourage resistance to the Soviets and, as part of that, to foster economic recovery. The memo was a further step in the development of the strategy of containment.

At the same time, the American president was becoming especially concerned with events in the Mediterranean and worried over Soviet actions in Greece, Turkey, and Iran. The British request for support was thus not unexpected, and Truman's quick agreement was consistent with his evolving policy of "firmness" toward the Soviet Union. He was careful, as Roosevelt had been, to consult members of Congress and bring them along. Not everyone was eager, of course, and some were generally resentful at the idea of rescuing Britain. That was at least one reason why, in his address to Congress on March 12, Truman justified the decision to provide aid to Greece and Turkey in universalist terms. As he explained, "I believe that it must be the policy of the United States to support free peoples who are resisting attempted subjugation by armed minorities or by outside pressures." Once again, he referred to the threat from totalitarianism but grounded it with just a bit of social analysis. "The seeds of totalitarianism," he argued, "are nurtured by misery and want."[17] The "Truman Doctrine," as it came to be called, was both specific in terms of who would be resisted and extremely general and open-ended in terms of who might be supported and what might be done as part of that effort. It is rightly seen as an implicit commitment to fight the Cold War on a global scale.

The initial Soviet reaction was measured, for the Soviets regarded Truman's stance as mainly rhetorical and underestimated his resolve. The

Soviets did, however, continue to shore up their position in Eastern Europe and to be difficult and obstructionist in the many venues where the former allies were daily engaged. The Soviets also began to encourage local Communist parties and their trade union allies in the West to become less cooperative within postwar coalition governments. In France, for example, PCF (French Communist Party) leaders and militants backed off the "battle for production" that sought to promote industrial peace in order to aid recovery and instead encouraged a wave of strikes and protests led by the CGT (General Confederation of Labor).[18] A more formal Soviet response—a kind of declaration of Cold War—would wait until September, when they founded the Cominform (Communist Information Bureau), a successor to the disbanded and much feared Comintern. At the founding meeting, Stalin's deputy for ideology, Andrei Zhdanov, proclaimed that the world had broken into "two camps" that were fundamentally at odds—an imperialist camp led by the United States and an "anti-imperialist democratic" camp led by the Soviet Union. If there had ever been a chance that democracy would survive in even a token form in the new states in Eastern Europe—and the chance was ever so slight—the new course adopted in the fall of 1947 extinguished it.

As Cold War rifts deepened, the two sides geared up for a sustained confrontation. The Soviet Union did not lack for leadership and cohesion, though the creation of the Cominform was in part an effort to exert greater control of Communists both in Eastern Europe and in the West. The United States and its allies, by contrast, were rushing to demobilize, and public opinion was less easily controlled. Government was also more fragmented and less centralized, most notably in the United States. The Truman administration did not seek ideological conformity and could not have achieved it even if it had tried, especially given the new Republican majorities in the House and Senate. It could and did work to rationalize what came to be called the security establishment. Even before the British request to aid Greece and Turkey, there were plans to reorganize and improve the efficiency of defense and intelligence activity. The National Security Act, signed into law in July 1947, established a new Department of Defense that would supervise the army (formerly the War Department), the navy, and the newly independent air force; made the Joint Chiefs of Staff permanent; and created the Central Intelligence

Agency from the remnants of the wartime Office of Strategic Services (OSS). The act also established the National Security Council to coordinate intelligence and advise the president. Not everything worked out quite as planned, but the result was nevertheless a more functional structure than the chaotic system it replaced.[19]

What truly animated the new bureaucratic structure was the determination to wage the Cold War. That was not a given in America in 1947, for the public was weary of war and remained suspicious of "foreign entanglements." The resurgence of Republicans in Congress also meant that at least some of the old voices of "isolationism," silenced since Pearl Harbor, could be heard again. Republicans were also still mostly hostile to the New Deal and its legacy. To the extent that US involvement in the creation of the postwar world had been understood by supporters as a means of bringing about a "New Deal for the World," there was every reason to expect that opponents of the New Deal would find fault with the project. That largely failed to happen and Truman's key initiatives received bipartisan support. It was in a meeting to discuss aid to Greece and Turkey that Republican senator Arthur Vandenberg is reported to have said that Truman had to "scare hell out of the country" in order to win public backing for such a broad effort. He also urged that the situation in the Mediterranean be linked to basic principles and a broader struggle between Communism and democracy. Vandenberg and Governor Thomas Dewey were vocal and consistent in support and even Robert Taft, reluctantly, voted yes.[20]

Besides Truman's (and before him Roosevelt's) political savvy, the president was able to secure this bipartisan support because of the strength of anti-Communism. Before 1939, anti-fascism was controversial; anti-Communism, even after the wartime collaboration, was easier to sell. It is hard to imagine that the American commitment to the Marshall Plan, to NATO, and to allies in Asia would have occurred absent the Cold War and the rivalry with Communism. Waging the Cold War successfully, of course, required not just will but also policy. Probably the most innovative and successful policy undertaken by the Truman administration was the Marshall Plan.[21] It was an economic measure in the first instance, but it had huge political effects. Its origins lay in the economic crisis that confronted the allies at the end of the war and in the

hunger and desperation of people across Europe, East and West, among
the vanquished, among those they had so recently occupied and brutal-
ized, and even, though to a lesser extent, among the victors. The devastation wrought by the war had destroyed not only cities and factories and
farms and roads and railway lines, but also the commercial relationships
that allow market economies to function. The effect was to prolong the
postwar crisis so that by 1947 the economies of Europe were still not
working. The prospect that economic revival would be delayed also
meant, or so it was feared, that political stability would be hard to achieve
and that instability would provide opportunities for the advance of undemocratic forces. These considerations led political leaders in the US
and Britain to reconsider policies toward Germany. Germany had been
the largest economy in Europe, and hopes for a revival across the continent were increasingly seen to depend on restoring its industrial strength
and harnessing that to stimulate growth in its neighbors. That would of
necessity mean scaling back the effort to punish and reform Germany
and instead providing aid to help it prosper again.

That shift was awkward for leaders everywhere, but much harder
for those in countries like France that had suffered so much and so recently at the hands of the Germans. It was more or less impossible for the
Soviet Union, which had not only lost millions of people and much productive capacity to the Nazis, but which also staked its material future on
reparations. The Soviets therefore not only had solid geopolitical reasons
for wanting to keep Germany weak and its industrial and military capacity dismantled; they also had a major economic interest in doing so. The
stark reality of continued economic distress nevertheless compelled the
US and Britain to proceed with efforts aimed at the economic revival of
the defeated enemy. The harsh winter of 1946–47 added even greater
urgency and convinced Secretary of State George C. Marshall and his
aides of the need for economic assistance.

Marshall would announce his plan at the Harvard graduation on
June 5, 1947. The decision to propose the huge aid package had been in
the works even before the Truman administration had received the request from Britain that prompted the Truman Doctrine and was developed further as the details of US involvement in Greece and Turkey
were being formulated. It was finalized when Marshall himself returned

from the foreign ministers' meeting in Moscow that began March 10 and dragged on for six weeks. Potsdam was the last time the Big Three had met, and decisions regarding postwar issues—occupation policy, peace treaties, and other concerns—were supposed to be taken at regular meetings of the foreign ministers of the UK, the US, France, and the Soviet Union. After the explosion of the first atom bombs, Stalin felt that the Americans would use their new position "to force us to accept their plans on questions affecting Europe and the world" but, he told Andrei Gromyko, the Soviet ambassador to the US, "that is not going to happen."[22] He told Molotov not to make any concessions at these meetings; the Soviets were likewise uncooperative at meetings of the Allied Control Council for Germany. The meeting in the spring of 1947 was predictably difficult.

The main topic was Germany and the need to shift policies to enable its economic revival. The US and Britain had merged their occupation zones in early 1947 and had stopped reparations well before that. The French were coming around to that position, but the Soviets were firm in demanding further reparations and extracting all they could from their zone. In theory, both sides wanted Germany to be a single state with a unified economy, but they diverged completely over the shape that its economy and system of governance should take. In fact, a major reason the Soviets wanted Germany united was to be able to extract reparations from the British, American, and French zones. As that possibility receded, the Soviet stance was to block progress toward the creation of a prosperous democratic and capitalist Germany in the West. With the talks essentially stalemated, Marshall insisted on meeting directly with Stalin. The meeting occurred late on the evening of April 15. Marshall made clear to Stalin, "We are frankly determined to do what we can to assist those countries which are suffering from economic deterioration" because if "unchecked, [this] might lead to economic collapse and the consequent elimination of any chance of democratic survival."[23] Stalin and Molotov were unmoved, and the meeting ended without reaching any substantial agreement.

The meeting did succeed in convincing Marshall that the United States needed to act on its own. The people working under him saw things in much the same way. Will Clayton, undersecretary for economic affairs, explained in May that "we grossly underestimated the destruction to the European economy by the war. . . . Europe is steadily deteriorating. The political position reflects the economic. . . . Millions of people in the cities are slowly starving. . . . Without further and prompt aid from the United States, economic, social and political disintegration will overwhelm Europe."[24] Even before Marshall returned from Moscow, officials had begun drafting plans. George Kennan, now head of the Policy Planning Staff at the State Department, was tasked with putting them together and making sense of the whole. Dean Acheson was delegated to give a speech in Mississippi on May 8 explaining why providing aid to Europe was in the interests of the United States. By mid-May Kennan had a draft that would be further refined with input from the major players and readied by the time of Marshall's speech. The speech itself was relatively brief and low-key, but notable in three ways: first, it proposed a major aid package, but lacked a price tag; second, it stressed that the initiative for the program, its details and costs, should come from Europe, and from European states coordinating their requests; and third, the program would in theory be open to all of Europe, including the Soviet Union and Eastern Europe. Marshall added a warning, however, that it would not be open to states unwilling to cooperate in the recovery program or seeking to sabotage it.[25]

The vision behind the speech involved a new and unprecedented level of European cooperation, if not quite a United States of Europe. It thus anticipated, and would eventually help to foster, developments like the formation of the European Coal and Steel Community and later the Common Market. None of this was entirely clear in mid-1947, for it was not known who would participate in the Marshall Plan and who would not. That was the critical matter to be decided over the next month.

The United States did not want the Soviet Union to join, but American leaders did not want to be blamed for the division of Germany or Europe. US policy makers wanted simultaneously to set conditions on participation that would keep the Soviets out, but still leave the responsibility for crafting the plan to the Europeans. It was a complicated issue, with real risks. If the Soviets joined, it was assumed that they would work from within to wreck the program. If the Soviet Union chose not to, and told its "satellites" (as the Soviets themselves called the regimes in

Eastern Europe) and the Communist parties in Western Europe to oppose it as well, they would maintain their tight grip on the East but likely suffer setbacks in the West.

Shortly after Marshall's speech, British foreign secretary Ernest Bevin called the State Department to say that he would take the lead in organizing European countries to put together the request that would lead to the grant of US aid. The first stop would be Paris, where Bevin met with his French counterpart, Georges Bidault. The cooperation of France was necessary if the Marshall Plan was to succeed, but it was not easily secured. The French had designs on Germany that were the opposite of what the US and UK now sought; and France had hoped to make independent agreements for its security with both the United States and the Soviet Union. Only in 1947 did it become clear that working with the Soviets was not a practical option and that German economic revival was vital to France's hopes of prosperity as well. Even then, French leaders worried that teaming up with the Anglo-Americans would not be popular. The French Communist Party remained strong, and De Gaulle and his followers were resentful and restless. Nevertheless, when Marshall asked Bidault if the US "could rely on France," the answer he received was yes; and Bidault chose to work closely with Bevin.[26] They decided, with American approval, to invite representatives of the Soviet Union to meet in Paris in late June.

The Soviets were wary of the Marshall Plan from the moment it was announced, warning, as *Pravda* claimed on June 17, that its aim was the "quick formation of a notorious western bloc under the unconditional and absolute leadership of American imperialism." Despite such rhetoric, Molotov agreed to attend the Paris meeting and arrived on June 26 with a large delegation. He was not there to cooperate, however, and in his initial statement objected to the requirement that states seeking aid should essentially open their books to foreigners and coordinate their economic plans. The Soviets were also opposed to helping Germany to recover and had no interest in seeing Europe come together in any formal way. After several days of fruitless and increasingly acrimonious discussion, Molotov walked out of the meeting on July 2. He acted on orders from Stalin, of course, and he ended his participation with vague threats directed at the French and the British.[27]

The Soviet decision to oppose rather than participate in the Marshall Plan was hugely consequential. Most important, it ensured that the plan would go ahead. Had the Soviets and their "satellites" joined the effort, it is highly unlikely that the US Congress would have approved it. The Soviets would also, by cooperating, have reaped considerable goodwill in European countries east and west and strengthened the position of Communists all around. By rejecting Marshall aid, demanding that the new states in Eastern Europe do likewise, and instructing Communist parties in places like France and Italy to oppose it, they lost on every front. The Soviets themselves would get nothing and reparations from Germany would cease, Eastern Europeans would get nothing and resent their Soviet masters for it, and Communists in the West would forfeit much of what they had gained in popular support for the role they played in the resistance to the Nazis and the liberation and reconstruction of their countries. The US had taken a risk in leaving open the possibility of Soviet participation; the Soviet Union had shown that the risk had been worth it. Leaders in the US and UK were happily surprised at what they saw as the Soviets' mistake. They probably should not have been, for the decision was consistent with the nature of the regime late in Stalin's reign.

It would take months for the Europeans, with US "assistance," to come up with a request and a rationale. It would take still more time for Congress to debate, hold hearings, and pass legislation to make the Marshall Plan a reality. Truman would sign the bill on April 3, 1948. All the while the Soviets and their client parties would attack it. Emergency aid to Europe continued, and when the plan was approved it flowed more freely. The economic effects were overwhelmingly positive; even before the law's passage, the boost to European confidence had a palpable effect. The economic situation remained dire, but was better, and it would steadily improve. Equally important were the political effects. The Marshall Plan was a major step not only toward recovery but toward the division of Europe that would endure until 1989. The founding of the Cominform in late September 1947 was largely aimed at blunting the effects of the plan. Its creation was also a means of imposing the new, more rigid policy of the Kremlin on Soviet-dominated parties in Eastern Europe and in the West. Stalin had been particularly angered by the initial enthusiasm for the plan displayed by political leaders in Poland, Czechoslovakia, and Yugoslavia. They were brought to heel with blunt orders from Moscow. The Czech leaders would be called to Moscow shortly after the Soviet withdrawal from the Paris meeting. Jan Masaryk commented later, "I went to Moscow as a Foreign Minister of an independent state. I returned as a lackey of a foreign country."[28] Masaryk would not survive the brutal coup in Czechoslovakia in February 1948. He was found dead on March 10 beneath a window in the Foreign Ministry, though it was not clear if he had jumped or been pushed.[29] The coup ended any pretense that the government was not under the control of the Soviets and sent a terrifying message to the rest of Europe.

Communist party leaders in France and Italy were instructed to oppose the program and to do what they could to foment unrest by encouraging strikes and demonstrations by the unions over which they had influence. The strategy proved counterproductive: Communists did not stop the Marshall Plan and they lost political support. In France the PCF had been pushed out of the ruling coalition in May 1947, but it was still the largest party in the National Assembly. Its leaders hoped to reenter the government, but the party's behavior angered potential allies, who blocked the Communists from participation in government. The era of "Tripartism," coalition governments that included the Communists, came to an end and was replaced by a series of coalitions of the center-left and center-right that would be labeled "Third Force" governments. The Communists and their CGT allies responded by leading waves of strikes in 1947–48. The most bitter and prolonged were in the nationalized industries, coal most prominently, and were accompanied by enough violence to make some fear "insurrection." The aims were not insurrectionary, but they were both economic and political. The strikes were eventually put down as the government shored up police forces and brought in troops. The CGT suffered serious losses and witnessed the beginnings of a schism in its ranks.[30]

Italy followed a parallel path. As in France, the Communists emerged much strengthened after the war. They commanded armed militias forged in the resistance and the giant trade union federation, the Confederazione generale italiana del lavoro (CGIL), was mostly controlled by the Italian Communist Party (PCI). They also, like their French comrades, followed the Soviet-approved policy of participating in coalition governments in the first two years after the war. Differences with coalition partners would, nonetheless, lead to their exit from government in May 1947. Alcide De Gasperi, the leader of the Christian Democrats, resigned on May 13 and formed a new coalition without the Communists and their socialist allies, the Italian Socialist Party (PSI). The Communists responded as they had in France, encouraging industrial unrest and vociferously opposing the Marshall Plan. The formation of the Cominform provided an occasion for criticism of the Italian Communists for lack of revolutionary zeal and "parliamentary cretinism," as one Hungarian Communist declared. The party leader, Palmiro Togliatti, responded with vocal calls to protest: "Go into the piazzas for the defense of democracy and the republic," he urged his followers; and they did.[31]

The confrontation was sustained and tensions mounted through the winter and spring in anticipation of April elections. The Communists did prepare for an uprising, but neither Togliatti nor Stalin wanted to go that far. Instead, the focus remained on the election and the Soviet Union provided substantial material support for the party. The Americans provided even more for the Christian Democrats and other non-Communist parties. Much of the US effort was quite open: the US ambassador traveled the country; Italian Americans were asked to write letters to relatives back in Italy; the Sons of Italy got involved; so, too, did Frank Sinatra and Joe DiMaggio. Some of the support was not visible, and purposefully so—this constituted the first major effort by the CIA to intervene in the domestic politics of another country. The US also worked openly and secretly with the Vatican, which of course had its own reasons for opposing the Communists. Local priests acted like election agents, bishops and archbishops denounced the Communists from their pulpits and threatened Catholics tempted to vote for the Communist-led Popular Democratic Front. Visions of the Blessed Virgin were reported across the country and, of course, she did not approve of Communism. These massive efforts worked: just six weeks before the election George Kennan was worried the Communists would win; when the country voted on April 18, the Christian Democrats won 48 percent of the vote and a majority of deputies while the vote for the PCI/PSI Front fell to just 31 percent.[32]

At its core, the Marshall Plan was initiated to deal with Germany. Its economic needs were dire, its depressed state impeding recovery all over Europe, and disagreements among the occupying powers meant that its political future remained unsettled. The Marshall Plan was intended to address both problems and, in the western zones of occupation, would have dramatic effects on the economy and the nation's political life. The creation of the Bizone was an indication that the future would likely involve the division of Germany and the establishment of two states and two systems. It took more than two more years of debate and tension for that to occur. The foreign ministers of the Four Powers met in London in November–December 1947, but could not agree on a way forward. The Soviets continued to insist that the deal worked out at Potsdam be adhered to. Most of all they wanted reparations. The US and UK had different plans, and the French were coming around. With the impasse at the foreign ministers' meeting, the British and Americans decided to proceed on their own, turning their joint occupation zone into a new state. An initial step would be the introduction of a new currency. On March 5, 1948, the decision to merge the Bizone and the French zone was announced and it was decided to bring Germany into the formal structure of the Marshall Plan and to set up a West German state. This "London Program" was further advanced on March 17 with the signing of the Brussels Pact, which brought together Britain, France, and the Benelux countries into the Western Union Defense Organization. The Soviets condemned these moves, claiming that they were aimed at creating a "Western Bloc" directed at the Soviet Union. They were not entirely wrong.

Launching a new currency and taking steps to create a new political authority raised many questions, not least the status of Berlin, the former capital now controlled by the Four Powers. Berlin was located well within the borders of the Soviet zone in the east and exposed to whatever pressure the Soviets and their East German allies chose to inflict. As early as January and February 1948 authorities in the Soviet zone held up trains between the west and Berlin on the pretext of checking documents and inspecting cargo. In March, Stalin explicitly ordered his representatives there to ramp up pressure on the city and its inhabitants. Later that month the commander of Soviet forces walked out of the Allied Control Council, effectively ending its functioning. Further harassment of passengers and slow-downs in the transport of goods followed. In early April the US responded with an airlift to supply its forces in the city. Undeterred, the allies on June 7 announced plans to hold elections and create a constitution for the soon-to-be West Germany. The new currency was introduced less than two weeks later. On June 23, the Soviets chose to impose a comprehensive blockade on Berlin, restricting access by road, by train, and even by canal, and on the next day introduced its own new currency in the eastern zone.

The Soviets did not, however, cut off air traffic. It was clear that neither side wanted war and that Stalin's objective was to harass and impede and, he hoped, persuade the western powers to abandon their plans. The strategy failed, for the airlift, massively expanded, would be successful. While the contest played out in Berlin, there were negotiations in Moscow that came close to a deal, but by this point neither side trusted the other enough to make it happen. The process of creating a new state in the west had developed its own momentum. The Soviets, for their part, were confident that as winter set in, the people of Berlin would give up the fight. That calculation proved mistaken; something quite the opposite happened. West Berliners recoiled at Soviet moves and took an active part in making the airlift work. They built a new airport; and in December they voted in large numbers for the Social Democratic Party (SPD) in local elections in the western portions of the city. Elections were not allowed in the eastern sector, for the authorities feared an embarrassing defeat. The most popular politician in Berlin was Ernst Reuter, leader of the SPD. When the US general Lucius Clay asked Reuter how the people of Berlin would respond to the blockade, he told Clay, "You worry about the airlift, let me worry about the Berliners."[33] In fact, Reuter, the SPD, and many Berliners were determined to resist the blockade and to make sure that the Western allies not abandon Berlin. He used a speech to a huge crowd at the Brandenburg Gate on September 9, 1948, to address the world: "You people of the world, you people in America, in England, in Italy! Look at this city and realize that you must not, that you cannot surrender this city and this people. . . . People of the world, look at Berlin! And people of Berlin, be certain of this, this struggle we will, this struggle we shall win!"[34] The blockade was ended on May 12, 1949.

The Berlin blockade failed on its own terms. In February 1949, the airlift was supplying twice the amount of supplies considered essential.[35] The failure also had decisive political consequences, easing the establishment both of the new West German state and of NATO (the North Atlantic Treaty Organization). It was the determination of the western occupying powers to create a new German state that had provoked the blockade, so the decision to resist its effects through the airlift implied that work on shaping that state would be pushed forward. The key event was the decision of the three occupation powers—the US, the UK, and France—to convene on September 1, 1948, a Parliamentary Council to draft a de facto constitution. Meeting in Bonn, the council chose Konrad Adenauer, an old and to this point not very well-known Christian Democrat, to lead it. The council finished its work in April. The new constitution was labeled the Basic Law, a gesture to the idea that it was provisional and would be superseded by a proper constitution when Germany was reunited. It became effective in June. The new state was to be a decidedly federal state, with central power restricted and much authority residing in the Länder, the state governments. The first elections to the Bundestag were held on August 14, 1949, and Adenauer became the state's first chancellor a month later. He would retain that position for thirteen years, ensuring that West Germany would take shape under the political domination of the Christian Democrats. Its economic policy would be shaped by an economic liberal, Ludwig Erhard, who was appointed head of economic administration in the Bizone in March 1948. The model would be essentially a hybrid, a "social market economy" mixing the social protections supported by Christian Democracy and the economic liberalism of Erhard and his advisors.

The move to establish NATO was also facilitated by the blockade's failure, though the initial move was the creation of the Western European Union in March 1948. An additional spur was the recent Czech coup in February. It led to fears of similar moves elsewhere and to a more general fear of a war between the superpowers, for which the West was largely unprepared. The Brussels Pact that established the new organization was pushed hard by the British foreign secretary, Ernest Bevin, who would also be a forceful advocate for the airlift a few months later. The pact was in itself a modest affair, directed initially at defending against Germany, but it produced a sense that any worthwhile security arrangement would need American support and participation. There was also a developing sense that the Marshall Plan, an economic collaboration designed to bring economic security to Europe, would require a military complement to ensure security in matters of defense. This was ironic in that one of the arguments for the Marshall Plan was that it would make it unnecessary for the United States to take responsibility for European security because it would allow the Europeans to provide for themselves. By December 1948 the State Department concluded just the opposite: "a North Atlantic Security Pact [was] an essential supplement to the Marshall Plan."[36] That was also the thinking of Senator Vandenberg, who introduced a resolution supportive of enhanced collective security arrangements. His resolution was approved in June 1948 and encouraged the State Department to undertake mutual-defense planning in July.

In his Inaugural Address in January 1949 Truman promised a "collective defense arrangement" linking the US, Canada, and Europe. The logic leading from the Marshall Plan to military alliance was powerful, and by early 1949 the effort had gained serious momentum. On April 9, 1949, the treaty setting up NATO was signed in Washington. The decisions that produced the Marshall Plan, NATO, and the new West German state were countered with parallel moves by the Soviet Union. The Soviets began making bilateral trade agreements with the states of Eastern Europe in 1947 and these were then turned into a regional grouping, Comecon; and the German Democratic Republic was founded on October 7, 1949. The Warsaw Pact, which was hardly necessary given the looming and commanding presence of Soviet forces in Eastern Europe, did not come into being until 1955. Still, the symmetry seemed appropriate, even though cooperation and alliances in the West were largely voluntary, if often the fruit of argument and at least subtle manipulation, while those in the East were simply coerced.

Taken together, the Western initiatives were a dramatic reversal of previous policies and long-standing traditions. It is certainly an oversimplification to say that the United States went from being an isolationist power as late as 1940 to being an involved and committed world citizen by the end of the 1940s. America had never been completely disengaged. It began life as an offshoot of European empires; its independence was secured against one empire with aid from another; its Declaration of Independence was addressed to other states, mainly empires, and insisted that the new state be treated as one of them.[37] Its economy was always integrated in global circuits: its original capital came from outside, and much later it exported capital all over the world; its labor force came mainly from abroad, as free immigrants or captive slaves; its raw materials were mostly generated internally, but then exported widely; its industrial products were consumed locally and exported; its supply chains started locally but became widely dispersed; and it started as and had long been a trading nation. It was never isolated economically or politically.

Nevertheless, the US was separated from external threats by oceans, and its diplomatic and geopolitical stance had typically been a kind of offshore balancing. And there was a strong tradition of remaining aloof from alliances and the entanglements supposedly characteristic of the Old World of Europe. The elaboration of new levels of connection represented by the Marshall Plan and NATO was in this sense a departure, and something that took persuasion to achieve. It was no easy thing for the Truman administration to devise these policies and institutions, and selling them to the public and to Congress was a major task. Not surprisingly, those responsible for bringing about this new direction in US global policy regarded their success as a signal achievement.[38] They could and would take special pride in the success of the Marshall Plan in stimulating an economic revival in Europe. Americans had hoped that the framework of international economic policy hammered out at Bretton Woods would, more or less automatically, allow the world economy, and the economy of Europe, to recover without further intervention. Those institutions and the policies they espoused were not up to the enormous tasks of providing relief and encouraging growth in Europe after the war. Something like the Marshall Plan was needed. The fact that it was forthcoming, and that it was conceived and approved and implemented so rapidly—with $13 billion going to Europe over four years—is in retrospect quite remarkable.[39] That the political consequences of the plan were so unfavorable to the Soviets and the Communist parties of the West and so helpful in producing more or less stable political regimes of the political center was a bonus, but perhaps an earned bonus.

The policies and institutions put in place between 1947 and 1949 would provide the framework within which the Cold War would be fought out over the next several decades. It would take a bit longer for the nature and dimensions of the contest to become clear. That the struggle would involve a nuclear arms race became apparent on August 29, 1949, when the Soviets successfully tested their own atom bomb. The United States had estimated that it would take longer for the Soviet Union to develop an atomic weapon. They had been helped by spies in the US and Britain—not greatly, but the revelation of the Soviet spying network sparked a Red Scare that turned a real but manageable security threat into a nearly paranoid search for spies and traitors. Less than five weeks later, on October 1, the People's Republic of China was proclaimed. The Chinese Communists, led by Mao Zedong, had thoroughly defeated the Nationalist Guomindang under the leadership of Chiang Kai-shek. Mao's victory meant that the most populous country in the world joined the country with largest land mass, the USSR, as allied Communist states.

The Soviet atomic bomb and the Chinese Revolution rendered the Cold War global and nuclear. The reaction in the West was to ramp up its ability to fight the Cold War. The manifestation of this new resolve was a document produced by the Policy Planning Staff of the State Department, NSC 68, in April 1950. NSC 68 argued that the Soviet bomb and events in China required as a response "the rapid building up of the political, economic, and military strength of the free world." This would mean specifically a massive increase in conventional and nuclear forces in the United States and smaller increases among NATO allies. Defense spending in America tripled between 1950 and 1954, to over 14 percent of GNP. Not everyone in the Truman administration agreed with NSC 68 when it was presented, but the invasion of South Korea in June 1950, backed by the Soviets and the Chinese, swept away doubt and opposition.[40] With the mobilization prompted by the Korean conflict, the Cold War had become thoroughly militarized and violent and it had now spread to Asia.[41] The Korean War was also, in a basic sense, a war about the legacy of colonialism and a sure sign that subsequent battles over decolonization and the end of empire would be intensified by and framed within the context of the Cold War.[42]

The Korean War ended in a stalemate whose borders and conditions were becoming visible by mid-1951. It dragged on for two more years, partly because both the North and South Koreans wanted to continue fighting in hopes they might prevail and because Stalin, who stood behind and supplied the Chinese and the North Koreans, believed that prolonging the war benefited the Soviets and weakened the US. An armistice would be signed only after Stalin's death in 1953.[43] The outcome in Korea meant an effective stabilization in the battle lines of the Cold War. Further advances, by either side, would be piecemeal and would come slowly, as the two sides were becoming more deeply dug into their respective positions. The arms race was accelerated in terms of conventional and nuclear weapons, and the two giant security blocs became more solidly entrenched. Over the next decade Communist regimes everywhere consolidated their grip over society and politics; and in the West, along with Japan, non-Communist democracies also became more firmly established. Securing these domestic stabilizations and reconstructions was a critical task in waging the Cold War.

The world envisioned in 1945 was meant to be peaceful, ordered, and liberal. By 1950–51, what had come into existence was a Cold War world order.[44] Though actual war was being waged only on the periphery, in Korea, it was hardly a world at peace. The US and the USSR confronted each other armed with nuclear weapons and with large arsenals of conventional weapons; and they were at the center of rival blocs that spanned much of the globe. It was becoming a more ordered world, as the political vacuum of 1945 was filled with new states and institutions, but order was coerced in the East and not uniformly stable in the West. The occupations of Germany and Japan were winding down, but democracy was new and untested, and stability was by no means assured. New states and governments had been established in Italy and France, but the political systems seemed fragile.

Was the emerging Cold War order truly liberal or conducive to liberalism? In the vast territories controlled by Communist states, liberalism and democracy were not so much alien as forbidden by the ruling parties. It was also hard to characterize political order as liberal in those large sections of the world that remained part of European empires.

Colonies are by definition illiberal, for they exclude the ruled, the subaltern who are invariably the majority of the population. The United States had a long tradition of opposing colonialism, with key exceptions, but during the early years of the Cold War it became more tolerant of the efforts of its British and French allies to hold on to their imperial possessions. Gradually, decolonization would prevail, but the persistence and legacy of empire would long taint the image of the so-called free world. So, too, would the routine practice of propping up and tolerating dictatorships that, while anti-Soviet, were nevertheless brutal and oppressive.

So, the world was divided behind two expansive systems, a frankly illiberal bloc and a Western bloc (including Japan) that was in theory committed to liberalism in politics and to an economy that was capitalist, but with varying degrees of state control and social protections. Within that liberal bloc were numerous illiberal anomalies—some vestigial, some more anchored and unlikely to disappear—but its liberalism was not merely incidental. It was the vision that inspired its creation as a bloc, that would largely govern the relations between its members, and that mostly characterized the internal politics of those states. The fact that the bloc was not now the world meant that the reach of liberal politics and institutions was limited, but operating within distinct boundaries meant that the system would develop on a smaller, but more manageable, scale. It was, after all, a new order that would require time to take root and would need to be consolidated before it could be regarded as stable. That process would, of course, take place within a broader Cold War balance that had a huge impact on how liberal systems and the liberal order would evolve. Understood thus, the liberal order that existed in that non-Communist world was still a project, an aspiration, and its future would be worked out within the framework of the Cold War. Whatever its flaws and limits, it was a considerably more attractive order than what had existed in 1939 and that, if the Germans and Italians and Japanese had succeeded, would have existed after their triumph.

In Search of Stability and Prosperity

By the middle of 1951, the Cold War world was taking on a recognizable shape, with borders soon to be clearly defined. Although its geography was becoming more established, the content of life and politics within the two huge spheres was still to be worked out. Stability was probably closer at hand in the East, for political systems there did not rely on the consent of the governed. In the more open societies outside the Communist world, politics involved more uncertainty, and creating stable polities would require more tending and bargaining and, for that to happen, more time. In both East and West, much would depend on whether the new states and regimes could generate prosperity. Prosperity would confer legitimacy in a way that mere politics, democratic or authoritarian, on its own probably could not. Economic conditions in the West had improved significantly since 1947, but less so in the East, and nowhere was the future of the economy certain.

The Fate of Liberalism in the East

The repressive orders installed in the East of necessity varied from country to country, but the objective was uniformity. In Eastern Europe the new regimes became more "Stalinized" in the late 1940s and early 1950s; the ruling parties were expected to fall into line with Moscow and adhere closely to the Soviet model. The economies of the new states were to be centrally planned as they were in the Soviet Union and, except in Poland, agriculture would be collectivized. Politically, these would all become single-party states and would have their own versions of the secret police. The best known and feared would be the Stasi in East Germany, but its equivalents were ubiquitous. In places, there were even "show trials" and purges of the sort pioneered under Stalin. The victims were ordinary men and women, liberals and socialists and Catholics, but also Communists who somehow managed to displease the Soviets. A significant number were Jews. Examples came from Albania, Bulgaria, and Romania, but particularly notorious cases occurred in Hungary and Czechoslovakia. These included among their victims the Hungarian László Rajk, a loyal Communist who was nonetheless arrested, forced to confess, and executed in 1949. Not long after, a similar move was made in Czechoslovakia, where the party's general secretary, Rudolf Slánský, urged his comrades to "unmask the enemies in our own ranks, for they are the most dangerous enemies." Vladimir Clementis, the foreign minister, was among the first to be targeted, but soon enough it was Slánský's turn. His show trial in November 1952 was scripted, the script personally approved by Stalin. Of course, he was convicted, and in December 1953 he, Clementis, and nine others were executed.[1]

The move toward rigidity and dictatorship in Eastern Europe mirrored what was happening in the Soviet Union itself. There had been some hope that there might be an opening up of the regime after 1945. The Soviets had wanted to continue the wartime alliance and it seemed just possible to imagine that the spirit of the "popular front" might gradually loosen controls. It did not happen. If anything, Soviet policy after the war aimed to close down opposition and eliminate oppositional spaces. Besides Stalin, the name most closely associated with the restoration of hard-line orthodoxy was Andrei Zhdanov, who was in charge of ideology and cultural policy under Stalin. In 1946 he introduced a resolution to the Central Committee denouncing bourgeois tendencies in literature. The resolution signaled a new policy—*Zhdanovshchina*, as it was called— and it developed into a broad campaign that affected literature, music, the arts, and even the sciences. Criticism was directed at poets like Anna Ahkmatova, denounced as "half-nun, half-harlot" and expelled from the

Writers' Union, composers such as Prokofiev and Shostakovich, and many others.[2] The effect on Soviet culture was devastating. Equally dangerous were the consequences for science. This was the era when the Soviets denounced relativity theory and promoted the biological theories of Lysenko, who argued against recent developments in genetics and for the belief in the inheritance of acquired characteristics.

It was the very same Zhdanov, of course, to whom Stalin entrusted the task of founding the Cominform in September 1947—the Soviet answer to the Truman Doctrine and the Marshall Plan. Zhdanov died in 1948, but the policies associated with him remained and were pursued into 1953. The turn in Soviet policy meant that the last years of Stalin's rule represented a continuation of prewar policies, with roughly 2.5 million still in the gulags in 1951 and with recurring rounds of purges. An egregious example occurred not long before Stalin's death. On January 13, 1953, Radio Moscow proclaimed the discovery of a "criminal group of killer doctors" whose goal was the killing of Soviet leaders. Most of those arrested were Jews. The "doctors' plot" was the climax of an intensified anti-Semitism that had begun in 1948. Stalin's death led his successors to abandon the charges and release the arrested doctors.

The death of Stalin again raised hopes for a loosening or "thaw," but these hopes were to be thwarted yet again. The man mostly responsible for carrying out purges and eliminations for Stalin, Lavrentiy Beria, was initially seen as a likely successor. Not only had he led the NKVD, the secret police, but he had played a crucial role in setting up the states in Eastern Europe and he had been put in charge of the Soviet atomic bomb project. These strengths struck fear in his rivals and they turned against him. Arrested in late June, he was tried and executed in December 1953. His death is regarded as the last instance of the explicit use of terror and murder among the Soviet leadership. Ironically, before his arrest Beria had overseen a modest lessening of repression: about a million prisoners were released from the gulags. But his background and his naked ambition doomed him.

Beria was also an indirect victim of the German uprising of June 17, 1953. Encouraged to think that Stalin's death might in fact allow more scope for compromise and a recognition of local conditions and needs, East Europeans in the more urban centers began to push for better conditions. In Czechoslovakia a currency reform at the end of May triggered unrest and led to a strike at the Škoda plant in Plzeň (Pilsen in German) on June 1. The protests passed, but a more serious movement developed in East Germany: workers protested the recent decision to raise work norms and impose higher prices and taxes. The Soviets urged a "new course" on the regime and on others in the region, but opposition continued to escalate and spread beyond Berlin to cities like Rostock, Magdeburg, Dresden, and Leipzig as well as to smaller towns all over the country. As it grew, it became bolder, and protesters demanded free elections and the removal of Soviet troops. In response, the "new course" was effectively abandoned and martial law was declared. Even so, the East German Communists were reportedly ready to evacuate. What saved the regime was the direct intervention of Soviet troops and tanks. The repression was severe: nearly three hundred were killed by Soviet forces; of the several thousand arrested, roughly fourteen hundred were sentenced to extensive prison terms and a further two hundred were shot. The outcome made clear the limits to any easing of Soviet control in the region. Beria's role, as it happened, was quite indirect, but he was reported, not unreasonably, to have regarded East Germany as a weak state hardly worth defending and to have considered abandoning it in return for a unified, neutral Germany and Western aid to the Soviet Union. It was in the immediate aftermath of the uprising that he was arrested on the initiative of Nikita Khrushchev, who was emerging as the top leader after Stalin's passing.

In practice, Stalin's death did little to alter the character of the Soviet regime or to open up those newly installed in Eastern Europe. There would be yet another moment when hopes for a more open and less repressive system rose in 1956. On February 24 Khrushchev gave a lengthy speech to the Twentieth Congress of the Communist Party in which he denounced Stalin, the cult of personality that surrounded him, and the purges he carried out. The contents of the "Secret Speech," quickly leaked, caused a stir inside and outside the Soviet bloc. Within the bloc, it was believed that the speech would finally produce the opening that had failed to occur after the war or following Stalin's death. Hope was widespread, and serious unrest emerged in Poland and Hungary. Khrushchev himself went to Poland to assess the situation in mid-October amid talk of violence between troops loyal to the Soviets and those loyal to the local government. "Finding a reason for an armed conflict right now would be pretty easy," Khrushchev reported, "but finding a way to put an end to such a conflict later on would be very hard." A deal was reached in which some noxious Soviets who were in charge of the Polish army, like Marshall Rokossovskii, would leave and, in turn, the Polish government under the reform Communist Władysław Gomułka agreed to remain within the Soviet bloc.[3]

Events in Hungary followed a more confrontational, and ultimately more violent, path. The Communist government in Hungary, led by Imre Nagy, had chosen to follow the "new course" adopted in 1953, backed off from the extreme repression of the period of "high Stalinism," and eased up on the drive for collectivization of agriculture and overly ambitious industrial targets. This modest liberalization had been resisted by hard-liners in the party, like longtime general secretary Mátyás Rákosi, and in March 1955 the Soviets denounced Nagy for "rightist deviations." Rákosi and his allies returned to power. They were, of course, stunned by Khrushchev's speech and soon the Soviets came to believe that allowing Rákosi to stay in office was not in their interest. They engineered his ouster and had him replaced in July by the lackluster Stalinist Ernő Gerő.

Unlike in other countries in Eastern Europe, genuine opposition existed in Hungary. Within the party there was a reformist group around Nagy. Beyond the party there were groups of writers, students, and intellectuals who, again uniquely in the region, established ties with workers. The most interesting and effective was the so-called Petőfi Circle, named for a poet who had been a leader of the 1848 revolution. Dissent also infected organizations like the League for Working Youth and the Hungarian Writers' Association. These opposition groups began to come together, encouraged by the successful protests in Poland. On October 22, a meeting of five thousand students voted to leave the League for Working Youth and form an independent organization. By midnight, they had come up with a call to arms, the Sixteen Points. Their numbers quintupled the next day and kept growing; the crowds chanted, "Russians go home," and by that night they had seized the radio station and toppled a statue of Stalin. They demanded the return of Nagy, who became prime

minister on October 24, and much more. The events, largely spontaneous, took a revolutionary turn over the next two weeks: military officers
(at least some) and many soldiers defected, the head of the police in
Budapest came over to the rebels, more statues fell, workers' councils
sprang up in factories, political prisoners were released, members of the
secret police were lynched, and on October 30 the party's headquarters
in the capitol was stormed. Nagy, angered by the presence of Soviet
troops, chose to side with the revolutionaries by negotiating on key demands, agreeing to set up a multi-party government, and insisting that
the Soviets leave. He went on to promise to abolish the secret police and
said that Hungary would leave the Warsaw Pact. On November 1, Nagy
announced that Hungary was now a neutral country and requested that
the UN recognize it as such.

The Soviets hesitated at first, sending troops and then holding
them back, but the progress of the revolution convinced them they had
to act. They installed a new government led by János Kádár and on November 3 began the counterattack. Soviet tanks entered Budapest the
next day and subdued the rebellion in three days. Elsewhere resistance
continued through November, December, and into January. It has been
estimated that 2,700 died directly in the struggle, nearly 350 were tried
and executed, 22,000 were imprisoned, and 13,000 were sent to camps.[4]
Nagy was executed. Despite the effort to involve the United Nations,
there was little or no international opposition to what the Soviets did.
The United States had occasionally called for the "rollback" of Soviet
power in Eastern Europe, but had no serious intention of doing anything to make it happen. Containment meant containment, not an effort
to push the Soviet Union back by force. It was also a bad moment for
Western governments to coordinate action against the Soviets, for the
British and French were just then involved in their own folly at Suez,
which the United States reasonably opposed. The distraction was extremely convenient for the Soviets and their minions elsewhere in Eastern Europe, who joined in condemning the uprising and endorsing its
suppression.

The fate of Eastern Europe under the Soviets had probably been set
as early as 1947 or 1948, but the precise extent and form of its domination
would remain unclear until 1956. By that date any hope of reform, of

creating in the region "socialism with a human face," was gone. From that date dictatorial rule in that part of the Soviet bloc would in fact be somewhat milder than it had been before 1953, and the Soviet model would be implemented with at least some concession to local conditions. The basic outlines were set, however, and if reformers' hopes were kindled once more in the Prague Spring of 1968, they were again dashed late that summer. It would become obvious later, much later, that Soviet rule and that of the regimes they protected were never really accepted, but those who lived through the era had little reason to hope for a better world anytime soon. They were forced to accommodate, and while many surely continued to hope for a more humane version of socialism, efforts at reform achieved very little. The year 1956 also served to demonstrate that prospects for a serious breakthrough for the left in the West were no more realistic, let alone desirable. Khrushchev's speech and the crushing of the Hungarian Revolution caused Communist parties outside the bloc to hemorrhage members. They entered a crisis from which they would never recover.

Beyond Eastern Europe and the Soviet Union, there were now Communist regimes farther to the east. The spread of Communism to Asia was among the most dramatic developments in the post–World War II era. It was a source of excitement for Communists everywhere and a cause of dread among its opponents. Much about its effect was inevitably unknown in the early years of the Cold War. Did the triumph of Communism in China, North Korea, and later North Vietnam signal a steady advance across the world? Would Communism in Asia mean something different from what it meant in the Soviet Union and in Eastern Europe? Would there be scope for variation and the possibility for a more liberal and attractive type of economy and political system? Or would the same model be applied in what were very different societies?

Answers to these questions would come only slowly, and they would be provisional, for there would be substantial shifts over time. Two things stood out fairly clearly early on, however. The first was that the Communist states in Asia would have deeper roots and more genuine popular support than those recently set up in Eastern Europe. The main reason was that they were created from broad-based movements of national liberation and so saw themselves, and were seen by others, as securing independence for the nation against outsiders, imperialists, and invaders. The Chinese Communist Party had taken the lead in the fight against Japan and it styled itself as the vehicle for the reestablishment of Chinese sovereignty after a century of domination and humiliation at the hands of the West.[5] In Korea, the national enemy had been the Japanese, who had begun the subjugation of their neighbor in the 1870s and formally annexed it in 1910. In Vietnam, the imperial power was France, whose rule began in the 1880s. Even though the population in these separate nations consisted mainly of peasants, not in theory the natural base of Communist support, leadership of the national and anti-imperialist struggle created mass support for the Communists.

The second clear fact about the Asian Communist states was that, at least at first, there was no real alternative to the Soviet model and no serious effort to develop one. To those who directed the building of Communist states and societies in Asia, the Soviets appeared as major benefactors. Moreover, the Soviet Union had built a system that worked. The Soviets had survived and triumphed in the Second World War and as of 1949 they had their own atomic bomb. The Soviets were also generous with their support—not always as generous as Mao and others might have wanted, but overall their help was enormous. They aided the Chinese and Korean parties before they came to power, then again during the Korean War, and throughout the 1950s with massive development aid. By one estimate, between 1946 and 1960 the Soviets provided assistance to the new Chinese state worth the equivalent of $25 billion, larger than the Marshall Plan, and also assisted with the transfer of technology and by deploying an array of Soviet advisors.[6] In the early 1950s, there was thus no reason to develop an alternative approach to building socialism.

As a result, the new regimes put in place command economies very similar to that of the Soviet Union and repressive political systems closely resembling what they understood to be the practice in the Soviet Union, replete with secret police and the apparatus of control that accompanied its existence. Circumstances obviously differed in the three Asian Communist states. North Korea was at war into 1953, and the exigencies of war overrode all other concerns. War did not, however, make the regime any less harsh. The Vietnamese were also at war until 1954, and that meant that there was no "normal" until after that; even then, normal would not last long before the nation was at war again.

Building the institutions of a new state, and building socialism, would therefore be shaped by the decision to follow the Soviet model but also by the distortions of war. War was also a reality for China because of its involvement in Korea, both as a participant and as the country that supplied the North Koreans, but the regime consolidated itself fairly quickly after 1949 and its development hewed closely to the Soviet model.

Later in the 1950s, China under Mao Zedong would begin to follow a divergent and distinctive path. The Chinese Communists were unhappy with Khrushchev's "Secret Speech" and subsequent moves to distance the Soviet Union from the Stalinist past. Mao's assessment of Stalin remained mostly positive. Soon after Stalin's death, he became impatient with the slow path to the building of socialism that the Soviet experience of Five-Year Plans implied. Bizarrely, he argued, "The Soviet Union has been building socialism for forty-one years and it couldn't make a transition to socialism in 12 years. They are now behind us and already in panic." He wanted to move faster and in 1958 launched a campaign to speed up development in agriculture and industry in the so-called Great Leap Forward. Results were disastrous: by 1961, roughly 40 million had died and the campaign was abandoned.[7] Mao never conceded that his plan was mistaken, instead blaming his opponents. That perception in turn fueled his desire to shake up the party and its leaders, which would produce the Cultural Revolution in 1966. The Great Leap Forward represented an explicit repudiation of the Soviet model and it was accompanied by increasing antagonism between China and the Soviet Union. The Sino-Soviet split would have major geopolitical consequences and put an end to the notion that Communism was monolithic and that the path to socialism would be the same in every country. Whichever path was chosen, none involved anything remotely like democracy or liberalism, and there would be no model available for a less repressive road to socialism.

In Pursuit of Democracy and Stability

The prospects for democratic outcomes and for the creation of a liberal international order would therefore be confined to what came to be called the West in the Cold War world. There, at least, there was no official ideology that disdained and proscribed liberalism and democracy. Equally important, the dominant power in the West exercised its hegemony through bargaining and mostly subtle pressure rather than by force. If the United States built a kind of empire, it was not unreasonably described as an "empire by invitation."[8] The United States served as a model to its allies, and emulation was as important as coercion in the choices countries made as to whether, and to what extent, to follow it. Part of the reason was that America's allies had substantial prior experience with both democracy and capitalism, even if democracy had been temporarily snuffed out in key places—Germany, Italy, and Japan most notably.

Still, the quest for a stability that was basically democratic was not simple. Democracy had obviously been on the defensive before the war, and if it was to become more stable and secure, it would be necessary to do things differently. A prerequisite would be a functioning economy. There was no way to ensure that, but important steps had been taken as the war ended. The Bretton Woods agreements were intended to replace the autarchic, protectionist policies that characterized responses to the Great Depression and to prevent financial and currency crises from crippling the economy. Would they deliver? On their own, probably not, for the sums available to the International Monetary Fund (IMF) and the World Bank were insufficient and the rules about their use lacked flexibility. With the Marshall Plan, however, countries gained the ability to trade and invest that would allow the potential of the European economies to be realized. The leap in military spending produced by the Korean War added a further stimulus as the funds for the European Recovery Program were running down. Unlike after the First World War, growth was not held back by debts and reparations. Britain, the United States, and France had stopped reparations from their zones to the Soviet Union during the late 1940s, and the London Debt Agreement of 1953 forgave a large share of (West) German debt. These choices facilitated Germany's reemergence as an exporter, as trade within Europe increased. Overall, the opening up of the world economy envisioned by those who designed the Bretton Woods system would happen only slowly, but the agreed objective set the direction of change.

The making of economic policy, and ideas about it, had also shifted dramatically since the 1930s. Among economists and policy makers the ascendance of Keynesian theories and the willingness to use Keynesian techniques to govern the economy were key differences. The ability to draw upon Keynes and the macro-economic tools he advocated facilitated the commitments of governments to guaranteeing full employment. The commitments were partly rhetorical, and the capacity of governments to deliver on them was untested and unlikely to be adequate, but what governments say and promise their citizens has, and had then, a real effect. In the United States, for example, the Employment Act of 1946 proved controversial and the version that passed into law was much less robust than what the Truman administration had proposed, but it did send a message that the government accepted that it was its duty to ensure a high and stable level of employment. Governments in Europe and in Japan made similar commitments, though the means adopted to realize them varied greatly.[9]

The French had carried out extensive nationalizations during 1944–46. In December 1945 Jean Monnet, then head of the General Planning Commission (Le commissariat général du plan) and later a founder of the European Community, had produced a "plan for the modernization" of France. Efforts to generate growth routinely made use of nationalized firms to accomplish key development tasks, but the goal was to create a balanced or mixed economy, an économie concertée. The preference was for what would be called "indicative planning" rather than for any detailed blueprint. Nevertheless, the role of the state would be essential.[10] Italy also used the state to mobilize capital: the Institute for Industrial Reconstruction (IRI), founded under Mussolini, continued to control numerous firms after the war and on its own employed over two hundred thousand people in 1948, and the National Agency for Hydrocarbons (ENI), the Ministry for State Holdings, created in 1956, and the Cassa per il mezzogiorno together exercised control of much of the economy and played a major role in directing investment.[11] In Germany, it was the links between banks and business that provided a constant flow of investment in the "social market economy" established under Erhard's liberal direction; and in Japan powerful firms worked closely with the Ministry of International Trade and Industry, established in 1949, to coordinate industrial policy. In Britain, the nationalizations of the 1940s gave government a role in industrial policy, but because state ownership was concentrated in older industries,

new investment flowed elsewhere and came mostly from the private sector. A vogue for planning would come later, as would more active industrial policy. The United States relied rather more on the market to steer
the economy, but the huge role of defense spending meant that its economic policy was perhaps most accurately characterized as a kind of
military Keynesianism.[12]

These distinct models of intervention were underpinned by welfare and labor market policies that were, if not everywhere the same, at
least somewhat comparable across the range of countries. The scourge
of the Great Depression had been made worse everywhere by the lack of
social supports. Governments were forced to respond, but did so unevenly. Coming out of the war there was a widespread commitment to
building better systems of social protection. Inevitably, new commitments and funding came on top of existing institutions and mechanisms, though new policies could also require the creation of novel
structures. In Great Britain, the major innovation was the National
Health Service, created in 1948, though even that built on the network
of hospitals already in place. The principle of universalism and the notion that health care was a right and that government had a duty to provide it were new, however. In other countries, legacies were more visible
and sometimes rather awkward. Germany had a long tradition of providing welfare going back to Bismarck that involved collaboration between the state, industry, and private organizations. In France, a number
of policies were carried over from the prewar period, but extended and
made more universal. Policies in Italy also manifested continuities from
the fascist era under a disorganized institutional structure. In the United
States, welfare provision had been meager and localized before the New
Deal, but under the Roosevelt administration had become more expansive. Much was left to the states, of course, and that translated into serious inequities. African Americans were excluded from many of the
benefits of the New Deal or received less generous benefits than whites.
After the war, the Truman administration proposed a Fair Deal designed
to make New Deal programs larger and more equitable. Much was
achieved, but benefits were nevertheless distributed unevenly.[13] The
transformation across the democratic countries was registered most
dramatically in massively increased budgets for social provision—in

health care, pensions, unemployment and disability payments, housing, education, and maternal and child welfare.

Policy affecting work and workers was transformed as well. A distinguishing feature of fascism was its attack on free trade unions. Appropriately, the right to form unions and bargain collectively became a defining part of anti-fascism. After the war, such rights became more or less universal outside the Soviet bloc. The right to join a union was actually written into the French constitution. In Britain and the United States, union membership had grown massively during the war, and employers were pressured to recognize and bargain with unions. After the war, the unions were powerful political actors. Unions had been repressed in Germany, Italy, and in occupied France and under Vichy during the war. In Italy and France, they regrouped in and through the Resistance and emerged much strengthened after the war. In Germany, new and old unions were reconstituted after the war and were accorded new rights in the workplace.[14] Essentially, the new model of capitalism put in place across the West gave unions a solid place within industry. The Marshall Plan, which had strong support among American trade unions, further encouraged progressive industrial relations policies. None of this precluded bitter strikes—particularly in France and Italy— and fierce battles about how much control workers and unions should exercise in the workplace. In the United States, employers launched a sustained effort to take back control of the shop floor and to limit the scope of bargaining, and Congress passed the restrictive Taft-Hartley Act in 1947 over Truman's veto.[15] Despite these reversals and countermoves, union strength persisted, and unions would be a novel and critical part of the landscape of industrial relations just about everywhere. Their presence would ensure that as the economy recovered, ordinary workers would get a reasonable share of the proceeds.

The combination of governments committed to preventing unemployment and willing to deploy new tools and resources to make that promise real, much enhanced social services to relieve poverty and to provide security for ordinary citizens, and stronger trade unions represented a new framework for economic life. It was a vision that in America grew from the New Deal and in Europe fulfilled many of the aspirations of social democracy.[16] It was a product, however, not of one party but of the variety of forces unleashed by depression and war and then by political mobilization at the end of the war. Progressives, whether they considered themselves social democrats or New Deal liberals, played a vital role, but in some cases the new model of capitalism was overseen by Christian Democratic parties. The Marshall Plan pushed in this direction and so, too, did the occupation policies of the United States and its allies in West Germany and of the US in Japan. It was a set of policies and institutions that were, or became, more or less consensual in the West and Japan. It would also prove to be a highly effective framework for generating sustained economic growth.

Three other factors contributed to what became a "golden age" of capitalism. First came the gradual opening up of trade. Advocates of free trade were disappointed that it did not happen faster, but it happened and it was sustained. The creation of the European Payments Union in 1950 and the subsequent founding of the Common Market eased trade within Europe, and trade beyond Europe became more open as well. The second was the growth of population both in Europe and the United States. Europe's baby boom was less dramatic than that of the United States, but it reversed the interwar trend and provided an extra stimulus to demand. In addition, there was a huge reservoir of underemployed agricultural labor across Europe that could move into cities and industries to supplement the existing labor force, and it was relatively cheap labor whose employment did not add to inflationary pressure. The movement of African Americans from agriculture to industry and from the South to the North and the West or to new industrial centers in the South had a similar effect in the United States. An additional source of population growth was migration. The quarter century after the war was not a period of mass migration, but in Europe there were substantial flows of people fleeing Communist regimes in the East, of workers moving from southern Italy, Greece, Spain, and Turkey to jobs in the north, and of immigrants from the colonies. In theory, many of these workers were supposed to be only temporary residents, and some were, but they came to constitute a large portion of the workforce in Western Europe. In general, the new workers not only provided additional labor for the postwar boom but also consumed the relatively cheap manufactured goods produced by these growing economies.[17]

The third factor that aided growth after the war was the more equitable distribution of income. Important recent work has shown that during the depression and the Second World War inequality was reduced by economic collapse, by wartime destruction, by increased wages due to the spread of unionization, and by the high rates of taxation required to wage war.[18] That compression of income and wealth created a novel structure of demand that allowed for mass consumption and steady income growth for the working and middle classes. It lasted until the 1980s and, according to numerous estimates, has been replaced in recent decades by growing inequality, with very different consequences for growth and welfare. The narrowing of inequalities in income and wealth that prevailed from the end of the war until the mid- or late 1970s was, by most measures, a unique moment in the long history of capitalism. The facts that it was in those years that the economy grew faster and in a more sustained fashion than ever before and that the fruits of that growth were enjoyed by the large majority of the population presumably owed much to this more equal starting point.

The data on economic performance in the West are indeed impressive. France grew on average 5 percent per year from 1947 to 1973; Germany achieved a growth rate of 8 percent per year throughout the 1950s; the Netherlands economy saw an increase on average of 3.5 percent per year from 1950 to 1970; and, because the base was lower and Italy could make great gains catching up, growth there was 5.5 percent during the 1950s and further accelerated in the next decade, reaching roughly 8 percent in the late 1960s. Britain was, of course, already a more developed country and with older industries. Still, it banished the curse of unemployment: unemployment that had averaged 13.4 percent during 1921–38 fell to 1.6 percent in the period 1950–69. Japan managed to grow by 7.1 percent per year during the first postwar decade (1946–56); by the 1960s, its economy grew by nearly 10 percent per year. The United States, another mature economy that was not devastated by war, nevertheless grew by an average of 2.5 percent from 1948 through 1973. These results led commentators to speak of a *Wirtschaftswunder* in Germany, of "economic miracles" in Italy, Japan, and Greece, of *les trente glorieuses* in France.[19] Growth was sustained, it affected almost every Western nation, and its proceeds were shared more equitably than ever before.

The economic boom also brought structural changes to the countries where it occurred. Everywhere people left the countryside for the city and into jobs that were much more productive. Workers moved in huge numbers into industries organized on the basis of mass production technologies. This "Fordist" pattern of industrial growth had critical feedback loops and favored further growth. In the Fordist model, workers in mass production industries churned out goods that were of basic quality at relatively low cost. They were paid reasonable wages and could consume the sorts of things they produced, increasing demand still more. Of course, the shift toward Fordism was not universal. Sustained growth at the levels achieved in the postwar era also meant a demand for products produced in more artisanal fashion, and it also required an expansion of services, particularly in transportation and retail. Still, the widespread adoption of Fordist techniques was a defining feature of the postwar boom. Mass production also meant mass consumption, and the boom allowed increasing numbers of ordinary workers to afford better housing, to have indoor plumbing, to buy better clothes, refrigerators, televisions, and eventually automobiles. The wealthiest citizens and the most advanced countries got access to these goods more quickly, but by the 1970s many such items were owned and enjoyed by most people in the West. It constituted a consumer revolution and created a standard of living that was unimaginable in the 1930s or even in 1945.

Shaping Democratic Political Systems

Prosperity made it easier to establish political systems that were democratic and whose legitimacy was widely accepted, but political creativity was also essential. The decisive achievement of postwar politics was to make the political center stronger. That might involve shifting the beliefs and behavior of existing parties in that direction; or it might mean creating new parties; and it might also mean excluding some parties and some beliefs. Exclusions—efforts that were to a certain extent illiberal— were, in fact, essential to establishing liberal political regimes.

The key groups to be excluded were the extreme right and the far left. Defeat in war meant that parties on the extreme right were disabled and discredited. In Germany and Japan, they were proscribed and punished, though not as thoroughly purged as they perhaps deserved to be. Italy and France also witnessed purges and punishments, though again some fascists and collaborators survived and held onto positions of authority and influence. Even where individuals escaped punishment, the ideas that animated the far right fell very much out of favor. Racism, extreme nationalism, and anti-Semitism undoubtedly lived on in the culture and in the minds and hearts of individuals, but they were less visible, and less easily voiced and acted upon. The destruction of the right was particularly extensive because many traditional right-wing parties had been tainted by actual collaboration with Nazis, Fascists, and the authoritarian regime in Japan.

The exclusion of the extreme left, which meant the Communists, was more complicated because the Soviet Union was held in high regard in 1945 and the local Communists in places like Italy and France had acquitted themselves well in the Resistance and liberation. Soviet behavior in Eastern Europe did much to reverse the positive image of the Red Army and Uncle Joe. So, too, did the decisions by the Communists in France and Italy to oppose the policies of the postwar coalitions, of which they were part, as Cold War tensions mounted. The turning point was 1947, when the PCF and the PCI more or less excluded themselves, first by encouraging strikes and protests by their supporters, and then by opposing the Marshall Plan. The parties remained strong long after, retaining a firm base of support within the working class and close links to the largest trade unions, but they never again entered government. The parties often held power locally, but they were shut out of power at the national level. Elsewhere in Europe, the exclusion of the left was simpler. In Germany the depredations of the Red Army made the Soviet Union and the Communists extremely unpopular. The old Communist Party, the KPD, would be banned in the West; and the new party controlled by the Communists in the East, the Socialist Unity Party (SED), had trouble finding support even there, where it ruled.

Effectively banning the right and excluding the left narrowed the political spectrum by cutting off its extremes. The effect was to limit choices for voters—an inherently illiberal move—but by doing so it aided parties and movements committed to democratic politics. The extreme right had made it clear between the wars that even if it came to power democratically, it would abolish democracy when it could; and the Communists had demonstrated a comparable unwillingness to tolerate dissent and to allow democratic choice in Eastern Europe after 1945. Parties of the center were thus accorded political space in which to compete for support. As a result, center-left parties like the Social Democrats (SPD) in Germany and the Socialists (SFIO) in France were able to re-emerge and to play key roles in postwar politics. The most significant new force to emerge was, however, on the center-right: Christian Democracy. In France, it was the Mouvement républicain populaire (MRP) that played this role in the early postwar years; in Italy, it was Democrazia Cristiana (DC) that occupied the center-right into the 1990s; and in Germany it was the Christlich Demokratische Union (CDU) allied with the Christlich-Soziale Union (CSU) in Bavaria that did so even into the twenty-first century. Christian Democratic parties were also strong in Belgium and the Netherlands as well as in Austria and Switzerland.[20]

The success of Christian Democracy was one of the more important, and somewhat surprising, facts of postwar. The parties' main predecessors were Catholic parties, and these did not distinguish themselves in the 1930s or during the war. They had, as a rule, come to terms with Fascists and Nazis and were often collaborators. Nor had the papacy come through the war with its reputation intact, for its record on the persecution of the Jews was at best mixed and its relations with the regime of Mussolini disturbingly close.[21] To many, it seemed that the future belonged not to Christian parties but to the various social democratic parties, which had been genuinely anti-fascist and had suffered greatly for that. What would make Christian Democracy so attractive and viable after the war was in part its anti-Communism. Whatever the record of Catholic parties or of the pope, they could be counted on to oppose the Soviet Union, its policies in Eastern Europe, and its allies in the West. Social democratic parties, despite a history of opposing both Fascist and Communist parties, were not such useful vehicles for a politics organized around opposition to Communism.

It would be a mistake to think of Christian Democracy as merely anti-Communist, though, for at least three reasons. The new parties incorporated both Catholics and Protestants and were that much less sectarian as a result. Christian Democrats were also not simple enthusiasts for capitalism, and in fact were committed to reforms that would constrain the workings of the market within a more solidaristic social model. Everywhere, Christian Democrats helped to build the welfare state, even if their vision was centered on the family more than the individual and their policies devolved more responsibilities onto private, often religious, organizations or on business. Such a model and vision could be suspicious of democracy and sympathetic to the pretensions of corporatist and authoritarian politics, but the experience of fascism and war led Christian, especially Catholic, thinkers to a greater appreciation of political democracy.[22] Another distinctive feature of Christian Democracy was its support for Europe as a political project and hence for the movement that led to the European Coal and Steel Community, then the Common Market and the European Community. This was a fundamentally anti-nationalist stance that effectively repudiated the prior Catholic or Christian dalliance with extreme nationalism.

The ascendancy of Christian Democracy or, in France, the social Catholicism of the MRP, mattered most in the late 1940s when the occupation in Germany was being wound down and the coalition governments in France and Italy were breaking apart. In France, the break with and then rivalry with Gaullism would reduce their influence over the following decade. Elsewhere they would remain strong, often presiding over coalitions with liberal parties like the Free Democrats in Germany. The German Social Democrats were the main competition, but lost the elections of 1953 and 1957. Stung by repeated defeats, the party adopted a more modest and reformist program at Bad Godesberg in 1959. It made impressive gains in the election of 1961 and in 1966 formed a grand coalition with the Christian Democrats. Three years later the party gained power on its own. In Italy, the Christian Democrats were typically compelled to govern in coalitions, sometimes with liberals and later with the socialists. The need for allies and incessant factionalism led to the rise and fall of numerous governments, but the DC would remain dominant for decades. Despite this instability—and instability of this sort was also characteristic of France during the Fourth Republic—political systems across Europe became relatively more stable during the quarter century after the war. The extreme right and the Communists were everywhere excluded from power; ordinarily, center-right parties competed with each other and with the center-left for the right to form governments. It was not the most inspiring scenario, but it persisted, and voters and citizens became accustomed to living in stable, if imperfect, democracies.

An essentially similar outcome occurred in Japan, though the route to it differed. To start, the US occupation there was more control-ling and showed less deference to local traditions than the occupation of Germany.[23] Its new constitution was drafted by the Japanese, but with strong guidance and input from the Americans: parts of it were first written in English. It made the legislature, the Diet, "the highest organ of state power"; it stripped power from the emperor; and Article 9 re-nounced war as a "sovereign right of the nation." The constitution was controversial, but it endured.[24] The landscape of parties, initially chaotic, had by the late 1940s stabilized around three main parties—the Liberals, the Progressives (or Democrats), and the Socialists. The Socialists won a plurality of votes and seats in 1947, but the two coalitions the election produced—one led by a Socialist, the other by a Democrat—had failed by October 1948 and pushed the Democrats into an alliance with the Liberals. That shift, which was made more concrete by the merger of the two parties into the Liberal Democratic Party in 1955, resulted in center-right governments that would rule Japan for decades. The Social-ists continued to attract about a third of the votes in later elections, but were kept from power. Though their origins and traditions differed markedly, the Liberal Democrats would serve more or less the same function for Japan that the Christian Democrats (CDU/CSU, DC) did for Germany and Italy throughout the Cold War.[25]

The Liberal Model in Great Britain and the United States

If there was to be a truly liberal core within the broader Cold War order, it would be found in the United Kingdom and the United States. The two countries had the longest history with liberal democracy and they were committed, if unevenly and inconsistently, to an open world economy. The British and Americans had also taken the lead in the effort to craft the institutional framework for a liberal international order after 1945.

Together, the two countries worked to bring democracy to a defeated Germany, and the United States had overseen that task in Japan. Success in this endeavor presupposed that the internal politics of Britain and America would remain stable and democratic. Maintaining a commitment to liberal democracy at home would also be necessary for political leaders to convince voters in the two nations to support a foreign policy aimed at enlarging the sphere of liberal democracy. How well, then, did the systems in Britain and the United States live up to their claim to be liberal democracies? And how did parties and leaders get ordinary citizens to sustain their ambitious and costly plans? It would be deeply ironic if the two pioneers and advocates of liberalism should backslide toward an illiberal politics while they were seeking to promote democratic politics elsewhere. How was that avoided?

British politics after the war were less contentious than politics elsewhere. The immediate reason was that the victory of the Labour Party in 1945 was extremely convincing and had an enduring effect. Labour laid out a range of policies in its election campaign and managed to fulfill most of its promises by the time it left office in 1951. It essentially built the welfare state in those years. The most notable achievement was the creation of the National Health Service, but the party also oversaw the consolidation and extension of social protections and the expansion of efforts to build housing and plan urban development. Educational reform, initiated under the wartime coalition, moved forward under Labour. The Labour government also nationalized large swathes of industry, giving the state enhanced leverage over the direction of the economy. The Labour Party inherited a depleted economy and was forced to continue austerity; it even expanded rationing. It needed a massive loan from the United States right after the war and would have needed further loans had it not been for the Marshall Plan. Despite all this, Britain came through the late 1940s with an economy beginning to grow and a welfare state that was solidly entrenched.

A signal of the popularity of the welfare state, and much else that Labour had constructed, was the fact that by 1950 the Conservative Party came to accept these new policies and institutions and did little to dismantle them when the party returned to power in 1951. The Tories promised to end rationing and to build more houses, largely for private purchase, but they did not depart from the basic policies of the Labour governments. Indeed, commentators took to referring to the mix of social and economic policies of the 1950s as "Butskillism," a coinage derived by combining the names of Rab Butler, the Tory chancellor (1951–55), and Hugh Gaitskill, his Labour shadow minister. The term was to some extent misleading, for the differences between Tory and Labour policies were more than trivial, but it captures well the sense that the gap between the parties was less than it had been in the past, and that narrowing of the partisan gap was the true measure of Labour's achievement.

Labour and the Tories were also not that far apart on questions of foreign policy. Both were firmly committed to the alliance with the United States, although the Americans treated Britain pretty shabbily after 1945, scrapping Lend-Lease and offering a loan on fairly harsh terms. Nevertheless, when the United States went looking for allies in the contest with the Soviet Union, the British were the most reliable partners. Bevin, the foreign secretary, played a major role in making the Marshall Plan a reality and he was later a strong advocate for NATO. British choices were, of course, not disinterested. Britain's global influence had peaked long before, and the nation's leaders understood that its ability to play a significant role internationally could only occur with support from, and in alliance with, the United States. The Labour government also took the decision to develop its own nuclear weapons. Within the Labour Party, those in favor of Britain staking out a role as a "third force" standing between the superpowers published a manifesto entitled "Keep Left" in 1947. They were a minority, however, and were unable to shift the party's policy. This was due in large part to the fact that the leaders of the party and the trade unions had a lengthy history of dealing with the British Communist Party that left them strongly opposed to its influence and to that of the Soviet Union.

Labour's international policy therefore did not differ greatly from what the Tories would have done. There could have been a row over Churchill's "Iron Curtain" speech in 1946, but there was not. There could well have been a bitter divide over empire, but that, too, did not happen. When the government decided to grant independence to India and to withdraw from Palestine, even the Conservatives understood that the alternative was simply not practical. Britain lacked the resources and the will to hold onto the subcontinent and had no desire to stay involved in the toxic issues at play in Palestine. Nor did the Tories object to the decision to create a British atom bomb. It was Labour that took the decision to get involved in the Korean War alongside the United States, but it was the Conservative government in power after 1951 that continued that policy. The Tories were and would remain a party with a much greater fondness for military adventure and empire than Labour, as the embarrassment of Suez would demonstrate, but what was most remarkable was the overlap and compatibility of Labour and Conservative policies, domestically and internationally, in the early postwar years.

There was also a political convergence in the United States, but differences between the parties were sharper and confrontations more serious. The New Deal had worked a revolution in the role of government in the economy and in providing a measure of security for ordinary Americans, but opposition to the New Deal never went away. Republicans were routinely critical and sought to scale back the scope of New Deal programs, and business never quite reconciled itself to the new power of trade unions. The structure of American government, with much authority residing in states and with numerous veto points across the system, ensured that even a popular president like Roosevelt could be checked by opponents in Congress or the judiciary and that federal policies could be vitiated at state level. This dispersal of power was made more serious by the fact that both major parties were split. Republicans in the Northeast tended to be relatively liberal and internationalist, while those from more rural areas in the Midwest and the West were more conservative. The split among Democrats was more extreme: Democrats in the big cities of the North and Midwest were liberal and had deep support in the labor movement and ethnic communities, while southern Democrats were conservative on several dimensions, but especially on race.

The main consequence was that Democratic presidents were often unable to get their programs through Congress. Roosevelt had won a huge victory in 1936, but in 1938 his party lost seventy-two seats in the House and seven in the Senate. Democrats retained their majority, but a coalition of Republicans and conservative southern Democrats blocked efforts to expand the New Deal. The same thing happened again in 1942, with Democrats in formal control but unable to break the conservative hold over legislation. They fared worse in 1946, when Republicans gained outright majorities in both houses of Congress. Truman's upset victory in 1948 put Democrats again in charge in Congress, but without the strength to implement the "Fair Deal." In 1950, the Republicans again assumed control of Congress and were able to block much of the legislation proposed by Truman.

The same structure of politics also meant that Republicans were unable to make much legislative progress when they held the presidency. Eisenhower would handily win the election of 1952 and Republicans added seats in Congress as well. That would prove to be a high point, as it was the last year Republicans would control the House of Representatives until 1994. For most of Eisenhower's two terms, Republicans would therefore be unable to make much headway with their legislative agenda. The effect was that much of what Eisenhower accomplished had to be negotiated and was, as a result, more or less consensual. Republicans hoping for a more serious effort to roll back the New Deal were inevitably disappointed. Disappointment would turn to fury when Democrats recaptured the White House in 1960 and when Lyndon Johnson managed to pass legislation that guaranteed enhanced and enforceable civil rights, added Medicare to existing social provision, and sought to use government to create the "Great Society."

The alternation between parties and the checks on the ability of whoever held office to exercise power produced a pattern of policy making marked by fits and starts and without programmatic consistency. Indeed, there was much comment on the weakness of American government by politicians, party members, and academics. In 1950, the normally reticent American Political Science Association was moved to issue a report calling for the creation of a more responsible party system in which parties would become more coherent, more programmatic, and more disciplined.[26] The authors clearly had in mind something closer to the "Westminster model," where the Labour Party was in the process of successfully carrying out a coherent and radical program.[27]

Just because policy making was messier and less consistent in the United States does not mean that policy making did not occur. Under Truman, for example, the New Deal was consolidated: benefits were improved and access to them broadened. The Truman administration also did what it could to extend benefits to African Americans. During Eisenhower's presidency, New Deal programs were actually expanded and the government undertook to build the interstate highway system, a huge infrastructure project that ensured a continued role for the state in the economy. To fund all this, Eisenhower resisted pressure from Republicans to lower taxes and the top marginal rate remained at just over 90 percent through his two terms of office. What this amounted to was that the "New Deal order" would be a more or less permanent fixture of life in the United States into the late 1970s.[28] The outcome was less a matter of consensus between the two parties than a sign that the peculiarities of the political system resulted in the inability of either side to fully implement its agenda: Democrats would not be able to move toward a European welfare state and Republicans were unable to undo the New Deal. It was an uneasy compromise that left many unhappy, but so long as the economy boomed, it stuck.

The contours of this compromise were largely determined by the results of the presidential elections of 1948 and 1952. The Republican congressional majorities returned in 1946 had raised the possibility of serious pushback against the New Deal. Although Republicans acceded to most of Truman's requests on foreign policy, they were eager to lower taxes to levels that would cut the budgets for domestic programs and diminish the power of organized labor. A huge wave of strikes followed the end of the war. In October 1945, 43,000 oil workers went out on strike; a month later, 225,000 workers at General Motors downed tools in a strike with an unusually bold set of demands: a 30 percent increase in wages without a corresponding increase in prices and the insistence that GM "open the books." In January electrical workers, meatpackers, and three-quarters of a million steelworkers struck; coal miners came out in April and railway workers in May. There were also citywide general strikes in Lancaster, Pennsylvania; Rochester, New York; Akron, Ohio; and Oakland, California. Employers agreed to higher wages, though they sought to recoup by raising prices. On other issues they resisted, especially on matters of corporate control, and were joined by Republican allies in Congress, who passed the Taft-Hartley Act in 1947.[29] President Truman vetoed the act and denounced it in a national radio address: he called it "a shocking piece of legislation . . . deliberately designed to weaken labor unions." It would "take fundamental rights away from our working people," and certain provisions were actually "dangerous to free speech and our free press."[30] The veto was overridden and the bill became law, but the law drew attention to the desire of Republicans to undo a critical achievement of the New Deal. Truman would campaign against the law in 1948 and propose a series of social reforms and civil rights initiatives that gave him an unexpected victory.

Truman's victory did not usher in a wave of social democratic reform, but it did convince enough Republicans that it was not good politics to seek to overturn the New Deal. Tired of losing to Democrats, Republicans chose to nominate Dwight Eisenhower for president in 1952. It was a closely run affair, with conservative Republicans pushing to nominate the former "isolationist" and inveterate opponent of the New Deal, Senator Robert Taft. The contest was extremely bitter, for it pitted longtime Republicans opposed to the New Deal and suspicious of America's new global role against Republicans in the Northeast and in the large cities who had come to see the New Deal as a fact to be reckoned with and who supported recent US foreign policy. Eisenhower was a popular war hero who drew support from people who were not traditional Republicans. Taft's supporters resented these recent converts, who might vote for Eisenhower but not for other Republicans, and local primaries and caucuses were marked by irregularities. The behavior of Taft supporters in Texas was notorious, but Eisenhower's team played rough as well. In the end, it came down to who was thought to have the best chance of winning, and Taft lost out. He was gracious enough but aggrieved, and characteristically blamed his loss on New York bankers and the media.[31]

Eisenhower's victory meant an end to two decades of Democratic rule and a turn to the right in domestic policy, though not a sharp turn and in no way a reversal of recent policy. It also meant a decisive defeat for the conservative Republicanism that Taft symbolized. Taft had opposed the fundamental thrust of the New Deal and continued to denounce it, and Truman's Fair Deal, as creeping socialism. The Taft-Hartley Act demonstrated his sustained antipathy to organized labor. He had also been a staunch opponent of American intervention in the early years of the war, and after the war he was a reluctant and highly ambivalent internationalist.

He voted for the Marshall Plan, for example, but against NATO the following year. Taft supported Truman's decision to enter the Korean War, but was soon carping over the details and blaming Truman for projecting weakness that led to war.

In office, Eisenhower was able to govern without serious worry about criticism from the right of the party. The effect of these two presidential elections, then, was a de facto centering of US politics. The progress of the left was blocked, even if minor reforms continued, and the possibility of a return to government of the anti–New Deal right was also prevented. As Eisenhower later confided to his diary, "Should any party attempt to abolish social security and eliminate labor laws and farm programs, you would not hear of that party again in our political history."[32] What caused this move to the center? A major factor was the simple fact that most Americans did not want a return to the 1930s. The reforms and policies of Roosevelt were widely accepted and had become part of the more or less permanent landscape of American politics. The other reason why political differences and choices had narrowed was the Cold War. Whatever judgment one renders on the wisdom or effectiveness of Cold War policies in the first postwar decade, what is not in dispute is that most voters, in both parties, lent their support to the effort. Fighting the Cold War had become the objective on which the two parties agreed; and much subsequent debate was focused on who could or would pursue it more effectively. Parties could differ on a range of other issues, but that much was shared, and the commitment to pursuing the Cold War set the boundaries within which politics would be played out.

The Truman and Eisenhower administrations effectively established those boundaries and worked within them. The constraints did not render them ineffective, nor did they preclude partisan disagreement. Political conflict was sharp during Truman's presidency. Truman nonetheless pressed on and notched up at least modest gains. The minimum wage was increased; Social Security benefits were doubled and coverage was expanded to include new groups like farm and domestic workers and the self-employed. Disability benefits were added to Social Security and Aid to Families with Dependent Children extended. Funds were provided to double hospital construction. With somewhat surprising support from Senator Taft, the 1949 National Housing Act allowed a modest effort at slum clearance and the building of public housing. The wisdom of such programs has lately been called into question, but the effort itself was not unworthy. The Truman administration failed to get Congress to approve its plans for education and, most significantly, for a national health system, but such failures set the agenda for future battles. It was also unable to repeal Taft-Hartley, though not for want of trying.

Truman and his advisors understood the limits within which they worked, particularly on matters affecting race, but the recognition did not lead to inactivity. On his own Truman set up the President's Committee on Civil Rights in 1946. Its report called for the establishment of a civil rights division in the Justice Department and a permanent Civil Rights Commission.[33] As part of his election platform, Truman proposed setting up a permanent Fair Employment Practices Committee (FEPC), and on July 26, 1948, he issued two dramatic executive orders aimed at eliminating discrimination in hiring in the federal workforce and desegregating the armed forces. There would be resistance to both these efforts, but they were ultimately successful. Another executive order in 1951, as military spending and rearmament ramped up, banned discrimination by defense contractors.

Eisenhower came into office with a less ambitious program, for even this advocate of "modern Republicanism" did not wish to expand the range of government programs. What was notable, however, was that Eisenhower chose not to seek to repeal any of the major achievements of his predecessors. Though supporting a balanced budget, for example, he further expanded Social Security. He also resisted calls from the right to dramatically lower taxes. Instead, his administration passed the Internal Revenue Act of 1954, which restructured the tax code for at least a generation. The law added numerous deductions and benefits but kept overall rates high and progressive: incomes up to $2,000 were taxed at 20 percent, those over $150,000 at 90 percent, and those over $200,000 at 91 percent. Eisenhower's most distinctive contribution to the nation's development was the interstate highway system, created and financed by the Federal Aid Highway Act of 1956, which led to the building of a network of over forty thousand miles of linked roads. The act and the system had major economic and social effects, knitting together the national economy, lowering transportation costs, stimulating the car industry, and encouraging the expansion of suburbs. In the long term, the problems that came with sub-urban living, the excessive reliance on automobiles and cheap oil, the de-cay of inner cities, and the neglect of public transportation would provoke a reassessment of the value of building highways, but that was still to come. In the meantime, the United States grew along the lines the system laid out.

Eisenhower was, of course, committed to Cold War policies, and he oversaw the steady buildup of nuclear weapons. It was on his watch, moreover, that the arms race became a space race. The Soviet Union beat the United States into space with the launch of Sputnik on October 4, 1957. The US put its first satellite into space on January 31, 1958. During the 1950s, the arms race became qualitatively and quantitatively more serious and deadly: the explosion of the first hydrogen bomb by the United States on November 1, 1952, ratcheted up the lethality of nuclear weapons; five years later, Sputnik opened the possibility of delivering nuclear weapons by missiles rather than airplanes. The United States and the Soviet Union not only pioneered these new technological pos-sibilities, they also massively increased the production of bombs, bomb-ers, and later missiles. The competition kept defense budgets high, providing a sustained fiscal stimulus and increasing the influence of what Eisenhower would warn against, the "military-industrial complex." He knew of what he spoke.

Eisenhower did not know as much about civil rights, nor was he particularly committed to expanding them, but he was forced to deal with the issue and did more, and better, than might have been expected. He followed through on Truman's plans to ban discrimination in federal employment and to desegregate the armed forces. The Korean War was a further spur to creating a military in which African Americans had more equal rights, and Eisenhower's prestige as a wartime leader gave him additional leverage to make the new policies effective.

On May 17, 1954, the Supreme Court delivered its opinion in *Brown v. Board of Education,* holding that separate was not equal and segregated schools were unconstitutional. Eisenhower did not much like the ruling, but agreed to obey it. The court did not specify any precise remedy, but ordered states to make plans to desegregate. Opposition was immediate and spread across the South. Senator Harry Byrd of Virginia called for a campaign of "massive resistance" and Prince Edward County actually closed its public schools rather than integrate them. In Little Rock, Arkansas, the governor used the National Guard to prevent nine Black students from entering Central High in 1957, and when the National Guard stood down, a mob of whites blocked the students' entry. Eisenhower responded by sending in the army. Progress would be slow, as whites across the South mobilized against desegregation, but the administration stood firm. In fact, the administration moved to pass the Civil Rights Act of 1957, establishing the United States Commission on Civil Rights and setting up a civil rights office in the Justice Department. Enforcement lagged, predictably, but under Eisenhower the power of the federal government was used to advance rather than to retard the cause of equality for Black Americans.[34]

The steady advance of civil rights under both Truman and Eisenhower was testimony to the deep and abiding racism of the United States and, equally important, to the sustained efforts of African Americans to defeat it. It also owed at least something to the peculiar politics of the Cold War. The Cold War was a matter of guns and bombs, of alliances and borders, and of tough diplomacy, but it was also a contest of ideas and images. The Soviet Union's treatment of its subjects, at home and in Eastern Europe, provided a huge stock of images that could be used by its opponents. By contrast, the United States was often associated with more upbeat and attractive images, but the discrimination and mistreatment of African Americans was visible and appalling, and the Soviet Union and its supporters made it a staple of their propaganda. The attack on the racism and, by implication, the hypocrisy of the United States was particularly effective in the Third World, where the two superpowers struggled to win support from nonwhite peoples emerging from colonialism. In this context, American political leaders, and even the Supreme Court, felt pressured to support an end to racial discrimination. Truman had not been known as a strong advocate of civil rights over his long career; and Eisenhower preferred not to be involved. Nevertheless, the Cold War pushed both presidents, and many other US political leaders, to lend their support to the growing civil rights movement.[35]

Overall, the political stabilization of postwar owed much to the Cold War. In the East, little mattered but the overwhelming dominance of the

Soviet Union. In the West, American power mattered greatly, but its effects were less direct and threatening. Still, the Cold War forced political leaders to choose sides, and political systems on both sides had to accommodate to the imperatives of the Cold War. In the West, a key effect was to exclude the far left and the far right. That inevitably meant a forced narrowing of the range of acceptable politics and a centering of parties and policy choices. In Britain, the parties converged around the institutions and policies put in place by the Labour governments of 1945–51. In the United States, a more fragmented and less responsive political order congealed around the legacy of the New Deal. Everywhere in the West the achievement of a level of political stability was accompanied and helped by economic recovery and unprecedented growth. This happy coincidence was a sign that, however imperfect the workings of the political system, the economic and social model worked. The reform and refounding of capitalism after the war and the elaboration of social protections that occurred in most every country led to an era of prosperity that made it possible to build democratic polities that provided the liberal international order a distinctive and attractive domestic content and a solid political anchor.

Political Stability

Preconditions and Discontents

The politics put in place early in the postwar era would eventually become less effective and pull apart, but it was remarkable how long the systems remained stable. In the East, the end would come dramatically in 1989. In the West, the economic crises of the 1970s undermined the shared prosperity that made stability the rule rather than the exception. Politics began to shift in response, but the most serious challenges would not come until after the Cold War had ended. Regimes in the East relied mostly upon repression for their maintenance, so their relative stability prior to their collapse requires little explanation.[1] Politics in democratic countries were less predictable. Voters needed wooing, and parties competed to do so. So, too, did leaders within parties. Interests and constituencies gradually shifted, of course, and parties built around particular interests were forced to find new constituencies as interests and identities changed. The salience of issues also shifted, with certain questions seemingly resolved for decades or longer becoming the focus of critiques, protests, and new coalitions.

The more or less enduring strength of the systems in the United States, Western Europe, and Japan therefore does require explanation. That strength was in good part the product of a buoyant economy, which allowed parties and leaders to claim that their policies were working. History and memory mattered, too, for the legacy of fascism kept the right from drifting to the far right, anchored instead to some version of centrist politics. The constraints of the Cold War also served to keep the right united behind the social compromises worked out in the early postwar years, and they served to keep Communists on the margins. There was also, it appears, a rather good fit between the dominant parties and the interests of voters. The connections were largely a matter of class and institutions linked to class, but occasionally also of religion and ethnicity. Conservative parties were more or less faithful representatives of the middle and upper classes, of rural voters and, in continental Europe, of Catholics. Center-left parties—Labour in Britain, socialists and social democratic parties elsewhere in Europe, the Democrats in the US—drew support from urban and working-class voters and boasted close ties to trade unions. In Italy and France, large numbers of workers belonged to Communist-affiliated unions and gave their votes to the PCI and the PCF, but their minority status kept them out of power. Shifts in social and economic structure would weaken such attachments, but they endured for decades.

It would be a stretch to label this state of affairs as stable. In France, after all, the Fourth Republic collapsed, or was overthrown, and Charles De Gaulle came to power in 1958 in what was effectively a coup.[2] The Fourth Republic had fallen over the Algerian War, but on key issues the Fifth Republic did not constitute a sharp break from the Fourth. Outside France, continuity was more marked, though everywhere there were stresses and conflicts, and these became more frequent from the mid-1960s. It would seem better to characterize the period as one of managed instability, or of sufficient stability to keep the show on the road, with major crises averted or overcome.

What helped to make this relative calm possible, in addition to the economy, the systems of representation, and the centering effect of the Cold War, was the fact that potentially divisive issues were not especially salient. Political conflict between center-right and center-left was a constant, but the issues were familiar and for the most part reinforced existing political alignments. Issues that might cause more serious ruptures were few. Questions of war and peace, for example, and of the role of the military in society were largely removed from contestation, displaced upward and to some extent beyond the nation-state because of the Cold War and the alliances and policies it involved. Even the United States, powerful as it was, was constrained by past commitments and the alliances and institutions established to make them real. The major foreign policy that could divide allies and domestic opinion was decolonization, but its impact was mostly confined to France until the massive protests over the Vietnam War. Other issues that could rip apart the major parties and coalitions were not high on the political agenda. Specifically, debates about trade and immigration were less central to politics in the quarter century after the war than they had been before and would become in recent years. In many countries, the question of race was linked primarily to that of immigration, and so rose and fell in importance when immigration, or debates about it, rose or fell. In one country, of course, race was a constant. In the United States, discrimination against African Americans was so extreme that it could not be ignored; and because racial division was closely entwined with party politics, race and civil rights deeply affected and ultimately reshaped American politics. Understanding the strains that these different questions put upon parties and politics—or, conversely, how and why for long periods they did not much intrude on the superficial stability of postwar politics—requires the detailed examination of trade, immigration, race, and decolonization.

On Trade

Trade in theory benefits the entire economy, but it also creates winners and losers and is often the subject of bitter rivalries that can split apart those who might otherwise be allies.[3] Workers and owners in infant industries might well want protection, as would those in declining sectors. Industries that are more competitive will not worry about imports and crave the exports to be gained by unimpeded trade. When thinking as consumers, workers will want the lower prices that come with freer imports; when focused on their jobs, they will fret over foreign competition. Farmers can be equally schizophrenic: they want to expand exports and imports when they benefit from them, but seek to protect local markets when imports flood the market at cheaper prices; and when they succeed in getting protectionist policies in place, they chafe at the rising cost of imported farm implements and inputs. These splits and contradictions characterize most economies, but they have been particularly pronounced in the United States, with its size and complex variety of industries and with an agricultural sector eager to export but vulnerable, as agriculture is almost everywhere, to the ups and downs of commodity prices.

Between the wars trade, finance, and reparations became tangled up in toxic fashion and the issues also pitted countries against one another. In response to the Great Depression, there was a worldwide retreat from free trade and toward protectionism. The United States, the country that had to buy imports from Germany in order for the Germans to pay reparations, instead passed the Emergency Tariff Act in 1921 and then replaced it in 1922 with the Fordney-McCumber Act. US tariffs remained high throughout the decade. When depression hit, Congress passed and Hoover signed the Smoot-Hawley Tariff Act in 1930, raising barriers still higher. As economists and others predicted, twenty-five countries imposed retaliatory tariffs; and international trade decreased by over 65 percent between 1929 and 1934. Particularly significant was the response of Great Britain, the country that had been committed to free trade since the repeal of the Corn Laws in 1846. Britain adopted a policy of imperial preference worked out in the Ottawa Agreements of 1932 and moved toward an economic policy that privileged its empire and former colonies, reinforced by the commitment to sterling.

Witnessing the steady collapse of world trade, the Roosevelt administration changed course. In early 1934, it set up the Export-Import Bank and shortly after the president signed the Reciprocal Trade Agreements Act. The act gave the president the main role in trade negotiations and restricted Congress to votes on whether to renew his authority every three years. Initiative passed from Congress, whose structure and processes had long served to impede moves toward freer trade and allowed for all sorts of exemptions and special provisions. The act also allowed the inclusion of "most favored nation" clauses, which meant that decisions to lower tariffs in bilateral deals were applied to all other countries to which the US had granted that status. That meant that the thirty-two agreements negotiated between 1934 and 1945 applied to a much wider range of countries.[4]

The US push for a world with more open trade would continue through and beyond the war. There was a widespread belief that the division of the world into competing currency and trading blocs, often based on imperial or quasi-imperial connections, had helped to create the political divisions and alliances that led to the Second World War. The link between protectionism, empire, militarism, and war weighed heavily on the minds of those who designed and bargained out the framework for the postwar economy. The Bretton Woods system and institutions were designed to foster more open trade, both by facilitating the exchange of currencies and the movement of money and by lowering tariffs and eliminating nontariff barriers. Critical adjustments had to be made in the late 1940s and early 1950s, for America's allies were simply not capable of opening their economies in the immediate postwar years.[5] Currency convertibility was delayed for a long time, and trade barriers had to be abolished gradually. The most dramatic adjustment was the Marshall Plan, which provided the funds with which Europeans could begin trading again. The effort to create a formal International Trade Organization (ITO) as a complement to the IMF and the World Bank was also deflected into a new channel: it elicited resistance from America's trading partners and also fell afoul of key interest groups in the United States with defenders in Congress. Its charter, agreed upon in Havana in March 1948, was not ratified. Before the charter was drafted, however, a preliminary and provisional agreement—the General Agreement on Tariffs and Trade (GATT)—was reached by twenty-three countries, including the US and the UK, in October 1947. The existence and functioning of GATT made it less essential to create the ITO and that organization would regulate world trade until it was superseded by the World Trade Organization.

The Reciprocal Trade Agreements Act had served to move disputes upward, out of Congress and to the president. GATT would move questions of trade outward, further removed from domestic policy debates and into the international arena, and a highly technical arena at that. The displacement was critical in the United States, but equally so in Europe. The Marshall Plan required states to coordinate policies and encouraged trade. This would be accomplished administratively through the Organization for European Economic Cooperation, established to supervise the aid program in 1948, and trade was further facilitated by the creation of the European Payments Union in 1950. Britain, having turned to protection and imperial preference in 1932, saw its future as the economic center of its empire and Commonwealth, but with substantial and more or less free trade with countries beyond that.[6] The internationalization of economic policy making, including over trade, was taken a step further with the setting up of the European Coal and Steel Community in 1951. The decision was taken primarily for political reasons, but it had major economic effects and was a further move toward European integration.

The European Economic Community (EEC) explicitly took the responsibility for negotiating trade away from individual states and vested it in the Community. That would mean that when new states joined, they also gave up national control over trade and tariffs. The most important step was the first, when the six countries involved decided that economic cooperation should replace the competition of the interwar years. The linking of the fates of Germany and France was particularly notable, for both world wars had a Franco-German confrontation at their center. It is likely, too, that embarking on a joint European project reinforced the political stability of the original Six. It would overstate the case to say that trade was thoroughly depoliticized by the 1950s, but the venues in which it was bargained were further removed from partisan and interest group politics, and with trade policy made elsewhere, party politics was focused on other matters and became, it would seem, less intense.

The GATT would provide the framework for a series of negotiations from 1958 to 1995. In several stages, or rounds, member states agreed to a steady lowering of tariffs. The first round occurred even before the agreement was signed: meeting in Geneva, the founding members agreed on forty-five thousand concessions affecting trade worth $10 billion. Two quick rounds occurred in Annecy in 1949 and Torquay in 1950 that together produced agreement on nearly fourteen thousand additional concessions, while reducing tariffs by 25 percent. A further round occurred in Geneva in 1956, bringing Japan into the organization and enacting reductions on $2.5 billion in trade. The so-called Dillon Round of 1960–62 was devoted mainly to matters related to the European Community but also reduced levies on nearly $5 billion worth of trade. The Kennedy Round (1964–67) led to concessions worth $40 billion and included anti-dumping provisions. The Tokyo Round (1973–79) agreed to tariff reductions on no less than $300 billion worth of trade and began to address nontariff barriers as well. By this point, tariffs worldwide had decreased to a very low level. The last set of negotiations, the Uruguay Round (1986–94), shifted to new terrain, to trade in agriculture and services and to intellectual property rights. Participating states also worked out the details of the new World Trade Organization, which would come into existence in 1995.

The dispersal of responsibility for trade matters—to the president in the US, to the European Community in Brussels, to the negotiators at GATT—had yet another effect beyond removing trade as a major source of contention in domestic politics. It also slowed the process of liberalization and probably made its short- and long-term outcomes more acceptable. It took many years to wean Europeans, for example, from protectionist policies. There were endless negotiations at all levels in every venue, and those who took part were regularly frustrated, but the results were seen more as an evolution than as an abrupt imposition of free-trade doctrine in the interests of the dominant power. The European Community, for example, has long been criticized for its overly gentle treatment of farmers and the piling up of mounds of butter that could not be sold at the right price, but the Common Agricultural Policy (CAP) was the price to be paid for the gradual integration of European markets. Similarly, the United States has reasonably been accused of double standards for preaching the virtues of free trade while maintaining agricultural subsidies and quotas and for protections afforded to textiles, automobile manufacturing, and other industries. Despite these exemptions and compromises, progress toward a more open economy continued from the late 1940s through the early 1990s with only occasional backsliding. Eventually, trade would become more controversial: the economic slowdown of the late 1970s and early 1980s brought the issue to the fore during the Reagan administration; more recently, discontent with the consequences of rapid globalization led to eruptions like the so-called battle of Seattle in 1999 and, more consequentially, the election of Donald Trump. Much else had to happen before that became possible, however, and it took time for that story to unfold.

On Immigration

The United States might well be a nation of immigrants, but the country has also fought bitterly over immigration. Resentment of immigrants—many fleeing the Irish famine, plus a large number fleeing Germany after the failure of the revolutions of 1848—led to the rise of the Know-Nothings as an explicitly anti-immigrant and anti-Catholic movement. They flourished briefly in the 1850s before fading as the issue of slavery came to overshadow most other concerns.[7] The strength of the Know-Nothings was in the Northeast. On the West Coast, the focus of anti-immigrant sentiment was on the Chinese who had come to the United States during the boom prompted by the gold rush and then by the need for labor to build the transcontinental railway. Local restrictions were put in place in California, and in 1882 Congress passed the Chinese Exclusion Act.[8] Another large wave of immigration came later in the century, composed mostly of migrants from southern and Eastern Europe—Italians, Slavs, and Jews. Nativist sentiment rose again, this time with a more distinguished pedigree and armed with the new "science" of eugenics. Efforts to limit immigration followed, and anti-immigrant legislation was passed and signed into law by Calvin Coolidge in 1924. The Immigration Act of 1924 sharply limited immigration overall and set quotas for people of different "national origins," targeting the places from which recent immigrants had mostly come.[9]

America's distinctive demography made immigration a recurring issue in local politics, but the restrictions enacted in 1924 prevented its emergence in national politics for several decades. Fear of foreigners, outsiders, and minorities was common enough outside the US. What was remarkable about the 1950s and 1960s, though, was that hostility to immigrants and immigration was rarely expressed in the US, and was not especially prominent or vocal in Western Europe. No doubt private views were often intolerant, but outward expressions of antipathy were few. Part of the reason was the simple fact that Nazism had done a lot to discredit racism.

Another reason, it would seem, was that earlier policies and events made immigration less of an issue. European states, for example, were more ethnically homogeneous than before the war. The expulsion and slaughter of Jews removed a regular target of prejudice from much of the continent. In the 1940s, moreover, vast numbers of "displaced persons" were moved from one state to another and landed in what were seen as ethnic homelands. It has been argued that the settlement after the First World War created new states for people where they were, but that after the Second World War people were moved to, and removed from, states. The largest group was ethnic Germans, who were expelled from the east, where they had often lived for centuries, and forcibly returned to Germany. Of course, the German armies had displaced many more as they marched to the east, but millions of Germans were forced back ahead of the Red Army and large numbers of Poles, Ukrainians, people from the Baltic states, Cossacks, and others fled with them for fear of being punished by the locals as collaborators or captured by the Soviets. During the war, the Germans had also imported hundreds of thousands of people, many of them prisoners of war or deportees from occupied lands, to work in German factories. Over a million French citizens—some prisoners, some expelled Jews, some simply workers— were in Germany in May 1945. There were also close to 2 million Soviets working in Germany at the end of the war. Many were war prisoners, and they did not all wish to go home, for they knew the conditions they would find there. Besides, Stalin was deeply suspicious of those who had spent time in the West. Poles were moved and removed and moved again. Some were expelled by the Soviets in 1939–41; others were moved at the end of the war because borders moved to the west. There were also forced exchanges of Ukrainians and Poles. And, of course, Poland had been home to the majority of Jews killed by the Nazis.[10]

With all this forced and unforced movement, the contribution of migration per se was hard to assess. As people were settled and economic revival set in, immigration of a more familiar sort resumed. The context was now different, however, from what it had been before the war. Labor shortages now replaced mass unemployment. In addition, the war left populations depleted. In France, there had been worries about declining population since the late nineteenth century, but they became much more acute after the First World War, and governments of all stripes adopted policies to encourage people to have children. The effort became more intense and was mixed with racism, regressive notions of women's proper place, and notions of ethnic hierarchy under Vichy. French losses in the Second World War ensured that the need to encourage population growth and immigration after the war was widely accepted, and there was at least a rhetorical move away from the nastier aspects of Vichy's policies on these issues. The French moved aggressively to recruit migrants for its mines and factories, and in 1946 the Planning Commission called for between 1 million and 1.5 million to be brought in over the next five years. As early as November 1945, a new Office national d'immigration (ONI) was established under the Labor Ministry to facilitate the process. The ONI set up recruitment centers in Milan, London, Copenhagen, and in selected German cities where they could possibly attract Germans but, failing that, recruit displaced persons from elsewhere.

The ambitious plans to attract immigrants did not produce the desired result, as it was hard to convince people who were not forced by economic necessity to come and work and live in France. France had a terrible housing shortage and there were opportunities in other countries. There was also a shake-up in the government in 1947 and a purge of Communists in 1948 that forced the removal of key personnel from the ONI, which was reorganized and reduced in size, its responsibilities transferred to other departments. Still, the very existence of the office pointed to the fact that France needed immigrants and would largely welcome them, with exceptions.[11] The main exceptions would be migrants from North Africa, particularly Algeria. How, given the difficulties, did France find the labor force for its economic recovery? Partly with immigrants from the poorer districts of Italy, Spain, and Portugal; and partly with native Frenchmen. Though there were fewer French than many wished, a baby boom began near the end of the war and continued into the mid-1960s. French social policies such as the building of day care centers and nursery schools facilitated the steady rise in women's participation in the labor force while encouraging couples to have children. Equally important, there remained a large reservoir of labor still engaged in agriculture; and throughout *les trente glorieuses* hundreds of thousands of them moved to cities and factories. Again, the much-derided CAP probably eased the move. Over that span of time, the urban population increased by 16 million while the rural population continued its decline.

The French were by no means unique in the problems they faced or in how they were resolved. Western European nations in the north had stable or declining populations and in the postwar boom experienced labor shortages; in the south, surplus labor was trapped in agriculture. The demand for labor would be met by draining the countryside within the most developed economies and by migration from south to north. In Germany, movement from the countryside into industry and urban areas was supplemented by the continued arrival of people fleeing not only East Germany but other states in Eastern Europe. As economic growth accelerated, more formal provisions were developed to recruit, classify, and set rules for "guest workers" (*Gastarbeiter*) from southern Europe and Turkey. They were in theory temporary workers, with few rights, but many stayed for a long time and formed stable ethnic enclaves. Some managed to become citizens. By 1973, there were 2.8 million foreign workers in West Germany—close to half a million Italians, 535,000 Yugoslavs, and 605,000 Turks; and in France, there were 2.3 million such workers, or 11 percent of the labor force.[12] Italy served as both a destination and a source. It was a sort of split society, with a thriving industrial north and a much poorer south, which sent workers to northern cities like Milan and Bologna and abroad to France, Belgium, Germany, and Switzerland. Most of these migrants had few skills and little education, but they were capable of staffing the new and growing mass production industries that defined the era and of working in service industries like construction or, for women, service sector work—nursing, teaching, and retail sales—as well as in less desirable service jobs such as cleaning and maintenance.

Great Britain also confronted a tight labor market in the 1950s and 1960s, but its problems and solutions differed considerably from the European pattern. Growth there was steady, but slower than elsewhere, so the demand for labor not as intense as in Germany, France, and other northern European countries. Britain had long been a country of net emigration. In the nineteenth century it developed policies aimed at "shoveling out paupers" and sending convict labor to Australia. It needed people to run the empire and to populate the colonies of settlement. Those needs continued, for Britain still had an empire after 1945, and its economy had long been outward-looking.[13] After the war, the government put in place programs to encourage white immigrants to move to Australia and New Zealand.[14] Immigrants did come, but emigration exceeded immigration every year from 1946 through 1979, if not by much. The needs of British industry during these years of full employment would therefore be met from other sources. Unlike much of Europe,

Britain did not have great reserves of labor still working in agriculture, but there were some who moved to the cities; and there were migrants from Scotland. The main source, however, was the large reserve army of labor nearby in Ireland. The Irish came and went in large numbers, but without much fuss or any formal apparatus of recruitment and control. They worked in less skilled and more poorly paid jobs, as they had before the war. Gradually, immigrants began to come from other places, first from the West Indies and later from the subcontinent, primarily from Pakistan. The numbers were small, but they did not find a particularly warm welcome.

Because Britain remained broadly committed to the empire, it was eager after the war to convince colonials of the benefits of continued membership, and the British Nationality Act of 1948 granted liberal citizenship rights to people from within the empire.[15] Together with the high demand for labor, the effect was to encourage immigration from places like the Caribbean. On June 22, 1948, eight hundred Jamaicans disembarked from the *Empire Windrush* at Tilbury Docks just outside London. Their arrival marked the beginning of a modest nonwhite immigration to the UK. Small numbers kept arriving, with many getting work in transport or the National Health Service, and many experienced anti-immigrant and racist hostility. In August 1958 there was a riot in Notting Hill, where a Black neighborhood had grown up. Shortly before, an anti-Black riot had occurred in Nottingham. The incidents did not spread, but they provoked a backlash that led to successive acts to curb immigration. The Commonwealth Immigrants Act of 1962 required immigrants to obtain work vouchers before entering the country, and a subsequent act in 1965 restricted the number of vouchers available. To make restriction less objectionable, in the same year the Labour Government passed the Race Relations Act outlawing racial discrimination. This dual policy did not satisfy opponents of immigration and resentment was ongoing. In April 1968 the Conservative MP Enoch Powell gave an incendiary speech in Birmingham during which he spoke of "wide-grinning picaninnies" and shared a vision of "the river Tiber foaming with much blood." The speech was denounced by respectable opinion, but in a Gallup poll conducted shortly after, fully 74 percent indicated their support. As Parliament debated a new Race Relations Act, a thousand dockers marched to Westminster to show their support for Powell, and the next day four hundred workers from Smithfield Market delivered a ninety-two-page petition on his behalf. His fellow Tories turned on Powell, however, and he was removed from the front bench by the party leader, Edward Heath.

The furor over Powell was telling. It demonstrated that beneath the liberal and tolerant surface of British life there was much racism. At the same time, the incident showed that neither Labour nor the Conservatives were interested in stoking that racism or profiting from it politically. Those dockers and meatpackers all would have been members of trade unions and most would have voted for Labour. The Labour Party itself walked a fine line, imposing restrictions on immigration but passing race relations acts to protect the rights of those people of color already living and working in Britain. Rather more Tories might well have quietly agreed with what Powell was saying, but the party chose to sack him rather than back him. The implicit prohibition against explicit racism held.

Immigration was not at this point a major issue in the United States. The simple explanation is that the 1924 legislation meant that there were relatively few immigrants. The Cold War mattered as well. Just as attacks on America's treatment of African Americans predisposed political leaders to at least feign concern for civil rights, the same critique of US hypocrisy led the US gradually to modify its restrictive policies. Part of the Cold War competition with the Soviet Union meant a desire to win favor among peoples fighting against colonialism and for national independence. A racist immigration policy did not help, and efforts to revise the 1924 formulas were ongoing. The result was the Immigration and Nationality Act of 1965, which abolished the transparently racist national origins quotas of the prevailing law.[16] It was a remarkably bipartisan effort: the House vote was 320-70 in favor; in the Senate the vote was 76-18 in support, with twenty-four Republicans voting yes.

The thrust of US immigration policy in the 1950s and 1960s was liberalizing, but it was not proof of the prevalence of liberal attitudes among Americans. It was primarily the result of the effectiveness of earlier illiberal legislation having reduced the flow of immigrants and evidence, too, of the pressure that the global role of the US put upon domestic policies and practices. In consequence, immigration was not an issue of great political salience on the national level. It resonated locally, of course, in places where large numbers of Mexicans were employed in agriculture. The politics were nevertheless complicated. Businesses and farmers benefited from cheap Mexican labor, while opposition came from diverse sources and waxed and waned. The federal government recognized the need for Mexican labor during the war and instituted the Bracero program to recruit workers on a temporary basis. Alongside this legal immigration, there was considerable illegal border crossing. The ambivalence surrounding this stream of migration in the US was matched by the contradictory attitudes of the Mexican government, which worried that the drain of labor to the north retarded the development of Mexican industry and deprived Mexican farmers of seasonal labor. The most notoriously illiberal policy of the era was "Operation Wetback," a US initiative worked out in conjunction with Mexico. It began in 1954, was intensified in 1955, and deported millions from the US, some of them US citizens, often sending them far beyond the border to regions that were supposedly in need of labor. It was gradually wound down, but inflicted real pain on those affected, while businesses dependent on Mexican labor continued to find ways to bring workers to the United States. The issue it addressed and the "operation" it produced did not, however, become a national issue.

On Race in America

If immigration did not disturb the political landscape of the United States for several decades after 1945, the question of race certainly did. In fact, it produced a major realignment of the party system. The driving force of the transformation was demography, specifically the "great migration" of African Americans from the agricultural South to the cities of the North, the industrial Midwest, the West Coast, and the growing industrial cities in the South itself.[17] That movement began during the First World War, slowed between the wars, and accelerated during the Second World War. The effect was to make the question of how Blacks were treated a national issue, not merely a matter for the rural South. It also empowered African Americans by creating large and vibrant Black communities across the country and by opening up new venues and opportunities for political action. It became increasingly possible, and attractive, to make claims on the national government as opposed to the entrenched and racist regimes in the South and to make alliances with a broader spectrum of interests and organizations, including the newly powerful labor movement.

The civil rights movement was the great political mobilization of the postwar era. It was led by African Americans, but also enrolled substantial numbers of white supporters. Political leaders and the courts responded, and their actions led to further action on the ground. These in turn had repercussions on party politics and elections. Harry Truman largely owed his reelection to the labor movement and to Black voters. His support for the permanent establishment of a Fair Employment Practices Commission and for ending segregation in the military and in federal employment was a key part of the implicit bargain. Even before these promises could be redeemed, southern Democrats defected and formed the States' Rights Democratic Party, nicknamed the Dixiecrats, with Strom Thurmond as its nominee for president. The party's platform was explicit: "We stand for the segregation of the races and the racial integrity of each race. . . . We oppose the elimination of segregation . . . [and] the repeal of miscegenation statutes."[18] The party received over 1.1 million votes and won thirty-nine electoral votes, but did not manage to defeat Truman. The Dixiecrats dissolved quickly, but they had delivered a clear message: the "solid South," a Democratic stronghold since Reconstruction, was no longer solid.

The weakening of Democratic support in the southern states presaged a realignment of parties along ideological and racial lines, but it would not happen quickly.[19] Neither party was quite ready to make the leap, for too many careers were invested in the existing party divisions that were based as much on geography as ideology. The questions of race and civil rights did not go away, however, and they served to prepare the grounds for an eventual shift. The Republican defeat in 1948 led the party to nominate Eisenhower four years later and, though no crusader for civil rights, he was not interested in moving backwards on the issue. He therefore agreed to obey the *Brown v. Board of Education* decision outlawing segregated schools and sent federal troops to enforce it. The decision sparked a wave of protest and organization across the South that preached and practiced resistance to integration. African Americans continued to organize, to march, to sit-in, to protest. They also kept pushing Democrats on the issue; and Democrats responded despite the reluctance of southerners like Lyndon Johnson and Sam Rayburn. John F. Kennedy was regarded as a moderate supporter of civil rights, but he chose Johnson as his running mate in 1960 and during the campaign sought to assure southern Democrats that he would not cause them difficulties. Shortly before the election, however, Martin Luther King Jr. was arrested at a sit-in sponsored by SNCC (the Student Non-violent Coordinating Committee) and imprisoned in Georgia. Kennedy sought to defuse the issue by asking the governor, Ernest Vandiver, to find a way to get the civil rights leader out of jail. Later that day, he defied campaign advisors and called Coretta Scott King to offer his sympathy and support. King was released the next day, October 27; he praised Kennedy for his help and expressed disappointment at Richard Nixon's silence. Robert Kennedy, his brother's campaign manager, was furious, worried about the loss of white voters across the region. Kennedy won, but barely, and there is at least some reason to believe that Black voters were critical to his victory.[20]

The Kennedy and, after his assassination, Johnson administrations would be pushed repeatedly on civil rights and forced to take sides on the protests sweeping the South over desegregation and voting rights. Two key pieces of legislation resulted: the Civil Rights Act of 1964 and the Voting Rights Act of 1965. Kennedy had proposed the Civil Rights Act in June 1963, but it was blocked by a Senate filibuster. Johnson reintroduced it, it quickly passed, and was signed into law on July 2, 1964. It outlawed racial segregation in public places and employment discrimination based on race, color, religion, sex, or national origin. Johnson was clear about the political risks that passage posed for the Democrats, remarking to an aide, "It is an important gain, but I think we just delivered the South to the Republican Party for a long time." The Voting Rights Act was passed the following summer amid large-scale mobilization by African Americans. It took aim at various restrictions and obstacles placed in the way of the ability of Black Americans to exercise their right to vote and targeted specific districts guilty of past discrimination for special monitoring and supervision (preclearance).

The new federal commitments to defend and enhance the civil rights of African Americans undoubtedly moved southern whites closer to the Republicans, especially when the party made clear its opposition. Barry Goldwater, the Republican nominee for president in 1964, voted against the Civil Rights Act and made it a campaign issue. Republicans increasingly deployed what some referred to as "the Southern strategy" to break Democratic control in the region. It did not always work, however. Goldwater's massive defeat in 1964 was a bitter lesson and Nixon's Watergate disaster would mean that, at least in the short run, a realignment in favor of the Republicans was not yet at hand. Still, the trend was obvious enough; and eventually, with the election of Ronald Reagan in 1980, it would triumph.

The reaction against the civil rights and Black protest movements was intensified, spreading to the North and West, with the urban uprisings of the 1960s. They were often provoked by instances of police brutality, but were built on a long history of grievance and a more recent determination by victims to fight back. An early example came in Harlem in July 1964 and another came later that summer in Philadelphia. Much bigger protests occurred in the Watts district of Los Angeles in August 1965. In 1966 it was Cleveland's turn, and in 1967 outbreaks of violence spread to Newark, New Jersey, Detroit, and the Minneapolis/St. Paul area. The assassination of Martin Luther King on April 4, 1968, produced widespread and sustained protests across the country.

These uprisings produced a backlash among whites, northern and southern, and helped to fuel the election campaign of George Wallace in 1968. Wallace, the former governor of Alabama, was a staunch opponent of integration, his opposition most famously expressed in a speech at the University of Alabama. "Segregation now, segregation tomorrow, segregation forever," he vowed in 1963.[21] He ran for president as a third-party candidate against Nixon and Humphrey and drew substantial support from whites. His rhetoric stressed "law and order" and "states' rights," not very subtle code for opposition to civil rights and Black protest. Two months before the election, a poll of union members showed that a third supported Wallace. Both parties responded aggressively and drove the Wallace vote down, but in the November election, he received over 9.9 million votes and won Alabama, Arkansas, Georgia, Louisiana, and

Mississippi. This was not enough to throw the election into the House of Representatives, which was his plan, but it was an unmistakable sign that the question of race was now highly salient and would continue to transform American politics. The surprise, in a way, was that it took until 1980 and the election of Ronald Reagan for it to happen.

On Decolonization

Trade, immigration, and race were all connected, for they were all about "the other." They threatened to disrupt political attachments and coalitions by pitting insiders against outsiders, defined as such because they were foreigners competing in the same markets, immigrants taking away jobs or invading cultures and communities, or racial minorities feared and despised for so many reasons. The alignments worked out by the early 1950s were spared deep divisions over trade and immigration because the politics of trade had been displaced from elections and from legislatures and because immigrants were few and from familiar places. Race did divide people in the most important democratic country, but the party system was reconfigured rather than torn apart. Whites, mainly but not exclusively in the South, moved to the right into the Republican Party, but their numbers were more or less balanced out by the movement of African Americans to the Democrats.

The issue of decolonization was closely linked to immigration and race and had explosive potential. It had definite political effects, but for most of the early postwar period did not seriously disturb the political systems that were forced to confront it. The most obvious reason was that the pain that accompanied moves toward independence was felt primarily in the colonies.[22] The Indian subcontinent descended into nasty sectarian clashes when the British left, but it hurt Indians and Pakistanis. Where national liberation movements faced resistance and led to civil war, the battles were not fought in the metropole. The British deployed brutal counter-insurgency tactics in Malaya and Kenya, but not only did they happen far away from the UK itself, they were covered up rather successfully. Yet another reason decolonization did not produce deep fissures was that elites and parties recognized early on that the cause of empire was mostly lost. There were, of course, Tory diehards who did not approve of the Attlee government's decisions to leave India or Palestine, but not many. The outcome on the subcontinent had been decided long before 1947; and few in Britain wanted to stay involved in the conflict between Jews and Arabs. The Dutch also figured out pretty quickly that they could not hold Indonesia. There, too, the issue had been decided before the Dutch came to recognize it. Indonesia was occupied by the Japanese early in the war and the Dutch West Indies administration relocated to Australia. Nationalists declared the country independent, and the Japanese surrendered in September not to the Dutch, but to the British. The Dutch did not return until early the next year, and not in full force. After more than three years of fighting, and many Indonesian casualties, the Netherlands recognized the country's independence in late 1949.

Were there still any doubts about the ultimate fate of empire, they would have been cleared up by the Suez Crisis of 1956. British leaders had long believed in Egypt's supposedly critical role in the Mediterranean and the Middle East. Even after leaving Palestine and having asked the United States to take over its position in Greece, Turkey, and Iran, they held onto the fantasy of a special destiny in the region. This was challenged directly in 1952 by the Egyptian coup carried out by the Free Officers Movement, led by Mohammed Naquib and Gamal Abdel Nasser. By 1956 Nasser was dominant, heading a government determined to transform the country and to assert Egypt's regional predominance. In July his government nationalized the Suez Canal. France had less at stake, but it did have a continuing interest in the canal, and its leaders were worried about Nasser's influence across North Africa. The British, the French, and the Israelis—always at odds with their Arab neighbors— concocted a scheme in which Israel would invade Egypt, then France and Britain would send in troops as peacekeepers—who would also take back control of the canal. The operation, which began on October 29, was a failure, and the British prime minister, Anthony Eden, declared a ceasefire on November 6. The intervention of the US president, Dwight Eisenhower, was decisive. He made it clear he opposed the invasion and was prepared to cause Britain financial difficulties if it persisted. The Egyptians kept the canal and could gloat about their victory: Eden resigned; the French withdrew. The lesson of the failure was that any hopes the British and French still harbored about maintaining their empires were doomed.

Decolonization became unstoppable after Suez and swept away much of the British and French imperial presence in Africa and elsewhere in the late 1950s and early 1960s. A host of new states were created and quickly joined the United Nations, where they began to assert their influence in the General Assembly. The transfer of power was typically peaceful, with the notable exceptions of Kenya and Algeria. The British fought a "dirty war" against the Mau Mau during the mid-1950s and 1960s, with concentration camps, torture, murder, and tactics first developed in Malaya. Majority rule was achieved in 1960, formal independence in 1963. The story of Britain's repression remained largely hidden away for another forty years, however, and did not become a major political issue at the time.[23]

The Algerian War, by contrast, disturbed France a great deal. Like Kenya, Algeria was a settler colony, administratively a formal part of France, and much more than that in the country's political imagination. French involvement had begun in 1830 and by the 1950s over a million French had settled there, occupying the best land. These *pieds noirs* were resolute in refusing to grant rights to their Arab and Muslim neighbors. The French also had a rather distinct vision of themselves and their empire. Britain might rule over native populations, but the French were bringing them civilization and inviting their subjects to become French. The insistence of the majority of Algerians on independence meant rejecting this universalizing mission.[24]

The war was extremely brutal.[25] The rebel forces, led by the National Liberation Front (FNL), waged a determined guerilla struggle against the authorities and the French army. The army deployed torture and terror against them. Protests by Algerians and their supporters in France were violently repressed. Public opinion in France became deeply split: the left opposed the war and supported independence, while the right backed the *pieds noirs* and the army. And it was generals in the army in favor of continued repression and French domination who effectively brought down the Fourth Republic in 1958. De Gaulle came to power with their support and made clear his sympathy for their cause: "Vive l'Algérie française!" he said on June 6, 1958. He would in the end renege on his implied pledge and accept Algerian independence in 1962. Fortunately for him, he escaped unscathed from more than one assassination attempt.

The United States ought to have been spared the consequences of decolonization. After the Philippines became independent in 1946, the US had no formal colonies. It had, however, Cold War allies that still ruled over empires. The country had long styled itself as anti-imperialist, even if its actions looked and often felt like those of an imperial power, especially to its neighbors in Latin America. After 1945, America also claimed to be the leader of the "free world" that had played a key role in ridding the world of fascism and now stood ready to defend it from Soviet domination. Giving aid and comfort to imperial powers seeking to retain their colonial possessions, and using deadly force to do that, was an obvious contradiction, and the Soviets routinely attacked the US over the issue. The United States wavered and walked a fine line in dealing with decolonization. It helped to ease the Dutch out of Indonesia, and the US was in theory in favor of national self-determination more generally. It was also happy enough to see the British Empire shrink. On the other hand, fear of Communism in Asia led the US to bankroll the French in Indochina. US opposition was, conversely, critical to the failure of the invasion of Suez, and that failure led to the collapse of the British and French empires across Africa. On balance, the US probably assisted decolonization in a modest fashion, and it would be eager to win allies in the former colonies after they became independent.

Its nearly obsessive anti-Communism nevertheless pushed the United States to get involved in actions that made a mockery of its pretensions. The problem was that the national liberation movements that took over from colonial rulers often leaned to the left or were willing to accept Soviet support and often adopted a statist model of economic development after gaining independence. Such a move led the US to intervene and to support unsavory rivals. The most visible efforts were in Latin American countries that had long been free of colonial rule but were typically in a dependent relationship with the colossus to the north. The Cuban Revolution of 1959 was a particular spur to US efforts to police the south for signs of Communist influence and to support a host of authoritarian regimes that boasted of their anti-Communism. Africa was farther away and not a major focus of US policy, but the Eisenhower administration was worried enough to work with the British and the Belgians to organize the overthrow, and subsequent murder, of Patrice Lumumba in the Congo in January 1961.

The most serious intervention was to come in Vietnam. The French long had an interest in Indochina, but effective control dated only from the 1880s. During the Second World War, Vietnam was controlled by the Japanese, with the assistance of the governor-general appointed by Vichy. Japan stationed thirty thousand troops in Vietnam and used it as a key staging area during the war. The remnants of French rule were ousted by the Japanese in 1945, and with Japan's defeat the emperor Bao Dai declared Vietnam's independence. Vietnam had an effective Communist party since 1925, and in 1941 its leader, Ho Chi Minh, helped to create the League for the Independence of Vietnam, the Viet Minh. The Viet Minh seized control from the relatively powerless emperor in August 1945. The French were determined to reassert their authority and, aided by British forces, gained control of the south of the country in 1946. By December the French and the Viet Minh were at war. The triumph of the Chinese Communists in 1949 gave a substantial boost to the fortunes of the Viet Minh, while the US stepped up aid to the French. The French nevertheless suffered a massive defeat at Dien Bien Phu in May 1954; in the Geneva Accords of 1955, they agreed to leave the country.

The struggle in Vietnam would soon become a matter for the United States and the Vietnamese. The Geneva Accords left the Viet Minh with control of the North, with nationwide elections promised for 1956. They never happened, mainly because the rulers of the South and their American advisors knew that the Viet Minh would win. Instead, both sides struggled to build up rival states. The North Vietnamese effort was far more successful, but massive US aid allowed some progress in the South. Ngo Dinh Diem, a Catholic, was chosen as the leader of the southern state. It became quickly obvious that war would come again soon. In 1959 the Vietnamese Communists decided to launch a "people's war" in the South and the National Liberation Front was established in 1960. The North Vietnamese could count on support from both the Soviets and the Chinese who, though feuding, were eager to shore up their revolutionary credentials. That backing was a major reason why the

United States felt compelled to respond by aiding the regime in the South. By 1963, the US had sixteen thousand advisors and had begun to participate in the fighting. Despite this, the war did not go well, and the US encouraged the overthrow of Diem at the beginning of November 1963 in the hopes of creating a more effective government.

President Kennedy was assassinated three weeks later, on November 22, 1963. There has been much debate about what Kennedy would have done had he not been gunned down. There is evidence that he was rethinking the US position, but it is not definitive. Whatever he might have done, his successor chose to escalate US involvement, and in 1964 Johnson convinced Congress to support the Gulf of Tonkin resolution allowing him "to take all necessary measures to repel any armed attack against the forces of the United States and to prevent further aggression."[26] Soon the US began to bomb North Vietnam. In July 1965, Johnson decided to send 175,000 troops to Vietnam and by 1967 there were close to half a million US forces there. The Soviets were content to continue aid to the North Vietnamese and to use the issue to discredit the US in the Third World, and the Chinese actually stepped up their assistance. The Johnson administration persisted in viewing the conflict as an essential Cold War battle and in failing to recognize that the enemy in Vietnam had the support of the bulk of the population. Johnson feared that withdrawing from Vietnam would send the wrong message to allies. Remembering the bitter debates over "who lost China," he worried that allowing South Vietnam to fall would provoke a "mean and destructive debate that would shatter my Presidency, kill my administration, and damage our democracy."[27] He was probably correct in thinking that his expansive domestic program would be in jeopardy.

The more America intervened, the more the South Vietnamese government and military faltered. The decisive moment was the Tet offensive in January 1968. The North Vietnamese and the NLF launched a general uprising and hit the US embassy in Saigon, seized the most important radio station, and engaged soldiers at the presidential palace. The offensive failed in a strictly military sense, but it succeeded in demonstrating that the US and its South Vietnamese allies could not win the war. US leaders, Democrats and Republicans, came to understand the dilemma, but struggled to find a way to end the war. Richard Nixon, who succeeded Johnson, recognized the inevitable, but undertook a dramatic escalation of the war as a means of putting it off and pressuring the North Vietnamese and their allies to agree to a deal that would disguise and delay defeat and "save face" for the United States.

Protests against the war within the United States had begun as early as 1965 and grew massively in 1967. They were fueled in part by TV images of the war and its devastation, but even more by the fact that all young American males were subject to the draft. Fear of being conscripted and forced to fight far away, in a war that was not going well and that few believed in, turned young people from skeptics into serious political opponents. The antiwar movement gained strength from the civil rights movement that was peaking at more or less the same moment. Malcolm X had first linked the struggle of African Americans to anti-imperialist struggles like Vietnam in 1964, and in 1965 SNCC issued a statement saying that Black Americans should not "fight in Vietnam for the white man's freedom until all the Negro people are free in Mississippi." Martin Luther King condemned the war with growing passion in 1966 and 1967.[28] The antiwar and student movements fed off the energy and the ideas of the civil rights movement, and their combined strength produced massive unrest and demonstrations. King's assassination in 1968 led to the biggest wave of urban uprisings of the 1960s, and Nixon's invasion of Cambodia produced a huge student rebellion in the spring of 1970.

Both movements died down in the early 1970s. The abolition of the draft and the beginnings of peace negotiations removed the two main stimuli to antiwar and student protest; a combination of repression against the Black Panthers, the most radical Black organization, and a sense of political exhaustion among other civil rights leaders dampened enthusiasm for further action among African Americans. Still, the movements left their mark on America in a way that the issues of race, decolonization, trade, or immigration had not done in Europe or Japan. The American protest movements did find echoes in Europe and Japan, however. The use of Japan as a staging area for the US during the Vietnam War caused protests that resonated deeply with the broader pacifism that characterized postwar Japanese politics. Highly visible protests against the Vietnam War also took place in Great Britain; and in Ger-

many US foreign policy in both Vietnam and Iran likewise sparked protests. The spectacular events of May 1968 in France had many local
causes, but criticism of the war in Vietnam certainly played a part. The
left in France displayed a distinct *tier-mondist* sensibility and that, too,
was linked to a critique of US imperialism in Vietnam and elsewhere. In
this curious fashion, the problem of decolonization, which rightly belonged to the former colonizers, came indirectly to cause the greatest
unrest in the country without formal colonies, and this American unrest
came back in turn to ruffle the politics of Europe and the rest of the
Western alliance.[29]

The Postwar Political Order Tested

The protests of the late 1960s and early 1970s generated great hopes of
social transformation and apocalyptic fears of what that would mean.
Both were exaggerated. Hopes of reform and, for some, revolution were
fleeting; the fear and resentment of the political and cultural changes of
the period were more lasting, but intermittent in their effects. Objec-
tively, what mattered most was that the political systems put in place
after the war survived a severe challenge and endured. Inevitably, they
evolved, but avoided collapse. Specifically, the parties and party systems
adapted. France managed to remain stable without De Gaulle and elected an ally as his replacement. Germany, Japan, and Italy demonstrated
an ability to respond to protest without recourse to repressive violence.
The United States survived Nixon, and his fall led to an array of reforms
that constrained the abuse of power by subsequent presidents.

Perhaps the key to this relative stability was the durability and orientation of the major parties. Center-right parties did not react to protest
by moving sharply to the right. There were expressions of extreme right-
wing sentiment from Italy and Japan to the United States, but conservative parties remained largely immune to their appeals. Republicans in
the United States might use the question of race to win votes, as Nixon
did with the "Southern strategy," but his actual policies were closer to the
political center. The center-right remained committed to the political
and economic compromises that were worked out in the 1940s and early
1950s. The Cold War, which persisted despite the beginnings of détente

and arms control, prevented conservative parties from departing too much from established formulas for governance.

Parties of the center-left also retained their strength and were not particularly tempted by the brief upsurge of ultra-left sentiment among the young. They were and continued to be anchored in labor movements and trade unions that were still growing in strength. Workers became noticeably more militant and launched waves of strikes in Britain, the United States, France, Italy, and Germany.[30] Unions and workers across the West had greater rights and representation than ever before, and low levels of unemployment had given them leverage, though they seldom made full use of that leverage and their wage demands were rather modest. That began to change during the 1960s, and workers insisted on higher wages as the potential of mass consumption became more visible and available. Employers were often willing to acquiesce, for the economy kept growing and allowed them to offset increased costs through automation or to pass them along to consumers through higher prices. The waxing strength of workers added to that of the center-left parties for which they mostly voted. Such parties would also replenish their ranks as youthful rebels, no longer so rebellious but still energetic, joined up. There would be debates, of course, about whether parties of this sort should move further to the left on issues like civil rights and race, the environment, or women's rights, but their relative openness to these new causes probably made them stronger overall.

What appeared as a series of crises at the time therefore proved not to be. For a genuine crisis to occur, the parties that made the political systems work would have to lose their social and ideological anchoring. That would happen, and it would pose a threat to the politics that had provided stability after 1945, but it would require both a deep recession and a reorientation of the economy and a break in the geopolitics of the Cold War. Economic problems would come first and redefine what liberalism meant; and then the end of the Cold War would determine the reach and meaning of liberalism and liberal order.

Liberalism and Liberal Order, Modified

L iberal democracy sustained, and was sustained by, a liberal international order for the quarter century after 1945. Internal and external politics reinforced one another even when behavior and policies deviated from strict liberal norms. What largely kept the system going was the prosperity that suffused the liberal democratic world, and that economic success was based on a specific model of political economy. The mixed economy, with its balance between states and markets and more or less generous social provisions, worked. It allowed mass production along Fordist lines and the beginnings of mass consumption to operate in tandem, creating positive feedback across the economy. The policies that governed the international economy, implemented by the Bretton Woods institutions and policy makers in individual countries, also worked. The world economy became gradually more open; trade and the exchange of currencies became easier and so expanded.

Unfortunately, but perhaps inevitably, *les trente glorieuses* could not and did not last. The fundamental reason was that the postwar model of growth fulfilled its potential and then began to slow down. The industries that prospered during the 1950s and 1960s—automobiles, home appliances like televisions and washing machines, and the construction of roads and houses that created the modern suburb—faced slack markets and lower profits when most households had cars and TVs and the demand for new homes lagged as those who could afford them got them. Profits were threatened when the techniques of mass production spread beyond the United States and the industries in which they were first applied. The production of cars, for example, expanded massively in countries like Germany and Japan, whose exports soon found willing buyers in the United States; and countries like Britain, France, and Italy ramped up their own car industries, even if most buyers were domestic. Televisions and other consumer electronics came to be produced in Japan and, with a lag, in Taiwan and South Korea. The dispersion of the latest techniques meant that supply came to outpace demand, and increased competition led to falling prices and profits. All of this meant that the Fordist model, for all its strengths, became less effective at generating prosperity during the 1970s.

This weakening of the engine of growth was not obvious at first. That was because the consequences of the changing world economy were visible most immediately in the crisis of the international financial system and in inflation. The two were related: inflation increased in the United States during the Vietnam War and began to shift the value of the major currencies. This meant that the United States could not maintain its policy of exchanging dollars for gold on demand at the parity agreed in the Bretton Woods arrangements. The effect was that in August 1971 the Nixon administration proclaimed a "New Economic Program" that suspended the dollar's convertibility into gold, froze wages and prices, and imposed a 10 percent import surcharge.[1] It took some time for the implications of this departure, directly linked to Nixon's prospects for reelection, to register internationally, but currencies began to fluctuate and a new element of uncertainty entered the calculations of businessmen and policy makers.

As the significance of Nixon's abandonment of Bretton Woods became clearer, the global economy experienced yet another shock that would be immediately visible to everyone. Israel was attacked over the Yom Kippur holiday in 1973 and its Arab opponents made initial gains. The Israelis countered and were soon threatening to extend their control over traditionally Arab territory. The reversal of fortunes had required that Israel be resupplied shortly after the war had begun. The main source was the United States, but the US relied, or sought to rely, upon bases and equipment in Europe. In response, the Arab states called for a boycott on the sale and shipment of oil to the US and its closest allies and imposed cuts in production. Oil prices were also ratcheted up; by December, they had quadrupled. The boycott, cutbacks, and price increases were made possible by the existence of OPEC, the Organization of Petroleum Exporting States, which had been founded in 1960. OPEC was weak at first, but over the next decade became more powerful, forcing oil companies to negotiate new agreements with states where oil was found and pumped. OPEC gained leverage mainly because economic growth led to ever greater demand for the product its members sold. The United States had a huge domestic oil industry, but by 1973 was importing 36 percent of its oil.[2] European countries were even more dependent on oil imports, and virtually all the oil used in Japan was imported.[3]

The impact of the oil crisis was dramatic, pervasive, and ongoing. Oil did not just heat homes and provide fuel for cars and trucks. It was also a key factor in production, and it was essential for the manufacture of fertilizers. Rising oil prices and diminished supplies caused shortages of gasoline and heating oil and increased costs of those products right away, but higher oil prices also led to higher prices later on in economic sectors that did not seem at all connected to oil's use as a fuel. There was, in addition, a second oil shock on the occasion of the Iranian Revolution in 1978–79 that came just as the world was beginning to adjust to the effects of the first. Its effects continued into the early 1980s. The impact of the recurring crises was ubiquitous, and almost every country that imported oil suffered. The economically advanced countries were hurt, but so, too, were developing countries because for most such countries efforts to generate growth depended on increasingly expensive energy imports. Oil producers and exporters benefited, of course, but since the Middle Eastern nations with the largest oil reserves were seldom democratic, it was their rulers who benefited most. The regimes in Saudi Arabia, Iraq, and Iran made use of the extra money to buy military and police equipment that could be used to threaten their neighbors or to control their own populations. The Soviet Union, with huge reserves, also did well, and its earnings from oil provided resources that helped keep the system going.

Rising prices for oil and related products, and then for the entire economy, meant that combating inflation became a top priority in just about every advanced country. It was not the only problem, however, and its prominence as an issue was in part a political choice. Who gains and who loses from inflation is not as obvious as it might first appear, and choosing to make the taming of inflation the main goal of policy making has unequal consequences. When policy makers put the battle against inflation at the top of the agenda, they are deciding to protect the interests of finance, creditors, and pensioners, not those of workers and debtors and probably not those of industry or agriculture.

Measures to reduce inflation also had different impacts on different interests and were seldom seen as neutral in their effects. Wage and price controls could be fair or not, depending on timing and the details of the controls, but they were typically resented. Workers and trade unions in Britain, for example, understood wage controls as a mechanism to reduce their earnings at a moment when their bargaining power was at a peak and when they could finally get what they believed they deserved. Businessmen disliked price controls on principle, for they implied a level of scrutiny by the public and the state that reduced their flexibility and, they feared, threatened their profits. Monetary policy to combat inflation meant rising interest rates. That raised the cost of borrowing and led to reduced investment and demand and to higher unemployment. Fiscal austerity had similar effects and also threatened public budgets and benefits, which affected the poor more directly than the well-off. Before and into the 1970s the objectives and techniques of macro-economic policy in the US, the UK, and other Western countries were for the most part Keynesian—specifically, to promote economic growth and to provide relatively full employment while seeking to maintain price stability.[4] The oil shocks and price increases of that decade rearranged these goals so that ensuring price stability came first while guaranteeing high and stable levels of employment became a secondary concern.

This shift in priorities would take the form of a turn toward policies that favored the market and pushed back the role of the state in the economy.[5] Before that could occur, existing governments and their policies had to be discredited and rejected. The process was not merely a matter of persuasion. It also involved the mobilization of money and power. It was the main outcome of the contentious politics of the 1970s. The transformation occurred across the democratic capitalist world, but it happened earliest and most dramatically in Great Britain and the United States. The political consequences wrought in these two countries would spread and become a global phenomenon. It is common to discuss the economies and economic policies of the two countries together on the assumption that they were both examples of "liberal market economies."[6] They were then and are now comparable in the extent to which policy in the United Kingdom and the US is more market-oriented than in places like Germany, France, or Japan. In the 1970s, however, neither country was as committed to free markets as market enthusiasts wanted. Britain had followed a more "national" strategy of using the state to build up the economy in the postwar era, deploying a broad repertoire of policies to stimulate and control growth. The United States was more traditionally liberal, but the state played a major role there as well, even if it was not regularly acknowledged. More important and interestingly, the challenges of the 1970s led initially to more, not less, involvement by the state in both of these "liberal market economies."

Turning against the State in Britain

Labour and the Conservatives largely shared the goals of promoting growth through policies that privileged the "national" over international interests. Though Britain had a deep, historic attachment to free trade and economic liberalism, that had been eclipsed during the depression and the Second World War, and policy was more or less protectionist long after the war. The UK resisted US pressure to open up its economy, but acquiesced eventually and grudgingly. British policy makers also resisted the lure of the more free-market Common Market until they realized that their European competitors were growing faster than Britain and that the enlarged internal market would likely help to spur British economic growth as well. While they waited to join, they sought to utilize planning to encourage faster growth. The Tories set up the National Economic Development Council (NEDC) in 1962 to bring business and the unions together to coordinate plans. Labour would build on this initiative when it took office in 1964 and add a Department of Economic

Affairs charged with drafting a national plan. These efforts were largely unsuccessful, but they revealed the shared goals of the major parties. Success was elusive because the state lacked the levers to compel action on the part of industry or labor and because funding never reached the level needed for a sustained "dash for growth." That was itself a product of Britain's recurring balance of payments problem, which produced what was labeled a "stop/go" pattern of development. The economy would begin to heat up, prices would rise, exports would increase less than planned and imports would grow to feed both production and consumption, and the balance of payments would turn negative. That led governments to apply the brakes to the economy through fiscal and monetary policy and put an abrupt end to the growth spurt.

To overcome this chronic constraint, political leaders came to the decision that wages had to be controlled to keep the price of exports down and to discourage the consumption of imports. The new planning institutions became the venues in which wage policy was bargained. The most important bargaining, however, occurred outside official channels in negotiations between unions and bosses and in unofficial strikes. Strikes in Britain began to rise in industries like motorcars in the late 1950s, and by the mid-1960s there was a wave of strikes that continued into the early 1970s. Union membership also grew steadily. The Labour government of Harold Wilson became desperate to avoid strikes, for they seemed to threaten the government's economic strategy. It turned for help to the union leaders who were so critical in the party's affairs, but learned that the leaders were often unable to control their members. To remedy the situation, the government published the white paper *In Place of Strife*, which called for the reform of trade unions. The proposal would enshrine new rights for workers and unions, but in return union leaders were to be given authority to help prevent strikes. The plan served only to alienate trade unionists and their leaders, and it was soon withdrawn. Strikes continued at a high level, and inflation continued to rise.

The Conservative government elected in 1970 passed its own trade union legislation and instituted wage and price controls. These moves provoked massive protests by the trade unions and were defied. The most spectacular acts of defiance came from the miners, who were traditionally underpaid and could boast of broad public support. The miners' strike of 1972 featured a new set of aggressive tactics. The Heath government caved and granted substantial wage increases. Price increases quickly ate away the miners' gains, and they went on strike again in late 1973. The miners' militancy coincided with, and was aided by, the first oil crisis. Coal became more essential as oil became scarce and more expensive. The government felt compelled to institute a three-day work-week. Neither side could find a way to break the deadlock and so Heath called an election for the end of February 1974. It was fought, at least implicitly, on the question of "who governs?"—the government or the unions. The result was a clear repudiation of the Tory government, but otherwise the message from voters was ambiguous. The biggest winners were the Liberals, who secured 19 percent of the vote but, as usual in Britain's "first-past-the-post" system, won far fewer seats. The Tories actually won slightly more votes than Labour, but not enough to continue in government. After they failed to form a coalition with the Liberals, Labour, again under Harold Wilson, took over. A second election in October gave Labour a slim overall majority in Parliament.

The Labour government of 1974–79, led by Wilson until 1976, then by James Callaghan, was populated by talented leaders, but its narrow and then nonexistent majority rendered it ineffective. So, too, did Labour's internal politics. The party came into office with two new sets of commitments: it had adopted a quite radical program in 1973 committed to increasing government control of the "commanding heights" of the economy by the creation of a National Enterprise Board and by requiring businesses to develop planning agreements with unions and workers. Separately, party leaders and the leadership of the Trades Union Congress agreed to a "social contract" that would give the unions more say over policy in exchange for cooperation in holding down wages. In return for keeping pay settlements in check, the government would increase "the social wage"—for example, pensions, assistance for the lowest paid, and other benefits. These two sets of commitments were not always in contradiction, but together they added up to a great deal more than the government could afford or deliver. Inflation continued to grow, hitting 25 percent in 1975, and the budget situation deteriorated. In 1976, the government was forced to ask for a loan from the IMF, which demanded substantial cuts in return. Callaghan pushed the deal through the Cabinet, but incurred the wrath of the left within the party.[7] The industrial strategy proposed in the party platform was largely unrealized, but the bargain with the unions held until the fall of 1978. The government proposed a 5 percent norm for pay increases for 1978–79, and union leaders could not deliver the support of their members. Len Murray, the head of the Trades Union Congress (TUC), explained later, "We warned Callaghan that he would have industrial trouble if he tried to impose a 5 per cent wages policy," but he persisted.

Industrial trouble was not long in coming. In September workers at Ford Motor Company went on strike, and by December they had won an increase of 17 percent.[8] Other unions in the private sector followed— and asked for even more. Soon the strikes spread to the public sector; a million and a half workers participated in a "day of action" on January 22, 1979. The "winter of discontent," as it came to be called, dragged on before petering out in March. On Valentine's Day, the government and the TUC announced that they had agreed to a concordat on "The Government, the Economy and Trade Union Responsibility." The agreement did not end the discontent, but it did signal the failure of the Labour Party's approach to governance.

Labour's strategy of governing was a mix of ideas and policies with mechanisms to implement those ideas and policies. The party believed in government, in the public sector, and in state-led policies to bring about fairness, prosperity, and growth. The policies varied: the bulk of the leadership favored classic macro-economic policies to expand—or at times limit—demand, and the inspiration for such policies was Keynesian; the left was more interventionist and supported the creation of public institutions to mobilize investment and state enforcement of requirements that industry carry out plans made in consultation with government and workers. During the 1970s, the government primarily stuck to the former, though there were moves toward more dirigiste policies as well. Critical to the macro-economic policies pursued by Labour were its efforts to control wages and, where possible, prices. The voluntarist traditions baked into the history of collective bargaining in Britain meant that government could make incomes policy work only with the cooperation of the trade unions. During the 1970s, in fact, Labour's main argument for why it could govern more effectively than the

Tories was that Labour could work with the unions. To the extent that the "social contract" held, producing gains for workers, lower costs for employers, and less rapid price rises for the economy, the claim was vindicated. With the "winter of discontent," the claim lost credibility.

The failure was not a refutation of the tenets of Keynes. Before, during, and after the crises of the 1970s, Keynesian predictions and policies were routinely effective in managing the national economy. They were temporarily overwhelmed, however, by the extreme external shocks delivered by oil price increases. When those shocks were absorbed and dealt with, policy makers continued to make use of what were basically Keynesian techniques. What failed in Britain was the effort to run the economy by the quasi-corporatist strategy that got government involved in detailed negotiations with business and trade unions and whose success required the cooperation of government, business, and unions and the ability of employers and unions, especially the unions, to control their members and get them to acquiesce in decisions made by their leaders. That failure of governance did not, of course, prevent critics of Keynesian economics and policies from proclaiming the failure of Keynes and promoting their more market-oriented alternatives.

Among those critics were Margaret Thatcher and the "neoliberal" economists with whom she consorted. Particularly fashionable in 1979, when Thatcher led the Conservatives to victory in the May general election, was a variant of market-based thinking referred to as "monetarism," which focused on the supply of money as the key to fighting inflation. Monetarist remedies were tried over the next few years, with mixed results. The pace of inflation did eventually come down, but the keys to that achievement were high interest rates, mainly in the United States, and the severe recession of 1981–82, which reduced demand for oil and pushed prices down. The critique of Keynesian theory and techniques was part of a broader attack on the role of government in the economy. Under Thatcher, that would lead to a determined effort to lower the expectations of what government could do to control the economy and, more specifically, of how effective it could be in generating growth and employment. The stance was a direct repudiation of the assumptions of postwar economic policy making, which had given priority to maintaining employment.

The new assumption was that the best government could do was to create stable conditions in which business could feel confident enough to invest. Such a limited assumption did not, of course, prevent the Thatcher government from pursuing policies that it claimed would aid growth and that would benefit the prime minister's wealthy supporters. The most important was reducing the rate of tax paid by the well-to-do and businesspeople. Top rates of income tax were cut sharply and the lost revenue was made up for, at least in part, by increased "value added tax" (VAT), which was nearly doubled in Thatcher's first budget. VAT was and is a variation on a sales tax, which is typically more regressive than income tax. The second policy was deregulation, designed to make it easier for businesses to invest. The third, and perhaps most controversial, policy was privatization. Privatization involved both the selling off of state-owned industries and allowing tenants in public housing (council housing) to buy their own flats. The government owned key industries, and privatizing them involved restructuring so as to make shares more attractive to investors and then selling them off. The Tory governments of the 1980s and early 1990s took in hundreds of millions of pounds through these asset sales and divested the state of stakes in industries that could have been profitable and provided leverage over industrial policy. That, of course, was the point.

The sale of council housing was less about money and the economy and more about politics. The Conservatives believed, not unreasonably, that tenants in council housing tended to vote Labour, in part because it was often the Labour-controlled local council that built and maintained their homes and set their rents. Studies did show that the strongest predictors of Labour voting were living in council housing and union membership. Giving council house tenants title to their property would, it was hoped, remove that incentive to vote Labour. So, too, would weakening trade unions by discouraging membership, and the Thatcher government worked hard at that as well. Crushing the miners' strike of 1984–85 was the symbol of the anti-union crusade, and it worked. Union membership fell steadily through the decade-plus of Conservative rule. Neither policy created Tory voters to the extent hoped for, but the transformation of institutions was real and had long-term consequences.

The American Embrace of the Market

The United States opted for pro-market policies with the election of Ronald Reagan in November 1980, just eighteen months after Margaret Thatcher won her first election. Of course, Americans knew as little about what this meant as did those who voted for Thatcher. What voters in both countries knew was that current and recent policies, and the politicians trying to make them work, were failing. The Carter administration inherited problems it did not know how to solve, and then they got worse. Inflation and a slowing economy greeted Carter when he took office in 1977; in 1978, the second oil shock reversed whatever progress his administration had achieved on inflation. That was accompanied by, and was largely caused by, the revolution in Iran that toppled the Shah. The Shah had long been seen as a creature of the United States, and when he was admitted to the US for medical treatment in October 1979—at the urging of old friends like Henry Kissinger—students in Teheran broke into the US embassy and seized sixty-six hostages. The United States tried desperately to negotiate their release, but there was nobody with whom to strike a bargain in Iran. The new Islamist leader, Ayatollah Ruhallah Khomeini, was still in the process of consolidating power. Increasingly frustrated, the Carter administration mounted a rescue operation on April 24, 1980, but it failed disastrously. Eventually a deal was made, but the fifty-two remaining hostages would not be released until January 20, 1981, the day Reagan was inaugurated president. Meanwhile, oil prices continued to rise, pushing up the price of everything else, and the economy tipped into recession.

In the context it was somewhat surprising that the election of 1980 was close until very near the end of the campaign. Even then, Reagan's margin of victory was modest. He received a narrow majority of votes cast, 50.8 percent, though he won handily in the Electoral College. It would seem that Reagan's preference for market-based solutions, and his hostility to the activist state, were as yet not widely shared views. Over time, they would gain wider acceptance and anchor a new governing consensus, but during the late 1970s and into 1980 there was little agreement on how to deal with the problems that Carter faced. There was nevertheless a widespread view that what had worked before was no longer effective. The lack of consensus was fitting testimony to the scale of the difficulties that the United States confronted during the 1970s, but answers remained elusive.

The term invented to describe the economic problems of the '70s, *stagflation,* was itself an admission of the inability of policy makers and economists to figure out just what was wrong and needed fixing. Inflation made the headlines, and taming it came to dominate political debate, but the Nixon, Ford, and Carter administrations were also aware of rising unemployment.[9] Policy under Nixon, as might be expected, was eclectic and unorthodox, dominated by Nixon's desire for reelection. Jettisoning the constraints of Bretton Woods was a precondition to devaluing the dollar, a remedy that was indeed a dramatic departure but which fell within the range of traditional Keynesian techniques. So, too, did the imposition of wage and price controls. The surcharge on imports was a departure from the free-trade principles that Americans rhetorically supported and sought to impose on the world, but the United States had always reserved the right to protect domestic producers, farmers in particular. Nixon was also not afraid to tax and spend and use the power of government to regulate markets for energy. He adopted these policies less out of conviction than as the means to get himself reelected and to hold onto power. His dramatic fall from power because of Watergate had little immediate effect on policy, but it did make any policy harder to implement because of the distrust his behavior elicited from ordinary Americans.

His successor, Gerald Ford, was a more orthodox, small-government, anti-tax Republican, and he surrounded himself with market fundamentalists like William Simon, who became his treasury secretary, and Alan Greenspan, chair of Ford's Council of Economic Advisers. Policy remained more ambivalent, for the Ford government lacked the authority for any serious departures in policy. Democrats had made major gains in the congressional elections of 1974, and Ford was actually pushed into adopting a mildly expansionary budget in 1975. The move briefly served to restore growth and reduced the incentive for new policies. Also, the recession caused by the first oil crisis led to reduced demand and moderated the rise in prices. Between 1974 and 1978, oil prices rose less than inflation, which meant a de facto price reduction.

The temporary easing of the upward pressure of oil prices did not prevent the incoming Carter administration from focusing on energy. That focus would become part of its undoing due to the second oil price crisis, but the effort was misconceived from the start. Carter was a new type of Democrat: a southern moderate without the historic ties to labor and the deep attachment to the New Deal of fellow Democrats. On the questions of the relative role of the market and the state and the proper size and role of government, he was further to the right than most of his party. Carter was also a man of faith, personally austere, who had taught Bible classes; and his governing style and vision reflected these traits and preferences. His moralism—and, some would say, moralizing—may have played well in Georgia and did provide a useful contrast to the corruption and immorality of Nixon. These attitudes also lent credence and credibility to Carter's emphasis on human rights in foreign policy. In domestic policy, especially on energy, they were less effective, for they led Carter to argue for austerity and sacrifice at a moment when Americans felt they were suffering enough from higher prices and rising unemployment.

Carter was sworn in as president during a severe cold wave. In December 1976 OPEC had raised the price of oil by 10 percent. There were also shortages and increases in the price of natural gas, which warmed households throughout the northern part of the country. Carter was in favor of loosening controls on natural gas, whose price and distribution were strictly regulated. The pain caused by higher prices would have to be offset by conservation, which meant consuming less gas and oil. Americans were already required to adhere to a fifty-five-mile-per-hour speed limit; now they were told to keep thermostats at sixty-five degrees during the day and fifty-five degrees at night. "All of us," Carter told the country on February 2, 1977, "must learn to waste less energy."[10] The president followed this up on March 1 with a bill to create a new Department of Energy, which would come up with a plan to make America energy independent. The core of the plan would be "strict conservation" that would "require substantial sacrifices on the part of the American people."[11] On April 18, Carter proposed his energy plan, labeling the effort "the moral equivalent of war."[12] It was a curious if not totally coherent mix of proposals: more controls on natural gas, despite Carter's preference for decontrol; a tax on crude oil that would bring US prices to world levels but would then be returned to consumers; more stringent fuel economy standards and a tax on gas guzzlers; new efficiency standards for industry and a requirement that utilities convert from oil and natural gas to coal; and tax credits for energy conservation and the use of renewables.

The package pleased nobody, arousing opposition from across the political spectrum, from business and energy companies to environmentalists. Speaker Tip O'Neill managed to get it through the House in August, but it more or less died in the Senate. Rather than burying it, the administration continued to negotiate and accepted compromises that stripped the legislation of its most important provisions, even reversing the proposal to extend controls on natural gas. The National Energy Act was finally passed on October 15, 1978. Carter had devoted more than a year and a half to getting his energy proposals adopted. He ended with little to show for the effort and he had made enemies on all sides. When the second oil crisis hit shortly after, he had no reservoir of support upon which to draw.

The president's troubles stemmed from real and largely intractable problems that would have stymied the interventions of even a much more skilled hand. Still, Carter was poorly suited to the needs of the moment. His ideas put him on the right of his party when the party had moved left in response not only to the failures of Nixon and Ford, but also as a reaction to the oil crisis and economic slowdown. Many Democrats blamed the oil companies for high prices and multinationals for taking capital and jobs away; they wanted government to intervene to restart economic growth. The liberal advance in the 1974 elections reflected this shift, and in 1975 there were popular proposals for economic planning and a development bank. These would be incorporated into the Humphrey-Hawkins bill that called for massive public works and committed the state to guarantee everyone a job. Carter pledged support for the bill during the 1976 election, but backed away once in office. A much watered-down version was finally passed in October 1978.

The poor fit between Carter and the party he led was also evident in the administration's fiscal policy. Carter was skeptical of government and wanted to rein it in, but Democrats wanted to use it to address the needs of their voters. Carter's first budget was mildly expansionist, but a disappointment to the party. Soon after its passage, moreover, Carter cancelled the planned tax cut that constituted a third of the stimulus in the budget. Reluctant to do much to encourage growth, the administration sought to get other countries—specifically Germany and Japan—to adopt more pro-growth policies. This was a sort of Keynesian policy at the international level understood at the time as the "locomotive strategy": strong countries would adopt pro-growth strategies in a coordinated fashion and pull the world economy out of recession. At the London summit in spring 1977 Carter failed to elicit firm commitments from Germany and Japan, largely because of his own unwillingness to stimulate the US economy. He did much better the next year at the Bonn summit, with Germany and Japan agreeing to stimulus in exchange for a US promise to cut oil imports. The plan seemed to work for a while, but was rendered irrelevant by the second oil shock.[13]

From late 1978 there was no question that Carter's top priority would be the fight against inflation, specifically high oil prices. Again, he told the country that "the path of fiscal restraint" was the way to go. "Reducing the deficit will require difficult and painful decisions," he explained.[14] His grim message was obviously sincere, but voters were not pleased to hear about the need for further austerity. Carter's plans would entail budget cuts, the removal of controls on oil prices, and tax increases. They were in stark contrast to Republican promises of tax cuts, as proposed in the Kemp-Roth bill unveiled the previous summer. Oil prices continued to increase, as OPEC announced a hike of nearly 15 percent on December 17, 1978, and just days later production stopped altogether in Iran. By spring there were shortages and Americans were once again in a panic: they waited in long lines at the gas pumps to get their share of scarce supplies, and fights broke out over people jumping the queue. Carter's response was to use his authority to begin the process of decontrol of oil prices on June 1, which did nothing to make gas more available but did increase the cost. He proposed to couple decontrol with an excess profits tax on oil companies. Consumers continued to panic, however, and put the blame more or less equally on the companies and the Carter administration. Facing growing unpopularity, the administration began directing criticism at OPEC and advocating programs to

develop solar power and alternative fuels. On the first official day of
summer, truckers went on strike demanding more fuel at lower prices.
The administration had no answer and shortages persisted. In late June
Carter traveled to Japan for another summit and while there OPEC announced yet another, and bigger, price increase.

Carter's advisors themselves began to panic about the growing
crisis and urged the president to give a major speech to the American
public on his return from Japan. Carter at first agreed, but then canceled
the speech on July 4. Instead, he convened a week-long retreat at Camp
David where he discussed with selected leaders and academics the crisis
of confidence that Americans were supposedly experiencing. He would
give a different speech on July 15. The president was strongly influenced
by his young pollster and advisor Patrick Caddell, who fretted over
America's spiritual crisis. Carter's speech went all in on the spiritual,
moralistic message. It effectively blamed the American people for the
country's current difficulties. "Too many of us now tend to worship self-
indulgence and consumption," but such behavior was not working,
Carter lectured. "We've learned that piling up material goods cannot fill
the emptiness of lives which have no confidence or purpose." He went
on, "On the battlefield of energy we can win for our nation a new confidence and we can seize control again of our common destiny."[15] Conservation and austerity were the keys to progress, but they would be coupled
with a crash program to produce and exploit synthetic fuels.

The exhortation to conserve and to live with less did little to assuage angry truckers or other consumers. What did help was the decision of Saudi Arabia to increase production. By the end of July, the lines
at the gas stations had disappeared. Quickly, support for the president's
ambitious proposal on synthetic fuels began to dissipate, politics returned to normal, and Carter had little or nothing to show for his dramatic public intervention. He kept pushing for the creation of an Energy
Security Corporation, asking for $140 billion over twelve years. The plan
drew much criticism from both right and left. Though a version was
passed in the wake of the Iranian hostage crisis as political leaders briefly rallied behind the president, Congress refused to approve the Emergency Mobilization Board that would have actually carried out its
provisions. Even so, whatever support Carter received because of the

hostage crisis dissipated rapidly. When the administration used the moment to push for a substantial tax on gasoline, resistance exploded. The Kemp-Roth bill had already showed the attraction of schemes to lower taxes, as had the passage in June of Proposition 13 in California, which aimed to roll back and then permanently limit property taxes. The nation had not fully embraced the free-market doctrines that Reagan would advocate and implement, but the massive inflation and straitened circumstances of the late 1970s made talk of increasing taxes massively unpopular. Carter seemed not to understand.

Carter stumbled through the spring of 1980 fending off the challenge of Senator Edward Kennedy for the nomination and watching Ronald Reagan march to the Republican nomination with relative ease. The Republicans made much of the government's incapacity to solve the energy crisis and tame inflation, using it as an argument against government more generally. They could hardly have asked for a better example of state failure and, implicitly, of the superiority of market solutions. Carter himself had seemed to concede the argument with the appointment of Paul Volcker as chairman of the Federal Reserve back in August 1979. Volcker's overwhelming priority was to tame inflation, and he moved quickly to use controls on the money supply to accomplish that. The new controls were accompanied by high interest rates and were designed to engineer a recession. The administration also adopted a budget that reduced expenditures by $13–14 billion and added that much in tax. Together, these measures worked to put the brakes on the economy. GDP fell by nearly 8 percent in the second quarter of 1980, and by mid-April two key measures of interest rates topped 20 percent.[16] The wonder is that Carter did not lose the election of 1980 by a much wider margin.

Reagan's victory ended a decade of debate, confusion, and experimentation in economic policy. The new administration moved decisively to implement its philosophy of reliance on the market and to put limits on the role of the state. The key was tax cuts, which Reagan turned to in his first budget. Overall rates were lowered, but the most distinctive feature of the plan was the reduction in top rates and in what businesses could deduct. The second major thrust of Reagan's policies was deregulation. Deregulation was for the Reagan administration what privatization was for the Thatcher regime. The zeal with which the market fundamentalists took to deregulation was impressive, although they also faced considerable opposition, for most Americans did not want to lower environmental standards, to eliminate the regulation of food and medicine, or to give corporations license to write their own rules. It was also the case that some of the people Reagan appointed to positions concerned with regulation, like James Watt at the Interior Department and Ann Gorsuch at the EPA (Environmental Protection Agency), were rightly seen as fringe characters. Watt was explicit about his peculiar religious views, telling Congress, "I do not know how many future generations we can count on before the Lord returns."[17] His beliefs presumably rendered conservation unnecessary. Watt also famously banned the Beach Boys from playing at the annual Independence Day celebrations on the Mall in Washington and replaced them with Wayne Newton, a friend of the president's.

Battles over deregulation inevitably went back and forth, with market advocates and interested industries winning some struggles and losing others. Officials of the new administration knew that this would likely happen, and they understood that many of their detailed policies were unpopular. Grasping that reality, they adopted a blunter but broader and, they hoped, more effective strategy. They would deny funding, and where possible staffing, to the agencies tasked with regulating the economy and overseeing the care and tending of the environment. The plan worked by increasing the budget deficit, which would pressure Congress and subsequent administrations to make cuts in specific programs. Reagan's first budget director, David Stockman, understood how this would work; and so, too, did other advisors. It meant that despite incessant talk about reducing deficits, Republicans understood that they were a potent weapon. The reason for deficits, of course, was the decision simultaneously to cut taxes and increase defense spending. It was rationalized by talk of improving the "supply side" of the economy, but as Stockman conceded, such talk was a "Trojan horse" that would permit the reduction of the top rate of tax.[18] In later iterations, the strategy was described as "starve the beast," meaning government, but the origins of the plan dated to 1981. Alongside this plan to use deficits to cripple the state and constrain any future Democratic administration, Republicans also sought to gain control of the courts and developed strategies to embed the "market revolution" in the law. This involved efforts to win over the courts and to secure conservative control of the Supreme Court (and lower courts as well) by nominating sympathetic justices. Ed Meese, Reagan's second attorney general, explained that his aim was to use the legal system to "institutionalize the Reagan revolution so it can't be set aside no matter what happens in future elections."[19]

Reagan's successes and failures traced an arc similar to that of Margaret Thatcher. Both were in office during the most severe recession since the 1930s, and their standing in the polls reflected that. The results of the midterm elections of 1982 were extremely bad for the Republicans, and the new Congress would force concessions from the administration, most notably on taxes. The two conservative leaders nevertheless survived and eventually prevailed. Buoyed by victory in the Falklands War and aided by a split opposition, Thatcher won reelection with a large majority in Parliament in 1983. Economic recovery had also begun, appearing to vindicate at least some of her policy choices. Reagan faced the electorate a year later, by which time the economy was growing rapidly. Inflation had also eased, due to weakened demand during the recession, discord within OPEC, and new supplies of oil. Being reelected by comfortable margins allowed Reagan and Thatcher more time to implement their market-oriented policies. It was in Thatcher's second term, for example, that she took on the miners and defeated them. Reagan turned his focus to foreign policy after reelection, with rather surprising results, but his allies and appointees continued efforts to push back the frontiers of the state. Thatcher won election again in 1987, and Reagan was succeeded by his vice president, George Bush. Prolonged control by the Tories and the Republicans meant that their analytical framework and policies became embedded in the practices of government and assumptions about what government could and should do in both the UK and the US. When the Democrats finally won back the presidency in 1992, their leaders had come to accept much of what Reagan and Bush had done. So, too, had Labour in Britain. Tony Blair and Gordon Brown, the main leaders and creators of "New Labour," were committed to modifying Thatcher's legacy by humanizing it, taking the sharper edges off its harsher policies, and restoring a measure of public funding for social services. That was more or less what they did in office after 1997. In neither country was there the aspiration to reverse the transformations so recently effected or to undo what had become a more market-oriented consensus.

The Washington Consensus

Yet another marker of success was the extent to which Reagan and Thatcher had pushed, or encouraged, other nations to adopt more market-friendly policies.[20] In Western Europe, the Germans had long combined state aid to business and a paternalistic array of social protections with fiscal prudence. They did not need much encouragement to lean further toward austerity. With the Christian Democrat Helmut Kohl taking office in October 1982, the tilt was ensured. The French were, by contrast, quite out of synch with the policy shifts in London and Washington and in 1981 elected a socialist government under François Mitterand. Mitterand and his ministers presided over a move to the left, nationalizing banks and key industries, increasing benefits, and pursuing an expansionary fiscal policy. The effect was rising prices, capital flight, and pressure on the franc. Within two years the government was compelled to reverse course. With British, German, and then French leaders becoming more supportive of market-based solutions, the European Community itself moved in the same direction.[21] It was under the former French finance minister and now head of the European Commission, Jacques Delors, that the European Community adopted the plan for the "single market" in 1986. The hope was that encouraging greater competition and the free movement of goods, money, and people across the EC would be a spur to growth that would overcome the economic slowdown of the 1980s. The opening up of capital markets was a crucial step everywhere: the United States had abandoned controls in 1974, the UK in 1979; Japan followed soon after; the EC announced in 1988 that capital controls would be abolished by July 1, 1990; and in 1989 the Organisation for Economic Co-operation and Development (OECD) had urged the "full liberalization of capital markets." The European Community's conversion to markets was a much more measured thing than the turns executed in Britain and the United

States. The EC coupled its market opening policy with talk, and not just talk but policy initiatives, designed to ensure that members of the Community would create a "European model of society" with substantial social provision and efforts to bring about equality and harmony between "social partners" and between men and women.

The move toward more market-centered policies internationally had a particular bite in the developing world. Non-Western countries had pushed the United Nations to declare the necessity of establishing a "new international economic order" in 1974; and support was forthcoming from the European Community and the World Bank. The demand was a product of Third World countries' long-term efforts at development and the belief that what was required were higher prices for the commodities they produced, controls on imports to protect domestic producers, and substantial government intervention to make it all work. To this package of policies—typically labeled "import substitution industrialization" or ISI—was added in the early 1970s the example of the world's most powerful producers' cartel, OPEC, which used its control of production and prices to extract enormous resources from developed countries. If other producers of commodities could unite and get higher prices for what they grew or extracted, the proceeds could be plowed back into development. This was the inspiration for the New International Economic Order (NIEO).

The demand for a new international order would not succeed, but it would generate much talk as part of the ensuing "North-South Dialogue," which became more formal with the creation of the Brandt Commission. Its report, published in 1980, led to a high-level meeting in Cancun the next year. Reagan and Thatcher both attended, if only to delay and obfuscate, and it ended with no serious commitments to meet the demands of the South. What really doomed the effort was the debt crisis that soon gripped the developing countries, beginning in Mexico in 1982. Inflation, and especially the rise in oil prices, had led developing countries to borrow extensively in the 1970s. There was plenty of money, much of it recycled from the oil-exporting countries, but interest rates were high. They were still not much above the rate of inflation and so, for the moment, were a good deal. With the recession of 1981–82 oil prices and broader measures of inflation declined, but the high interest rates remained. One nation after another, and some more than once, default-ed or came close to defaulting on their loans. Rescue packages were put together in negotiations between the debtor country, its creditors, and international organizations like the IMF, the World Bank, and various development banks. No fewer than thirty of these were hammered out between 1982 and 1984, and more were agreed throughout the decade. To say that they were "agreed" is perhaps the wrong word, for the debtor countries had little leverage and were largely forced to accept the condi-tions proposed by the bankers and international financial institutions. These would normally require austerity, the adoption of pro-market policies, and commitments to open up trade and remove barriers to for-eign investment. Such "structural adjustment" packages aimed to make the market-oriented policies first embraced in Britain and the United States into a requirement for participation in the international economy. By 1989, an official involved in bargaining out these agreements sug-gested that the conditions attached to these agreements on debt relief represented something he called "the Washington consensus."[22]

The turn to the market that began with Thatcher and continued with Reagan therefore represented a dramatic shift in the framework and philosophy of economic policy—not only domestically but interna-tionally. It can be understood in part as a paradigm shift produced by the lengthy efforts of free-market advocates going back to the 1940s, when their ideas had been relegated to the margins of political and eco-nomic discourse.[23] Shut out of policy making and out of favor within the economics profession, they retreated to their own networks, like the Mont Pelerin Society, and institutions to keep their ideas alive. The best known of these market fundamentalists was, of course, Friedrich Hayek, but he was not alone: he was joined by his mentor and fellow Austrian Ludwig von Mises, his contemporary Lionel Robbins at the London School of Economics, and the younger Milton Friedman at Chicago. Gradually, as the luster of Keynesian thinking began to dim and as prob-lems arose that the tools of Keynesian demand management were not equipped to handle, they gained influence among conservative politi-cians and think tanks like the Institute of Economic Affairs, the Adam Smith Institute, and the Centre for Policy Studies in the UK, and in the United States the American Enterprise Institute, the Heritage Foundation, and the Cato Institute.[24] The growing influence of such market-friendly thinking was not mainly a reflection of the steady intellectual work of its adherents. The timing and circumstances of their impact suggests that they were responding to opportunities opened up by the ending of the long postwar boom. The American Enterprise Institute, for example, remained a shaky organization on the margins of political and economic thought until the 1970s, and so, too, did the Institute of Economic Affairs. The Heritage Foundation was not founded until 1973 and would not have seen the light of day without funding from Joseph Coors; the Centre for Policy Studies was founded in 1974 by the Conservative leader Keith Joseph, who got funding from fairly traditional Tory backers; and the Cato Institute, also established in 1974, was the creature of Charles Koch. It is better to think of this emergence of pro-market and anti-statist thought and policy advice as a revolt of the wealthy against the welfare state and the compromises of the early postwar period than as either an intellectual movement or a popular grassroots phenomenon.

The Postwar Liberal Order Remade

The sharp turn to pro-market policies would have long-term effects that were probably hard to predict at the time. In the short term, inflation was tamed and growth resumed in the United States, Britain, and most of Europe, though growth was nowhere near as robust as it had been in the three decades after the war. What was or should have been clear right away was that the social compact and accompanying political compromises of postwar had been disrupted. Just about everywhere in the West, strong unions and progressive tax systems in place after 1945 produced a more equitable distribution of income than had ever been the case in the lengthy history of capitalism. The market revolution would alter that balance. During the 1980s, the strength of unions was severely diminished by the rundown of old industries and regions. Deliberate efforts to weaken unions' bargaining power, most notable in the United Kingdom but real elsewhere, would mean that when growth resumed, unions would not regain their strength and influence. The tax changes passed under Thatcher and Reagan had equally drastic effects:

they lowered taxes overall, but mostly for the well-to-do and for business. Taxes whose incidence was less progressive, like VAT, were raised to make up the lost revenues. And in most countries, the return to growth would tend to exacerbate broader trends that heightened inequality. Straitened government budgets would reinforce such trends, for they forced cuts in services and benefits that fell most harshly on those who needed them most. This much was inevitable and clear at the beginning of the neoliberal turn.

The implications for politics and political stability would not be apparent until changes in policy had time to take effect, but they would be serious. The postwar settlement had brought forth a capitalism that put restrictions on what business, corporations, and the wealthy could do. It was more regulated than capitalism had been before the depression, and the poor and the working classes had more of a voice and more of a stake than before. The compression of income around the mean was also good for economic growth. Indeed, a relatively equitable division of the proceeds of industry facilitated the growth of manufacturing and rising standards of living. There could be no talk of affluence or the "affluent worker" before the late 1950s and early 1960s; and mass consumption was truly a postwar phenomenon.

It was clear that this postwar settlement would be transformed when the choice for market-oriented policies was made with the elections, and then reelections, of Thatcher and Reagan. Whether those who made the choice understood that it represented a decisive break with what had been a successful quarter century of growth, material progress, and social peace is unclear, though some undoubtedly did get it and were happy with it. In the United States, for example, many conservatives—particularly so-called movement conservatives—had been determined to reverse the New Deal since it had come into existence. That had been the original aim of the oldest free-market think tank, the American Enterprise Institute, when it was founded in 1938. Hayek first came to widespread attention with the publication of *The Road to Serfdom* in 1944.[25] In it, he took aim at the Labour Party, its program to expand the welfare state, and Keynesian economic policies. The Tories sought to use it in the 1945 election campaign, but the rationing of paper in the UK made it difficult to get enough copies. They were helped out by *Reader's Digest*, which printed an abridged version for early distribution. It did not help—Labour won a decisive victory—but the chronology indicates that neoliberals—and were they at all "neo"?—were denouncing the welfare state as and even before it was built. It is unlikely that their followers missed the fact that the stability of postwar was built on a reformed capitalism with an activist state, strong social protections, and social compromises that gave labor and its representatives a say and a stake in the postwar order. Those who understood matters this well, and who knew the history from living it, must necessarily have realized that the imposition of market-oriented policies constituted a repudiation, a ripping up, of the implicit contract that underpinned the postwar order.

Perhaps the strongest argument for the choice for markets was that it was at least a choice. The era of postwar growth had been superseded not simply by a slowdown and readjustment, which would have had to occur with the exhaustion of the Fordist model, but by a genuine set of intertwined and poorly understood crises in the 1970s. These were caused largely by external shocks, and it was by no means obvious to policy makers and voters that these shocks would be temporary. To them, what seemed clear was the failure of current policies, and that the frameworks from which they were derived were not working. Put more politically, what the parties of the center-left offered as responses to rising prices and increasing unemployment had not worked, and by 1979 or 1980 their prescriptions seemed unlikely to work in the future. In that context, the lurch to the right was not inexplicable, even if there remained considerable and thoughtful opposition to the move. The neoliberal turn was also linked, as effect and as cause, to the increasingly global nature of the economy. The inability of the governments of the late 1970s to make the economy work as they wished it to had been at least in part a product of the fact that the economic problems they faced came from outside the nation. Technology had made production more mobile, and the international flow of goods and money had increased massively in the 1970s. Globalization would continue to advance during the next decade and beyond. Neoliberalism was to a considerable extent a manifestation of this new reality, the ideological accompaniment to globalization.[26] It would also, once in place, further that process. The connection was intimate.

Whether, and just how, the choice for markets would weaken the foundations of the postwar order politically would necessarily remain unclear until the dissolution was well underway, and its impact would be hard to disentangle from the dramatic events soon to occur in international relations. It would nevertheless matter enormously, for it would serve to undermine the conditions that had made political stability possible since the Second World War.

The End of the Cold War and the Expansion of Liberal Order

The Strange and Surprising Ending of the Cold War

The Cold War was the great structuring fact of the postwar order and that order, more or less liberal in the West and Japan, starkly illiberal in the East, was built on and around that geopolitical divide. The same divide had major consequences for other parts of the world as well. As late as the early 1980s, when Cold War tensions intensified, there was no sign or expectation that this most basic division would come to an end anytime soon. Less than a decade later, it had ended, and decisively so.

Where to begin the story of its ending? Probably in the 1970s, the moment when it appeared that the Cold War had been fought to a draw, a rough balance reflected in the policy of détente and then in the Helsinki Accords, signed in 1975. Détente was a recognition that the Soviet Union had achieved a rough parity with the United States and that further advances in nuclear weapons would not mean greater security. The result was a set of arms control agreements reached in the early 1970s. Helsinki was a further step in normalizing relations between East and West. The agreements in the accords fell into three "baskets." The first was concerned with easing military tensions in Europe and recognizing borders; the second involved trade and other economic exchanges; and the third involved measures to increase personal freedom and freedom of the press. The modest promises in basket 3 were not at first considered important, but they became a useful tool for those seeking to extend human rights in the Soviet sphere. The main significance of the agreements was that they were a de facto recognition of a rough equilibrium between East and West and represented the high point of détente, the policy response to that balance.

The fact that the agreement came not long after the fall of Saigon— the final victory of the North Vietnamese and their southern allies— actually led more than a few in the United States to estimate that the Cold War balance had in fact tilted toward the Soviets.[1] The economic crises that beset the US, Europe, and to a lesser extent Japan as *les trente glorieuses* drew to a close did nothing to cast doubt on such a judgment. If anything, economic troubles raised doubts about the supposed superiority of the capitalist economies over the systems of the Soviet bloc. Standards of living were in no way comparable, for the long postwar boom had lifted incomes massively in the West and Japan. Still, the difficulties encountered in managing the oil shocks implied that growth in the liberal capitalist world might well not continue.

In the competition for influence in the Third World, moreover, the United States and its allies did not seem to be faring terribly well. On the "southern flank" of Europe, Spain and Portugal were in the midst of democratic transitions that could turn out well, or not. Because Portugal remained a colonial power in Africa, its transformation would have ramifications in Mozambique and Angola, where the Soviets were backing insurgencies. The success of these movements would put further pressure on the apartheid regime in South Africa and the settler state of Rhodesia. Neither the United States nor Britain was eager to defend these racist and rogue states, but they did not want to see them replaced by movements and parties close to the Soviet Union. There were also troubles on the Horn of Africa, where it seemed that Soviet-backed forces were making progress. In both these regions, the Soviet presence per se was minimal, but its aid was important and its influence was spread by Cuban forces. In Latin America, insurgents were battling governments allied with the United States in El Salvador, Guatemala, and Nicaragua. The Sandinistas, with support from the Cubans, toppled the Somoza regime in Nicaragua in 1979. In the Middle East, the Iranian

Revolution chased the Shah of Iran, another longtime US ally, from power and from the country in early 1979. Iran shares a border more than five hundred miles long with its neighbor to the east, Afghanistan. The government in Afghanistan was controlled by pro-Soviet leaders who in the late 1970s confronted local insurgents inspired by Islamist sentiments. The Soviets sent thirty thousand troops to prop up their Afghan allies on December 24, 1979.

It made little sense analytically to lump together events in Afghanistan and Nicaragua, or Nicaragua and Mozambique, and even less to interpret the fall of the Shah as benefiting the Soviet Union. What these disparate events did have in common was that they could all be seen as in some sense defeats, or setbacks, for the United States and its allies. The fact that they occurred close together and that they could be attributed, fairly or not, to the weakness of the Carter administration served further to connect them. Together, they seemed to contradict the premises of détente and to undermine the reality of it. The belief that the Soviet Union was continuing to develop and deploy nuclear weapons even while proclaiming its support for détente was taken as a further indication that the policy was flawed and ineffective and that the balance of advantage, or what the Soviets termed the "correlation of forces," no longer favored the US, or the West more broadly. A key move was the Soviet decision in 1976 to station a new generation of intermediate-range nuclear weapons, SS-20s, where they could reach Western Europe. The Europeans were worried, for the new weapons could threaten Europe while sparing the United States, implicitly raising the question of whether the US would invite a global confrontation to protect its European allies. The Soviets clearly sought to encourage distrust within NATO. Helmut Schmidt, the German chancellor, raised the issue forcefully and James Callaghan did so quietly, and the ultimate response was the decision to deploy American Pershing and cruise missiles in Europe. These "Euromissiles," which Carter approved but would be delivered while Ronald Reagan was president, became hugely controversial and raised tensions with the Soviets and within the alliance.

The effect of these mostly unrelated developments was a serious intensification of Cold War rhetoric and a ratcheting up of the arms race. Defense spending rose by over 10 percent in the last year of the

Carter administration and by still more after Reagan's election. This "Second Cold War," as it has been called, would continue until the elevation of Mikhail Gorbachev as Soviet leader and the resumption of arms control talks.[2] While it lasted, it raised fears and elicited protests and wasted a ton of money. Cold War animosity reached a peak in 1983: Euromissiles were installed that year; Reagan referred to the Soviet Union as the "evil empire"; and the United States announced the Strategic Defense Initiative (SDI, or, more commonly, "Star Wars"), which raised the destabilizing prospect that America would try to develop a missile defense system which, the Soviets and others claimed, would give it a first-strike capability and increase the likelihood of nuclear war. Given the state of tension in the early 1980s, nobody would have predicted that the Cold War would be over by the end of the decade, that the "socialist" states in Eastern Europe would collapse in 1989, and that the USSR itself would cease to exist by December 1991.

The path that led from the Second Cold War to the end of the Cold War was not simple. It would require new leadership in the Soviet Union and a shift in the stance of the United States.[3] Upon taking office, the Reagan administration boosted defense spending and adopted a more virulently anti-Communist posture. It focused much of its attention on Latin America, where it abandoned the human rights agenda of Jimmy Carter and threw its support behind local strongmen. The rationale had been provided by UN ambassador Jeanne Kirkpatrick, whose famous article "Dictators and Double Standards" made the case that authoritarian leaders of the sort preferred by the US could be encouraged to become more democratic, whereas those supported by the Soviets could not be reformed.[4] Her views and priorities were shared by Alexander Haig, Reagan's first secretary of state. The administration's strategy was to put pressure on the Soviet Union by probing around the periphery of its sphere of influence on the assumption that it was weakest there. Latin America was the ideal place for such an approach, for it was a long way from the Soviet Union and very close, geographically and historically, to the United States. Afghanistan, where the Soviets were tied to unpopular leaders and opposed by indigenous Muslim fighters, was another potential weak spot.

The Reagan administration did not at first have much hope for more direct meddling in the Soviet Union or in Eastern Europe, but the emergence and then suppression of Solidarity, the union that began in the Gdansk shipyards and became a national resistance, opened up possibilities for pressuring the Soviets closer to home. Poland, long an uneasy Soviet satellite, had secured a measure of autonomy denied to other states in Eastern Europe. The Reagan administration decided to impose sanctions on the Soviet Union after the declaration of martial law in December 1981 and began calling out the Soviets for violations of human rights. Reagan and his advisors had previously eschewed talk of human rights because of its association with Carter and the fact that a focus on human rights would make it harder to work with dictatorial regimes battling left-wing insurgencies in Latin America and elsewhere. That began to change when the invocation of human rights became a stick with which to beat the Soviet Union.

Efforts to encourage trouble on the peripheries of Soviet power and to denounce its suppression of rights in Poland were probably of less importance to the administration than its defense buildup. Intensifying the arms race was, of course, the opposite of disarmament, and for much of Reagan's first term there would be no dialogue with the Soviet Union on the issue. The administration's attitude began to change in 1983, partly because of the reaction, domestically and in Western Europe, to its aggressive moves and words. A precondition for the shift had occurred in August 1982, when George Shultz replaced Alexander Haig as secretary of state. There were also large-scale protests over Euromissiles that forced Reagan, as well as European leaders like Thatcher, to adjust at least their rhetoric. In the United States, the nuclear freeze movement garnered widespread support among the public and in Congress. Reagan apparently felt compelled to surround the administration's more controversial policies with verbal commitments to pursue arms control; and he went as far as to say that if the US succeeded at creating a missile defense system, it would share it with the Soviets. Two other considerations pushed the US to become more interested in arms negotiations: the fact that, after two years of increased spending, Reagan was himself impressed at the strength of the US military; and intelligence reports that in November 1983 the Soviets had interpreted a series of NATO military exercises labeled Able Archer as the beginning of an actual attack and gone on full alert.[5] The time had come, it seemed, to cool things down in the new Cold War, which was dangerously warming. Shultz soon began exploring the possibility of talks with Moscow.

Talking with Moscow would prove complicated. Soviet leaders expected little from Reagan and were not eager to accept whatever terms and proposals the Americans would come up with. There was also the practical question of who among the aging Soviet leaders would be able to speak. Leonid Brezhnev, the longtime Soviet leader, died in 1982; his successor, Yuri Andropov, presided over the country from November 1982 but died in February 1984; and his successor, Konstantin Chernenko, was sick when he took over, could barely do his job, and died in March 1985. He was succeeded by Mikhail Gorbachev. Gorbachev was of a younger generation and brought new energy and ideas to the job. He would last until the Soviet Union ceased to exist and he would be largely responsible for ending the Cold War. It was Margaret Thatcher, not Reagan, who met Gorbachev first and took his measure. She told a BBC interviewer: "I like Mr. Gorbachev. We can do business together."[6]

Gorbachev would surprise everyone with the ambition of his plans to reform the Soviet Union and his willingness to begin the process of disarmament. While he undertook to open Soviet society, the economy, and the political system, he also participated in five separate summit meetings with Reagan between November 1985 and December 1988. The two leaders clearly had chemistry, but it was also in their joint interests to rein in the arms race and to begin to disarm. The most concrete agreement was the INF (Intermediate-Range Nuclear Forces) Treaty, signed in December 1987. It called for the elimination of an entire class of weapons, which included the Euromissiles that had been stationed in Europe only in 1983. The summits were famous for what they achieved and for the range of topics on which progress was begun, but they were even more famous for the visionary proposals made by the leaders of the two superpowers. At Reykjavik in October 1986, for example, the Soviets proposed cutting stores of nuclear weapons in half, and the US countered with an offer that was not quite so good. As the talks continued, Reagan said, "It would be fine with me if we eliminate all nuclear weapons," to which Gorbachev replied, "We can do that."[7] In the end, the issue of Star Wars precluded an agreement, but the willingness of Reagan and Gorbachev to speak of a world without nuclear weapons was catalytic.

The talk was serious enough to worry Reagan's more hawkish advisors, and Margaret Thatcher flew to Camp David to remind Reagan that the United States and Britain still relied upon nuclear weapons.

Negotiations and eventual agreements on nuclear weapons removed the most threatening feature of the Cold War. They were accompanied, moreover, by the resolution of a host of regional confrontations stretching from Latin America to southern Africa to Afghanistan. Essentially, Soviet leaders chose to pull back from global competition in order to focus on domestic reform. The United States had in large part moved away from its support of local authoritarians and begun to advocate democratic transitions during the 1980s. The effect was an easing of tensions in parts of the world where Cold War rivalries had previously sustained conflict and caused huge damage. Probably the most potent symbol of this new and more thoroughgoing détente was the cooperation, however brief and grudging, between the US and its allies and the Soviet Union over Iraq's invasion of Kuwait in 1990. Geopolitical tension would return soon enough, but the shift wrought by the ending of the global Cold War was palpable and widely welcomed.

Of course, since the Cold War was a confrontation between states with distinct and opposed economic systems, its definitive end would come only when the "socialist" states in Eastern Europe and the Soviet Union collapsed. These endings were closely interconnected, but nevertheless distinct. Because "actually existing socialism" had been imposed on Eastern Europe from outside, it had never acquired legitimacy there. With the exception of Yugoslavia, the parties that ran the countries of Eastern Europe were likewise not organically linked to the peoples over whom they ruled. They had been cobbled together from the remnants of local Communists who survived the Second World War and other social democratic or peasant parties, with a sprinkling of anti-fascist liberals, held together by the looming presence of the Red Army. Over time, the members and leaders of these parties would inevitably become invested in the institutions that afforded them power and privilege, but those institutions remained fragile constructions. The states in Eastern Europe were brittle, despite their formidable repressive powers.

In consequence, the regimes in the East were reliant on the fear of Soviet intervention to keep their subjects cowed. That fear had been

repeatedly reinforced by repression. A poignant example was the suppression of the Prague Spring in 1968, but memories had begun to fade
two decades on. The more interesting and recent example was in Poland,
but that taught a rather different lesson. The Soviets certainly encouraged the imposition of martial law and the banning of Solidarity in December 1981, but they did not intervene directly, leaving the job to locals
like General Jaruzelski. The repression was not very thorough or effective. The regime felt compelled to issue an amnesty to political prisoners
in 1986, and Solidarity survived to continue its efforts. By 1988, it was in
"Roundtable" talks with the government over policy. In June 1989, Solidarity swept to victory in elections and by August was the dominant
force in government. What happened in Poland reverberated throughout the region. The fact that the weakening of the regime was allowed to
proceed without intervention seemed to confirm what Gorbachev said
about recognizing the right of peoples to form their own government in
his speech to the UN in December 1988. The "Brezhnev doctrine," announced in the aftermath of the suppression of the Prague Spring,
was no longer operative. It was becoming clear that the Soviet Union
lacked the desire, and maybe even the capacity, to intervene to protect its
clients.

It was this perception as much as the specific example of Poland
that led Eastern Europeans to revolt and overthrow the local Communist governments from Germany to Bulgaria in the fall of 1989.[8] There
was little violence, except in Romania, and even there it was not widespread; and it was quickly over. Government and party leaders in East
Germany came close to unleashing forces against the protesters, but
backed down.[9] In other countries, the existing leadership largely acquiesced in Communism's demise, although Yugoslavia was disintegrating
in its own unhappy fashion. Ceauşescu in Romania held out, but the
army and other leaders abandoned him, and he was shot on Christmas
Day. The rapidity and thoroughness of the collapse was telling proof of
the weakness of the socialist regimes. The nature of their ending was
also an indication of what was to follow: socialism would not be replaced by some halfway house between socialism and capitalism, by a
humane and democratic socialism or social democracy, but by capitalism, with all its dynamism—and all its iniquities. The new states would

in theory be democratic, for no other model seemed viable, but because the old regimes had suppressed normal politics for forty years, the parties and movements that took over were weak and not deeply rooted. Parties of the center-left were particularly disadvantaged: they had no organizational presence and would have considerable difficulty distinguishing themselves from the discredited Communist parties.

The collapse of socialism in Eastern Europe did not help Gorbachev in his efforts to open up and liberalize the Soviet Union. Gorbachev had encouraged reforms within the Soviet bloc, but had not expected that the bloc would completely disintegrate. Its disappearance did not necessarily represent a security threat to the Soviet regime, but Gorbachev's opponents in the military and intelligence services claimed it weakened the country by leaving it exposed to attack from the West. The very same people were also unhappy at the gathering pace of arms control. Gorbachev's agenda was encapsulated in two words: *perestroika*, which meant transformation in the economy and in society, and *glasnost*, or transparency and openness. His problem was that every move to reduce the controls on which the command economy relied threatened the interests of those who ran it, while initiatives to open up the party and loosen its grip were a threat to those whose lives and livelihoods depended on holding onto their positions atop the party and the economy and in the state apparatus. Together, these people were often referred to as the *nomenklatura*. Gorbachev faced constant resistance from them, which in turn led him to propose more drastic measures to weaken those who opposed him.

The struggle was never resolved under Gorbachev, because the crisis it precipitated caused the state itself to unravel. As the center lost its grip, Gorbachev came to realize that the state would have to be reconstituted by redistributing authority between the central state and the republics. In 1991 he and his allies worked on a new treaty between the republics of the USSR. Power was already leaking out from the center as its paralysis grew and was being grabbed by the republics, most importantly the Russian Republic, then led by Boris Yeltsin. Just before the treaty was to be signed, an old guard of military and KGB leaders staged a coup. On August 18 its leaders flew to Crimea to meet Gorbachev at his dacha, demanding that he order a state of emergency and empower the coup's organizers while he was confined in the south. He refused, but they proclaimed the emergency the next day on their own. Yeltsin held out at the White House in Moscow and urged the military to join him. Preparations for an attack were made, but it was called off because the troops were unwilling to carry it out. Gorbachev returned to Moscow on August 22, and leaders of the coup were arrested. Several committed suicide. Gorbachev thought he was back in control, and he officially was, but it was Yeltsin and his allies who had defeated the coup and it was they who emerged as the de facto leaders of the country. Yeltsin and the leaders of other republics signed their own union treaty in early December, effectively abolishing the USSR, and Gorbachev soon resigned as president of the nonexistent state.[10]

After the Cold War, After Socialism

The demise of the Soviet Union was messier than the collapse of the smaller states in Eastern Europe, but it was equally decisive. The events left an enormous gap, for it meant that governance and economic life needed to be re-created on a new basis over a huge swathe of the world's territory, containing hundreds of millions of people. What would replace socialism as an economic system, and what sorts of new governing arrangements would be worked out when Communist states and parties were gone? Who would decide, and how? And what would be the implications for the international order? Would the new economies be fair and open, would the political systems be more or less democratic, and would the reshaped global order be genuinely liberal?

The reach of the liberal order that the United States, Britain, and their Western allies sought to set up after World War II had been limited by the very existence of the Soviet Union and its control of Eastern Europe. Communist states remained immune to liberalism. Those places and peoples that were still part of the European empires after the war could also not really be considered part of any liberal order. They could perhaps join up after decolonization—they did typically join the UN and engaged in world trade—but they were seldom liberal democracies. The other exception involved those Third World states run by local authoritarians whom the United States, and occasionally the Soviets, helped to hold onto power for fear that, if they fell, the Soviets or the US would gain influence. The policy of propping up dictators had begun to change in the 1980s, but until then it further restricted the reach of liberal order.[11]

The dissolution of the regimes of Eastern Europe and the Soviet Union presented the possibility that a fuller and more meaningful version of liberal order could be put in place. In order for this to be realized, much would have to go right after 1989. The political systems established in the formerly Communist states would need to be democratic; economies that had been state-run and state-owned would have to be replaced by economies in which the key decisions would be made via markets and more or less private actors; new states and economies would have to be integrated into the institutions that governed the world economy and the system of states. And if the emerging liberal order were to be truly global, it would have to allow for the resolution of local crises in the Third World, many of which had been exacerbated and allowed to fester because of Cold War rivalries. A truly global regime would also seek to include China, though how and on what terms would never be resolved. Still, there would be at least some effort to bring China into the global order, or at least into a stable relationship with that order. How much of this would be possible in the decade or so after the end of the Cold War was not clear in 1989–91, nor would it be that much clearer by the turn of the millennium. Even a partial review reveals serious initiatives and some real progress on each of these fronts, but nothing approaching the full realization of the vision of a truly global and effective liberal order held by its advocates.

The political transitions in the formerly socialist countries would, if they were to succeed, have to be led by citizens of those countries. They were hampered by the fact that those nations' experiences of democracy were not of long standing and not much worth celebrating. In the late 1930s, authoritarian rulers had been in charge across much of Eastern Europe until they were swept away or incorporated by the Nazis and their machinery of war and repression. These regimes and leaders had in turn been crushed by the advancing Red Army and thoroughly repressed after 1945. That meant that local right-wing and nationalist parties were largely wiped out. That did not mean that ethno-nationalist and right-wing sentiments vanished from the hearts and minds of people in Central and Eastern Europe, but expressing them had not been possible. On the other hand, after 1945 the Communists overwhelmed the forces of the center-left, forcing them to collaborate and therefore lose whatever integrity they might have possessed or driving them underground. The consistent attempts by these regimes to crush or control the institutions of civil society made it extremely difficult for center-left or liberal oppositions to establish roots within the political cultures of the Eastern European states. When the states began to crumble in 1989, it was not obvious who would succeed the leaders who had fallen.

An exception was Poland, where Solidarity could provide a basis for a new government. It had become a force because it was first and foremost a trade union and enjoyed working-class support and because of its ties to the Catholic Church, which had preserved its role in Poland as churches elsewhere in the bloc had not. In Hungary, the existing leadership had begun to undertake a gradual liberalization before the collapse and the political transition there was less abrupt. In Czechoslovakia, the liberal playwright and poet Václav Havel had participated in the Prague Spring and become a founder of Charter 77, a group committed to holding the state to its Helsinki commitments. The Civic Forum he led in 1989 propelled him into the presidency, but the nation split into the Czech Republic and Slovakia in 1993. The liberalism he represented was sincere but not very robust. In East Germany, the leaders of protests in 1989 were mostly liberal Protestant clergymen, and they briefly entered government along with a few centrist politicians as the regime fell apart. It quickly became clear, however, that such leaders were themselves transitional; and almost immediately, the major parties in West Germany, the Christian Democrats and the Social Democrats, expanded to the east and were the dominant forces in the March 1990 elections, whose results ensured that East and West Germany would reunite in short order.

Further south, Yugoslavia descended into a civil war that eventually occasioned intervention by the United States and NATO. Internal political developments there thus became the subject of international negotiations. In Romania, the National Salvation Front (FSN) emerged as the dominant political actor. It spoke of revolution and claimed a social democratic heritage, but it derived real strength from its ability to take over the apparatus and use the resources, and some of the personnel, of the old Communist Party. It splintered, but each faction practiced clientelist politics and took part in corruption by seizing privatized state assets as the opportunity to do so presented itself. In Bulgaria, the Communists labeled themselves "social democrats" and dominated the new government as the Bulgarian Socialist Party. As in Romania, the successor party to the Communists could build upon their infrastructure, resources, and, to a considerable extent, social base in the working class. The new parties sought to distance themselves from Marxism and the repressive policies of the old regimes, but governing in the new environment proved difficult.

It was in large part the lack of rooted and trusted political parties and institutions, a direct legacy of Communist rule, that made it so hard to govern these new political entities. The difficulty was seriously compounded by the fact that these countries needed to transition from a socialist to a capitalist economy while creating new political institutions. Moving from a command to a market economy involves two sets of tasks. This first is dismantling the command economy, which requires ending controls on prices, including rents and wages, opening up trade, and imposing budgets sufficiently balanced to instill confidence. The second involves turning state assets into private property and getting production going again. What is ordinarily the first step, abandoning controls, is the most painful, and it is risky, for it leads to higher prices for basic needs that are seldom accompanied by wage increases that might allow consumers to cope. Across the former Soviet bloc, in fact, few businesses were economically viable, for they produced shabby goods with outdated technologies. The result was not merely that wages would not rise, but that they would fall or, more likely still, that uneconomic businesses would simply cease to operate. Eventually, and sometimes rather quickly, decontrol would bring more goods to market, but people could seldom afford to buy them. Everywhere this passage was painful and led to bitter disputes about whether to proceed in stages or to move to market prices all at once and administer a kind of "shock therapy" to the economy. Inevitably, political leaders wavered on the question and often paid a price, being forced from office very quickly. This happened both to those parties and leaders who chose to go slow as well as to those who did not; and it ensured that when new parties and leaders came to power, they were faced with the same tough choices and often experienced similar fates. It might well have been expected that liberal, pro-market parties and advocates would be best suited to the moment, but they were often blamed for the chaos that followed decontrol. The effect was that liberalism as a political force suffered serious long-term damage. Instability was widespread.

Eventually, decontrol occurred, but at great cost in terms of living standards, economic growth, and political stability. The cost was all the greater because it was mostly borne locally. There were loans and some grants from the IMF and other institutional lenders, and some aid from wealthier countries, but it was woefully insufficient. There had been calls in the early transition years for a new Marshall Plan for Eastern Europe and the former Soviet Union, but they were not listened to and little was done. The main reason for this lack of support was that economic policy making in most capitalist states and in international economic institutions was decidedly market-oriented, and the first rule in such a framework was to keep taxes and spending low. A more generous policy from the international community might have eased the pain of the move to market prices, but it was not forthcoming.

The other major task in making the transition was to privatize state assets. This would include, though often at a lag, housing. The complications in this process were daunting. To begin, many state industries were not worth much and there were few likely buyers. These could be sold off in a more or less democratic fashion by giving shares to their workers, but what then? Would industries resume operations, and how? There was also the lack of functioning capital markets and, in many cases, the absence of legal frameworks to regulate purchases. In the confusion and uncertainty insiders had huge advantages. So, too, did criminals who had made money from the black markets that had flourished because of the failures of the old system. As a result, state assets were often seized by the people who had run them before the collapse, enriching the very interests whose privileged rule had produced systemic economic failure or those who had thrived on its chaos and corruption. The most valuable assets were in any case extractive industries, and the Eastern European countries possessed few of these. Occasionally, manufacturing plants would be bought by foreigners, Germans most often, and in these cases Western firms could make better use of them than local party-appointed managers had. Still, these were all assets of the states, and ultimately of the workers whose coerced and underpaid labor had built them up. Few ordinary Eastern Europeans received much benefit from their transfer.

Privatization did not have to be a driver of inequality, and in rare instances it was not, but in much of the formerly socialist world it was. It was especially extreme in the former Soviet Union. Mikhail Gorbachev's efforts to open up the economy had been thwarted by the resistance of vested interests. Two of his advisors—Yavlinsky and Shatalin—came up with a plan for decontrol and the transfer of assets from the state to the people in "500 Days," as the plan itself was known. By this time, Gorbachev was trying to placate the less reform-minded of his colleagues and so his support was lukewarm and the plan was never really implemented. Nor, in fact, was an alternative plan authored by Nikolai Ryzhkov put in place, even though it was approved by the Supreme Soviet. Later, Yeltsin would give his strong support to the idea and in January 1992 told his economics minister, Yegor Gaidar, to make it happen. A form of shock therapy, it caused substantial hardship, but it did gradually ease shortages. It was meant also to privatize the economy, though that process went more slowly. The results were nevertheless similar to those in Eastern Europe, with insiders and criminals benefiting disproportionately. Russia's continuing financial crisis made things worse there. With the government unable to collect taxes, in 1995 it instituted a "Loans for Shares" program in which wealthy bankers would loan to the government in return for shares in privatizing industries.

The speed and thoroughness of the fall of the Soviet Union belied the fact that support for the old regime was substantial. After 1991, the opposition was led by Communists or former Communists, operating under different labels, or by Russian nationalists. Between them, they made life difficult for Yeltsin and slowed the progress of his reforms. By March 1993 supporters of Yeltsin were outnumbered in the Russian parliament by those adhering to the Russia Unity bloc, composed of former Communists, nationalists, and a motley collection of other political forces. Confrontations continued from March through September, even though Yeltsin prevailed in a referendum on April 25. On September 21, Yeltsin declared Congress and its Supreme Soviet dissolved; the Constitutional Court quickly decided that the president's actions were unconstitutional; and the Congress voted to impeach Yeltsin. Members of parliament and their allies occupied the parliament building and a standoff ensued for nearly two weeks. For a time, it was unclear what position the armed forces would take, but they rallied to Yeltsin. The White House was stormed on October 4. Yeltsin went on to consolidate power, and he managed to secure approval of a new constitution. In new elections in December 1993, however, his opponents largely prevailed and Yeltsin was forced to govern through the use of emergency powers. The main source of contention was economic reform, whose fate would remain in the balance for several more years. The new state would also have to contend with the separatist movement in the mostly Muslim region of Chechnya, to which Yeltsin responded with force. Democratic transition did not come easy to Russia; and it would not be fully established before Vladimir Putin rose to power. Putin would initially proceed with pro-market reforms and bring a measure of stability, but his Bonapartist style of rule became increasingly authoritarian.

If liberal order was to be successfully extended to Eastern Europe and the former Soviet Union, effective transitions to democracy and market economies were essential. A decade after the end of the Cold War market economies had been established across the vast region, though their performance was uneven and they were marred by stark inequalities stemming from flawed privatizations. The move toward democracy was less straightforward. Elections and parliaments had become pretty much universal, but the formal adherence to democratic processes could not disguise the illiberal practices and corruption that affected political outcomes and rewards. A more robust commitment to democratic norms was evident in those countries that joined or sought to join NATO and/or the European Union, for those international organizations demanded it as a condition of membership. Ideally, membership ought to "lock in" democratic practices and enforcement of human rights. Once a country was admitted to NATO or the EU, however, it would prove difficult for either institution to prevent backsliding, the growth of illiberal politics, and the emergence of illiberal leaders. There had been progress toward both political democracy and liberal economies during the 1990s, but things remained precarious.

Reshaping International Institutions

Efforts to reshape international institutions and security alliances after the Cold War were rather more successful, both formally and in practice. Eastern European states had been in the United Nations long before 1989, but they were forced to follow the Soviet line. That was no longer necessary. The former Soviet republics could also now participate as independent states and they, too, could act independently. And in its last years the Soviet Union had become more cooperative and less likely to use its veto to frustrate actions that had broad international support. That would continue for some time when Russia assumed the USSR's place on the Security Council, except on issues involving areas of long-standing interest, as was the case with Serbia. The effect was to raise hopes that the United Nations would begin to fulfill the promise of those who had created the organization in 1945. Such hopes were accompanied and fostered by a growing interest in expanding human rights and protesting their denial or violation. The discourse of human rights was everywhere in the early post–Cold War era; commitments to honor rights were written into international treaties and incorporated into the mission statements and programs of a host of international organizations and agencies.[12] So, too, were pledges to foster democracy and responsible government. NATO membership required that members commit to these principles, for example, as did the European Union. Even the IMF began evaluating countries in terms of governance. A trade agreement between the EU and South Africa offers an example of the ubiquity of such rhetoric and formal commitments. Its preamble read, "Recognising the historic achievements of the South African people in abolishing the apartheid system and building a new political order based on the rule of law, human rights and democracy . . . [and] recalling the firm commitment of the Parties to the principles of the United Nations Charter and to democratic principles and fundamental human rights as laid down in the Universal Declaration of Human Rights . . ."[13]

The rhetorical invocation of human rights, good governance, and democracy did not make them real, but it mattered because it affected decisions about money, alliances, and membership in international organizations. Aid and loans, opportunities for increased trade, and access to the international community increasingly depended on adherence to these commitments. In tough cases, more rigorous enforcement was required, and the discourse of rights and democracy was less useful. The crisis in Rwanda was the most obvious example, and the international community and the United Nations were found wanting. The reaction to this genocide was nevertheless significant, for it led to a growing recognition that local atrocities occurring within states might well compel intervention by outside forces and prompted a series of debates about "humanitarian intervention." Action of this sort was legally and politically complicated because it contradicted the principle of national sovereignty. After Rwanda the most egregious case was in the former Yugoslavia, with Serbia in conflict with Croatia and Bosnia. It was in this civil war that the phrase "ethnic cleansing" had its origin. The United States and its NATO allies eventually intervened, and the Dayton Accords of 1995 imposed a solution to the civil war, but it was controversial. The Russians chose to oppose it, but did not act; and there was much debate in the US and Europe about the wisdom of intervention. Critics even spoke of "the imperialism of human rights," while advocates began to craft arguments about what came to be called "the responsibility to protect." The crisis over Kosovo in 1999, again involving Serbia, occasioned another intervention and another round of debate. US and NATO intervention was effective in ending the crisis, and after it was over a UN commission declared the intervention technically "illegal" but "legitimate." Later, in 2005, the UN approved a document outlining the "responsibility to protect."[14]

By the time the United Nations, "the parliament of man," figured out its position on humanitarian intervention, the United States had put together two "coalitions of the willing" to invade first Afghanistan and then Iraq. The mixed results of the interventions in the 1990s and the fierce opposition aroused by the invasion of Iraq caused the notion of humanitarian intervention to fall out of favor. Even before this, the high hopes that some had entertained for the UN in a post–Cold War world had begun to fade; in their stead, states and peoples chose to trust their security to more traditional alliances. The most important of these was NATO, which expanded and redefined its mission. NATO expansion was welcomed by those Eastern European states that feared Russian revanchism but, not surprisingly, opposed by Russia, where it fueled that revanchism. Whether an alternative path was possible that would have led to a more stable world order, with Russia feeling less threatened and more involved, remains a matter of debate, though it is reasonable to suggest that the main determinants of Russian policy were not what outsiders did, but internal pressures and choices.[15]

Probably the greatest advance of liberal order took place in international economic relations. The world economy was becoming more global from the 1970s, particularly in matters of finance. The trend accelerated in the 1980s with the turn toward more market-oriented policies in the US and the UK and their efforts to convince other major nations to further open their economies. The member states of the EC signed the Single European Act in February 1986 and agreed to complete the internal market by the end of 1992. The beginning of serious bargaining in the Uruguay Round of GATT talks in 1986 added to the momentum behind opening international trade and finance. The "big bang" in the City of London in October 1986 was yet another step toward freeing up the movement of capital and a sign that London would be open to American banks and investors and that the British and the Americans would compete in European markets.

After 1989 sustained efforts were made to integrate the economies of the formerly socialist countries into the world market and the institutions that governed it. The IMF and the World Bank would focus much of their attention on assisting the transition to market economies in the East through grants, loans, and advice. So, too, would governments in advanced capitalist countries, directly and via central banks and private financial institutions. A new bank, the European Bank for Reconstruction and Development, was created in 1990, with Europeans very much taking the initiative, specifically "to foster the transition towards open-market economies." The United States joined up and, in agreement with other founding governments, insisted on "political conditionality of a democratic nature," and the new bank's charter restricted its lending to countries "committed to and applying the principles of multi-party democracy, pluralism and market economies."[16] The European Community (after 1992 the European Union) made a rather more serious commitment of resources than did others, and played an active role in guiding the economic and political transitions. It also offered Eastern European countries the prospects of membership in the EU and worked closely to lay out the steps needed for that to happen. Much of the success achieved in the region was due to Europe.

As rapid, if rough and turbulent, transitions were transforming Eastern Europe and Russia, the Uruguay Round of trade negotiations dragged on. They were focused on politically sensitive issues whose resolution—agriculture, textiles, services, and intellectual property—engaged the interests of sectors previously untouched by moves to open trade. The United States and the European Union were at odds over agriculture, and developing countries were eager for easier access to the markets of developed countries. The successful conclusion of the North American Free Trade Agreement (NAFTA) in 1993 was a spur and something of a model. Ultimately, compromises were reached and the Round was concluded in 1994. The final agreement not only ratified the deals reached but created the World Trade Organization (WTO), which came into existence on January 1, 1995. It was genuinely meant as a global organization that all countries could join. Among its founding members were not merely those countries that had long participated in the GATT regime, but most Eastern European nations—Poland, Hungary, Romania, the Czech Republic, Slovakia, and, in 1996, Bulgaria—emerging economies like Brazil, India, Indonesia, and South Africa, and many developing countries. The European Union was a formal member from the beginning and what had been East Germany, now reunified with the rest of the country, was also there from the beginning. The Baltic states would enter a few years later. China was admitted in 2001 and Russia joined in 2012. The establishment of the WTO meant that the framework governing the world economy had been updated in a fashion that was more market-friendly and inclusive. It was a framework within which those economies transitioning from state to market could operate in world markets, and it served to accelerate globalization. The long-term consequences of globalization were as yet largely unforeseen, but it was very definitely on the march. It would take another major step forward when China joined the WTO, again with effects on employment that were not yet fully in evidence.

Liberal Order, Recast

The international order that came into being after the Cold War was, almost by definition, more liberal than the order that existed during the Cold War. It was more liberal because of the simple fact that the reach of political and economic liberalism was vastly extended. The end of socialism in Eastern Europe and the Soviet Union meant that authoritarian regimes sitting on top of command economies over an enormous geographical area, with large populations, were now gone; and whatever was put in their place would of necessity be more "liberal." Various measures of the spread of democracy peaked in the decade after the Cold War ended; so, too, did estimates of the openness of markets.

It is nonetheless reasonable to ask how deep and thorough the transformations were, how secure the apparent advance of democratic rule, and how firm the commitment to the maintenance of open markets. During the 1990s there did not seem to be a viable alternative to liberalism. Given that, and the opportunity it created, how successful were the efforts to plant democratic roots in places where democratic traditions were weak; how effective were the campaigns and laws meant to instill respect for human rights; and were the new, emerging market economies more dynamic than what had come before and capable of generating wealth for ordinary citizens?

Outcomes varied from place to place, and over time, but the record was very mixed. By the year 2000 transitions to market economies probably had produced more concrete results that were likely to stick than had the shakier and more uneven transitions to democracy. The creation of market economies had not yet brought much economic growth, however, and had been accompanied by enormous inequalities. The privatization of state assets had almost everywhere benefited insiders, doing little for workers, farmers, and people not connected to the old regime. Ordinary people fared better in the Eastern European states that attracted investment from the West or that retained capacity in the few industries that were not outdated and backward. There was not much of either, but some. Farmers in the East sought markets in the West and the leaders of those nations were eager to get access to the EU, but the EU had its own farmers to protect; and it did. The other path to economic growth was the export of raw materials. Russia could and did benefit from that, but the countries of Eastern Europe had few resources to export. Even then, the export of commodities like oil and gas, although it put vast wealth in the hands of those who controlled the resources, added few jobs. Those who became wealthy were more likely to send their newfound fortunes abroad, for they understood the lack of investment opportunities locally. So, the economic transition was done and settled, but hardly a great success.

Democratic transition proved to be an even harder task. In Western Europe after the Second World War, stable democracies were built on growing economies. With anemic growth, political stability was more difficult to achieve after 1989 in the East. Again, the countries of Eastern Europe did better than the nations left behind by the implosion of the Soviet Union. The Baltic states—Latvia, Lithuania, and Estonia—had more robust protest movements than other Soviet republics; and they boasted civic cultures and national sentiments that could and did provide the basis for political stability and democratic practices once they had broken away from the Soviet Union. Elsewhere in the former Soviet republics there had not been much agitation for reform, and in a number of these countries rulers from the Soviet period, or those who emerged from the wreckage that attended the collapse, continued to govern much as their authoritarian predecessors had, though, having dispensed with ideological tests of loyalty, they would add more nepotism, clientelism, and appeals to nationalism to their repertoire of rule.

In Russia itself, Yeltsin's appointment of Yevgeny Primakov as prime minister in September 1998 brought a measure of stability. His popularity and effectiveness were seen by Yeltsin as a threat, however, and he was dismissed in May 1999. He would be replaced by Vladimir Putin in August. In December, Yeltsin resigned and Putin became acting president. He was then elected to the post in March 2000. Primakov and Putin were both part of the political and bureaucratic establishment and had backgrounds in the intelligence services. Primakov headed up the Foreign Intelligence Service (SVR), formerly the First Chief Directorate of the KGB, from 1991 to 1996. Putin had served in the KGB from 1975 until 1990 and was stationed in East Germany from 1985 to 1990, where he saw the coming dissolution of Communist rule. In 1998, Putin became director of the FSB, successor to the KGB. The backgrounds of Primakov and Putin were a stark reminder that in the new Russia there was much continuity with the Soviet regime. In eastern Germany, the fall of the government was followed by the dismantling of the secret police, the Stasi; in Russia, the security and intelligence agencies got new names but remained much the same in practice and retained a prominent role in the new government. Putin would preside over the consolidation of a market economy and implement the reforms needed to do that. He would work hard to ensure that the oligarchs who controlled so much of the economy submitted to his political domination, but in exchange they got to keep their money. No thoroughgoing reform of institutions and norms occurred, though Putin's government itself became increasingly secure.

The imperfect and incomplete transitions to democracy would make the states in the east vulnerable to parties and leaders whose commitment to democratic norms was at best superficial. The economies of the new states also fared less well than had been hoped for after the fall of Communism. Markets and property rights were established, but robust growth was elusive. The international order constructed during the 1990s was thus liberal in form and in rhetoric and its economies operated roughly according to market principles, but the political systems in these newly liberal spaces were only partially democratic and as yet lacked the institutions and political cultures that would allow them to endure as democracies.

These modest outcomes were no doubt due in large part to the fact that the project of creating a liberal order on a nearly global scale was a giant, and perhaps impossible, undertaking. There had never been an economic transition to a market economy so vast, so thorough, and so rapid as Eastern Europeans and the peoples of the former Soviet Union were forced to carry out. The extent of the effort required was possibly best illustrated in Germany. Under Helmut Kohl, it was decided to thoroughly integrate the former East Germany into the newly unified German state and to bring wages and living standards there up to those prevailing in West Germany. The government also chose to undertake infrastructure investments so that people living in the east would have resources and services comparable to those in the west. The costs proved enormous and arguably depressed economic growth for a decade. Implementing similar programs elsewhere was unimaginable.

Setting up viable democracies in the region proved equally daunting; success would be partial, superficial, and at risk of being reversed. The disappointing outcome was not for lack of effort, internally or externally. Internally, advocates of democracy, rights, and transparency worked valiantly to make their principles the law of the land and to introduce and entrench appropriate practices. They were handicapped by lack of experience and of money, but also because the tasks they confronted were so great. They had to build parties from nothing, to found newspapers and media where the old models were corrupt or bankrupt, and to develop policies and programs amid great uncertainty. It proved almost impossible for post–Cold War parties and leaders in the region simultaneously to guide the transition to a market-based economy and oversee the implantation of democracy. They were helped by assistance from outside. Grants and loans came from the West and financial experts offered their advice. Western NGOs sprang up in the formerly socialist world and sought to mentor locals committed to democracy. Initiatives of this sort were, however, insufficient; they were seldom effective and often resented. Advisors from the IMF or the World Bank knew little of local conditions and typically offered rather formulaic prescriptions. Economists from Ivy League universities were technically clever, but lacked detailed knowledge and had little practical experience on which to base their recommendations. Foreign governments also tried to help, but their efforts lacked support from their own people. Even in the two countries that had pioneered in the creation of a liberal order after 1945, the US and the UK, the task of stabilizing the newly enlarged post–Cold War order was not especially popular.

Thatcher may have played a constructive role in ending the Cold War by serving as the bridge between Gorbachev and Reagan, but she was out of office by the time the Soviet Union fell apart. She had also forfeited the opportunity to take a lead in the reconstruction of Europe by opposing the reunification of Germany. And while Thatcher had been critical to making market-oriented policies the default stance of the re-structured economic order, her subsequent attacks on European integration and her worries over German reunification meant that Britain was not in a position to help craft European policies toward Eastern Europe. Her successor, John Major, was a dutiful ally of the US on such matters, but his administration was largely on the defensive, plagued by petty scandals and made ineffective by the growing Euroscepticism of the right within the Conservative Party. When Labour finally returned to office in 1997, Blair steered the country's foreign policy toward greater involvement in Europe, especially on matters of human rights. He even pushed President Clinton toward humanitarian intervention in the Balkans, a not entirely successful venture for the UK and the US. After 9/11, Blair would reaffirm his commitment to the alliance with the United States and to intervention abroad; and he joined the US not just in the invasion of Afghanistan but also of Iraq. The disasters attending those ventures led to a dramatic reversal in public opinion in both Britain and America.

In the United States, the administration of G. H. W. Bush was committed to aiding the political and economic transitions in the East, and the president himself spoke about a "new world order" that he saw emerging during the First Gulf War. Bush has been credited with following a cautious policy toward the Soviet Union that would avoid giving ammunition to Gorbachev's enemies and ensuring a peaceful end to the Cold War. His decisions not to boast and gloat, not to dance on the Berlin Wall, and not to upstage leaders in the East, were surely sensible. At the same time, the US under Bush was not terribly generous with aid that could be used to ease the economic transitions in the East. His painful experience over tax increases taught him that opposition to higher taxes was now at the center of Republican politics. The administration managed to keep defense spending at a level higher than liberals wanted, but Bush proposed no major program to assist the states of Eastern Europe or the former Soviet Union. He also had the strange experience of watching his approval ratings, which had soared during the Gulf War to reverse Saddam Hussein's invasion and seizure of Kuwait in 1990, drop precipitously after it ended, presaging his election defeat in 1992.

Bill Clinton would draw lessons from Bush's failures; he quickly understood that voters had a deep aversion to paying taxes and little appetite for foreign entanglements. These lessons were reinforced by events in Somalia in early October 1993. President Bush had dispatched twenty-five thousand US troops there in December 1992 to assist in a UN relief operation. The UN effort followed a coup in 1991 that left rival warlords battling one another and the nation on the brink of starvation. Continued fighting bedeviled the UN operation. Clinton, skeptical about the effort, reduced US forces to a mere one thousand by June 1993. He was persuaded, however, to send in four hundred special forces in August and to seek to capture the most dominant and troublesome warlord, General Aydid. These modest forces undertook several unsuccessful missions in September and prepared for yet another with the aim of seizing Aydid at a hotel in Mogadishu on October 3. It failed spectacularly: two Black Hawk helicopters were shot down and US troops surrounded by militia fighters. By the end of a day of harsh fighting, eighteen American soldiers were dead and another eighty-four wounded; hundreds of Somalis, both fighters and civilians, also lost their lives. The incident led Clinton to remove all US troops and convinced the administration that interventions of this sort were potential disasters. It was no accident, therefore, that the United States did not get involved in the Rwandan genocide the following year or that it was to be so slow to step in during the civil war in the former Yugoslavia.

With the Clinton administration reluctant to send US troops abroad and fearful of making commitments that it might be unable to fulfill, it developed a national security strategy that proposed reliance on diplomacy and the indirect effects of US involvement in international institutions and alliances. The strategy was based on "engagement and enlargement." The idea was that the US should foster engagement with the global economy and induce new states to participate in the global community and its institutions. The lure of the world market and international recognition would convince countries that it was in their interests to so engage. In the process, they and their leaders would be encouraged to adopt democratic norms and practices and follow market-oriented policies. The effect would be to enlarge the sphere of market democracies and make those democracies more secure. It was suggested that engagement would tempt even the Chinese to open up their society and political system.

The argument was not completely wrong, for opening up markets and trade and tourism could produce shifts in opinion, but it was also a bit mystical and naïve. Clinton's national security advisor, Anthony Lake, explained in September 1993, "The strategy of 'enlargement' of democracies would replace the doctrine of the containment of communism."[17] His statement predated what happened in Somalia; after that fiasco, the administration would begin redrafting the policy to make it less ambitious. When *A National Security Strategy of Engagement and Enlargement* was finally issued in July 1994, it reeked of caution and made clear that the administration's primary focus would be on the domestic economy: insisting that "the line between our domestic and foreign policies is disappearing—[and] that we must revitalize our economy if we are to sustain our military forces, foreign initiatives and global influence, and that we must engage actively abroad if we are to open foreign markets and create jobs for our people."[18]

The explicit connection between security and the opening of markets could be understood as a sign of America's long-term commitment to a capitalist future in which its role would be central—or as something rather different. The United States had a long tradition of seeing the expansion of free markets as a key foreign policy goal.[19] What was different in the 1990s was the extent to which market-friendly policies had displaced other priorities and redefined the role of government. Similar shifts occurred across the advanced democratic countries. The change was most marked in the United States and Britain, and it informed their vision of the world and how it should work. The turn to markets in the 1980s, to "neoliberalism," had thus ensured that the expansion of liberal order after 1989 would be qualitatively different from the establishment of liberal order in the 1940s. American policy makers during and after the Second World War understood their aim as creating a "New Deal for the world," and their British allies largely agreed. The states and political systems set up and stabilized after 1945 would be capitalist, of course, but it was a reformed capitalism constrained by commitments to full employment and more social support and by bargains struck between capital and newly empowered labor. The model promoted after 1989 was something else again. Its priority was to establish market economies and to constrain states from interfering with their functioning.[20] The order would be formally democratic and members would affirm their support for human rights, but the social and economic vision accompanying it was narrow. The new and expanded liberal order failed to inspire.

Constrained by the commitment to the new orthodoxies of market fundamentalism, policy makers chose not to spend the money and expend the effort that might have been required for a thorough economic and political reconstruction of states and societies emerging from socialist stagnation and authoritarianism. That would have required tax increases, and the leaders and parties in power in the US and UK in the 1990s were unwilling or unable to make such bold—and perhaps enlightened—choices. Whether such efforts would have succeeded cannot be answered, and the results from later in the decade, when a new set of leaders had assumed power, were not encouraging. The sad thing is that efforts on the scale of what might have been required were never attempted.

The Center Ceases to Hold

The strength and stability of the postwar order had largely been based on the prosperity that the Fordist model delivered and the centering of politics it encouraged. Economic growth faltered in the 1970s and a new framework for how to run the economy—prioritizing markets and lower taxes and minimizing state intervention—became predominant. The move did not restore the rates of growth of the 1950s and 1960s, but it unfortunately did remove the economic and social foundations of stability. The political basis of the system continued to hold for a time, but it was gradually eroded or abandoned as parties of the center-left and center-right either weakened or moved away from the political center. Center-left parties became weaker as their social and institutional supports weakened. Center-right parties made more conscious choices to vacate the center ground of politics and policy making and move to the right. It is common to say that politics became more polarized, but polarization implies a symmetry between left and right. There was no symmetry, for the center-left continued to advocate a politics of moderate reform but had to operate in a context in which social and economic structures were working against it, while the center-right deserted the center and embraced right-wing ideas and politics.[1]

The Center-Left and Its Shifting Bases of Support

The difficulties confronting center-left parties—socialists and social democrats in Europe, Labour in Britain, the Democrats in the United States—stemmed mostly from social and economic change. The center-left was never simply the party of the working class, for the successful pursuit of electoral politics always required broader support beyond manual workers. Workers and the trade unions that spoke for them were nevertheless routinely the core backers of such parties. Modern manufacturing industry required a mass of workers, and their numbers expanded as one country after another industrialized. The numbers would peak in the most developed economies during the long postwar boom. In the US, it did so in 1979. Fordist growth by definition made greater use of machines and assembly lines than ever before, but also required workers to tend and service those machines and to perform the labor needed to get goods to and from the market. As growth proceeded, however, businesses became more efficient, and the numbers of workers ceased to increase. Even before this, the industrial working class had begun to decline as a proportion of the labor force. For some years, the service sector had grown faster than industry. Jobs in services varied enormously, encompassing, depending on the criteria used to measure class or status, bankers and highly paid professionals, people working in retail sales and in restaurants, truckers and hairdressers. Incomes varied greatly, as did the conditions in which these employees worked. The sustained rise of these mostly white-collar occupations meant that those involved in actual production were outnumbered in the working population. The political consequences of the shifting occupational structure were not always clear, but they did force center-left parties to rethink their appeal.

So, too, did the fact that during the long boom wages and conditions improved for ordinary workers. Real incomes rose steadily from the 1940s through the 1970s. It was a bit of an exaggeration to speak of this as "affluence," as so many did in the 1960s, but it was reasonable to suggest that higher incomes took the edge off working-class grievance and may well have reduced the attachment of workers to center-left parties. Probably more important than the lessening of grievance was the fact that the coming of mass consumption allowed more working-class families to live a lifestyle that was less cut off from the middle classes than previously. The effect was at least a slight blurring of class distinctions.

Parties of the center-left also had to deal with the rise of new issues that did not reinforce the ties of sympathy and interest between parties, their leaders, and their working-class base. The student movements of the 1960s were fueled mostly by anger at the war in Vietnam, but they were accompanied by the spread of a distinct counterculture. The center-left had difficulty speaking both to the war and the rather amorphous youth culture. Race was another issue that fit uneasily into the political culture of such parties. To the extent that Black protest was about poverty and exclusion, the center-left could rely on its long-standing support for redistribution and economic fairness, but the focus on identity was a challenge. The women's movement, more a phenomenon of the 1970s than the 1960s, presented further challenges to a tradition that had been largely the preserve of men, whether they were male workers in manufacturing or a political leadership made up mainly of men. Support for gay rights was also something that did not come easily to center-left parties and the institutions to which they were linked. In theory, their skepticism toward business ought to have made center-left parties better equipped to respond positively to the concerns of environmentalists, but the trade unions with which they were allied often viewed things differently. The coming together of these diverse issues involving identity and values rather than interests vastly complicated and threatened to weaken the connections between moderate parties of the left and their historic sources of support.[2]

In the US, the tensions ruined the chances of Democrats in the presidential elections of both 1968 and 1972. In 1968, antiwar sentiment bolstered the candidacies of Eugene McCarthy and Robert Kennedy, leading Lyndon Johnson to drop out of the race. Vice President Hubert Humphrey took Johnson's place, inheriting his convention delegates and the support of the party establishment but also the enmity of the antiwar movement. He would secure the nomination at the Democratic convention in Chicago in August, but an antiwar plank garnered the votes of 40 percent of the delegates. The meeting itself was overshadowed by antiwar protests and the brutal policing ordered and overseen by Mayor Richard Daley. In addition, the issue of race was ubiquitous and highly consequential. African Americans had been moving toward the Democrats, and Johnson's civil rights legislation confirmed the shift. As late as 1964, however, Democrats from southern states resisted. There was a nasty and public battle over whether to seat the delegation sent by the Mississippi Freedom Democratic Party or the official—segregated and Goldwater-supporting—slate at the 1964 convention. A messy compromise of sorts was worked out, but the legacy of the fight was a commitment to prevent discrimination in the selection of delegates that was included in the formal "Call to the 1968 Convention." African Americans were as a result more fully represented in 1968, and arguments in the Credentials Committee over whom to seat had more favorable outcomes. It was the alternative delegation, not the delegation selected on a more discriminatory basis, that was seated for Mississippi; and in the case of Georgia, two separate slates were seated, one led by the segregationist governor, Lester Maddox, and one led by the African American leader Julian Bond. Most of the Maddox delegates walked out early in the meeting.[3]

Racial discrimination had become a national issue and the urban uprisings by African Americans during the 1960s were inspiring to some, frightening to others, and highly consequential. They were a sign that many in the civil rights movement had concluded that nonviolence had not produced the desired results—what was required was to turn civil rights into a more radical Black liberation movement. The move, and the violent protests themselves, were not popular with white voters either in the North or the South and made a least some of them reluctant to vote for a Democrat.

The weakening of the electoral coalition behind the Democrats was still more manifest in 1972. Revulsion at the spectacle of the 1968 convention in Chicago led the party to implement further reforms in its procedures. The reforms had been a long time in the making, but the work of making them real fell to the Commission on Party Structure and Delegate Selection (the McGovern-Fraser Commission) appointed in early 1969. It made formal the requirement that the nominating contest would rely on primaries or caucuses rather than party machines and insider deals. It also moved beyond prohibiting discrimination in delegate selection to insisting that, in terms of race, there be a "reasonable relationship between the representation of delegates and representation of the minority group to the population of the state in question."[4] The same logic was applied to the representation of women and youth. The resulting guidelines came close to mandating quotas for African Americans, women, and youth. The rationale was that as the base of the party was shifting, its membership and leadership should reflect that. As civil rights leader Channing Emery Phillips explained, "New coalitions of big-city Blacks, Youth and suburban young to middle-aged must be brought into the party, if for no other reason than numbers." At a moment when "the lower middle-class, blue-collar vote erodes," commission member Fred Dutton argued, these new voters were desperately needed to replenish the ranks.[5]

Opening up the party and its procedures and trying to make it look more like its voters, or those it aimed to rally behind its standard, had the unintended effect of exacerbating divisions within the party and exposing its weakened ties to working-class voters. George McGovern easily won the nomination for president, but would be beaten badly by Nixon. He faced opposition and de facto sabotage from the party's more conservative supporters. A key figure was the president of the AFL-CIO, George Meany, who accused McGovern of being "an apologist for the Communist world."[6] Meany had led the American Federation of Labor (AFL) since before its merger with the Congress of Industrial Organizations (CIO) in 1955 and he had strong support among the skilled trades. It was among those workers that discontent over race and over the Democrats' drift to the left was most intense. Other labor leaders, like Walter Reuther of the United Auto Workers (UAW), were more supportive of shifts in the party's demography and its politics. Meany's refusal to endorse McGovern gave Nixon a substantial boost. That the president cheated, as the Watergate controversy would demonstrate, was not known at the time of the election, but it is unlikely that knowledge of it would have saved McGovern.

Watergate and Nixon's resignation in 1974 did massively benefit Democrats, serving to obscure for a time the growing disaffection of more traditional working-class voters. In fact, the Congress elected in 1974 was probably the most liberal in American history and led to the passage of critical reforms. Democrats kept these gains in 1976 as revulsion over Nixon and his handiwork helped Jimmy Carter win the presidency. The reaction against Nixon and the Republicans was not enough, however, to sustain Carter through the difficulties of his presidency. Carter was undone primarily by the economic crisis he faced after the second oil shock in 1978–79, though the Iran hostage crisis did not help. The inability of the Democratic president to tame inflation and restore even a semblance of economic growth robbed him and the Democratic Party of the confidence that they could govern the economy effectively and in a way that protected the interests of ordinary Americans, be they middle class or working class. When Reagan prevailed in the election of 1980, a good part of his success was attributed to his ability to win the votes of what were labeled "Reagan Democrats."[7]

Reagan would continue to siphon off Democratic support among the white working class in 1984 and it would seem that his successor, George Bush, did so as well in 1988. Democratic losses were compounded by economic trends. The recession of 1981–82 cut deep into the workforce of industrial America. What was labeled the "Rust Belt" in the Midwest and parts of the Northeast lost jobs that would never come back. The term *de-industrialization* began to be used to describe the experience of these regions. Some of these jobs were exported to low-wage countries; some were eliminated by employers seeking to cut costs. Manufacturing employment continued to decline throughout the decade and beyond: nearly 9 percent of manufacturing jobs disappeared between 1979 and 2001.[8] When growth occurred, it happened elsewhere, in different places and different industries. In the post-Fordist and post-industrial economy growth was concentrated in services, including retail, and later in information technology. Defense production was boosted, but more in high-tech fields than in the routine production of weapons and transport vehicles. The fastest-growing occupational category was that of professionals, and there was a steady increase in the number of women working full-time.

Information technology was to become the most dynamic sector of the economy. IBM, playing catch-up against rivals who had pioneered the minicomputer, launched its personal computer in August 1981. It soon dominated the market and the industry would grow massively, becoming the engine of growth for the larger economy. The employment consequences would be mixed, for IT employed workers with different skills who tended to live and work outside the traditional regions of heavy industry. Overall, growth was slower after 1980 than before, and the economy produced fewer of the well-paid blue-collar jobs that had been a distinguishing feature of the previous era.

The less than robust economic performance of the late 1980s and early 1990s helped to prevent the neoliberal turn from becoming completely hegemonic and offered modest opportunities for alternative politics. The Democratic Party's difficulties did not go away after Reagan, but the party managed to recover the presidency in 1992. Clinton's formula for success revealed both the party's now chronic liabilities and certain emerging strengths and the delicate and complicated maneuvering required to put together a winning coalition. Democratic support among African Americans was solid and the party did increasingly resemble its base, and in 1992 it was not torn apart by debates about this. Many southern Democrats had long since left for the GOP. Clinton also benefited from the fact that the economy had experienced a brief but still painful recession in 1991–92. This brought at least some traditional working-class support back toward the party. Clinton was himself a moderate who had played a prominent role in the Democratic Leadership Council, a group that worked to counter Republican dominance by pushing the Democrats toward the center. He was also, like Jimmy Carter, a southerner; and that identity would allow him to win the electoral votes of Missouri, Tennessee, Arkansas, Louisiana, and Georgia. Clinton was, in addition, a clever and wary campaigner who made sure that he was not viewed as too liberal or too beholden to Black supporters. During the primaries Clinton had flown back to Arkansas to oversee the execution of a mentally impaired Black prisoner, Ricky Ray Rector. Later, in June 1992, he stood next to Jesse Jackson and denounced Sister Souljah, an African American hip-hop artist, activist, and writer who, during the civil unrest in Los Angeles over the acquittal of the police officers who had savagely beaten Rodney King, had said that "if black people kill black people every day, why not have a week and kill white people."[9] Clinton clearly sought to preempt attacks aimed at driving a wedge between Black and white supporters. His perceived need to do so suggests that he understood the fragility of his coalition; his behavior in office showed the same sensibility and provided evidence that the divergent pieces of the Democratic base demanded continued attention if they were to be held together.

Clinton's electoral success also demonstrated that economic and social trends did not uniformly favor the right. Democrats had been able to win votes from women, especially working women; minorities; sections of the traditional working class; and from many people, both professionals and those with fewer credentials, employed in services. In 2002 two rather bold writers published a book titled *The Emerging Democratic Majority*, laying out an argument about how demographic and occupational changes would create opportunities, not just risks, for Democrats.[10] Still, the party could not take the allegiance of any part of its base for granted.

The problem US Democrats faced was how to hold onto as much of its base in the working class as possible, find new sources of support among minorities, women, and the growing ranks of professionals and service sector workers, and bring these new and old constituencies together around a shared message and program. The same conundrum confronted center-left parties elsewhere, but its expression varied considerably. In France and Italy, for example, center-left parties lacked the history and rootedness of the Democrats in the United States or Labour in Britain. Quite large numbers of the working class had continued to support Communist parties well into the postwar years. Socialists or social democrats were correspondingly weaker, with narrower social roots and less robust traditions. The question was whether, and if so how, such center-left or socialist parties could ally with or take votes from the Communists. In Italy, the Socialists had been mostly junior partners to the Communists. Frustrated with the absence of alternatives, various small factions of the left took to terrorism. The most prominent was the Red Brigades (Brigate Rosso), which kidnapped the Christian Democratic leader Aldo Moro in March 1978. His dead body was found nearly two months later in Rome. Terror on the left was more than matched by terror on the right; and right-wing terror had connections with the police and the Christian Democratic Party. For its part, the PCI moved to end its exclusion from power by adopting a politics of Eurocommunism and in 1973 proposing a "historic compromise" with other parties.

Since the most predominant other party was obviously the Christian Democrats, working with them left little political space for the center-left.[11] As part of its effort to prove its loyalty to the republic, the PCI condemned the actions of left-wing terrorists.[12] Doing so did not bring it any closer to power, and the distractions of the moment precluded initiatives that might have done more to improve the prospects of a viable center-left. The Italian Socialists did get an opportunity to become a serious political contender when their leader, Bettino Craxi, became prime minister in 1983. The party had secured only 11 percent of the vote in the recent election, but in alliance with the Christian Democrats it was able to form a government that lasted for four years. Its leaders hoped to displace the Communists and become a regular partner in government, but by 1987 the PSI vote had only increased to 14.3 percent and Craxi was replaced as prime minister by a Christian Democrat. The party remained in coalitions with the CD until 1992, when it became engulfed in scandals over illegal campaign funding and virtually collapsed as a result.

In France, the socialists had a long and not unworthy history, but they were fragmented for much of the postwar era and had been shut out of power since the 1940s. François Mitterrand was able to run for president with the backing of various left and center-left groups in 1965, but lost to De Gaulle. De Gaulle's resignation in the wake of a failed referendum in April 1969 led to an election in which the center-left was routed. The response was the founding of a new Parti socialiste. In 1971 it was effectively taken over and rebuilt by Mitterrand, who succeeded by working with a new generation of leaders and building a coalition with the Communists. A declining PCF formed an alliance with the socialists behind the "Common Program for a Government of the Left" in 1972. Mitterrand lost the 1974 presidential election to Giscard d'Estaing by a narrow margin, but the socialists were beginning to sap the strength of the Communists. When Mitterrand ran again in 1981, he solidly beat his Communist rival, Georges Marchais, in the first round and then bested Giscard in the second round to win the presidency. He did so at the head of a broad-based coalition of the left and center-left espousing a quite radical program. Communists participated in the new government, but in minor posts, and they would be pushed out in 1984. The

economic difficulties of the early 1980s forced the government to reverse its key economic policies when in office and prevented the parties
that led it from establishing the record of governance needed to create a
solid phalanx of support in the country. The largest trade union federation continued to be led by Communists, and when the structural transformations of the post-industrial economy reached France and Italy, the
political impact was to reinforce the historic weakness of the left and the
center-left.[13]

By contrast, the Social Democratic Party of Germany had a longer
record of success as a governing party and much closer ties to the trade
unions. Perhaps more important, unions in Germany were solidly entrenched and had established roles to play in collective bargaining and
the management of enterprises. Employers did not use the crises of the
late 1970s and early 1980s to erode the rights and status of unions, and
industrial employment held up better than elsewhere. Germany's high-
wage and high-skilled workforce fared better in the transition from
Fordism to post-Fordism, and German companies, already oriented toward exports, did better than their competitors in other countries. When
structural changes did eventually occur, they did so in the context of
reunification, which meant that instead of moving jobs overseas, companies moved them to eastern Germany. The shift was also less dramatic
than in other industrial economies. Eventually, the Social Democrats
would face the same defections as other center-left parties, but these
would occur a decade or two later than elsewhere.

The Labour Party in Britain experienced the challenges of new
economic and social realities at roughly the same moment as did the
Democrats in the US, and the effects were just as dramatic. That was
entirely appropriate, for the two countries and the two parties had much
in common. Labour, like the Democrats, had a proud tradition of reform
and strong ties to its base. What separated them most were the industrial or occupational bases of their support and the role of race. The
question of race was not absent in Britain or without significance for
Labour, but it was far less salient than in the United States. The Labour
Party's working-class supporters were employed in distinctly older industries than were Democratic voters and supporters in the United
States. The concentration of support in what were mainly declining

industries—mining, textiles, shipbuilding—and in the regions where these were located skewed Labour toward essentially defensive policies. The effect was that the party was less successful in rooting itself in new places and among the workers in expanding sectors. This orientation toward and attachment to the old and backward would make adaptation to social and economic transformation that much harder. The policies that failed in the 1970s were a clear manifestation of the problem.

Labour in Britain had been founded by the trade unions and it was the connection to the unions that had sustained it through good times and bad. The unions effectively dominated policy making through their control of the annual party conference. The party's leadership was typically a mix of people with trade union backgrounds and, increasingly, well-educated middle- and upper-class professionals whose ideological orientation attracted them to Labour. After the great reforming ministries of the late 1940s and early 1950s Labour remained strong, though it was out of office from 1951 to 1964. After losing the election of 1959, some Labour thinkers began to question the party's attachment to a set of traditional slogans and its ability to win the votes of the expanding numbers of white-collar workers and of newly affluent workers in newer industries.[14] They wondered more specifically about whether the party should abandon Clause IV of its 1918 constitution, which committed it "to secure for the workers by hand or by brain the full fruits of their industry and the most equitable distribution thereof that may be possible upon the basis of the common ownership of the means of production, distribution and exchange, and the best obtainable system of popular administration and control of each industry or service." By 1959, few took this commitment literally, and it was seen as a liability with voters. It had, though, huge symbolic importance within the party. The party's leader, Hugh Gaitskell, and his allies floated the possibility of abandoning Clause IV after the defeat of 1959, but they botched the job and were forced to back off. The effect was to delay what its advocates called the "modernisation" of the party until the late 1980s and 1990s.[15]

It would take four general election losses in a row—in 1979, 1983, 1987, and 1992—before the party could be convinced to reform and restructure. The critical votes in those elections were those of the skilled working class that British pollsters denote as C2s: in 1974, they voted for

Labour by 49 percent to 26 percent; in 1979, their votes were split evenly, 41 percent each for the Conservatives and for Labour; in 1983 40
percent voted for the Conservatives and just 32 percent for Labour; four
years later, again 40 percent voted Conservative and 36 percent voted for
Labour.[16] The party's task was to reverse those numbers. Labour began
its revival under Neil Kinnock. His signal contribution was to break the
power of the left of the party. He also introduced more modern methods
of campaigning and moved policy back toward the center. After losing
the election of 1992 to John Major, Thatcher's successor, Kinnock was
replaced by John Smith, who managed to weaken the grip of the trade
unions on party policy making by curbing the "bloc vote." After his un-
timely death, he was replaced by Tony Blair who, alongside his fellow
reformer Gordon Brown, continued the work of Kinnock and Smith.
They reaffirmed the move to the political center, made it clear that they
were prepared to accept, or at least not reverse, major Thatcher policies,
and worked to rebrand Labour. Central to that effort was the decision to
replace Clause IV in the party constitution. They succeeded and won a
huge election victory in 1997.

New Labour was criticized at the time, and later, for its choice not
to seek to overturn Thatcher's policies on taxes and on privatization.
Promising to do so, however, might well have risked further electoral
defeats. Delivering on such promises would also have been hugely expensive and for that reason close to impossible in practice. It was equally impossible to turn back the social and occupational changes of the
previous decades. The old industries where Labour drew so much support in the 1950s and 1960s had shriveled during the Thatcher era. Coal
mining entered a terminal decline, while textiles and shipbuilding kept
shrinking. Labour's political recovery would of necessity require building a new party with different appeals to a changed electorate. And it
worked, at least for a while.

The Center-Right Moves to the Right

While parties like Labour in Britain and the Democrats in the United
States remained close to the political center even as they contended with
structural changes in the economy and society in order to attract new

voters to replace declining constituencies, parties on the right decided more or less on their own to vacate the center. They also had to navigate social, demographic, and cultural transformations, but the challenges they faced were more amorphous and less dramatic and allowed for a more deliberate response. The center-right was to this extent not compelled to move further to the right, but deliberately chose to do so.

Parties of both the left and the right have to pay attention to the changing needs and interests of supporters and potential supporters, and so have to adjust their appeals on a regular basis. For the right, the most threatening shifts over the postwar era were the movement of population from the countryside to the cities and suburbs and from farming to industry, and the steady erosion of religious belief. Conservative parties had historically found their strongest support in rural areas, but rapid postwar growth lured farmers and their children to jobs and lives in cities and more commercial and industrial regions. In these new settings, the ties connecting them to conservative politics were severed, or at least attenuated, and center-right parties needed to rebuild the connections. Whatever new links were established were never as solid as those that had existed in older, rural communities. Conservatives would instead rely on a sympathetic press and on the fact that for many such voters their movement into the cities would lead to improved living standards, which might incline voters to the right, and on appeals to patriotism, traditional religion, and anti-Communism. Playing the patriot card was not so easy in the aftermath of the Second World War and the discrediting of nationalism, and that meant that the preferred appeals involved linking Christian faith with anti-Communism. Indeed, the belief that Communism was a direct attack on religion meant that anti-Communism and the profession of Christian faith strongly reinforced each other.

The waning of Christian faith was for this reason a continuing challenge for conservatives. In most of Europe, attitudes toward religion shifted gradually in the 1950s and then rapidly in the 1960s. Mass entertainment, with its largely secular message and values, had come to Europe before the war. Genuine mass consumption, which would reinforce the message, came later during the 1950s and 1960s. Then came the counterculture of the late 1960s and 1970s, which was very much at odds with the pieties and structures of a once-dominant Christianity. It was not all sex, drugs, and rock-and-roll, but the urban and youth subcultures of the '60s and '70s were a distinct challenge to traditional Catholics and Protestants—and the churches did not respond well. A prime example was the decision by Pope Paul VI to issue the encyclical *Humanae vitae* in 1968: by forbidding contraception to young Catholics, the church ensured that it would be increasingly ignored when Catholics made the most important decisions in their intimate lives. The decline varied by country, with France and Britain moving earlier and most fully away from their faiths and Italy more slowly. In Eastern Europe, the Polish Catholic Church remained strong, but elsewhere attendance and belief waned. Ireland stayed Catholic for a long time, but when people did begin to leave the church, they did so quickly and in large numbers, often expressing deep bitterness toward the priests, nuns, and bishops who had exercised such domination over their lives. The United States was something of an exception, but perhaps less than is sometimes assumed. Its mass culture was decidedly irreligious and hedonist since at least the mid-1960s, and the crisis among Catholics began at the end of the decade. By the early 1970s, the seminaries were emptying out and younger Catholics stopped going to church.

In much of Europe, the churches had been a major social and cultural support for conservatism. As belief and practice faded, parties of the right lost that routine cultural reinforcement. It forced them to make other, usually more pragmatic and economic appeals. Catholics in the urban centers in the United States had been pretty firmly attached to the New Deal and hence to the Democrats, and recent Hispanic immigrants also tended to support the Democrats. The more devout Catholics could be tempted away by emphasizing issues like abortion, but the devout were a dwindling minority. Protestants in America were more often Republicans, but the mainline churches were losing members. African American Protestants attached themselves to the Democrats. White evangelicals, by contrast, grew in numbers and in their attachment to the right.[17] They would become an increasingly important component of the Republican base, even as the influence of religion overall diminished in the country.

To remain electorally viable, then, the center-right everywhere had to keep refurbishing its appeal, and to do so while confronting cultural and social changes that pushed in the opposite direction. Anti-Communism was always part of the mix. It served two distinct functions: it provided an external enemy against whom to rally support; and it served to keep conservatives tethered to the political center. In order to fight the Cold War, it was assumed that the West had to offer a reformed and constrained capitalism as the alternative to Communism. That required that conservatives continue to demonstrate their commitment to maintaining the reforms of the 1940s. The importance of the Cold War and anti-Communism gradually waned, but not everywhere. In Italy, for example, the Christian Democrats were seen as critical to keeping the Communists from power from the 1940s until 1989. In Germany, the CDU/CSU combined a Christian social vision with opposition to the enemy to the east. In France, nationalism was not as discredited as it had been in Germany and Italy and so appeals to rebuilding France and restoring French greatness remained available; they were the essence of De Gaulle's politics. In Britain, the Tories made it clear that they would do little or nothing to dismantle the welfare state built by Labour, and they were able to claim credit for steady economic growth during the 1950s. The boast became hollow during the 1960s and early 1970s as growth became harder to engineer and the discourse about the British economy turned negative. Republicans in the US, by choosing Eisenhower in 1952, also benefited from their apparent moderation and steady economic growth.

The fortunes of the center-right dimmed somewhat in the 1960s, but the crises of the 1970s gave them new issues and lines of attack. The failure to maintain growth and fight inflation hurt those in power everywhere, but the most visible failures were Labour in Britain and the administration of Jimmy Carter in the United States. The response was the turn to the market and against the state. Big government was blamed for the crisis and attacked as an impediment to resolving it. Thatcher and Reagan were the strongest proponents of these arguments, but they were echoed more widely. When West German chancellor Helmut Kohl, who took office in October 1982, announced a new economic policy, he said that it would be a move "away from more state to more market; away from collective burdens to more personal achievements, away from entrenched structures to more flexibility, individual initiative and competitiveness."[18]

Could neoliberalism of this sort itself ever be a popular set of beliefs that could sustain parties of the right over the long term? Its belief in tax cuts as the best response to almost any problem certainly has an appeal to those who benefit directly. The belief can also be attractive to those who benefit very little, or not at all, from tax breaks, for it accords with a broader critique of government. Attacks on the state can be popular, for many people—and not just Americans—resent being told what to do by authorities they barely know and by groups of experts that do not include people like themselves. There are limitations, however, to both anti-tax and anti-state rhetoric: citizens across the developed nations routinely depend on government, and hence on taxation, for pensions, health care, education, and many other public goods, and polling has repeatedly shown that spending money on these services has wide support. As political strategy, then, the politics of market fundamentalism lacks enduring appeal and over time becomes rather threadbare.[19]

The right, or center-right, also lost the use of anti-Communism to rally its supporters after the Cold War ended. Indeed, the dominant conservative parties in Italy and Japan, the Christian Democrats and the Liberal Democratic Party (LDP) respectively, began to falter in the early 1990s. These were basically Cold War coalitions that could no longer hold together. In Italy, the Christian Democrats were overwhelmed by corruption investigations beginning in 1992 and broke apart in 1994; in Japan, the LDP was also tainted by corruption, but mainly fragmented because what had previously held it together no longer sufficed. Conservative parties fared poorly elsewhere during the 1990s, and as of 2000, democrats, social democrats, or socialists were in power in Germany, France, the United Kingdom, and the United States. Leaders like Tony Blair, Gerhard Schroeder, and Bill Clinton saw themselves as allies and claimed to be pioneering a "third way." Lionel Jospin, the French prime minister, kept his distance and was less successful.

As committed as conservative leaders might be to market-oriented policies and to the interests of the wealthy, these were not effective in cementing political allegiances with other groups of voters. Margaret Thatcher had tried to create a popular basis for her policies with her invocation of "Victorian values," but they failed to inspire in a society that was not terribly Victorian in its beliefs and practices. Increasingly, then, center-right or right-wing parties sought to use other appeals in order to cobble together coalitions capable of winning elections. They would turn to older staples in the conservative repertoire—to nationalism and resentment of foreigners, to "culture wars," to religion, and to immigration and race. Since it was in the US and Britain that neoliberalism had its greatest success, it was in those countries where conservatives would have the greatest need for different and additional appeals to mobilize voters. After Thatcher, British conservatives largely failed to come up with a reason for voters to support them, and the result was a series of successive defeats at the hands of Labour. John Major won the election as a more humane and less abrasive Thatcherite in 1992, but he was on the defensive soon after. British conservatives had, however, already hit upon a potentially effective appeal with Euroscepticism. Europe was a tempting target for those interested in stoking opposition to the state and its intrusions: it was distant and amorphous and its bureaucracy in Brussels contained lots of foreigners, even if Britain was fully represented. The British tabloids, and also the more sedate *Telegraph*, were filled with stories about the European Commission issuing silly but cumbersome regulations on the shape of bananas, the labeling of cheese and chocolate, and much else. The stories, quite a few told without regard for evidence by *Telegraph* columnist Boris Johnson, were entertaining regardless of whether they were true.

The Tory right's main objection to Europe was that it proudly proclaimed a social vision that qualified its commitment to open markets. The head of the European Commission, Jacques Delors, had led the effort to complete the single market in the late 1980s, but to balance that market-friendly move he and the commission began emphasizing the EC's commitment to social and economic rights. Delors had given a well-received speech at the annual Trades Union Congress at Bournemouth in August 1988 urging the TUC to help him craft and put in place a "social dimension" to the single market. Thatcher, always alive to threats to her policies, responded sharply in her "Bruges speech" of September 20, 1988, warning, "We have not embarked on the business of throwing back the frontiers of the state at home, only to see a European super-state getting ready to exercise a new dominance from Brussels."[20] In Euroscepticism, the Tories, or some of them, had found an issue that would bedevil the party for over two decades but that they would ride to electoral victory only after 2016. Much would have to happen before that occurred, but it would provide the sort of emotional appeal that the attachment to markets could not, an appeal that was capable of enlisting very old-fashioned but recently unfashionable, and possibly unspeakable, sentiments like nationalism, the resentment of immigrants, and a nostalgia for empire as well as new fears of Islam. A nasty concoction, though still only a possibility before 2000.

In the United States, Republicans had a longer experience in mixing support for business and markets with more emotional appeals. Although Eisenhower's policies had symbolized the "modern Republicanism" he preached to his fellow Republicans, he had to contend with a bloc of Republicans from the Midwest and the West who were united in their hatred of the New Deal and its legacy and eager to reverse it. Just after his victory in 1956, Eisenhower wrote, "I still have a job of re-forming and re-vamping the Republican Party."[21] He did not succeed at the task, although Nixon's selection as presidential nominee indicated that his opponents had not either. What sustained, indeed animated, the more conservative Republicans were resistance to desegregation and the waxing influence of what came to be called "movement conservatism." The 1954 Supreme Court decision in *Brown v. Board of Education* that outlawed segregation in public schools left it to the states to actually end it, and many across the South resisted. That meant that the federal government was forced to step in and enforce it. The battle over desegregation set much of South ablaze with white anger and provided an opening for conservatives. Taft Republicans had long argued for limited government, but now the principle could and would be invoked to defend "states' rights," which to many translated into the rights of states to maintain segregation. Republicans had long sought to convince conservative southern Democrats to join them in battling northern liberals who were pushing the Democrats toward greater support for civil rights. Such efforts made little progress because southern Democrats had built up seniority in Congress and held important committee chairmanships in the House and the Senate. The progress of the civil rights movement and desegregation gave those arguments new purchase, even if the actual realignment took a bit longer to become reality.

"Modern Republicanism," the vision of Eisenhower and his pragmatic backers, represented a kind of centrist, "middle way" politics that almost invited the critique that it had no principles. Such was the attack levied against it by a new generation of conservative intellectuals like William F. Buckley, Brent Bozell, James Burnham, Frank Meyer, and William Rusher, largely centered on the journal *National Review*. They attacked liberals, especially elite liberals at Ivy League schools, accusing them of furthering the interests of socialism and destroying Christianity; and they gained further attention by defending Senator Joe McCarthy. "McCarthyism," Buckley and Bozell wrote, "is a movement around which men of good will and stern morality can close ranks."[22] These conservative intellectuals remained marginal even as they became notorious, and their journal was a precarious enterprise until it embraced the segregationist cause over Eisenhower's decision to send federal troops to Little Rock.[23] When it did, its support and readership grew significantly.

The marriage between "movement conservatism" and the resistance to civil rights was to become a powerful political force. The vision behind the new alliance was dubbed "fusionism" by one of its creators, and it successfully "merged the economic libertarianism of Hayek with cultural traditionalism [read racism] and morally charged anticommunism."[24] The combination of ideas provided an umbrella under which wealthy businesspeople opposed to the New Deal and eager to avoid paying taxes, militant anti-Communists, disgruntled Catholics, and southern racists (and some from outside the South) could find common ground.

Movement conservatism was aided by the growth of unofficial local organizations that began to pop up across the Sunbelt. From these bases and with this emerging coalition, it could launch an effort to gain control of the Republican Party. To do that, of course, it needed a potential leader.

He was found in Barry Goldwater. Goldwater was the perfect embodiment of movement conservatism.[25] He came from Arizona, was born rich but thought of himself as a self-made man, was strongly opposed to trade unions, and had attacked Eisenhower's proposed budget in 1957 for its supposedly excessive spending.[26] He had supported Joe McCarthy, spouted a vitriolic brand of anti-Communism, denounced

Brown v. Board of Education, and opposed Eisenhower's use of troops to enforce desegregation. Predictably, Goldwater would vote against the Civil Rights Act of 1964. For all these reasons, he was adopted by the new right. Buckley's co-author and brother-in-law Brent Bozell actually wrote Goldwater's 1960 book, *The Conscience of a Conservative.*[27] There were efforts to nominate Goldwater for president in 1960, but they did not get far; Richard Nixon became the nominee. His loss to Kennedy seemed to vindicate the critique of Eisenhower and "Modern Republicanism" and inspired the right within the party to promote Goldwater for president in 1964. He won the nomination, but was trounced by Lyndon Johnson.[28] The Goldwater campaign failed, but it created new heroes and spokespeople for the right wing of the Republican Party. Phyllis Schlafly, a classic Taft Republican, published *A Choice Not an Echo* to bolster Goldwater and expose the machinations of the eastern establishment to control and manipulate the party, while fashioning a critique of feminism. Ronald Reagan gave a nationally televised speech late during the contest endorsing Goldwater that marked his emergence on the national political stage.[29] Goldwater's campaign also demonstrated that the rhetoric about small government and states' rights effectively signaled to southern voters Republicans' opposition to civil rights and desegregation. They responded as they were meant to respond, and Goldwater carried five southern states—Alabama, Mississippi, Louisiana, Georgia, and South Carolina.

Defeat convinced Republicans to get behind Nixon again in 1968, and he proceeded to win the presidency. Goldwater's loss might well have signaled the end of movement conservatism, but the politics of the 1960s kept its fortunes alive. Passage of the Civil Rights Act and the Voting Rights Act, as well as legislation aimed at bringing about the Great Society, outraged conservatives. So, too, did continuing civil rights protests and demonstrations of the mid- to late 1960s. Conservatives also recoiled at the student movement and escalating antiwar protests. Outrage and resentment at these phenomena meant that the new right was never reconciled to whatever variation of Republicanism Nixon stood for. Nixon himself understood that the path to electoral success was through a coalition of traditional midwestern Republicans, white suburbanites, especially in the Sunbelt, white southerners motivated by opposition to civil rights, and working-class whites who shared the same fears and antipathies.[30] Nixon developed a strategy to make that alliance real, though the candidacy of George Wallace complicated matters. Nixon used his "Southern strategy" to win the nomination, but then moved slightly toward the center in the general election. His favored theme was "law and order," which would be coded racially by those so inclined but was also meant to appeal more broadly. In office, Nixon adopted policies designed to appeal both to moderates and to the right wing of the party, though after the mass antiwar protests of 1970 he moved further to the right. He scored a big victory in 1972 against a weak candidate and a divided Democratic Party, but was forced on the defensive by Watergate. When Nixon resigned in disgrace in 1974, movement conservatives once more felt vindicated and resumed their efforts to take control of the Republican Party. This time their hopes were focused on Ronald Reagan. They fought for his nomination in 1976 and lost, but when the Carter administration found itself in trouble on all fronts, they nominated Reagan and saw him capture the White House in the 1980 election.

Reagan's victory in winning the nomination and then the presidency meant that movement conservatism had gained control of the Republican Party. His campaign touched all the themes favored by the new right. An early campaign stop in the general election was held in Mississippi, not far from where civil rights organizers had been murdered sixteen years earlier, and announced, "I believe in states' rights."[31] What Reagan was able to do that others with his politics could not do was to make his views seem reasonable and unthreatening. Reagan could do that, in part, because of his and the party's new commitment to tax cuts and supply-side economics. Republicans had long favored tax cuts, but had difficulty explaining why this would not force cuts in popular government programs like Social Security. Arthur Laffer's argument that reduced taxes would spur growth and somehow increase revenues gave Republicans a rhetorical ability to deny that cutting taxes would force cuts in benefits. The Kemp-Roth bill to massively reduce taxes, introduced in Congress in 1978, would become a central plank of the Republican Party program. The young congressman Newt Gingrich grasped its potential immediately: the new doctrine, he explained, "exceeds anything I have seen in 18 years of politics and 5 years campaigning in its potential to create a conservative majority in this country."[32] Of course, Reagan's victory owed as much to the failures of the Carter administration, but the promises implied by supply-side economics helped.

Once in office, Reagan worked to implement his agenda of cutting taxes, easing or ending regulations on business, and scaling back federal support for social programs. He secured policy victories on all of these fronts. Success brought its own problems in the long run, however, for market fundamentalism did not offer a very rich or expansive vision. It had provided an effective critique of liberal failure in the late 1970s, but with Carter gone and Republicans in charge, taxes lowered and economic growth more or less restored, what was left to inspire voters? The magic that supply-side nostrums invoked was ultimately not credible, and the economic revival of the mid-1980s was patchy. The same dilemma haunted British conservatives in the late Thatcher era, and it would trouble Republicans at roughly the same moment. There were key differences, however, between the Tories and the Republicans. In the United States there was the enduring matter of race, which affected everything. Americans were also more tuned in to what would be called the "culture wars," the battle between conservatives and progressives over matters such as minority rights, reproductive rights, and feminism. Religion also played a bigger and more political role in the US than in Britain or in most other developed countries.

It was in the 1970s that the Republicans formed an alliance with evangelical Christians.[33] In 1979 the Reverend Jerry Falwell, together with Paul Weyrich of the Heritage Foundation, founded the Moral Majority. Falwell had been spurred into action in defense of Christian schools, whose tax-exempt status had been challenged by the IRS in 1978 because they tended to be all white. The organization's first venture into politics was to support Catholic protests against abortion. In 1980, the Moral Majority strongly backed Reagan for president and, according to Jimmy Carter, Falwell organized the purchase of $10 million worth of airtime "on southern radio and TV to brand me as a traitor to the South and no longer a Christian."[34] The appeal of groups like the Moral Majority lay in their effective mixing of all variety of culture wars issues: race, most importantly, but also the defense of conservative religion and "family values" and an intense resentment of the legacy of the 1960s.

Republican positions on women and religion were linked and would be dramatically transformed. In 1972 the Equal Rights Amendment (ERA), having passed the House and Senate with bipartisan support, was sent to the states for ratification. It was initially approved by thirty-five states, but Phyllis Schlafly and her (mostly religious) allies organized a backlash that blocked its passage. They argued that women would lose from the Equal Rights Amendment: they would lose protections at work that women had secured; they would lose their privileged position when it came to divorce and child custody; and they would even be subject to the military draft. The campaign served as a model for how conservatives could appeal to women.[35] The same coalition would manage to remove support for the ERA from the Republican platform in 1980. Just a year after the ERA was approved by Congress, the Supreme Court legalized abortion in *Roe v. Wade*. The decision was popular when it was announced and at first aroused little opposition, but by the late 1970s it, too, was becoming an issue that could mobilize religious voters on behalf of conservatives. Public opinion would continue to favor abortion rights, but it was to become another front in the culture wars that Republicans routinely used to augment their support among key blocs of voters. And these—race, religion, women's rights, abortion, gay and lesbian rights, later gun rights—were issues that persisted and afforded the right emotional appeals that could be used when other policies and proposals, like budget cuts or "entitlement reform" or promises to increase defense spending, left voters unmoved. They were issues that produced outrage, and the outrage persisted between elections, for the people who cared most about them were already organized in churches or in the National Rifle Association and connected through numerous formal and informal networks.[36]

The effectiveness of such appeals would be demonstrated in the 1988 presidential election. George Bush had the unenviable task of following a very popular and successful leader. He had little of Reagan's charisma and lacked the easy but articulate style that Reagan had developed over decades as an actor and speaker. Bush was also not a true believer in "movement conservatism" and had mocked Reagan's economic program as "voodoo economics." These flaws, or virtues, meant that he found himself trailing the Democratic presidential nominee, Michael Dukakis, by seventeen points after the Democratic convention in 1988. To overcome that deficit, Bush moved sharply to the right and deployed a vicious and racist campaign to take down Dukakis. His top aide, Lee Atwater, worked with Roger Ailes to smear the Democratic candidate. They created an advertisement featuring Willie Horton, a Black convict who while on prison furlough attacked a white couple and raped the woman. The advertisement was not at all supported by the facts, but it worked. Atwater would later explain that his strategy for beating Dukakis was to "strip the bark off the little bastard." Unfortunately, Dukakis proved to be incapable of fighting back and proceeded to lose the election in decisive fashion.[37]

Bush went on to govern as the moderate politician that he in fact was, but it did him little good. By some measures, his administration was very successful. Bush presided over the end of the Cold War in a judicious manner that ensured it was accompanied by very little violence. He also negotiated, with Gorbachev and then Yeltsin, a series of disarmament agreements that did much to lessen the threat of nuclear war. The Bush administration also put together an effective coalition to drive Saddam Hussein and his forces out of Kuwait after the invasion of August 1990. Victory in the Gulf War in early 1991 boosted his popularity and convinced several leading Democrats not to run against him. Unfortunately for him, he had incurred the wrath of more right-wing Republicans by agreeing to modest tax increases in 1990. Bush had told the Republican convention in 1988 that there would be "no new taxes," but the budgetary situation was dire two years later. It led Bush to reach a bipartisan agreement on the budget, but Newt Gingrich convinced House Republicans to repudiate the administration's plan and torpedo the agreement. The final deal was pushed through with more Democratic input and so resulted in a somewhat greater tax increase than originally proposed.[38] Conservatives never forgave Bush for the alleged betrayal of his anti-tax pledge, even when he sought to appease them by nominating Clarence Thomas for the Supreme Court in 1991. Many went on to support Patrick Buchanan in the 1992 presidential primaries.

Bush's inability to please the right wing of his party was, in a way, not surprising. What had not been foreseen at all was how little benefit Bush would reap from presiding over the peaceful ending of the Cold War, largely on America's terms, and then inflicting a humiliating defeat on Saddam Hussein. Elections seldom turn on matters of foreign policy, but its irrelevance in 1992 suggests something deeper. It indicates how central the Cold War had been to keeping center-right parties tied to the center, and how, with its disappearance, parties of the right felt little or no reason to continue to pursue centrist policies. Instead, they could engage their baser instincts, and those of their base, and move further to the right. The need to fight the Cold War had, until it ended, encouraged a degree of bipartisanship that put limits on political polarization. These limits began to seem unnecessary to the party that had already turned away from the economic policies that were largely followed during the three decades after 1945. By the early 1990s, partisanship was becoming less and less constrained, at least on the part of Republicans, who became committed to a newly intense and comprehensive partisan competition.

Increased partisanship and polarization affected the internal politics of Republicans and their relationship to Democrats. Two figures embodied and themselves furthered the shift: Patrick Buchanan and Newt Gingrich. They both took aim at Bill, and Hillary, Clinton and seemed to take special relish in it. Buchanan, a speechwriter, broadcaster, and advisor who had worked for three Republican presidents—Nixon, Ford, and Reagan—had challenged Bush in the 1992 primaries and criticized him from the right.[39] He lost, but his strong showing in Republican primaries suggested that Bush needed to appease him and his supporters. To achieve that, he was allowed to give a prime-time address to the Republican convention. His speech became famous for its explicit invocation of the culture wars. Early in his address, he charged that the recent Democratic convention was a charade: a "giant masquerade ball . . . where 20,000 liberals and radicals came dressed up as moderates and centrists . . . in the greatest single exhibition of cross-dressing in American political history." He reminded listeners, "It was under our party that the Soviet Empire collapsed, and the captive nations broke free." Having disposed of the Cold War, Buchanan went on to speak at length about the new struggle for American identity. He displayed a particular animus toward Hillary Clinton, asking, "What does Hillary believe? Well, Hillary believes that 12-year-olds should have the right to sue their parents, and Hillary has compared marriage and the family as institutions to slavery and life on an Indian reservation." He answered for her: "This, my friends, is radical feminism. The agenda that Clinton & Clinton would impose on America—abortion on demand, a litmus test for the Supreme Court, homosexual rights, discrimination against religious schools, women in combat units—that's change, all right. But it is not the kind of change America needs. It is not the kind of change America wants. And it is not the kind of change we can abide in a nation that we still call God's country."[40]

Buchanan made it clear that he had moved on from the Cold War to what was essentially a domestic struggle. He insisted, "This election is about more than who gets what. It is about who we are. It is about what we believe, and what we stand for as Americans. There is a religious war going on in this country. It is a cultural war, as critical to the kind of nation we shall be as was the Cold War itself, for this war is for the soul of America. And in that struggle for the soul of America, Clinton & Clinton are on the other side, and George Bush is on our side." The country no longer needed to fear threats outside its border; the new enemies were within: radical feminists, gays and lesbians, and environmentalists. And, of course, racial animus was a central feature of the culture wars. Buchanan would, in fact, end his speech praising the soldiers who had been called in to quell the uprising in Los Angeles following the acquittal of the cops who had beaten up Rodney King. He recalled meeting with several "troopers" who, he recounted, "came up the street, M-16s at the ready. And the [Black] mob threatened and cursed, but the mob retreated because it had met the one thing that could stop it: force, rooted in justice, and backed by moral courage." He concluded melodramatically, "Greater love than this hath no man than that he lay down his life for his friend. Here were 19-year-old boys ready to lay down their lives to stop a mob from molesting old people they did not even know. And as those boys took back the streets of Los Angeles, block by block, my friends, we must take back our cities, and take back our culture, and take back our country."

Rhetoric of this sort was not unknown in US history, but it was hard to find it in the twentieth century, especially since the 1940s. It echoed the debates just before the Civil War, and those did not end well. Buchanan would run for president again in 1996, and again he would lose, but he had a major influence on the Republican platform on which Bob Dole was forced to run. Buchanan would revive fears of immigration, and he would talk and write about "America first" and about how the United States was being taken advantage of by its allies and by international organizations like the United Nations. He would earn the label "paleoconservative" for his views, but he was extremely popular with the base of the Republican Party.

Newt Gingrich was a different sort of political animal. He, too, fancied himself a thinker and writer—he had a PhD in history from Tulane University—but he was basically a politician who took no prisoners among his opponents and rivals. He came to national attention when he led an effort in the late 1980s to discredit the Democratic Speaker of the House of Representatives, Jim Wright of Texas, and effectively ended his career over improprieties so trivial that they are now scarcely remembered.[41] Gingrich would do whatever he could to derail the Clinton administration and played a major role in Clinton's impeachment. In 1994, he and his allies put together the "Contract with America" and convinced other Republicans to sign it.[42] Basically a campaign document, it promised that Republicans would institute eight reforms of Congress and congressional behavior and that they would introduce ten specific acts for debate and votes. The Contract with America was carefully crafted: its reforms of the House appealed to voters eager to eliminate corruption and shake up politics; and its proposed list of bills omitted controversial items like abortion. It likely helped Republicans to win control of the House, with a gain of fifty-four seats, and it provided the program for the new majority. Gingrich became Speaker and under his leadership Congress proceeded to pass the reforms and introduce legislation. Republicans achieved very little in terms of positive legislation, but their actions made the party more cohesive and disciplined, its ideological stance more consistent.[43] Those changes stuck even after Gingrich himself left Congress in 1999. He had clearly overreached in forcing two government shutdowns and in his pursuit of Clinton, and he resigned as Speaker and from Congress after losses in the 1998 midterm elections. Gingrich nonetheless remained popular and influential with Republicans.

The Republican Party had clearly become more right-wing than center-right by the turn of the millennium. So, too, had the Tories in Britain. Elsewhere, center-right parties struggled to find solid anchors in the electorate and a convincing appeal after the end of the Cold War and the ascendancy of more pro-market policies. In the context, more traditional invocations of national interest and identity became more attractive. Few outside the United States were eager to fight the culture wars, at least not yet, but absent that kind of emotional tie to a loyal political base, conservative parties lacked urgency and resilience. What kept them going and afforded them occasional electoral success was the growing weakness of their opponents. Overall, in fact, it might well be argued that the crises affecting center-left parties allowed center-right parties to carry on despite the waning attractions of free-market liberalism. Conversely, the difficulty of parties on the right in formulating a broad-based appeal enabled the Democrats in the US, Labour in the UK, and socialists and social democrats in Europe to remain electorally viable despite economic and social changes that were weakening their bases of support. It was, of course, an unstable situation that could not and would not last.

A decade after the end of the Cold War the liberal order which, prior to 1989, was far from global, had vastly extended its reach and now encompassed countries that had only recently been part of an alternative socialist world order. It also included countries in Africa, Asia, and Latin America whose political and economic arrangements had been anything but liberal a few years earlier. This expansion of liberal order came at a price, however, for it now incorporated states with vastly different histories and cultures that would necessarily make it less coherent. Equally important, the commitment to a liberal international order had been based on domestic politics in the West (and Japan) with a very strong political center. Parties of the center-right and center-left might alternate in forming governments, but the alternation did not lead to wild swings in policy. The centripetal tendencies in domestic politics had begun seriously to erode, however, in the 1980s and 1990s. Parties on the right adopted pro-market beliefs and policies that threatened to undermine the postwar social cohesion; and parties on the left had trouble adjusting to economic and social changes that weakened their connection to core constituencies. The contradiction, on both the left and the right, between the appearance of external strength and the reality of internal weakness would be dramatically revealed after 2000. The stability of the liberal international order and of liberal democracy itself would face severe tests over the next two decades.

Challenges to Liberal Order, at Home and Abroad

The phrase "liberal order" usually refers to the international order, and that is what its proponents mostly mean by it. What has been argued here is that any liberal order in international relations that is at all robust and durable is necessarily linked to the existence and promotion of liberal democracy. There is no one-to-one correlation between liberalism internationally and domestically, and the imperfection of the connection has often been noted and used to cast doubt on how liberal either international arrangements or domestic politics have been and whether, in consequence, the term *liberal* is justified in either context. The implied standard—that a liberal international order should have no laggards or outliers or inadequacies, and that liberal democracy should be without blemish—is nevertheless unhelpful, for liberalism as an ordering principle for external relations and internal politics is partly an aspiration and a set of principles and partly the messy reality of institutions, parties, and individuals.

An abstract and ahistorical assessment of liberal order also misses the obvious fact that liberalism was historically mixed up with other forces. It has been part of a world of nation-states, even though nations and nationalism have frequently been marked by illiberal beliefs and practices. It was also, early on, deeply implicated in empire, although over time it became clear that liberal order and democracy were incompatible with imperialism and the racism that was its constant companion and support. Liberalism after 1945 was also, and almost had to be, anti-Communist and thus implicated in that perspective's phobias and excesses; and liberalism was also deeply intertwined with the project to create an American hegemony which, though far more tolerable than many alternatives, did not always promote the multilateralism or democracy that proponents of liberal order preached. Adopting an abstract and ahistorical standard of evaluation—faulting liberal political systems for their incompleteness, exclusions, and compromises and liberal internationalism for its connections to the real world of nation-states, nationalisms, and empire—also distracts from the central fact that democracy and the project of creating and sustaining a liberal order among states have been closely associated and have depended critically upon one another.

External Challenges to Liberal Order

Grasping this mutual dependency is critical to understanding the ongoing crisis of liberal order. After 2000, the liberal international order was tested on multiple fronts, forced to confront challenges and challengers that the weakened domestic political order would have difficulty dealing with. Internationally, efforts to extend and deepen the liberal order were already meeting resistance in the late 1990s. The conflict in Kosovo elicited deep skepticism about humanitarian intervention from states and leaders who put their sovereignty above the rights of citizens. It also provoked opposition from Russia, which was unhappy to see a former ally the object of an international coalition and, after the collapse of what was left of Yugoslavia, to accept that Slobodan Milošević could be tried before an international tribunal for crimes against humanity. The fact that the NATO intervention in the conflict was led by Britain and the United States made it possible to argue that humanitarian intervention was a mere cloak for the expansion of Anglo-American, mainly American, power. Debate over the Kosovo War continued after its conclusion in 1999. Even though the intervention was effective in ending the conflict, very few ever accepted the logic of Tony Blair's "doctrine of international community" in which he made the case for it.[1]

Blair's formulation was intended partly to pressure Clinton into agreeing on more drastic action, a sign that Clinton understood that Americans were ambivalent about taking on the role that Blair, and many in Clinton's administration, thought they should. In the presidential election of 2000, the Republican candidate George W. Bush spoke to that ambivalence when he came out against "nation-building." Bush's narrow and controversial victory gave no mandate on foreign policy, a sign that there was no clear preference among voters. The attacks of 9/11 quickly changed Bush's mind, though he was also encouraged by his more hawkish advisors.[2] The shock of the successful terrorist action had enormous and lasting consequences. Its immediate effect was to provoke US retaliation, first against Afghanistan and then against Iraq. The invasion of Afghanistan had broad support at home and from America's allies; a number of countries signed up to join the "coalition of the willing" that waged that war. The decision to invade Iraq had less domestic support and elicited strenuous opposition abroad. Tony Blair brought Britain into the now much smaller coalition despite massive protests. The French denounced the US action at the United Nations.[3] The failure of the Iraq invasion to result in a stable, democratic regime would mean that, by the midterm elections of 2006, the choice to invade had few defenders.

The implications of the attack of 9/11, the violence it let loose in the world, and the futility of the response profoundly weakened the global influence of the United States and its claim to provide the leadership of a liberal international order. The sequence forced attention to the fact that in critical respects many, if not most, of the world's Muslims lived in countries or communities effectively outside the liberal order. There were few democracies among Muslim-majority countries and, even when the state was formally democratic, as in Indonesia or, less convincingly, Pakistan, support for the secular modernity and the accompanying package of rights that characterized most Western democratic countries was limited. Reactions to 9/11 also made it clear that many among the large number of Muslims living in Western Europe had not fully integrated, or been allowed to integrate, into their host societies. The fact that only a handful engaged in or materially supported terrorism in their new homes or set off to join jihadist movements and

forces abroad did not make their alienation and separateness insignificant, for they reinforced views about the incompatibility of Islam and
the West and encouraged Europeans and Americans to look with suspicion or hostility upon migrants from Arab and other Islamic countries.

The rift that the Iraq invasion caused among core countries within
the liberal international order would be patched up, but never truly
healed, for it had made clear that less held them together than had been
thought. The election of Barack Obama brought relief and hopes for a
revitalized and more cooperative relationship, but during the Bush administration both the world economy and the security environment
had changed alter, as Russia and China began to act more powerfully
and independently. The two powers were vastly different. China was becoming a genuine economic competitor and would inevitably seek to
translate its economic strength into geopolitical influence. The Russian
economy, by contrast, remained very much a mess, but the country still
boasted the world's second most powerful military with a huge store of
nuclear weapons. Where the two nations were alike was in the fact that
neither had ever really bought into the principles and expectations of
the liberal international order. Substantial efforts were made in the
1990s to bring Russia into the liberal order, and there were moments of
possibility, but fundamental incompatibilities and differences of interest
could not be overcome. Russia cooperated with the United States in the
aftermath of 9/11, but the rapprochement had ended by the time of the
invasion of Iraq in early 2003.

US actions in Afghanistan and Iraq not only aroused antipathy
among allies, rivals, and third parties, but also displayed the country's
inability to impose its will on Islamist insurgents and its relative isolation. The diversion of resources and attention also meant that while the
United States became bogged down in the Middle East and western
Asia, Russia and China became relatively stronger and more inimical to
liberal order. That may have happened even if the Bush administration
was not preoccupied, but it definitely occurred while it was.

China's emergence as an economic giant had its roots in Deng
Xiaoping's reforms of 1978–79.[4] Chinese economic growth was based
largely on exports made possible by the low cost of labor. China had a
huge peasant population that could be moved into industrial work

where they produced goods that could be sold cheaply on world markets. Its share of global exports, a mere 2.3 percent in 1991, would be close to 19 percent by 2013, and that share would continue to expand. Two political deals helped to facilitate the process: the US grant of permanent normal trade relations (PNTR) in 2000 and China's entry into the World Trade Organization on December 11, 2001. To get these prizes, the Chinese were forced to agree to a long list of reforms. It was thought that these would further open up not only the economy but also Chinese society and its closed political system. China would fulfill many of its specific promises, and its liberalizing and privatizing efforts probably made its economy more efficient. Such reforms undoubtedly contributed to the 8 percent annual productivity growth achieved between 1998 and 2007. That increased efficiency helped to fuel an export boom and intensified the "China shock" that, between 2002 and 2007, saw Chinese competition become a serious threat to domestic manufacturing in North America, Europe, and Japan. A well-known study estimated that the China shock caused the loss of just under a million (actually 985,000) manufacturing jobs in the United States and up to 2 million jobs overall.[5] Subsequent studies offered lower estimates of job losses, but it is clear that the center of global manufacturing had shifted in the early years of the new century.[6] The transformation, however, was not accompanied by an opening up of the political system, and under Hu Jintao and later Xi Jinping, the Chinese Communist Party began to tighten its control.

Russia's retreat from liberalism and reform was mainly the work of Vladimir Putin, although he had lots of help. A former KGB agent, Putin became active in the politics of St. Petersburg and began making connections and building support that would serve him well in Moscow. Yeltsin appointed him prime minister of the Russian Federation on August 8, 1999. In September, a series of bombs exploded in apartment buildings in Moscow and other cities. Chechen rebels were blamed and Russian troops sent to Chechnya. Putin emerged as the advocate of law and order and pledged a ruthless campaign to suppress the Chechens. At the end of the year, Yeltsin resigned and Putin became acting president. The election, scheduled for June 2000, was brought forward to March and Putin was elected president.[7] From the beginning, Putin's rule was heavy-handed and corrupt, though in his first years he pushed through economic reforms demanded by the West and international institutions. With a firm hand in charge, the economy recovered, mostly because of rising prices for Russia's main exports, oil and natural gas. Putin was reelected in 2004. He made peace with the wealthy oligarchs who had emerged on top from the economic transition by gobbling up state assets. Putin did so by becoming one of them, but also by persecuting those who opposed him. The most famous example was Mikhail Khodorkovsky, who in October 2003 was prosecuted and jailed for tax evasion and corruption and whose oil company Yukos was seized and sold off at a bargain price. Most of the assets went to the state-controlled energy conglomerates, Rosneft and Gazprom. Under Putin, the independent press and journalists suffered similar fates. The press was largely brought under the control of the leader's allies, and journalists were harassed and killed, most notoriously Anna Politkovskaya in 2006 and Boris Nemtsov in 2015. Opposition parties also faced hostility and repression.

Putin's victims were mostly other Russians, but his aggressive behavior had an external dimension as well. Russian leaders after 1991 had always displayed an interest in what was referred to as the "near abroad," places where the Soviet Union had once ruled without substantial opposition. There was little they could do about the now independent countries of Eastern Europe, especially as they turned to the West, seeking membership in NATO and the European Union, but Putin was eager to maintain Russian influence in the former Soviet republics. That influence was threatened by the series of "color revolutions" that swept aside Soviet-era leaders—the Rose Revolution in Georgia in November 2003 that brought down Eduard Shevardnadze, the Orange Revolution in Ukraine that between November 2004 and January 2005 brought the reform candidate to power, and the Tulip Revolution in Kyrgyzstan in March and April of 2005. Putin was appalled, not just at the passing from the scene of an older generation who might be more sympathetic to Russian interests, but also at the prospect that the events might encourage reform movements within Russia. He explained in December 2004, "If you have permanent revolutions, you risk plunging the post-Soviet space into endless conflict."[8] He and his government responded by blaming the United States, the CIA in particular, for fomenting the unrest, and their stance became steadily more hostile to the United States and its European allies.

This mounting concern was likely a key factor behind Putin's pugnacious speech at the Munich Security Conference of 2007.[9] The speech was a remarkably blunt attack on the United States and its role in the world.[10] His starting point was an explicit rejection of the idea of a "unipolar world that had been proposed after the Cold War" as "pernicious," "not only unacceptable but impossible." It had led to and would continue to lead to "unilateral and frequently illegitimate actions" that have "caused new human tragedies and . . . new centres of tension." Putin went on to say, "Today we are witnessing an almost uncontained hyper use of force—military force—in international relations, force that is plunging the world into an abyss of permanent conflicts." "I am convinced," he went on, "that we have reached that decisive moment when we must seriously think about the architecture of global security."

The Russian president explained that the economies of India and China were now bigger than that of the United States and that the combined output of the BRIC countries—Brazil, Russia, India, and China—was greater than that of the European Union. That meant that the balance of global power had to shift, for "there is no reason to doubt that the economic potential of the new centres of global economic growth will inevitably be converted into political influence and will strengthen multipolarity." The new security architecture should therefore be less centered on the United States and its allies and more "multilateral"; because of this, only the United Nations, not NATO nor the EU nor an ad hoc coalition, could authorize the use of force. Putin's criticism of the United States was in this sense also a critique of its European allies. There was no explicit mention of the supposed role of Europe and the United States in the color revolutions occurring around Russia, but Putin did attack the Organization for Security and Cooperation in Europe (OSCE). The OSCE, he insisted, had been transformed "into a vulgar instrument designed to promote the foreign policy interests of one or a group of countries" by "interfering in the internal affairs of other countries." It was the OSCE, of course, that had certified the abuses that led to the color revolutions, supervised new elections, and confirmed the legitimacy of the new regimes.[11]

US policies in the Middle East, especially the invasion of Iraq, were an easy target for Putin, and his speech might have won more support were it not for the fact that what he was understood to be advocating was the right of Russia to throw its weight around in what it regarded as its proper sphere of influence. And the corollary was that China and other powers should have the same right. It was also starkly obvious that one of Putin's main concerns was to limit efforts to promote democracy. If the speech was fundamentally disingenuous, it was nevertheless a real challenge to the existing international order and a sign that the post–Cold War order was by no means secure. Coming as it did at the same time that China was emerging as the world's second-largest economy, the speech made it clear that the unipolar moment—good or bad, real or imagined, hoped for or feared—was not an accurate description of the world as of 2007.

The passing of the "unipolar moment" as well as the disappointing results of efforts to foster liberal democracy would be demonstrated with regular frequency after 2007. China was beginning to assert its claims to regional influence in the South China Sea, and there was little that its neighbors or the United States could do but protest. Explicit conflict was avoided, but the reality of increasing Chinese power came to be accepted. In the Middle East, there was a brief moment of hope that the advance of democracy might be resumed with the Arab Spring. It began in December 2010, in Tunisia, where it led to the ouster of the government by mid-January and to new elections the following October. It spread rapidly to Syria, Egypt, Bahrain, and Yemen. The first protest in Egypt occurred on January 25; by February 12 Hosni Mubarak was gone. Large-scale demonstrations that began in Syria in January, coupled with the resignation of key aides and military figures, led to the expectation that the regime of Bashar al-Assad would soon fall as well. Protests began in Libya on February 15, leading to violence and threats of violence from the government controlled by Muammar Gaddafi. The prospect led the United States, Britain, and France to begin airstrikes in March 2011. Dislodging Gaddafi took several more months, until he was killed and his forces in Sirte overcome on October 20. His death did not end the civil war in Libya, and bloody fighting continued long after.

The hopes invested in, or projected on, the Arab Spring were dashed as pro-democracy movements faltered and the authorities regrouped and fought back. The most dramatic defeats were in Egypt and Syria. Mohamed Morsi, a leader of the Muslim Brotherhood, was elected president of Egypt and took office at the end of June 2012. He made critical mistakes and his government overreached; he was overthrown in a military coup led by General Abdel Fattah el-Sisi. A wave of stark repression followed. The battle in Syria was far more protracted and complex, in part because of the involvement of outside powers. Bashar's regime wobbled for a time, but then counterattacked with force. Rebels gained considerable territory and had strength in Damascus and Aleppo. The government's weakness allowed the jihadist group ISIL (Islamic State of Iraq and the Levant) to seize control of substantial territory in the east, where it set up the Islamic State and proclaimed a new caliphate. The United States had maintained a small, covert presence since 2012, and reports of the possible use of chemical weapons by government forces prompted President Barack Obama in August 2012 to threaten a broader use of force if Syria crossed that "red line." That line was definitively crossed when Bashar al-Assad's military used such weapons on civilians in Damascus the following summer. Obama announced on August 31, 2013, that he planned to ask Congress to authorize military force in Syria. He was in a difficult situation, for Congress was wary and there was no groundswell of public support for getting involved. He had hoped that Britain and France would take action along with the United States, but Prime Minister David Cameron lost a vote on the issue in Parliament the day before Obama's announcement.[12] Faced with a lack of support, the Obama administration backed off and instead announced a joint Russian-American proposal to remove chemical and biological weapons from Syria in 2014. The effect of the US decision was to legitimize Russia's involvement in the conflict and to signal America's unwillingness to play a serious role. The US did continue its attacks on the Islamic State, but Russia and Iran stepped up their aid and direct involvement on Assad's behalf. Assad eventually regained control of the country in what was to be a decisive and bloody defeat for the Arab Spring.

There was no obvious connection between the decisions of Britain and the US not to get further involved in Syria in 2013 and what transpired in Ukraine in 2014. It is possible that Putin was to some extent emboldened by the US/UK stance, but Russia and its leader had long-standing reasons for the Russian move into Crimea and the Donbas region of eastern Ukraine. The president of Ukraine, Viktor Yanukovych, leaned strongly toward Russia, but he had somehow been persuaded to sign an association agreement with the European Union in 2013. Just before signing, he reversed course and chose to stick with Russia and the proposed Eurasian Economic Union. Demonstrations against the famously corrupt Yanukovych began on November 21, 2013, growing in strength in December, January, and February. The so-called Euromaidan Revolution echoed the Orange Revolution of 2004 that also led to the ouster of Yanukovych, and Putin surely remembered. An agreement, which the EU and Russia helped to broker but Russia refused to sign onto, was reached to end the crisis on February 21, and a new government took over.

Almost immediately, Yanukovych and his closest allies fled to Russia. Russia sent armed loyalists, pretending to be local volunteers, to seize key locations in Crimea, Ukraine's major outlet to the Black Sea. Within days Russian forces had control of the region and held a referendum on joining the Russian Federation. Soon, troops loyal to Russia became active in eastern Ukraine, where a prolonged conflict ensued. The United States and its allies levied sanctions on Russia and its agents, but Putin did not budge. The sanctions hurt, and kept hurting, but Ukraine had lost Crimea and no longer had effective control in the eastern part of the country. Ukraine itself elected a new government and signed the agreement with the EU, but it remained a site of corruption and intrigue. The outcomes of the Arab Spring and the crisis in Ukraine were clear symbols of the weakening of the liberal international order.

 The inability of the United States and its allies to control geopolitics found a parallel in the economic sphere, where a financial meltdown originating in the United States led to a crisis engulfing most of the developed world. The Great Recession that began in 2007–8 and dragged on for several years demonstrated this incapacity in stark terms.[13] The problems may have begun in the United States, but they soon spread to Europe; and the increasingly dense connections that knit together the global economy meant that the recession came to affect virtually the entire world. The broadening crisis threatened the foundations of the international economy and would alter its institutions and rules and how it functioned. The Great Recession also had dramatic effects domestically, further reshaping economies, producing very clear winners and losers, and upsetting existing political balances. It was simultaneously an external challenge to the liberal international order and a threat to the domestic stability and commitment to democracy that were the system's proudest products and the basis of its effectiveness.

The downturn began in 2007, with weakness in real estate and those financial institutions most involved in that sector's previous growth. It became more visible as it worsened the following year: the collapse of Bear Stearns in March 2008 and of Lehman Brothers the following September signaled how deeply implicated the financial sector had become in dodgy loans and in new and untested kinds of investment vehicles. In the fierce debates that followed these calamitous collapses, the public learned a series of new terms to describe a confusing array of financial instruments and the unprecedented risks that these had introduced into the American economy and into the wider world of advanced capitalism. The new terms included *subprime mortgages* or the *subprime market, collateralized debt obligations* (*CDOs*), and *credit default swaps*. (*Derivatives* and *hedge funds* had a longer history, but were not much better understood.) Unpacking these goes some way toward explaining the crisis. Subprime mortgages were sold to people seeking loans to buy property but not qualified on the standard criteria—the value of the property and the wealth, earnings, and indebtedness of the borrower. Banks and mortgage brokers offered loans at low or, for a time, no interest to people who could not afford them on the assumption, or the hope, that the value of the property would increase and somehow allow the loans to be repaid. It was a bet that the real estate market would continue to boom, even as signs mounted that the boom was ending. CDOs were packages of loans sold to investors. Within the packages were tranches of subprime loans along with less risky loans. These were typically given high marks by the ratings agencies on the theory that it was unlikely that a market downturn would be serious enough to affect both good and bad loans. When the property market tanked, these assets became toxic or, in the legislative euphemism used to describe the subsequent government bailout, "troubled," as in the Troubled Asset Relief Program (TARP).[14] Large institutional investors understood that these new products were risky and had sought protection by buying credit default swaps, a form of insurance against high-risk bonds and products containing such assets. They bought these from insurance companies such as AIG (American International Group) whose Financial Products Division in London specialized in credit default swaps. Because banks and investment funds in the US, Britain, and elsewhere had heavily invested in these, AIG was considered "too big to fail," and the US government was forced to rescue it in September 2008.

Very few people outside the world of finance understood these terms or the instruments and practices they referred to. What the terms nevertheless clearly point to are three distinctive facts about the recession: its origins in the real estate market; the linkage between ordinary borrowers and high finance in the United States and abroad; and the way in which bad loans put at risk the entire international financial system and demanded government action to rescue it. The importance of real estate was itself a sign of the underlying weakness of the world economy. Real estate investing had become more attractive because of the lack of other profitable opportunities. Investing in property provided a further stimulus because rising asset prices encouraged existing homeowners to borrow through refinancing and allowed new borrowers to get into the market and profit as prices continued to rise. The effect was a boom in construction and in consumer spending, which was further aided by the flow of cheap goods from China. The *Economist* had warned on June 16, 2005, "The worldwide rise in house prices is the biggest bubble in history." It was bound to burst, but only when that had happened did it become clear just how risky the lending sustaining it had been.

The recession cost the United States 8.6 million jobs and enormous losses in output and wealth. Employment in manufacturing, already declining, decreased by 28 percent between 2001 and 2015.[15] Britain would experience similar pain, as would other countries in Europe. The decrease in global demand caused a pause to growth in China and led to actual declines elsewhere. It also produced a crisis in economic governance, with power shifting from the G-7 (the G-8 with Russia) to the

G-20, a much broader grouping in which China, India, and other emerging economies had a greater voice.[16] Equally significant, confidence in the ideas and practices governing the world economy massively declined. Since the late 1980s the Washington Consensus, a neoliberal blueprint, had been dominant, but important voices proclaimed the end of neoliberalism during the Great Recession.[17] For a time, there was a revival of interest in Keynes and numerous proposals to reform or reimpose domestic and international regulations on capital and the behavior of banks. That moment passed rather quickly, and in both Europe and the United States the emphasis had shifted away from stimulus to austerity by 2010. The reversion to free-market orthodoxy was no proof that it worked, but rather an indication that no alternative was compelling enough to displace it. Even so, its credibility was much diminished, as was the ability of the United States and its allies to exercise leadership over the international economy and the willingness of the rest of the world to follow their lead. The economic lure of liberal order was diminished; and less and less was it seen as an effective means to order the political and geopolitical relations between states.

Liberalism and Democracy at Home

The external challenges to liberal order were both geopolitical and economic. Its reach was resisted, the attractions of democracy were disputed and dimmed, and the limits of American and Western power were painfully revealed. Russia and China explicitly rejected the system's preference for democracy, and economic policies guided by free-market principles were shown not to work, or not to work as effectively as their advocates boasted. These setbacks occurred when Western political systems were much weaker and more fragmented than at any time since the late 1940s—and weakened them further.

Politics were less stable because the constituencies supporting center-left parties had declined and not been replaced by newer supporters and because center-right parties had moved further to the right. These parallel developments were not well understood as late as 2000. In fact, the long-run decline of the center-left was masked by the fact that, largely by coincidence, center-left parties were in power in the United States,

Britain, France, and Germany that year.[18] There was also much talk by political analysts about how little separated left from right, about how, for example, Clinton and Blair were not much different from their opponents on the right. The Democrats in the US and Labour in Britain had indeed felt compelled to update their programs and appeals as the center had moved to the right under Reagan and Thatcher. The policies pursued by the government of Gerhard Schröder in Germany, known collectively as Agenda 2010, also involved reforms long advocated by his opponents on the right. The French Socialists under Lionel Jospin had not adapted as their British, American, and German counterparts had been forced to do, and in office they followed a relatively incoherent mix of left and centrist policies.[19] The focus on the narrowing gap between left and right nevertheless failed to distinguish between the center-left's consistent efforts to reach for and hold onto the center ground while the center-right, especially in the US and the UK, chose not to.

The divergence of party fortunes and strategies would be intensified by the external shocks that marked the years after 2000 and that gave new salience to issues that the more consensual politics of postwar had marginalized. The most important of these were trade and immigration, with immigration closely bound up with matters of race. The first big shock was 9/11, and the attacks that day not only pushed the United States and its allies to a disproportionate and ultimately unsuccessful military response, they also unleashed fear and prejudice toward Muslims at large and Muslim immigrants in Western countries in particular. Despite centuries of often violent conflict between Islam and Christianity and/or the West, anti-Muslim sentiment had little purchase in the political cultures of Europe and the United States in the postwar era. The Iranian revolution of 1979, and the hostage crisis that followed, put the issue of political Islam on the agenda in the United States and Europe, stimulating debates about the fit between Islam, modernity, and democracy. The reaction to Salman Rushdie's *Satanic Verses,* published in 1988—burnings of the book, threats to its translator, and the Ayatollah Khomeini's fatwa calling for the author's death—kept debates about Islam alive. Such debates were not simple expressions of Islamophobia, though some voices displayed intolerance and insensitivity; they were a sign of growing uneasiness about the role of Islam, especially in Europe.

France and Britain had large numbers of Muslims who had migrated from the former colonies, and Germany was host to a substantial population of mostly Muslim immigrants from Turkey. These communities were not well integrated into the countries where they lived, either by choice or by exclusion. In addition, a lack of local religious leaders and educators provided an opening for proselytizing by clerics, trained and funded by Saudi Arabia, who brought their Wahhabist version of Islam with them. Inevitably, some believers in London or Paris bought into this set of views. For the most part, Islamist militancy occurred in Muslim-majority countries and its targets were other Muslims and regimes thought to be insufficiently pious, but occasionally it spilled over into Europe. A notable example came when the brutal civil war in Algeria, which began in late 1991 and continued until 1999, was extended to France with a series of bombings targeting transport systems in Paris and Lyon and a school near Lyon.

The events of 9/11 transformed what had been an ongoing debate—which was simultaneously a fear, an irritant, and a prejudice that was largely implicit—into something much more potent and explicit. The Bush administration declared a "global war on terror." It was narrowly focused on Islamist terror, but the political effects could not be so easily contained. Arguments over Islam became sharper and more contentious and there were attacks on Muslims and mosques. The relatively small population of Muslims in the United States meant that anti-Muslim sentiment was not a major phenomenon in the country, but it was more widespread and intense in Europe, where it contributed to, and in turn profited from, growing resentment against immigrants. For decades the National Front in France, led by Jean-Marie Le Pen, had agitated against immigration and had gained a substantial following, largely in the south and west of the country. In 2002 Le Pen ran in the presidential election and, because of fragmentation on the left, narrowly beat out Jospin, the Socialist prime minister, in the first round. He was trounced in the second round by Jacques Chirac, but the National Front began to attract support from older industrial districts in the north and east. Le Pen was succeeded by his daughter, Marine Le Pen, who ran in the 2012 presidential election and polled slightly better than her father had in 2002, though she failed to make the second round.

In France, opposition to immigration went along with opposition
to the European Union. The elder Le Pen, though a member of the European Parliament, loudly denounced the Lisbon Treaty of 2007, and the
party continued to oppose efforts to strengthen the EU. The antipathy
was shared by Marine Le Pen, under whose leadership the National
Front actually came first in the 2014 European elections in France. In
2015 she put together an alliance of right-wing, putatively populist parties from Austria, Italy, Poland, the Netherlands, and a Flemish grouping
in the European Parliament. They labeled their coalition "Europe of Nations and Freedom." In 2017, backed by funding from a bank in Moscow,
Le Pen ran again for president. In the first round, she won 21.3 percent,
second to Emmanuel Macron's 24 percent. In the second round in May,
Macron beat her handily, but she managed to garner over a third of the
vote.

Anti-immigrant and anti-EU sentiment went together across Europe. Member states in the European Union set their own policies on
immigration from outside Europe, but the EU did insist on free movement of labor within its borders. The EU was widely perceived, correctly
or not, as a relatively open space with more or less liberal policies on
refugees and asylum seekers. It was also expanding. What had been
East Germany entered the bloc in 1990; Austria, Finland, and Sweden
joined in 1995. After that, enlargement mainly involved bringing in
countries from the former Soviet bloc: the Baltic states, the Czech Republic, Slovakia, Slovenia, Hungary, and Poland joined in 2004, along
with Malta and Cyprus; and Romania and Bulgaria were admitted in
2007. There were temporary restrictions on the free movement of labor
in certain countries, but migration from east to west was nevertheless
substantial. Britain, assuming that its position off the coast of Europe
would discourage migrants, did not impose restrictions and experienced
higher levels of migration than expected. The increased presence of foreigners, and foreign workers, became more controversial and remained
linked in the popular mind to the European Union. In the United Kingdom, only 6.5 percent of the population had been foreign-born or the
children of foreign-born in 1971; by 2015, that number had risen to
13.5 percent and 27.5 percent of births in England and Wales were to
foreign-born mothers.[20]

Immigration also became more of an issue in the United States. Perceptions did not quite match reality, but perceptions were what mattered. The 1965 Immigration and Nationality Act led to a steady rise in migrants from around the globe, but especially from Asia. It was entirely legal. Legal immigration from south of the border increased in proportion, while illegal immigration from the region rose and fell with the demands of the labor market. It is estimated that when the economy was growing between 2000 and 2007, an average of 470,000 undocumented workers came each year; with the Great Recession, that number dropped dramatically and some undocumented workers returned home, and with the economy reviving only slowly, no more than about 70,000 came each year between 2010 and 2015. Overall, the number of undocumented workers fell from 12.2 million in 2005 to 10.5 million in 2017. Illegal immigrants represented less than a quarter of the total number of 44.5 million immigrants in 2017. The total share of immigrants in the population had nonetheless increased. It 1970, the foreign-born and their children were 4.7 percent of the population; by 2019, 13.7 percent were foreign-born and 26 percent of children in the US lived with at least one immigrant parent.

The politics of immigration in America did not closely track the numbers of migrants, for interests and ideology did not always align. Organized labor is a core constituency for the Democrats, and fears about the employment impact of large numbers of migrants could conceivably have pushed both into opposition to increased immigration. Democrats have also been the more liberal party, however, and in addition they receive lots of votes from Hispanic Americans. In terms of ideology, Republicans might naturally incline toward controlling or even decreasing immigration levels, but businesspeople, their key constituency, have profited from an ample supply of cheap labor. So, while anti-immigrant sentiment has long been strong among rank-and-file Republicans, party leaders have been more ambivalent. It would take a political outsider, Donald Trump, to turn the Republican Party into a resolutely anti-immigrant party.

Prior to Trump, Republicans had also largely been in favor of free trade. As with immigration, of course, that part of the Republican base that disliked foreigners on principle had long been open to seeing the United States as the victim of unfair trading practices by other countries, but the business elites so essential to Republicans' ability to fight and win elections favored economic openness. In fact, to the extent that trade mattered, it mattered more to Democratic voters. Organized labor had been wary of the impact of trade on jobs since the recession of the early 1980s, if not earlier, and Democratic opposition had forced the Reagan administration to take a hard line with Japan over car exports to the US. During the Clinton administration, the president had to rely on the votes of Republicans to gain approval for the North American Free Trade Agreement and the Uruguay Round and for normalizing trade with China. Democrats, especially labor but also environmentalists, were also skeptical about the benefits of the increased globalization that free-trade agreements were meant to encourage. The disruption of the WTO meeting in 1999—the so-called battle of Seattle—was mainly a set of protests over whether trade agreements would include appropriate rules on fair employment practices and on the environment; and it was led by labor unions, environmental groups, and a few random leftists.

What made trade a more salient issue was the combined effect of the China shock and the Great Recession. Chinese competition accelerated the ongoing loss of manufacturing jobs. So long as the job losses had been balanced by the creation of new jobs in services, the political effects were modest. When the recession hit in 2008, this ceased to happen, and resentment swelled. Still worse, the recovery from the Great Recession was slow, and it became clear early on that the jobs lost over the previous decade would not return. Voters in hard-hit regions became angry and were apparently ready to abandon old political allegiances.

Trade was a more important issue in the United States than in Europe, if only because trade policy was set at the EU level and so was not the responsibility of national governments. Still, job losses and increased economic insecurity had similarly corrosive effects politically. In Britain, for example, older industrial regions in the Midlands and the north of the country were hard hit, and this gravely weakened support for the Labour Party in what had been its heartlands. What such voters would do, and whom they would support, remained unclear for a time, but there was no doubt that they were now less attached to Labour. Much the same was true in France, Italy, and even Germany. Parties of the center-left were most affected, but traditional right or center-right parties were not always the beneficiaries. What had been fringe parties or movements, most of them on the right, often gained at the expense of mainstream parties of both left and right.

Immigration and trade were not the only issues straining party systems previously dominated by the center. They mattered because they disrupted rather than reinforced stable party allegiances. Equally important, they came on top of developments that had already served to weaken those systems. The market obsession of the 1980s and after, for example, had shifted the balance in the "mixed economy" away from the state, with its controls on business and its role in redistribution and the provision of social security, toward the priorities of capital. The same ideological shift made life harder for trade unions, as did the continued erosion of well-paid jobs in manufacturing. The most noticeable consequence was the relative stagnation of real wages for workers and an increase in inequality. All these trends eroded the roots of party allegiances.

The mainstream parties of the right had been converted to market-oriented policies in the 1980s. By the 1990s, however, the vision and political appeal on offer from parties committed to markets and neoliberalism had become rather thin. They were still useful in a negative way. Conservative politicians could use the enduring attachment of elites to low taxes and the broader public concern over government spending and deficits to resist the proposals of more liberal parties and leaders. But they had little to offer of a more positive sort. That was a major reason for the resort to appeals to fight the culture wars.

In the United States and, to a lesser extent, in Britain, the resort to issues associated with the culture wars was encouraged by the changed media environment. Arguments about fiscal policy or social policy can be boring and do not thrive on sound bites, but arguments on aspects of the culture wars play better on cable, talk radio, or on Fox News, which thrive on outrage. Cable TV had originated in the late 1940s as a technology for providing access to remote and mostly rural populations in the United States, but its real expansion did not begin until the 1970s and 1980s. By 1990, 57 percent of American households had cable; by

2000, 65 million households were subscribed; and by 2012 not less than 93 percent had cable access. The early channels carried sports, entertainment, and news, but a significant number were linked to televangelists and their proselytizing and fundraising efforts. A leading TV preacher, Pat Robertson, ran for president in 1988 on a socially conservative platform and lost. Other televangelists might also have been tempted into political activism, but they displayed a marked tendency to get involved in scandals involving sex, money, or both, and this meant that for the most part they chose to play supporting roles on the right.

The proliferation of new media was not limited to cable television. Talk radio was equally important. Again, the technology was not new, but its use expanded massively after the repeal of the "fairness doctrine" by the FCC (Federal Communications Commission) in 1987. Prior to that, radio and TV stations were in theory required to present both sides of an issue and allow roughly equal time to opposing points of view. After that, talk radio expanded massively and its most effective practitioners, like Rush Limbaugh, were consistently on the far right. As listeners interested in music switched to FM stations, with their superior technology, many AM stations devoted themselves to talk, either of sports or personal relationships or politics. By the late 1990s, viewers and listeners had many more options and a new ability to surround themselves with opinions they agreed with and that fit their beliefs and prejudices.

That ability, especially for those leaning right, was taken to a new level with the founding in 1996 of Fox News, a venture owned and controlled by the conservative media mogul Rupert Murdoch. Roger Ailes, the longtime Republican political strategist, was CEO of the new network. Devotees of Fox News lived in a world that provided them with answers, simplistic and often simply false, on a wide range of questions and sealed them off from alternative viewpoints.[21] It took differences in outlook and lifestyle and routinely sought to turn them into antagonisms. The well-educated, mostly urban, professionals who voted Democratic did usually inhabit a different world from that of the less well educated and well off. Commentators on Fox went further, insisting that these liberals were not merely different, and perhaps indifferent, but actively hostile toward and intent on attacking those "left behind" or harboring politically incorrect beliefs. Fox and other right-wing media outlets also encouraged the dismissal of the views of trained professionals and experts. Anti-intellectualism was not new in America—and it was not unknown in other countries—but what Fox did was to build jealousy and resentment into outright contempt and, equally important, to find and give airtime to rival experts. The rival experts, like the climate deniers who were prominent in their ranks, were typically less well trained and credentialed than their opponents, and they were often in the pay of industries that benefited from their views, but being accredited by Fox gave them a large and appreciative audience. The effect was to reinforce the effects of immersion in the right-wing media environment.[22]

The technologies behind this existed elsewhere, but the legal and regulatory framework was more accommodating in the United States. The effect is that there is no equivalent to Fox News in Europe or Japan, and no figures comparable to Rush Limbaugh, Sean Hannity, or Tucker Carlson. CNews in France aspires to a similar role, but lags. There are newspapers and magazines everywhere that lean right. In Britain, they are mostly tabloids: the *Mail*, the *Daily Express*, and the Murdoch-owned *Sun*. Newspapers and magazines clearly do not have the same pervasive (and persuasive) effects on their readers that radio and TV do, however; and they do not have the immediacy of TV and radio. To this extent, America is different.

The United States is not particularly different in the use of social media. Facebook, Twitter, and other platforms are much more recent phenomena, and they are American companies, but their spread has been global. Their effects have been much debated. They were seen at first as empowering and democratizing discourse, facilitating the mobilization of interests against political establishments, as seemed to be happening in the early stages of the Arab Spring. Increasingly, though, they have come to be viewed as allowing false information and conspiracy theories to thrive. They have also proved to be easily manipulated by forces seeking mainly to disrupt and provoke; and those charged with overseeing them have been unwilling or unable to prevent such uses. In theory, advances in technology and the rise of new media should be neutral, but that assumes a rough equivalence and symmetry of left and right and in the kinds of issues and appeals favored by each. That assumption does not hold, and there appears to be a real compatibility between new media and the messages and images of the right.

New issues and new media combined with prior political shifts— on the left and the right—to continue to weaken the hold of the center. This was true across the democratic world, producing a wave of populist or "anti-system" politics contemptuous of existing elites and their liberal, "cosmopolitan" values and claiming to speak on behalf of the "people" ignored by those elites. Populism, however understood, looked different in different countries and fared better in certain contexts than in others. The appeal of traditional values per se was perhaps greatest in Central and Eastern Europe, where religious belief and affiliation remained relatively strong, especially outside the metropolitan centers, and where democratic institutions were of recent vintage and so less deeply implanted. The Law and Justice Party in Poland and Fidesz in Hungary were the most successful of these parties and movements.[23] Law and Justice was founded in 2001 by the Kaczyński twins, Lech and Jarosław. Its appeal to law and order and traditional values allowed it to make electoral gains in 2005, and it ruled in coalition until 2007. In elections that year, the party lost, and in response it moved still further to the right. Lech Kaczyński died in a plane crash in 2010 and his brother became sole leader. The party won an outright majority in 2015 and after that moved in a decidedly authoritarian direction—packing the courts, controlling the media, banning or restricting the work of pro-democracy NGOs (Non-governmental Organizations)—while adopting social and economic policies modeled on the Christian Democratic parties of Western Europe, but with a more conservative bent.

The Fidesz Party has a longer history in post-Communist Hungary and its leader, Viktor Orbán, more experience in government. Orbán took an active part in the events of 1989 and was elected to the National Assembly in 1990. He first became prime minister in 1998 and immediately began to "reform" the bureaucracy and leading institutions by appointing loyalists. The party nevertheless lost the elections of 2002 and remained in opposition until 2010, when it won two-thirds of the seats in Parliament, enough to push through constitutional changes. The 2011 constitution not only contained explicit commitments to traditional values and to the church, but also cut the number of seats in Parliament. Orbán soon began to publicly criticize liberal democracy and since 2014 has openly advocated for "illiberal democracy," reason enough for Tucker Carlson to broadcast directly from Hungary with Orbán at his side in August 2021.[24] Orbán has also taken a leading role in supporting illiberal and populist politicians and regimes across Europe. His government is typically listed as the leading example of democratic "backsliding" in the region.[25]

Outside Central and Eastern Europe populist movements and parties have typically not managed to gain office, or have done so only briefly and in unstable coalitions. The most successful was the Freedom Party of Austria (FPÖ), which served in coalition governments led by the more traditionally conservative Austrian People's Party (ÖVP) beginning in 1999 and again, also as the junior partner, since 2018. Its program was much like that of Fidesz and Orbán: nationalist, culturally conservative, anti-immigrant, anti-Muslim. The opposition to immigration there was more consequential because Austria had a larger immigrant population than, for example, Hungary or Poland, and its actions to seal borders and deny entry to refugees and asylum seekers had more immediate impact. Populists have also been successful in Italy, where the collapse of the mainstream parties in the 1990s allowed for the rise of Silvio Berlusconi, who effectively broke whatever norms sustained the Italian political system. Corrupt, clownish, debauched, and clearly criminal, Berlusconi dominated the political stage from 1994 to 2011. His party, Forza Italia, was compelled by the fragmentation of the party system to make deals and alliances in order to get and retain power. A frequent partner was the Northern League, recently known simply as the Lega. It was a more genuine far-right, populist party with strong roots in the north of the country. Its leader since 2013, Matteo Salvini, started his career on the center-left but moved to the right over issues such as immigration. Its northern origins have meant that even when the party fared poorly nationally, local support sustained it. That connection has also meant that its program contained a strong commitment to policies of regional autonomy; the same link made it Eurosceptic and led to its talk of a "Europe of the regions." Since 2009, the Lega has faced competition on the populist right from the Five Star Movement (M5S), led by

the former comedian Beppe Grillo. M5S and the Lega both strongly oppose immigration, and their popularity has soared in large part because
Italy is uniquely exposed to immigration from North Africa, Libya in
particular. Though agreeing on immigration and Euroscepticism, M5S
also claims to be environmentalist and has boasted of commitments to
direct democracy, with a fondness for online means of expressing its
members' and, in theory, the people's will. The two parties both did well
in the election of 2018 and formed a populist-dominated government.
M5S was dominant, but Salvini served as deputy prime minister and
minister of the interior. Salvini was ousted over a scandal in 2019, but he
and the Lega have remained a powerful force.

Right-wing, populist parties have taken root and grown in other
European countries, but have mostly been blocked from power. The
Flemish Vlaams Belang, for example, had considerable support in Flan-
ders, but the major parties kept it isolated. The Spanish variant, Vox, received over 10 percent of the vote in the election of April 2019, but
found no allies among other parties, perhaps because its politics were
more traditionally nationalist than genuinely populist. It wants to weak-
en regional autonomy and return power to the central state. Vox is also
quite market-oriented in its policies, which prevents it from espousing
key parts of the populist message. Moreover, it is very extreme, proposing to expel Muslims—it had at one point called for a *Reconquista*—and
to repopulate Spain with immigrants from Latin America. Even more
extreme is Golden Dawn in Greece, which has attracted explicit fascists
and neo-Nazis and engaged in violent and, as the courts ruled in 2020,
criminal behavior. To the north, the Dutch Freedom Party, founded in
2006 and led by Geert Wilders, came second in the election of March
2017 with just over 13 percent of the vote. It has been kept out of the
center-right coalition that took power, but managed to push policy to
the right over immigration. The Sweden Democrats were able to garner
17.5 percent of the votes in the 2018 election, but again were excluded
from office. As in the Netherlands, their presence and appeal have led
their rivals on the center-right to adopt less welcoming and generous
policies toward immigrants. The Danish People's Party, with similar politics, won an even larger share of votes, 21 percent, in 2015, and was
accorded a place in several governing coalitions. From within the gov-

ernment, it secured the adoption of tough new immigration controls and pressed the case against the dangers of multiculturalism.

There are considerable variations among these populist parties and movements. Those in Eastern and Central Europe have been more vocal in defense of traditional values and nationalism, while those in Scandinavia have attacked Muslims for not appreciating freedom of conscience, not supporting the rights of women and gay people, and failing to assimilate. Some are more pro-market or neoliberal, others more Christian Democratic, in their social and economic policies. What most unites them, beyond a common populist rhetoric about elites versus the people, is opposition to immigration and to Muslims. Their support has risen along with the Muslim share of Europe's population, periodically stoked by occasional, but frighteningly real, incidents of Islamist terror. The surge of support for right-wing populism in 2015–16 seems in particular to have been propelled by an increase of immigrants and asylum seekers from the Middle East and by the nearly simultaneous jihadist attacks in Paris, Brussels, Berlin, and other cities. Roughly 1.3 million refugees arrived in Europe in 2015.[26] The increase was mainly the result of the chaos and violence in Syria and Iraq, but people seeking to get to Europe also included migrants and refugees from North Africa and from as far away as Afghanistan. Illegal entry to European countries was also facilitated by Turkey until the EU agreed in March 2016 to give Turkey €6 billion to defray the expense of refugees staying in the country. The EU had agreed earlier that member countries should each take a share of migrants and refugees, but many states refused. The effect was that over a million ended up in Germany, where the Merkel government was more welcoming. "Wir schaffen das" (roughly, "We will cope"), she explained. The move angered some in her coalition and outraged the right-wing Alternativ für Deutschland, but she stuck to the position and Germany did in fact cope.

The surge of migrants and refugees nevertheless boosted the fortunes of the populists. The fact that it largely coincided with a wave of terrorist attacks reinforced the anti-immigrant and anti-Muslim message and appeal. Ever since the attack on the US on 9/11, the possibility that terrorists would undertake deadly attacks in Europe and America was part of a new reality. It became deadly real with the Madrid train bombing of March 11, 2004, which killed 193 and wounded over 2,000, and then again with the London train and bus bombings of July 7, 2005, which claimed 56 lives and injured close to 800 more. The proximate cause was the invasion of Iraq, and the inspiration and leadership came from al-Qaeda. Yet another wave of deadly and highly visible attacks began in 2015. These were mostly connected to the rise of the Islamic State (ISIL or ISIS), which actively recruited volunteers from among Europe's Muslim population and urged them to focus on European targets. The most spectacular hit France in January and November 2015. On January 7, militants killed 17 at the offices of *Charlie Hebdo*, the satirical magazine that had published cartoons of the prophet Muhammad. The next day allies killed a policeman and, on January 9, took hostages at a kosher market, leaving 3 dead in addition to the perpetrator. A still bigger disaster occurred on November 13, when coordinated attacks around Paris left 130 dead and 368 wounded. Jihadists also sought to hit a soccer stadium, where they largely failed, but their co-conspirators took control of the Bataclan Theater during a rock concert, and 90 perished.

Terrorist operations continued the following year and into 2017. It emerged that the more recent attacks in France involved both French and Belgian nationals from Muslim backgrounds. Not surprisingly, Brussels experienced deadly incidents on March 22, 2016, when militants set off bombs at the airport and the central train station, killing thirty-two. Especially heavy casualties in 2016–17 occurred in incidents involving the use of a new tactic—driving trucks and other vehicles into crowded areas. On Bastille Day, 2016, a militant drove a truck into hundreds of people celebrating on the Promenade des anglais in Nice, killing eighty-six and injuring many more. Terrorists next took aim at Germany, carrying out attacks later in July. A deadly and frightening incident occurred on December 19, 2016, when a truck drove into a Christmas market in Berlin, killing twelve and injuring forty-eight more. London would see an attack near Parliament on March 22, 2017, and a truck slammed into a Stockholm department store on April 7, killing five and wounding fifteen. An even more deadly attack occurred at an Ariana Grande concert in Manchester on May 22, leaving twenty-two dead and over fifty injured. In June came the London Bridge attack, again making use of a truck against pedestrians, and in August 2017 a van drove into a crowd in Barcelona and killed thirteen. No location, it seemed, was immune from attack; and the responsibility for most of these incidents was claimed by, or linked to, the Islamic State and its supporters. The wave of attacks petered out in late 2017, but the political and psychological effects would obviously linger and serve to sustain the appeals of the populist right.

Brexit and Trump: Turning Right in Britain and America

The triumph of the "yes" vote in the referendum on whether to leave the European Union and the election of Donald Trump as US president demonstrated that the appeal of right-wing populism was as great in the world's two oldest democracies as it was in Europe. Because of the dominant role of the United States in anchoring the liberal order, and Britain's not insignificant role, the impact of the turn in these two countries would be even more consequential. It was possible to respond to the electoral shocks of 2016 by hoping and assuming that the results were aberrations and that Britain would find a way to finesse Brexit with minor adjustments to its relationship to the EU and that Trump, once in office, would be forced to abandon his campaign rhetoric and govern like a normal politician. Four years later, it was clear that such hopes were merely comforting illusions. Both Brexit and Trump were long in the making and have had major effects that show no signs of disappearing.

The roots of both phenomena can be traced most directly to the transformation of the two main parties and the party systems in Britain and the United States. The center-left and the center-right were both seriously weakened, and the weakening of the center created an unstable and potentially volatile situation. In Britain, the Conservatives struggled to appeal to voters as the attractions of Thatcherism became less compelling. They were unable to settle on a message or strategy from the early 1990s and through the first decade of the new century. Labour was more successful, at least for a while. It chose to accept that Thatcher had changed the political landscape and developed a package of policies to soften the hard edges of what Thatcher and the Conservatives had left behind. Labour under Blair and Brown would reinvest in public services that had been run down over the previous eighteen years and invest in education and training to improve workers' prospects and alleviate poverty. New Labour had decided to modernize the party's image and structure and in office sought to modernize the country as well.

It was a modest strategy of incremental reform, and it proved popular enough to secure three consecutive general election victories and thirteen years in government. Labour managed to reverse the underfunding of the National Health Service and boosted funding for training and education. What it did not and could not do was to rebuild the working-class communities in the north, the Midlands, Scotland, and Wales that had been devastated by the deindustrialization of the Thatcher era. Nor could it restore the power of the trade unions that were so closely linked to the party. These losses were permanent and left Labour vulnerable; its base was wider in social terms, with more professionals and service sector workers, but more fragile. Blair managed to survive the outcry over the Iraq War, winning reelection in 2005, but his successor, Gordon Brown, had the misfortune of being in office when the Great Recession hit. By most accounts Brown handled it reasonably well, but by 2010 the party was tired, the economy was desperate, and Brown was a relatively unattractive leader. Labour went on to lose the election, though it was close.

After negotiations between the two major parties and the revived Liberal Democrats, the Tories and Liberal Democrats formed a coalition with David Cameron as prime minister and Nick Clegg as deputy prime minister. That the Conservatives did not win outright was a sign that they had not yet settled on an effective strategy for appealing to voters during their long period in opposition. They remained largely Thatcherite in outlook, but had not discovered a way to make their policies attractive to voters. They had, for the moment, more or less passed on the option of emphasizing the culture wars, presumably because they sensed that British voters, few of whom were religious and fewer still evangelical, were uninterested and would disapprove. The lack of an appealing vision was manifested in the coalition agreement, which contained little to attract voters, instead promising above all else fiscal rectitude and austerity. The election had not been fought on the issue of government spending and the need to retrench, but it was at least different from what

Labour was offering. It had the unfortunate effect of undoing much of the good that Labour had done in office and slowing the recovery from the Great Recession. That stance more or less guaranteed that voters in older working-class constituencies outside London and the southeast became more impoverished and demoralized. Ironically, that would hurt Labour more than the Tories. The coalition's strategy would also do little for the Liberals, for Cameron successfully shifted the blame for the government's most unpopular policies—like the imposition of tuition fees—onto Clegg and the Liberals. The result was that the Conservatives won a very narrow victory in 2015 and could form a government on their own.

While Labour continued to weaken and the Tories kept searching and failing to find an appeal, one political force was emerging outside the two parties and gathering attention and support. That was the United Kingdom Independence Party, or UKIP. It was founded in 1991 as the Anti-Federalist League and became UKIP in 1993. It lingered on the margins of British politics for more than a decade until it began to pick up support under a new and flamboyant leader, Nigel Farage, after 2006. It was from the beginning focused overwhelmingly on getting Britain to leave the European Union, but under Farage it adopted a broader array of populist policies and antipathies. A nationalist party, it opposed devolution for Scotland and Wales and multiculturalism more broadly. It was more pro-market than some populists in Europe, but made sure to espouse traditional values. It was also, and with increasing vehemence, opposed to immigration and the growing role of Islam in British society. UKIP had been against the expansion of the EU in 2004, on general principles and because it allowed migration from the countries of Eastern Europe. In UKIP's rhetoric the EU was blamed for just about all the evils supposedly afflicting Britain. The new wave of immigrants from Eastern Europe contained very few Muslims, but the EU's relative openness and social liberalism allowed UKIP to conflate opposition to immigration and opposition to Islam, using the mix to encourage opposition to the European Union.

UKIP had little success in British general elections through 2010, but rather more success in elections for the European Parliament. Its support in local, EU, and then national elections began a steady rise under the coalition government, whose austerity policies began to bite in those working-class areas where Labour's hold was already weakening and where nobody as yet considered voting Tory.[27] As of late 2012 UKIP was polling at around 10 percent nationally but in the local elections of May 2013 its candidates won 23 percent of the vote where they competed and increased the party's representation from 4 to 147 seats. In the European elections of 2014, it attracted 27.5 percent of the vote and elected twenty-four MEPs. The outcome, which made Tories and the entire political class take notice, was a direct threat to the Conservatives—but also an opportunity. David Cameron, the party leader, was a Eurosceptic, but did not support leaving the European Union. He was nonetheless tormented by the committed Eurosceptics in his own party who, although never strong enough to prevail, were a constant nuisance that gathered lots of attention. Cameron chose to respond to UKIP's rise and the discontent within the Tory ranks by proposing to hold a referendum should the Conservatives win the next general election. The promise was included in the 2015 Manifesto. The idea, or so it seems, was to placate the Eurosceptics but in the process to defeat them. In any event, the promise to hold a referendum was not taken terribly seriously. After the Tories unexpectedly won the 2015 election, it became necessary to actually do it. Still, party leaders were not very worried because they had prevailed in the Scottish independence referendum in September 2014 and believed that exiting the EU was an even less popular cause. It was a major miscalculation.

The referendum was scheduled for June 23, 2016. The Leave campaign was split between Vote Leave, Leave.EU, and Grassroots Out. Vote Leave was closer to the Conservatives and led by Dominic Cummings, with Tory MPs Michael Gove and Boris Johnson its most prominent spokesmen; its message was that Brexit would bring economic benefits. Leave.EU and Grassroots Out were closer to UKIP, Farage was the most notable leader, and their pitch focused more on immigration. The Remain campaign was run by Britain Stronger in Europe. It was more genuinely nonpartisan, with representatives from the Conservatives, Labour, and the Liberal Democrats. Its arguments were largely negative: leaving the EU would mean losses across the entire economy. The campaign was bitter, and the polls showed that the country was very evenly split.[28] In the referendum Leave prevailed, winning 51.9 percent of the vote. It had appealed successfully to older voters, while the young, who mostly favored Remain, failed to turn out in large numbers. Leave also polled well in rural districts and in older and declining industrial regions.

How did Brexit win? The Leave campaign made promises that were clearly fanciful, but its overall message nevertheless resonated. It also had the support of the right-wing press, with its extensive reach. Leave also benefited from the relatively complacent and lackluster Remain campaign. A good part of the weakness of the Remain camp stemmed from the ambiguous stance of the new Labour leader, Jeremy Corbyn. Ed Miliband had resigned the Labour leadership after losing the 2015 election, and his replacement was a backbencher with a long history on the left of the party who had been opposed to British membership in Europe since he entered politics in the 1970s. Corbyn came out officially against Brexit, but there was no enthusiasm behind his opposition, and reports emerged after the vote that his leadership team obstructed the work of the Labour Remain campaign.[29] Leave was, in other words, fortunate in its enemies. It was also fortunate in its timing. Euroscepticism may have had deep roots, but the fact that the referendum was held in 2016, on the heels of the refugee crisis of 2015 and while the upsurge of terrorist violence in Britain and Europe continued, surely made a huge difference.[30] In the twelve months leading up to the vote television and the press were filled with images of migrants in Calais trying to sneak onto lorries or to break into the Eurostar terminal in order to get to Britain, of dead or bleeding victims of terror in France and elsewhere, and of what appeared to be hordes of refugees and immigrants crossing borders. It was one such image that served as the background of the infamous UKIP/Leave.EU poster headlined "Breaking Point," released a week before the vote. It featured Nigel Farage pointing to a long line of nonwhite people at the border between Croatia and Slovenia and saying, "Europe Has Failed Us All"; hence the desperate need to "Take Back Control." The poster was widely condemned, Boris Johnson and the official campaign distanced themselves, but it was likely effective—and it undoubtedly captured the moment.

The aftermath of the Brexit referendum was a complicated and contentious reckoning with its meaning. Brexit backers seem not to have believed they would win and had no idea what to do next. David Cameron resigned as prime minister and Conservative leader, to be replaced by the unimpressive Theresa May, who struggled unsuccessfully with the details of leaving the European Union. She would fail and resign in 2019. Boris Johnson took her place and pressed forward with the decision to leave. His accession to the leadership and to the premiership meant that the Tories were now the party of Brexit. They had effectively stolen the populist and nationalist clothing of UKIP, which rapidly dwindled into factionalism and irrelevance. Johnson ran on the program lifted from UKIP and handily won the election of December 2019.[31] The United Kingdom officially left the EU in January 2020.

Who and what actually won in December 2019? UKIP's policy had prevailed, and so had its message and tone. It was the Conservatives, of course, who gained seats in Parliament and got to run the country's affairs, but to do so they had to adopt policies and a political style with which many traditional Tories were not entirely comfortable. The alignment of Tory politicians and voters with populist policies and appeals was a poor fit that might well not endure.

Similar questions could well be raised about Trump and the Republican Party. Trump ran against a bevy of more traditional Republican candidates for president, beat them all, and forced many who had been repelled by his message and character to rally around and support him in government. Opinion polls showed that even after Trump's outrageous behavior in office and his defeat in 2020, Republican voters still supported him; and Republican politicians were afraid to break with him for fear that his supporters would punish them. Trump, it would appear, was an outsider who took over an established party. That is how Trump saw and understood it: his son-in-law Jared Kushner, presumably privy to Trump's views, told the author Bob Woodward in April 2020 that "he basically did a full hostile takeover of the Republican Party."[32]

That view misses a great deal, for it neglects all the different ways in which the Republicans were moving toward Trump, even if neither he nor they quite understood it. To begin, there was the emptiness of Republican appeals as the commitment to market-based policies grew weaker and less effective and, even more, when markets failed so spectacularly in the Great Recession. This lack was a major reason why Republicans kept having to resort to invocations of the culture wars. What Republicans lacked in appeal they made up for in money, organization, and discipline. It was under Newt Gingrich that congressional Republicans became a coherent group, and subsequent leaders like Dennis Hastert, John Boehner, and Paul Ryan ensured that they stayed united.[33] They were also well funded, both directly in campaigns and indirectly through the various think tanks, institutes, and super-PACs that worked so hard to shape political discourse.[34] These resources would ensure that, even when facing a historical defeat, as in 2008, they had the ability to regroup and, even if they had yet to settle on a winning message, to win elections with attacks and slogans that tapped into the grievances and prejudices of their base.

The array of grievances and prejudices shared by right-wing Republicans included the many culture wars complaints that kept audiences happily watching Fox News—abortion; the supposed threats to Christian values and freedoms, like the "War on Christmas" so deplored by Bill O'Reilly; immigration; resentment against Muslims and paranoia about the plot to bring Sharia law to America; and the supposed oppression of white Americans disadvantaged by affirmative action and other racial preferences. All of these resentments were intensified by the election of Barack Obama in 2008, none more than racial antipathy. His rise and triumph were a catalyst for an intensification of political conflict and an upsurge in negative partisanship. Former Fox News anchor Juliet Huddy remembered the shift that occurred at the network in 2009: "It became just a constant barrage of anti-Obama—criticizing Obama just non-stop."[35] In his memoir, Obama himself was very clear that "it was as if my very presence in the White House had triggered a deep-seated panic, a sense that the natural order had been disrupted." As Obama explained, this "is exactly what Donald Trump understood when he started peddling assertions that I had not been born in the United States and was thus an illegitimate president. For millions of Americans spooked by a Black man in the White House, he promised an elixir for their racial anxiety."[36]

The swearing in of Barack Obama therefore quickly elicited a mobilization on the right. It was not officially led by the Republicans, still embarrassed by the party's defeat the previous November. Instead, it took the form of the Tea Party, a supposedly grassroots movement of people outraged at the fiscal irresponsibility of the new administration. On February 19 Rick Santelli, a CNBC business reporter broadcasting from the Chicago Mercantile Exchange, engaged in a rant against the administration's plan to rescue homeowners who, unable to pay their mortgages, were at risk of losing their homes. "The government is rewarding bad behavior," he claimed and called the people whose homes were being saved "losers." He also proposed a Chicago Tea Party to show opposition to the government's plan. Santelli was cheered by the traders in the background, and the idea was picked up by various media. Fox News went all in, becoming a virtual co-sponsor of the Tea Party. The movement spread rapidly and widely, with Fox News anchors playing up its events in anticipation and with right-wing foundations and campaign groups like FreedomWorks and Americans for Prosperity contributing funds.[37] The movement held a series of "Tax Day" rallies on April 15, with Fox News promoting and sending its personalities—Glenn Beck, Sean Hannity, Greta Van Susteren, and Neil Cavuto—to watch, cheer, and report. Tea Partiers moved on to showing up angry and disruptive at congressional town halls during the summer recess and sponsored a march in Washington, DC, on September 12.

Members and supporters of the Tea Party claimed that their goal was "Fiscal Responsibility, Limited Government, Free Markets," but they displayed a special animus toward the "undeserving," among whom were counted illegal immigrants and, at least implicitly, many African Americans. Of course, the movement did not oppose Social Security and Medicare, not terribly surprising given that many of its members were older white males. Tea Partiers supposedly wanted to see economic issues take precedence over social issues like abortion, but most also admitted to being "socially conservative." The timing of the Tea Party's emergence makes it obvious that one social issue, race, mattered a great deal. The Obama administration had barely taken office when the movement emerged and spread. There had been no opportunity to see whether the government's policies would be successful or not. All that was really known at the beginning of Obama's first term was who he was. He was Black: to Tea Party enthusiasts and other Republicans and to Fox News and its talk-radio allies, like Laura Ingraham and Rush Limbaugh, he was not one of "us."

The Tea Party would help get Scott Brown elected to Ted Kennedy's Senate seat in Massachusetts in January 2010, and its efforts at the state level would help Republicans to their big win in the 2010 midterms. That victory was strategically important. It reinforced the party's relentless opposition to Obama and was the occasion for Republicans in Congress to reaffirm their decision not to work with the administration. John Boehner, soon to be Speaker of the House, proclaimed his intention to frustrate Obama's agenda just before the election: "We're going to do everything—and I mean everything we can do—to kill it, stop it, slow it down, whatever we can." His Senate counterpart, Mitch McConnell, was equally blunt: "The single most important thing we want to achieve is for President Obama to be a one-term president."[38] The election also gave Republicans enhanced influence in state legislatures and allowed the party to control the redistricting process after the 2010 census and engage in heavy-handed but effective gerrymandering. The plan to use redistricting to lock in Republican majorities in Congress and in state legislatures was known as REDMAP, the Redistricting Majority Project, and was led by the Republican State Leadership Committee.[39] States like Pennsylvania, Michigan, and Wisconsin were special targets. The project was able to boast that in the aftermath of the 2012 election, which Obama won with an Electoral College margin of 332-206 over Mitt Romney, the 49 percent of voters who supported Republican congressional candidates produced a House majority of no fewer than thirty-three seats.[40]

The willingness to brag about securing a frankly anti-democratic outcome was surely a sign that American politics had entered a new and nasty phase. So, too, was the vitriol of the Tea Party and the undisguised antipathy to Obama. A few Republicans felt uneasy about the party's direction, and an official "autopsy" on its defeat in the presidential election of 2012 recommended a broadening of the party's appeal that might win it more votes from ethnic and racial minorities. This recommendation was ignored by the party's base and most of its leaders, who chose instead to rally its mostly white, older, and religiously conservative supporters through appeals based on race and resentment. Underpinning this choice was a perception on the right that the United States was becoming a different country, one in which whites were no longer as dominant as they had been and where being white and Christian no longer secured the privileges that white people were accustomed to. Liberals and Democrats welcomed Obama's election as opening a new era of racial tolerance in which minorities would have a greater role in government and society. That very prospect terrified others who began to see politics as existential, as a threat to their identity. If it required voter suppression and crude gerrymandering to protect that identity and status, so be it.

The Republican Party was to this extent already moving in a direction that would lead to Trump's nomination and election in 2016. The very same forces and institutions that were pushing the party to the right and leading it to countenance—indeed, to carry out—transparently antidemocratic measures would also provide the environment in which Trump flourished. There were indications of this well before 2016. To take but one simple example: the Conservative Political Action Conference, a mainstay of the Republican right, had welcomed Trump as a guest speaker on February 10, 2011. There the audience applauded loudly as he laid out his stock argument that America had become a "whipping post" and a "laughing stock of the world." The country, Trump claimed, was being taken advantage of by its enemies but also by its allies and trading partners. Its NATO allies did not pay their fair share even as leading countries, like Germany, prospered by exporting their goods to the United States. Japan likewise was protected by the United States in Asia and benefited massively when America kept open the sea-lanes from the Middle East so that it could continue to import the oil it needed. Mexico stole jobs and sent unwanted immigrants to the north. None of this was new for Trump. He had paid for a full-page ad making these very points, with slightly different examples, in the *New York Times*, the *Boston Globe,* and the *Washington Post* way back on September 2, 1987. It began: "For decades, Japan and other nations have been taking advantage of the United States. The saga continues."[41] The conservatives who welcomed Trump may have differed with him on matters of trade and on other issues, but there was an underlying compatibility between them and Trump that was displayed on the stage at that meeting in 2011.

Trump was at exactly that time about to become the most prominent advocate of the "birther" conspiracy that claimed Obama had not been born in the United States and that his presidency was illegitimate.

The move endeared him to a wider range of right-wing voters and politicians and helped to boost Trump's political visibility.[42] He was also about to receive a huge gift of unearned publicity from Fox News. It is well known that Trump was rescued financially and that he refurbished his image through the NBC "reality" show *The Apprentice,* which began to air in January 2004. That exposure was about Trump the businessman, not as a possible political leader, but Roger Ailes of Fox News later stepped in and arranged for Trump to expand on the "birther" conspiracy on a call-in to the morning show, *Fox and Friends,* on March 28, 2011. That appearance led to a decision to create a regular segment on the program, "Monday Mornings with Trump." Trump would call in to talk about his favorite political themes, and viewers got to listen and watch as the Fox hosts nodded along or asked "softball" questions.[43] These regular appearances ended only when Trump declared his candidacy for president in 2015, though he would continue to call in to *Fox and Friends* even after he took office. He obviously enjoyed the admiring audience, much as he did in the evenings when he would regularly get on the phone with Sean Hannity. Trump's links to Fox were part of a broader circuit: Fox was all in with Republicans and their views before 2008, and when Republicans were defeated that year by Obama, Fox turned into a relentless critic and helped to engineer a "grassroots" opposition, the Tea Party; when Republicans' antipathy to Obama led to a rebound in their electoral fortunes in 2010, Fox cheered them on; and when Trump began his rise in 2011 it was largely through Fox that he connected with the Republican base.

It would therefore make more sense to understand Trump as emerging from the furthest right reaches of the Republican Party than to see him as having pulled off a "hostile takeover" of the party.[44] What Trump did and what earned him the loyalty of Republicans who might well have been put off by his crude and uncivil demeanor was to provide them with the sort of message they lacked. Republicans had tried on populism with the selection of Sarah Palin as vice presidential nominee in 2008, but to little effect. Throughout Obama's two terms Republicans had been obstructionist, but had little positive to offer beside the promise of austerity. Trump broke with the Republican fixation on fiscal restraint, cutting spending, and reneging on entitlements. He promised voters whatever they wanted. He would boost Social Security benefits, protect and improve Medicare, and launch a giant program to build or rebuild infrastructure.

Equally important, Trump gave prominence to the two issues that were agitating voters and for which neither party had good answers: immigration and trade. Prior to 2016, Republicans were split over immigration and had come close to making deals with Democrats on legislation to resolve the issue. Republicans were also the party of free trade and of multinational firms that had done well out of globalization and the opening to China. Trump gave new answers on both immigration and trade. He promised to cut down on immigration with new rules: a ban on migrants from Muslim countries and a border wall to keep out Mexicans and people from Central America. On trade, Trump proposed the revision or repudiation of trade agreements and said he would impose tariffs on imports from China and from US allies like Germany if they did not agree to whatever Trump demanded.

On neither of these questions could one detect a rising wave of popular discontent. There were more immigrants than many Americans were entirely comfortable with, but not many connected the presence of immigrants to threats to American jobs. Likewise, those who lost jobs in manufacturing due to Chinese competition had mostly been able to find work in the service sector so long as growth lasted. With the Great Recession, and the slow and painful recovery, such grievances intensified and it became more plausible to link them with immigration and trade. Trump managed to do that and to win support from voters who shared these grievances and who had become detached from previous political alignments. Trump was also able to pull in voters more concerned about the culture wars. He won an early endorsement from Jerry Falwell Jr., who had inherited his position at Liberty University from his father. Falwell's support helped to ease the consciences of evangelicals who might otherwise object to Trump's personal style and behavior, allowing the vast majority to vote for the serial liar, misogynist, and frequently bankrupted businessman.

Trump's victory was also, of course, contingent on the fact that his opponent was a poor campaigner and could easily be portrayed as part of an out-of-touch political establishment. Hillary Clinton had been an object of hate and derision from the right for decades, and it had taken its toll on her credibility. Trump benefited, too, though it is difficult to say by how much, from Russian interference that involved the hacking and leaking of the email accounts of key Democrats. Of rather more importance, it would seem, was the bizarre behavior of the FBI director, James Comey, in the conduct of the investigation into Hillary Clinton's emails. He first announced that she was not guilty of wrongdoing, but coupled that with an unusual and uncalled-for rebuke; then, shortly before the election, he announced that the investigation had been reopened—and then, shortly before the vote, that the reopened investigation was closed. The effect was that a nonissue, blown up into a fake issue by congressional Republicans, was validated and allowed to linger until right before voters went to the polls. It is not impossible that the sense of crisis in Europe and the Middle East, which was the background to the Brexit vote, also aided Trump, though the impact was unlikely to have been significant. Even so, the perception that the United States was less effective, and exercised less control, in the world fit easily into Trump's view of the world as a dangerous place in which America was not winning.

The precise contribution of contingent and long-term factors to Trump's victory in November 2016 is impossible to know, but it makes sense to argue that the local, the recent, and the superficial converged with more deep-seated trends in American politics to produce an unexpected result. In the aftermath, surprised observers and scholars sought to disentangle the reasons for Trump's win. The main debate was whether it was a kind of revenge vote by those who were "left behind" by shifts in the economy and by their lack of education and whose plight had been ignored by more successful coastal and cosmopolitan elites with better credentials *or* a reflection of the racism that has been an enduring feature of American life and that Trump was to nurture and elicit.[45] The answer, surely, is that it was both, and more.[46] A lengthy process of social and economic change, made more painful and permanent by the Great Recession, served to detach Americans from settled alignments and, in particular, from the Democratic Party. The Republican commitment to an austere neoliberalism made the party turn increasingly to the culture wars as a means to motivate voters. The choice by Republicans to abandon the political center and move to the right allowed more toxic ideas and sentiments—racism, opposition to immigration, resentment of foreigners close by and abroad, opposition to abortion and LGBT rights, ideas that had been confined to the margins of politics for decades—to be revived and given voice. Voices expressing such views were amplified in the new and less responsible media environment. The election of Barack Obama had turned commonplace racial resentment into a near-apocalyptic fear that America was turning into a country in which whites, especially white men and white Christians, would soon be swamped and ruled over by people of color. Trump's contribution was to bring all this toxicity and dysfunction together at a moment that was uniquely favorable to him and his message. No small achievement, but he had lots of help. The larger question still looms: to what effect?

Conclusion

Fragmentation, Democracy, and Liberal Order

The Long View

The votes for Brexit and for Trump in 2016 were dramatic ruptures, clear breaks from three-quarters of a century of political history. The impacts will be clear only in the long term. The analysis laid out in this book suggests, however, that neither outcome was quite as aberrant and unpredictable as first reactions implied. The vote against Europe was unexpected when it occurred, but consistent with a lengthy tradition of British unease about its ties to the European continent. Trump was not the first demagogue to attract a large following in the United States, nor were his appeals to race and xenophobia previously unheard of.[1] He was the only such figure who managed to ride these sentiments to the presidency, but they were familiar features of the dark side of American history. The traditions that produced Brexit and Trump never went away in either country, but they were eclipsed beginning in the 1940s and remained at bay until roughly the 1990s. Their revival since drove the victories of Brexit and Trump; and populists elsewhere, relying on comparable traditions and sentiments, had success as well. The precondition for this breakthrough was the lengthy process by which parties and political systems in Britain, America, and other Western nations became effectively detached from the political center, less secure and less firmly rooted.

Put differently, a measure of the effectiveness of liberal order internationally and of liberal democratic politics domestically was their ability to keep the kinds of sentiments that Brexit and Trump and populism played upon confined to the margins for so long. Liberal order had been the rule in international relations in the West since the 1940s, and then more widely after 1989, and democratic political systems functioned with minor disturbances for a prolonged period. That era lasted long enough to make liberal order and political democracy appear normal and natural and to obscure from view the considerable difficulties that attended the creation of liberal order in the 1940s and the establishment of viable political systems in the West and Japan. Also obscured were the challenges that had to be confronted internationally and at home in maintaining liberal order and functioning democracies throughout the postwar era. Large sections of this study have been devoted to clarifying what was previously obscure in order to reveal not just the sources of stability in the system but also its vulnerabilities. Understanding what made things work after the Second World War shows that whatever stability was achieved—and *stability* is a relative term—the project was never assured and needed constant tending.

If the duration of liberal order and democratic politics made it difficult to appreciate the achievement, the erosion of the conditions sustaining both was also not obvious until it was well underway. The economic troubles of the 1970s got the attention they deserved, as did the inability of governments using the tools and ideas at hand to cope. The resulting turn away from the state toward the embrace of the market was also visible enough and well chronicled. The implications of the neoliberal turn for liberal order and democratic stability would, however, not be visible for some time. The resumption of at least modest growth after the steep recession of the early 1980s diverted attention from the corrosive effects of market fundamentalism. Its policy triumphs tore up the social compact—the expanded commitment to social provision or the welfare state, the limits on what business could and could not do, a reasonably fair and redistributive system of taxation, and a balance between the rights of labor and capital—that made prosperity shared and politics more stable from the late 1940s into the 1970s. Critics of neoliberalism may have predicted negative consequences, but it required a couple of decades for those consequences to be registered decisively.

Before that, liberalism and liberal order secured a historic victory over socialism and authoritarianism in Eastern Europe and the Soviet Union. The end of the Cold War was undoubtedly a vindication of liberal democracy and capitalism. It can plausibly be argued that the capitalism that had prevailed in the Cold War was not the market-oriented variety recently in vogue and on offer in 1989. Rather, it was the variant of reformed and constrained capitalism that had generated growth and steadily rising living standards during *les trente glorieuses* that decided the contest between capitalism and Soviet-style socialism. It was capitalism nonetheless, and to insist on this distinction in 1989, or in the decade that followed, would have been seen as churlish and would not have made much difference, particularly since economic growth accelerated further during the 1990s and globalization, whose locally devastating side effects would emerge only over time, advanced rapidly as well. The post–Cold War order was in fact a victory for liberal order, for capitalism, and for democracy, which extended their global reach and became established in places where socialism had produced economic stagnation, where democracy was largely unknown, and where international order had meant being locked into a bloc held together by force and repression.[2] The victory was inevitably incomplete and subject to reversal, and the prospects for further expanding liberal order and democratic rule would soon diminish, but the achievement was real and gave the appearance that the new order was likely stable and secure.

It would turn out to be neither, for it would confront serious external challenges after 2000, and internal developments in democratic political systems would render them fragile, leaving governments and leaders incapable of responding creatively to a new world. Even during the 1990s, if not before, the center had begun to weaken politically. Center-left parties had to reorient themselves as their previous bases of support atrophied. As these parties sought to attract and cement connections with new constituencies, they remained committed to the political center. On the center-right, by contrast, parties abandoned the center ground and moved further to the right. Part of the reason was that market liberalism offered little besides austerity and tax cuts to voters, and conservative politicians responded by courting them with appeals to nationalism, resentment of immigrants and foreigners, and the culture wars. The right's willingness to move away from the political center was also facilitated by the end of the Cold War, for it had been the need to fight the Cold War that had pushed many conservatives to adopt more centrist positions, both on the economy and on questions of civil and social rights. With the Cold War won and done, compromise and moderation were not so necessary. The weakening of the political center, already in progress since the 1980s, would advance much further in the first decade and a half of the new century. Issues like terrorism, the role of Islam in the West, and immigration would gain increased saliency, and a new, more polarized media environment pushed right-wing parties further to the right and led them to adopt a more populist tone and appeal. The center-left continued to make gains among professionals, ethnic minorities, and women, but center-left parties remained coalitions of interests and therefore hard to manage and keep together.

The shifting character of politics in democratic systems made those systems vulnerable. So, too, did the nature of the external difficulties they faced. The first and perhaps most difficult was the matter of dealing with the causes and consequences of 9/11, as parties and leaders argued over the appropriate response and adopted policies that were largely ineffective or counterproductive. Less immediately pressing but equally resistant to easy solutions were the open challenges to liberal order, and to democracy, from Russia and China. While the consequences of these shifts in the global order were still unfolding, the Great Recession hit in 2008, depriving the advocates of liberal order and liberal politics of the most powerful argument in their repertoire: the claim that liberal capitalism was an engine of growth and prosperity. The recession cut deep, destroying businesses and further hollowing out the manufacturing sector in the developed West, and recovery was slow and painful. The inequality that had been increasing since the 1980s got much worse and its victims became further detached from prior political loyalties and open to more demagogic appeals. Political entrepreneurs like Nigel Farage and Donald Trump, like populists across Europe, saw the opportunity and prospered in just about every country. Their breakthrough victories came in 2016, with the "yes" vote prevailing in the Brexit referendum in June and Trump winning the presidential election in November.

After 2016

What made the shocking choices of 2016 so important was where they occurred. It had been worrying to see turns toward authoritarianism in Russia and in Turkey, but not entirely surprising. So, too, in Brazil. Nor were the triumphs of authoritarian populists in Hungary and Poland entirely unexpected. It was disappointing to note that China's further integration into the global economy was not accompanied by any loosening of the grip of the Chinese Communist Party, but it was always a stretch to believe that it would. More troubling was the turn to populist parties and leaders in Western Europe, but the fragmentation of Italian and French politics was more or less structural and provided space for such movements to gain a foothold. The nations of Western Europe also confronted the same forces that weakened the hold of the political center as were operative elsewhere—rising inequality, strained and less generous social protections, and the erosion of previously secure jobs in industry. These issues combined with resentment against immigrants, Muslim immigrants in particular, to create conditions in which populist appeals attracted support.

When right-wing and rhetorically populist movements like Brexit and leaders like Trump won elections in 2016, they triumphed in the two countries that had been central to the prolonged effort to create and sustain a liberal international order. Britain and the United States also boasted the longest histories of successful democracy, always flawed but functioning steadily and gradually improving. For right-wing populism to suddenly prevail in Britain and America was to demonstrate that it could succeed anywhere; and because of the outsized role played by these countries, the United States most importantly, in making and maintaining liberal order and promoting democratic governance, the liberal international order would in consequence become weaker and democracy more fragile. Whatever happened after 2016, serious damage to liberal order and to liberal democracy had already been done.

The politics of Brexit after the referendum was, in fact, a bizarre parody of normal politics, and the Trump administration was a chaotic mess with but a single legislative accomplishment—a tax cut that utterly contradicted its populist appeals and promises—along with often brutal and poorly crafted executive orders that were routinely blocked by the courts and that would mostly not survive a new administration. Nevertheless, the effects of these moments of right-wing populist dominance were real and would have consequences.

The saga of Brexit after the referendum was pathetic and humorous and troubling, all at the same time. The vote prompted David Cameron, who had called it and lost it, to resign as prime minister. He would be succeeded by Theresa May, a lackluster party loyalist who declared on assuming power that "Brexit means Brexit." That in itself meant little, for Brexit remained to be defined, but it did make it unlikely that it could be reversed and gave the upper hand in shaping it to those most keen for a clean break. It did not prevent more than three years of parliamentary wrangling over the terms of Brexit, and another year of bargaining with the European Union. May herself would not survive the process. She made a huge error by calling a general election in June 2017. Her hopeful assumption was that the promise of "strong and steady leadership" would give her a big majority over Labour and leverage over the Brexit fanatics in her own party. The assumption was really a gamble, and she lost. Labour, which had trailed badly in the polls, somehow managed to fudge the question of Brexit and instead offered a program to end austerity. The result was that May lost her majority and was forced to rely on the backing of Britain's most retrograde party, the Ulster Unionists (DUP). Rather than being strengthened in Parliament, she was crippled. Under May's leadership the Tories would be bested by pro-Brexit forces in the European elections of May 2019, and she was compelled to resign shortly after. Boris Johnson was selected as party leader and took over as prime minister in late July. Amiable and unprincipled, Johnson promised to finish Brexit, and on that basis fought the general election of December 2019. Labour, deluded by its success two years earlier, endured a catastrophic loss. Brexit would happen, though another year would pass before Britain secured a provisional trade deal with the European Union.

The practical impact of the Brexit decision was likely to be mixed, with more negative than positive results. By choosing to leave the grouping of European countries, Britain was reducing its role and impact on the world. For a while it seemed possible that other member countries, with their own inevitable grievances, might follow the British example and leave, or threaten to leave, the EU. It did not happen, as European countries presented a united front in dealings with the UK. The coalition that supported Brexit had many factions and preferences, but a core group of Thatcherite enthusiasts believed that Britain should and would become a kind of Singapore on the Thames, competing with low taxes and few regulations and pushing for free trade all around. Johnson's populist pitch, and the Conservatives' need to preserve the gains they made in 2019 in the "red wall" of seats in older industrial areas in the north and Midlands, presumably preclude that option, but Britain will struggle economically whatever the government's policy choices. All serious predictions foretell economic loss from Brexit, though it will be difficult to distinguish losses due to Brexit from those stemming from the COVID-19 pandemic. In terms of domestic politics, Brexit made the Conservative Party into the Brexit party, reinforcing the move toward populism. Will the Tories thrive with that new identity? It seems questionable, particularly given the erratic character of Boris Johnson. What seems more possible, if not yet likely, is that Brexit will convince the Scots to hold another referendum on independence. Such sentiments could also grow in Wales; and Brexit could unsettle many things in Ireland. Overall, the British decision to leave the European Union has, and will continue to have, its main effects within the United Kingdom. It has had, and presumably will have, only modest effects internationally.

Trump's election would have far greater impact, though his interventions were too scattered and erratic to have the decisive effects that his supporters wanted and that so many others feared.[3] The most immediate change was in the tone and rhetoric of foreign policy, which ordinarily proceeds with pledges of friendship and common goals before getting down to negotiating the testy matters on which states differ. Trump reversed that, putting anger and threats first before, more often than not, backing down on specifics. He attacked longtime allies in NATO and questioned the usefulness of the alliance before acquiescing to minor policy changes and reaffirming US security commitments. The administration was also prone to bluster, issuing threats to obliterate North Korea—before Trump decided he was in love with its dictator—and getting little in return. More generally, Trump could be counted upon to do, or at least to say, pretty much the opposite of what Obama had said and done. The most obvious case was Russia: the Obama administration had been sharply critical of Russia over its intervention in Ukraine and its annexation of Crimea and had imposed tough sanctions. Trump, deciding that he trusted Vladimir Putin more than his own intelligence and foreign policy advisors, indicated that he wanted to lift sanctions. He did not manage to do that, but he tried.

The Trump administration also softened or abandoned American criticism of authoritarian rulers and regimes: of Duterte in the Philippines, Bolsonaro in Brazil, Erdoğan in Turkey, Orbán in Hungary and his counterparts in Poland, el-Sisi in Egypt and, most shamefully, the Saudis. Whether the new US attitude mattered much, and whether it further empowered these rulers and governments to behave worse than they otherwise would have, is difficult to say, but it is obvious that the United States under Trump did little or nothing to promote democracy anywhere. Aside from rhetoric, Trump's achievements were mainly negative. He renounced the Paris Climate Agreement, pulled back from the Trans-Pacific Partnership, took the United States out of the Iran nuclear deal in 2018, and opted out of the World Health Organization in the middle of the COVID-19 pandemic in 2020. None of these moves led to the collapse of the agreements, but they did signal that the Trump administration was not interested in maintaining the multilateral cooperation, alliances, and institutions through which a rules-based, liberal international order must work. The Trump administration also signed up to a very bad deal with the Taliban in February 2020, though the fall of the Afghan government would happen during his successor's tenure.

A central feature of liberal order has been economic openness. It is on this issue that the Trump administration had the greatest effects, but its efforts were not terribly productive. Though Trump insisted on withdrawing from the North American Free Trade Agreement, the substitute arrangement negotiated with Canada and Mexico made few changes. The threat to impose tariffs on allies, including Canada, was mostly not

followed up; and when it was, the administration's measures were rid-
dled with exceptions and reversals. The recourse to protection against
China was more consistent, but the policy did little to redress the balance of trade with China, and it led to higher prices for consumers, including businesses. Businesses have felt compelled to think about
reconfiguring their supply chains with key links in China, but do not
seem likely to relocate operations back to the United States. Vietnam,
Bangladesh, Mexico, and other low-wage economies offer better prospects. It is likely that the shift in policy toward China and trade will
continue beyond Trump, but policies pursued together with allies would
seem to offer a much better chance of success.[4] The problem is that
Trump's legacy might well render multilateral approaches more difficult.

At home, Trump's record was weak on substance, if dramatic in
presentation. Outrageous tweets became a substitute for policy. The administration's most significant legislative accomplishment was the Tax
Cuts and Jobs Act of 2017. It was one of the most unpopular bills ever to
be passed by Congress, mainly because roughly 80 percent of its benefits
went to the top 1 percent. Republicans barely mentioned it during the
2018 midterms, in which they experienced massive losses. Trump also
promised legislation on health care: he pledged to replace the Affordable
Care Act (Obamacare) with a much better system. Republicans came
close to securing repeal but failed, and they never got around to putting
forward an alternative. "Infrastructure week" became a joke. With few
legislative achievements, Trump chose instead to make policy through
executive orders. These were plentiful and covered just about every major policy area, but most were so poorly drafted that they were blocked
permanently by the courts or had to be seriously modified to withstand
judicial scrutiny. Among those that survived, many have been or will be
reversed by the Biden administration. Potentially the most damaging
would likely be those that have allowed businesses to pollute by dump-
ing or drilling or making unsafe or less fuel-efficient products, though
many companies, looking further ahead, will have been wary about taking advantage of Trump's deregulating initiatives when they were unlikely to last.[5] Trump's executive orders do fit, of course, into a long
history of efforts to cripple the government's ability to police the behavior of businesses and to protect the environment. In that sense, Steve

Bannon's pronounced desire to work toward the "deconstruction of the administrative state" was merely an update on prior efforts to "starve the beast," with more than a touch of added venom and paranoia.[6]

The balance sheet of Trump's few domestic accomplishments, through legislation or executive orders, added up to a largely ineffective presidency. Such a traditional measure, however, does not offer anything like an adequate assessment of his impact on the country and its political life.[7] Trump's election in 2016 was a product of Republicans' long march to the right on policy; of his and the party's willingness to make appeals on the basis of racial, ethnic, and religious identity; of their relentless focus on culture war issues; of efforts to build on and make use of a history of attempts to control the rules of the electoral game, mainly by making it more difficult for nonwhites to vote; and of appointing conservative justices to the courts. To this rather toxic brew Trump brought explicit contempt for women, for immigrants and foreigners, for his political opponents, and for the media, at least those reporters, broadcasters, and newspapers that chose to question him. Trump as president also imported into the center of government the routine practice of lying. All this eroded the norms and customs that have been, and continue to be, essential in maintaining democracy.[8] Trump also chose to populate his administration with people who were very rich, had little experience or competence, and were often plainly corrupt. If and when any of his team showed a hint of independence, he turned on them— and they were soon gone. There had been hope early on in the administration that there were enough "adults in the room," typically military men, to restrain Trump's worst impulses. They were only partially successful, and over time they would be replaced by more pliant—indeed, sycophantic—characters.

The purpose behind such practices did not appear to be a desire to advance a program or ideology, for Trump had no set of stable ideas. The effect, though, was to further the agenda of the Republican right and to embed their views in government, particularly in the judiciary. Trump's purpose, it seems, was mostly to aggrandize himself and to garner as much power and attention as possible. It began with transparently false claims about the size of the crowd at his inauguration and absurd arguments about how he had really won the popular vote, insisting that Clinton's popular majority was due to illegal votes. The political battle over the completely justified Russia investigation provoked the president to new efforts to assert his authority, most notably by firing the head of the FBI. When that led to the appointment of a special prosecutor and a lengthy inquiry, Trump not only did his best to obstruct justice—as the Mueller Report documented in detail—but also decided to cast himself as the victim of the "deep state" and to do whatever possible to purge the government of officials insufficiently loyal to him.[9] Where possible, he also sought to use the state for his personal enrichment and to advance his boundless political ambition.

The effort to get American taxpayers to make money for the president, his family, and his businesses meant endless bookings of government events at Trump properties and encouraging foreign leaders and emissaries to do the same. It also meant promoting his daughter's brands and doing what he could to help family members, like Jared Kushner, with their own financial troubles. Odd behavior for someone who had promised to "drain the swamp" in Washington. Rather more important for the long term was Trump's effort to use his position to keep himself in power. He reportedly asked China to buy more agricultural products to help his reelection, for example, and sought to extract policy pronouncements and decisions from foreigners to advance his interests.[10] The boldest attempt to use the powers at his disposal to advance his narrow political interests came with Trump's pressure on Ukraine in 2019. It was the cause of his first impeachment. Trump tried to hold up essential military aid approved by Congress to force Ukraine to investigate Hunter Biden, the former vice president's son, and Joe Biden himself. Whistleblowers inside the government, in the National Security Council and the CIA, leaked the text of the phone call from Trump to the Ukrainian president, Volodymyr Zelenskiy. Congress investigated and voted to impeach the US president. The Senate chose not to dismiss Trump, but there was little doubt of his guilt. Shortly after the Senate vote on February 5, 2020, Trump proceeded to enact another purge of officials he regarded as disloyal.

As the Senate was debating Trump's fate, news began to trickle in about a previously unknown and quite lethal virus that had broken out in December 2019 in Wuhan, China. Coping with this new coronavirus and the illness it caused, COVID-19, was the first serious challenge of Trump's presidency. For three years Trump had been very lucky: he had inherited an economic recovery from the previous administration, and the tax cuts of 2017 helped to keep it going; there had been extremely destructive hurricanes and wildfires to which Trump responded ineffectively, but he managed to avoid taking the blame; and the absence of serious international crises meant that Trump's efforts to disrupt the international order had less effect than they might have had if circumstances had been different. The coronavirus, which by March had become a global pandemic, put an end to Trump's good fortune and threatened his reelection.[11] It need not have done so. Other leaders, in the United States and abroad, were seen to respond effectively to the virus and became more popular with voters. Trump, by contrast, responded in perhaps the worst possible way. His first reaction was to deny the severity of the disease, claiming that the United States had few cases and that its spread would be controlled and at the same time blaming China for exporting the virus. The president famously told the journalist Bob Woodward that he deliberately played down the seriousness of the virus and the accompanying health crisis.[12] He then, very briefly, decided to take it seriously and began to advocate a national lockdown, but he left state and local leaders to do the actual work of combatting the disease. Trump presided over shortages of medical equipment—ventilators and PPE (personal protective equipment)—and tests, leaving local officials, businesses, doctors and hospitals, and the public to fend for themselves. The result was that in the first year of the pandemic the United States suffered more cases and more deaths than any other country, rich or poor.

The pandemic brought with it economic collapse, as businesses were forced to close for safety reasons and as people stopped shopping in person and eating out. Restaurants and bars, sports facilities and gyms, theaters and museums closed, as did many schools and colleges. Unemployment rose rapidly. Trump, fearing that the disruption to the economy would weaken his reelection prospects, soon shifted his position and began to call for lifting lockdown measures only recently, and belatedly, imposed. He actually held out the prospect of reopening by Easter of 2020. With the virus spreading more or less uncontrolled, that was impossible, but a few businesses started up again in May and more did so in June. The move was grossly irresponsible—a summer of re-opening was followed by an autumn of rising infections. This second surge was not confined to the coasts, which had been hit hardest in the spring, but was more widely dispersed. By November, rates of infection were highest in the Dakotas, despite their sparse populations spread out over vast expanses of territory. The argument over reopening became increasingly polarized and nasty, with Trump urging his followers to blame state governors for imposing restrictions on economic activity and social gatherings that could spread the virus and to demand that they "liberate Michigan," or Wisconsin, or wherever they found them-selves. It also led to disagreement between the administration and public health authorities who resisted Trump's early moves to declare that the virus was dying out, that businesses could safely reopen, or that social distancing and the use of face masks were unnecessary. As health profes-sionals spoke out, Trump attacked them, proposing untested, ineffective, or even dangerous remedies, and turning for advice to people who lacked expertise in infectious diseases. He appointed Dr. Scott Atlas—a fellow at the Hoover Institution, Fox News commentator, former profes-sor of neuroradiology, and advisor to Rudy Giuliani's presidential cam-paign in 2008—as a special advisor, for example, in order to counter the influence of more widely recognized experts like Anthony Fauci. Attack-ing experts was nothing new for Trump or for his followers or for Fox News, but it was dangerous.

As the pandemic brought devastation to the nation's health and its economy, Americans also witnessed yet another reckoning with racial discrimination. On May 25, George Floyd was killed during an arrest in Minneapolis. A police officer knelt on his neck for over nine minutes while Floyd kept saying, "I can't breathe," and begged for relief. Three other policemen stood by, preventing onlookers from intervening. The event was recorded. People all over the country soon saw what had hap-pened, and by the very next day protests erupted in the city. They quick-ly spread to roughly two thousand cities under the banner of Black Lives Matter. Most protests and protesters were nonviolent and, at least ini-tially, opinion polls were strongly in favor and also showed support for reforming the police. As is normal with such large-scale social move-ments, there was occasional violence. Some was provoked by protesters, some occurred when protesters confronted police, and some was carried out by opponents of the protesters seeking to discredit their actions. The Trump administration reacted by invoking "law and order" and, here and there, by sending in troops or federal agents. Protests and minor violence continued through the summer and even into the fall, but Trump's efforts to use the federal government for what was routinely the work of local and state police elicited resistance from mayors, governors, and even from the military and the secretary of defense. The political effect of the Black Lives Matter protests was difficult to assess, for the early support the movement received was dissipated to some extent by continued violence and, it has been argued, by demands to "defund the police." The phrase and the demand, supporters asserted, were not meant literally, but were a way of saying that more resources should be directed at efforts to reform the police and to employ people trained to handle mental health crises and to manage confrontations. Trump and his allies insisted on taking the demand literally, using it to justify their emphasis on establishing law and order by supporting the police.

What mattered most for the presidential election of 2020, it seems clear, was the coronavirus pandemic and Trump's ineffective handling of it. The progress of the disease was relentless, and however much Trump and the administration sought to play it down and hope that it would disappear, it did not. The effect was not merely to undo the economic success that Trump hoped would be his main claim to a second term, but to further erode his credibility and to undermine his regular boasts. His opponent, Joe Biden, took the virus seriously and acted as public health officials urged—wearing a mask, social distancing, and urging the public to do likewise. He campaigned from home and eschewed the sort of in-person, and largely maskless, rallies that Trump craved. The Trump campaign engaged in the same personal attacks that it had used on previous opponents, but they were less effective against a familiar and nonthreatening candidate like Biden. As these attacks failed, the Trump campaign followed the predictable path of trying to garner support by appealing to fear, based largely upon race, and on familiar culture war issues. These efforts proved to be insufficient, and Trump lost by a solid margin. Biden's victory was not a rout, particularly in light of the solid performance of Republicans in Congress, but it was a decisive rejection of Trump.

As Trump contemplated the possibility of defeat, he began to make the argument that the election was rigged, that the only way he could lose would be if the election was stolen. This pitch, too, was predictable, for he had said much the same thing in 2016, when he assumed he would lose. But he obviously enjoyed winning more and, having tasted the perquisites of office, was not eager to relinquish them. The effect was a prolonged, ungracious, and frankly undemocratic effort to refuse to accept the results of the election and to overturn it. It required the promulgation of what has rightly been called "the big lie"—that the election had been stolen from Trump—and culminated in the January 6 riot at the Capitol. Nothing so effectively symbolized the dark side of Trump and his presidency as the way he chose to leave it. The political effects of the failed effort cannot be good, but it is impossible to predict if they will be lasting. The behavior was certainly of a piece with the Trump record before his election and during his term as president; and the acceptance of the "big lie" by many Republicans was consistent with the party's newfound loyalty to Trump and its contempt for voters who might disagree.

Liberal Order and Democracy, Reassessed

Efforts to establish a liberal international order enjoyed two great moments of successful expansion. The first came in the decade or so after the Second World War, when democracy was established in Western Europe and Japan. Though its reach was confined, it was maintained for a long time and accompanied by a shared prosperity. The second moment occurred after the end of the Cold War, when the reach of the liberal order was extended, becoming more global, as democracies and market economies were established in what had been the Soviet bloc and in a number of non-Western countries. The prior wave of democratization that began in the 1970s and 1980s in Latin America, Africa, and Asia meant that by the early 2000s at least formal democratic rule was in place more widely than ever before; and more countries and peoples participated in the world market than had ever done so before, even if the benefits were distributed unequally. Liberal order, internationally and domestically, had been limited and qualified until the 1990s; after that, limits were extended; qualifications were still in order, but perhaps not forever. There were even hopes that integration into the world economy and engagement with international institutions, the law, and civil society in the world of liberal order and liberal democracy would erode the isolation and repression that characterized China and illiberal systems elsewhere. It would not happen, but for a brief moment it seemed conceivable at least, if not quite likely.

The two decades since have been rather sobering for advocates of liberal order and the promotion of democracy. The grand hopes of the early post–Cold War period have not been realized, and setbacks have been far more frequent than advances. The events of 9/11, and their bloody aftermath, demonstrated with brutal clarity that large sections of the world were not pining for democracy or the liberal, mostly secular, culture of the West. They showed, too, the limits of the kinds of power—military and economic—wielded by the United States and its allies.

With Putin's rise to power, Russia chose a path quite different from that envisioned by its Western advisors after the Soviet collapse: its variant of capitalism turned out to be highly unequal and based not so much on manufacturing and services as on resource extraction, never a recipe for equity or the nurturing of a democratic culture; and it decided to reclaim its position as a great power in opposition to the perceived hegemonic aspirations of the United States. China pushed forward with rates of economic growth seldom seen and has sought an international and geopolitical role commensurate with its enhanced economic status. And lastly, economic failure stripped the United States and its closest allies of what had been the most compelling argument for their vision of global order, market-oriented economic policies, and democratic governance. Failure was manifest most obviously in the Great Recession, but also in the slow and uneven growth that followed and the rising levels of inequality that accompanied it.

Severe hits to liberal order and liberal democracy have also come from within, as illiberal policies and politicians gained increasing support. Right-wing populism took root and spread across the advanced democracies, putting into question the commitment to democracy itself. Until 2016, the most serious turns toward illiberalism had come in Hungary and Poland, but the electoral shocks of 2016 in the UK and the US were more dramatic and arguably of greater consequence. The success of the Brexit referendum meant that a founder and pillar of the liberal international order had chosen to opt out of the organization that helped to define Europe as liberal and democratic. Trump's election victory was a triumph of an extremely toxic type of populism—market-oriented or neoliberal in economics but nationalist, racist, and socially conservative in its appeal, a kind of "plutocratic populism."[13] It was also an authoritarian populism, limited in its ambition mainly by its leader's incoherence and short attention span.

The recent threats to liberal order internationally and to liberal democracy domestically mean that talk of liberal order and its prospects needs to be coupled with a frank recognition of its limits and contradictions, of progress and backsliding. Rather than speaking of liberal order as something that was once established, then extended, and is now threatened—a familiar story of rise and fall—it makes more sense to regard the efforts to create and sustain a liberal international order and to advance liberal democratic politics within states as a continual quest. As a corollary, when examining and assessing those periods when liberalism has appeared to be the norm, it has proved essential to probe more deeply and explore the conditions that made it possible and allowed it to be seen as normal and natural. The basic lessons to be learned are that the efforts to bring about liberal order and liberal democracy were routinely hard, the results impermanent and hardly normative, even when they seemed to be stable and enduring, and that the successes of the liberal project required specific historical conditions that will not be replicated.

Those conditions—in the 1940s and the 1990s—were unique. Imagining that they, or something very similar, will recur is delusional. Absent the circumstances that enabled earlier liberal advances, the prospects for restoring support for liberal order or extending and deepening democracy will undoubtedly be more limited. Of necessity, any such efforts must be built on a recognition of the altered geopolitical landscape and present economic, social, and political realities. The question then becomes a matter of figuring out what possibilities these new contexts open up.

Take, for example, the demographic trends that have elicited panic on the right over the "great replacement" and its threat to "Western civilization" and the status of white Christians. It is worth recalling that this fear is based on desperation, for the increasingly multicultural and secular character of modern societies is a real phenomenon; and continued progress in this direction will make people who share these sentiments even more of a minority. In their place will come cohorts without such worries and antipathies. Other trends will push in the same direction: the steady expansion of higher education and the proliferation of post-industrial jobs will undoubtedly continue. The political effects of such change will not be automatic, but it is reasonable to imagine that they can be turned against the forces of illiberalism and allow for a successful pushback against right-wing panic and against those who base their appeals on issues derived from culture war cleavages.

Likewise, the economic changes associated with neoliberalism and globalization, so corrosive of the ties that held together the center-left, need not have similar effects forever. Already there is a turn toward greater use of government to mitigate unrestrained competition and a determination to control globalization and repair its destructive effects. The COVID pandemic, which exposed the danger of reliance by the United States and other advanced economies on foreign sources for critical items and the potential bottlenecks in global supply chains, will reinforce this shift and encourage at least some "reshoring." Political creativity will be required to devise liberal and progressive responses to these questions, but the history of resistance to Trump suggests that there will be no shortage of innovative responses.

It may also make sense, if one wants to grasp the potential in the current era of political menace, to return in part to the mentality that the advocates of liberal order and democracy were forced to adopt and maintain during the Cold War. The Cold War was a global struggle of terrifying breadth and depth. Liberal order nevertheless existed within it and was worth pursuing and sustaining in the relatively protected realm of the non-Communist world. This limitation did not mean, however, that the international order was marked only by chaos, competition, and conflict. Even with illiberal regimes in place over vast territories and ruling over huge populations, bargaining, compromise, and occasional cooperation were possible and, within limits, effective. With the world much more connected today and intercourse between states, cultures, and economies much more intense, the potential for bargaining, compromise, and cooperation should be more extensive despite sustained rivalry and competition.

The great difference between the Cold War era and the present is that the relative power of the most powerful states has altered: the United States is no longer so dominant and its economic weight no longer so overwhelming; economic and political clout is now more dispersed, and likely to remain so. This fundamental difference means that the quest for a stable international order needs to operate with a more limited set of goals and ambitions. It means, too, that efforts to promote democracy should be undertaken with greater realism and less grand expectations, and with more specific goals. And finally, the lesson of the most recent past is that some of the most serious threats to liberal order and democracy come from within democratic states themselves. The causes of this erosion of support for the project need desperately to be addressed. This may seem a modest agenda, but it is not, and it is no less urgent than any that has come before.

Would a more limited vision and program fail to inspire? It might seem so, but it is useful to recall that the postwar order was not primarily a product of utopian hopes and soaring rhetoric. It emerged from revulsion at what the depression, fascism, and war had wrought and from a widely shared understanding of what needed to be done to prevent a recurrence. It was a positive program inspired by a negative and often fearful vision, and it served to guide the construction of a new world. Its successes then led to a more expanded sense of the possible. Ambition grew with the increased capacity to turn aspirations into reality. The potential for incremental success can beget boldness, while high and unrealistic hopes are routinely disappointed. The focus, then, should be on the illiberal enemy and the likely dire effects of its policies, on practical steps aimed at its defeat, and on nurturing the prospects that exist and that will continue to emerge for the advance of a liberal democratic world.

Notes

Introduction

1. Talk about the crisis of liberal order or of the post–Cold War liberal order has been ubiquitous since 2016. For a thoughtful treatment, see G. John Ikenberry, *A World Safe for Democracy: Liberal Internationalism and the Crises of Global Order* (New Haven: Yale University Press, 2020). Francis Fukuyama, famous for his celebration of liberal triumph in his article on "The End of History," *The National Interest* (Summer 1989), shares the belief that the liberal order faces a crisis in his essay "What the World Saw That Day," *New York Times,* January 9, 2022. Predictably, not every commentator is convinced that the situation is critical or that the order cannot be patched up. See, for example, Jussi Hanhimäki, *Pax Transatlantica: America and Europe in the Post–Cold War Era* (Oxford: Oxford University Press, 2021); and Rebecca Lissner and Mira Rapp-Hooper, *An Open World: How America Can Win the Contest for Twenty-First-Century Order* (New Haven: Yale University Press, 2020). The premise of this study is that the crisis is real and serious. And that was decided on long before the Russian invasion of Ukraine.

2. On the long history of ideas about liberal, and not so liberal, global order, see Mark Mazower, *Governing the World: The History of an Idea* (New York: Penguin, 2012); and, with a focus on the United States, David Milne, *Worldmaking: The Art and Science of American Diplomacy* (New York: Farrar, Straus & Giroux, 2014). For debates about the US and liberal order, see also Elizabeth Borgwardt, Christopher Nichols, and Andrew Preston, *Rethinking American Grand Strategy* (Oxford: Oxford University Press, 2021). The concern with grand strategy is controversial and has elicited criticism from different directions: see Thomas Meaney and Stephen Wertheim, "Grand Flattery: The Yale Grand Strategy Seminar," *Nation,* May 8, 2012; and Colleen Flaherty, "Yale Program Director Resigns, Citing Donor Influence," *Inside Higher Education,* October 1, 2021, https://www.insidehighered.com/quicktakes/2021/10/01/yale-program-director-resigns-citing-donor-influence.

There is a separate and thoughtful literature on liberalism among intellectual historians. The emphasis in this study is not on the history of ideas but on the practice of making and unmaking liberal international order and political democracy, for which ideas are obviously relevant.

3. The implication of empire and, inevitably, race in the liberal international order made it possible for its opponents, like the Soviet Union and China, to condemn it as merely a new form of imperialism. Even at its inception, representatives of colonized and "third world" peoples were critical, as Eric Helleiner shows in *The Forgotten Foundations of Bretton Woods: International Development and the Making of the Postwar Order* (Ithaca: Cornell University Press, 2014). There are also critics who discuss liberal order as yet another flawed product of the West that, like other such products, should be rejected by non-Western peoples and states. See, for a recent example, Pankaj Mishra, "Grand Illusions," *New York Review of Books*, November 19, 2020, 31–32; and for a more thorough exposition, Mishra, *Bland Fanatics: Liberals, Race and Empire* (New York: Farrar, Straus & Giroux, 2020). For a realist critique that stresses that the use of force and posits that "dark bargains with illiberal forces" were always part of creating and maintaining "liberal order," see Patrick Porter, *The False Promise of Liberal Order: Nostalgia, Delusion and the Rise of Trump* (Cambridge: Polity, 2020).

4. G. John Ikenberry made essentially this argument in *After Victory: Institutions, Strategic Restraint, and the Rebuilding of Order After Major Wars* (Princeton: Princeton University Press, 2001). His book was basically an argument that the United States should not abandon the institutions and policies that it helped put in place following the Second World War after the end of the Cold War. It was part of a broader debate on international relations after the Cold War that often pitted liberal internationalists and institutionalists like Ikenberry against realist, or neo-realist, theorists. Among the latter, see especially the work of John Mearsheimer, "Back to the Future: Instability of Europe After the Cold War," *International Security* 15 (Summer 1990): 5–57. See also Ikenberry, *Liberal Leviathan: The Origins, Crisis and Transformation of the American World Order* (Princeton: Princeton University Press, 2011). The debates among scholars of international relations are fascinating and informative, but only indirectly related to the argument made here, which is mainly historical and focused simultaneously on the international and the domestic.

5. Graham Allison, "The Myth of Liberal Order: From Historical Accident to Conventional Wisdom," *Foreign Affairs,* July/August 2018. Allison insists that the stability of the "liberal international order" was due primarily to the Cold War balance. On the structuring effects of the Cold War, see James Cronin, *The World the Cold War Made* (London: Routledge, 1996).

ONE An Illiberal World of Rival "Orders"

1. Tobias Straumann, *1931: Debt, Crisis and the Rise of Hitler* (Oxford: Oxford University Press, 2019).

2. For a thorough retelling of interwar developments in international relations, see the two magisterial volumes by Zara Steiner, *The Lights That Failed: European Inter-*

national History, 1919–1933 (Oxford: Oxford University Press, 2007), and *Triumph of the Dark: European International History, 1933–1940* (Oxford: Oxford University Press, 2011).

3. Price data from Adam Tooze, *The Deluge: The Great War, America and the Remaking of the Global Order, 1916–1931* (New York: Viking, 2014), 213–14. See also chapter 19 on "The Great Deflation" of 1920–21.

4. The classic critique is John Maynard Keynes, *The Economic Consequences of Mr. Churchill* (London: Hogarth, 1925).

5. D. E. Moggridge, *British Monetary Policy, 1924–1931: The Norman Conquest of $4.86* (Cambridge: Cambridge University Press, 1972). On whether the pound was seriously overvalued after 1925, see Harold James, *The End of Globalization: Lessons from the Great Depression* (Cambridge, MA: Harvard University Press, 2001), 68–69; and Charles Kindleberger, *The World in Depression, 1929–1939* (London: Penguin, 1973), 44–48. Churchill's admission in 1945 is cited in Andrew Roberts, *Churchill: Walking with Destiny* (New York: Viking, 2018), 315. He takes it from Lord Moran, *Winston Churchill: The Struggle for Survival* (London: Constable, 1966), 303.

6. On the League of Nations and its Economic and Finance Committee, in which the United States participated formally from 1927, see Patricia Clavin, *Securing the World Economy: The Reinvention of the League of Nations, 1920–1946* (Oxford: Oxford University Press, 2013).

7. Tooze, *Deluge,* 487ff.

8. Mellon's comments come from Hoover, *The Memoirs of Herbert Hoover* (New York: Macmillan, 1952), 30–31. They are cited and discussed in Heather Cox Richardson, *To Make Men Free: A History of the Republican Party* (New York: Basic, 2014), 201.

9. Barry Eichengreen, *Hall of Mirrors: The Great Depression, the Great Recession, and the Uses—and Misuses—of History* (Oxford: Oxford University Press, 2015), 155ff.

10. Smoot-Hawley was not specifically a response to the depression, but a result of a promise made by Hoover and the Republicans during the 1928 election. See A. G. Hopkins, *American Empire: A Global History* (Princeton: Princeton University Press, 2018), 579–80.

11. Craig VanGrasstek, *Trade and American Leadership: The Paradoxes of Power and Wealth from Alexander Hamilton to Donald Trump* (Cambridge: Cambridge University Press, 2019), 30.

12. Sir Frederick Phillips, cited in Neil Forbes, *Doing Business with the Nazis: Britain's Economic and Financial Relations with the Nazis, 1931–1939* (London: Frank Cass, 2000), 99.

13. Roosevelt, "Wireless to the London Conference," July 3, 1933, *The American Presidency Project,* https://presidency.ucsb.edu. See also Paul Jankowski, *All against All: The Long Winter of 1933 and the Origins of the Second World War* (New York: Harper-Collins, 2020), 336–45.

14. James, *The End of Globalization,* 128–33; Clavin, *Securing the World Economy,* 116–21.

15. Cordell Hull, *The Memoirs of Cordell Hull*, vol. 1 (New York: Macmillan, 1948), chapters 18–19, esp. 254–55.

16. See Philip Nord, *France's New Deal: From the Thirties to the Postwar Era* (Princeton: Princeton University Press, 2010); and Isser Woloch, *The Postwar Moment: Progressive Forces in Britain, France and the United States After World War II* (New Haven: Yale University Press, 2019).

17. On the meaning of the "Greater East Asia Co-prosperity Sphere," see Peter Duus, introduction to Duus, Ramon Myers, and Mark Peattie, eds., *The Japanese Wartime Empire, 1931–1945* (Princeton: Princeton University Press, 1996), xxi–xxvii.

18. See Adam Tooze, *The Wages of Destruction: The Making and Breaking of the Nazi Economy* (New York: Penguin, 2006), 38, for the Hitler quote.

19. On the working out of the process in Eastern Europe and the Balkans, see Larry Wolff, *Woodrow Wilson and the Reimagining of Eastern Europe* (Stanford: Stanford University Press, 2020).

20. Susan Pedersen, *The Guardians: The League of Nations and the Crisis of Empire* (Oxford: Oxford University Press, 2015).

21. Cited in Ian Kershaw, *Hitler, 1889–1936* (London: Penguin, 1998), 421.

22. For a recent reevaluation, see Oona Hathaway and Scott Shapiro, *The Internationalists: How a Radical Plan to Outlaw War Remade the World* (New York: Simon & Schuster, 2017).

23. Steiner, *Triumph of the Dark*, 56.

24. George Herring, *The American Century and Beyond: U.S. Foreign Relations, 1893–2015* (Oxford: Oxford University Press, 2017), 204–5.

25. Anthony Adamthwaite, *France and the Coming of the Second World War, 1936–1939* (London: Frank Cass, 1977), 41.

26. Maurice Hankey, "The Future of the League of Nations," July 20, 1936, The National Archives (hereafter TNA), CAB 63/51.

27. Statement of the prime minister, "The International Situation: The Prime Minister's Second Visit to Herr Hitler," September 24, 1938, TNA, CAB 23/95/6, p. 12.

28. Stephen Wertheim, *Tomorrow, the World: The Birth of U.S. Global Supremacy* (Cambridge, MA: Belknap Press of Harvard University Press, 2020), argues that those labeled isolationists were not literally in favor of isolation. They wanted US involvement in the world economy and "intercourse" with other countries, but opposed military commitments. See also Brooke Blower, "From Isolationism to Neutrality: A New Framework for Understanding American Political Culture, 1919–1941," *Diplomatic History* 38, no. 2 (April 2014): 345–76; and Charles Kupchan, *Isolationism: A History of America's Efforts to Shield Itself from the World* (New York: Oxford University Press, 2020). Kupchan's account covers the long history of US foreign policy, but it is explicitly aimed at deriving a strategy for the near future. For a not dissimilar take, see Michael O'Hanlon, *The Art of War in an Age of Peace: U.S. Grand Strategy and Resolute Restraint* (New Haven: Yale University Press, 2021).

29. America's empire was also in many ways obscured. On this, see Daniel Immerwahr, *How to Hide an Empire: A History of the Greater United States* (New York: Farrar, Straus & Giroux, 2019).

30. In the summer of 1939 Walter Lippmann told Winston Churchill that Ambassador Joseph Kennedy believed that war with Germany was inevitable and Britain would lose. Churchill responded forcefully that it would not, but he ended his lengthy response by saying that if Britain failed, he assumed and hoped that the United States would continue the struggle. As he explained, "It will then be for you, for the Americans, to maintain the great heritage of the English-speaking peoples. It will be for you to think imperially, which means to think always of something higher and more vast than one's national interests." Churchill, quoted in Harold Nicolson, *Diaries and Letters: 1930–1939* (London: Collins, 1968), 403, and cited again in Nicholas Wapshott, *The Sphinx: Franklin Roosevelt, the Isolationists, and the Road to World War II* (New York: Norton, 2014), 137.

31. The "reaction against international migration," as Harold James labels it, was not confined to the United States. See James, *End of Globalization*, chapter 4.

32. See Daniel Okrent, *Guarded Gate: Bigotry, Eugenics and the Law That Kept Two Generations of Jews, Italians and Other European Immigrants out of America* (New York: Scribner's, 2019).

33. This is effectively the argument in Tooze, *Deluge*.

34. For a short but cogent statement, see Ian Buruma, "This Is the True End of Pax Americana," *New York Times*, October 21, 2019.

35. There are numerous studies of this moment. Among them, see Lynne Olson, *Those Angry Days: Roosevelt, Lindbergh, and America's Fight over World War II, 1939–1941* (New York: Random House, 2013); and Wapshott, *Sphinx*. Surely the most effective re-creation of this moment is fictional: Philip Roth's *The Plot against America* (New York: Vintage, 2005). The only thing that feels unrealistic about it is the happy ending.

36. Charles Lindbergh, "America and European Wars," September 15, 1939, http://www.charleslindbergh.com/americanfirst/.

37. Brewster and Claw, "We Stand Here," *Atlantic Monthly*, September 1940, was a response to Arnold Whitridge, "Where Do You Stand?" *Atlantic Monthly*, August 1940, an "Open Letter to Undergraduates" by a professor in the Yale History Department. John F. Kennedy wrote a check for $100 to the America First Committee. These and other supporters are noted and their activities described in Olson, *Those Angry Days*, and in Wapshott, *Sphinx*.

38. Charles Lindbergh, "Des Moines Speech," September 11, 1941, http://www.charleslindbergh.com/americanfirst/.

39. Hans Mommsen, "Hitler's Reichstag Speech of 30 January 1939," *History and Memory* 9, nos. 1/2 (Fall 1997): 147–61. The key quote, which came toward the end of a two-hour peroration, was "If the international Jewish financiers should succeed in plunging the nations once more into a world war, then the result will not be the Bolshevizing of the earth, but the annihilation of the Jewish race from Europe."

TWO Defining the Enemy, Crafting Strategy,
Imagining a New World

1. The most thorough account of the war is Gerhard L. Weinberg, *A World at Arms: A Global History of World War II*, 2nd ed. (Cambridge: Cambridge University Press, 2005).

2. Bernard Wasserstein, *Barbarism and Civilization: A History of Europe in Our Time* (Oxford: Oxford University Press, 2007), 323–28.

3. George Herring, *The American Century and Beyond: U.S. Foreign Relations, 1893–2015* (Oxford: Oxford University Press, 2015), 251–55.

4. Gerhard L. Weinberg, *Visions of Victory: The Hopes of Eight World War II Leaders* (Cambridge: Cambridge University Press, 2005).

5. In 1940 John Maynard Keynes was asked to address the issue of the Nazis' plans for a new European economic order. See Robert Skidelsky, *John Maynard Keynes*, vol. 3: *Fighting for Freedom* (New York: Viking, 2000). Shortly after, talk turned to the more liberal world order that the UK and US would seek to construct. See, for example, the memo by the Foreign Research and Publication Service, "British-American World Order," July 1941, TNA, CAB 117/98; and the curious report by the same group, "The Non-white Races in a British-American World Order," June 24, 1941, TNA, AVIA 38/1129. These are briefly discussed in James E. Cronin, *Global Rules: America, Britain and a Disordered World* (New Haven: Yale University Press, 2014), 5, notes 6 and 7, 317.

6. American leaders and strategic thinkers began to expand their vision of the nation's interest began shortly before the US entered the war. See Stephen Wertheim, *Tomorrow, the World: The Birth of U.S. Global Supremacy* (Cambridge, MA: Belknap Press of Harvard University Press, 2020); and John A. Thompson, *A Sense of Power: The Roots of America's Global Role* (Ithaca: Cornell University Press, 2015).

7. For the United States, see Robert A. Divine, *Second Chance: The Triumph of Internationalism in America during World War II* (New York: Atheneum, 1967); and Townsend Hoopes and Douglas Brinkley, *FDR and the Creation of the U.N.* (New Haven: Yale University Press, 1997).

8. Elizabeth Borgwardt, *A New Deal for the World: America's Vision for Human Rights* (Cambridge, MA: Belknap Press of Harvard University Press, 2005). The text of the charter is reproduced at 303–4.

9. Stephen Schlesinger, *Act of Creation: The Founding of the United Nations* (Boulder, CO: Westview, 2003), 201.

10. On the Arcadia meeting, see B. J. C. McKercher, *Transition of Power: Britain's Loss of Global Pre-eminence to the United States, 1930–1945* (Cambridge: Cambridge University Press, 1999), 312–14.

11. Michael Howard, "The United Nations: From War Fighting to Peace Planning," in Ernest May and Angeliki Laiou, eds., *The Dumbarton Oaks Conversations and the United Nations, 1944–1994* (Washington, DC: Dumbarton Oaks Research Library and Collections, distributed by Harvard University Press, 1998), 1–8.

12. The treaty replaced the Anglo-Soviet Agreement of July 12, 1941. In both agreements a major point was that neither side would do a separate deal with Germany.

13. Wertheim, *Tomorrow, the World*, chapter 4.

14. Roosevelt appointed John Franklin Carter to direct this quasi-formal agency. See Bradley F. Smith, *The Shadow Warriors: O.S.S. and the Origins of the C.I.A.* (New York: Basic Books, 1983), 63 and passim; and Barry Katz, *Foreign Intelligence: Research and Analysis in the Office of Strategic Services* (Cambridge, MA: Harvard University Press, 1989).

15. Michaela Hoenicke Moore, *Know Your Enemy: The American Debate on Nazism, 1933–1945* (Cambridge: Cambridge University Press, 2010), chapter 5.

16. A. J. P. Taylor, *The Course of German History* (London: Hamish Hamilton, 1945); Geoffrey Barraclough, *The Origins of Modern Germany* (Oxford: Basil Blackwell, 1946); Hugh Trevor-Roper, *The Last Days of Hitler* (New York: Macmillan, 1947).

17. Cited in Smith, *Shadow Warriors*, 369.

18. See Moore, *Know Your Enemy,* for details. On attitudes toward the Japanese, see John Dower, *War without Mercy: Race and Power in the Pacific War* (New York: Pantheon, 1986).

19. Isser Woloch, *The Postwar Moment: Progressive Forces in Britain, France and the United States After World War II* (New Haven: Yale University Press, 2019). Domestic politics in Britain have been chronicled in classic studies by Paul Addison, *The Road to 1945* (London: Jonathan Cape, 1975); and Angus Calder, *The People's War* (London: Random House, 1969). The literature on the United States is enormous. For a useful if slightly outdated overview, see John Morton Blum, *V Was for Victory: Politics and American Culture during World War II* (New York: Harcourt, Brace, 1976). Developments within France occurred under occupation or Vichy, about which see Robert Paxton, *Vichy France: Old Guard and New Order, 1940–1944* (New York: Knopf, 1972). See also Philip Nord, *France's New Deal: From the Thirties to the Postwar Era* (Princeton: Princeton University Press, 2010).

20. James Cronin, *Labour and Society in Britain, 1918–1979* (London: Batsford, 1984), 241–42.

21. Cato, *Guilty Men* (London: Victor Gollancz, 1940).

22. Woloch, *Postwar Moment*, 80–82.

23. The shift would have a major impact on postwar geopolitics. See David Reynolds, *From World War to Cold War: Churchill, Roosevelt, and the International History of the 1940s* (Oxford: Oxford University Press, 2006), 264–75.

24. Keynesian economics meant rather more than this, but its core message politically was the compatibility of the interests of labor and the overall economy. On Keynes in Britain, see James Cronin, *The Politics of State Expansion* (London: Routledge, 1991), chapters 6 and 8. On the role of Keynes more broadly, see Peter Hall, ed., *The Political Power of Economic Ideas: Keynesianism across Nations* (Princeton: Princeton University Press, 1989).

25. See Weinberg, *Visions of Victory*, chapter 1.

26. Or Rosenboim, *The Emergence of Globalism: Visions of World Order in Britain and the United States, 1939–1950* (Princeton: Princeton University Press, 2017), 2–3. See also Patrick Hearden, *Architects of Globalism: Building a New World Order during World War II* (Fayetteville: University of Arkansas Press, 2002); Glenda Sluga, *Internationalism in the Age of Nationalism* (Philadelphia: University of Pennsylvania Press, 2013); Andrew Williams, *Failed Imagination: New World Order of the Twentieth Century* (Manchester: Manchester University Press, 1998); and Glenda Sluga and Patricia Clavin, eds., *Internationalisms: A Twentieth-Century History* (Cambridge: Cambridge University Press, 2017).

27. Robert Hutchins et al., *Preliminary Draft of a World Constitution* (Chicago: University of Chicago Press, 1948).

28. Mark Mazower, *Governing the World: The History of an Idea* (New York: Penguin, 2012), 233.

29. Julian Jackson, *A Certain Idea of France* (London: Allen Lane, 2018).

30. The texts of the four Moscow Declarations can be found on the website *Avalon Project: Documents in Law, History and Diplomacy* maintained by Yale Law School. Ironically, the historic document on atrocities cites as an example of an action that would be punished the "wholesale shooting of Polish officers." This was clearly a reference to the Katyn Massacre, supposedly carried out by the Nazis. In fact, it was the Soviets who killed the Polish officers. Mikhail Gorbachev confirmed this and apologized in 1990.

31. Yalta Conference Agreement, *Declaration on Liberated Europe*, February 11, 1945, Wilson Center Digital Archive, https://digitalarchive.wilsoncenter.org/document/116176.pdf?v=66b99cbbf4a1b8de10c56b38cf4fc50d.

32. *Potsdam Agreement, Protocol of the Proceedings*, August 1, 1945. Text available at: https://www.nato.int/ebookshop/video/declassified/doc_files/Potsdam%20Agreement.pdf.

33. On Keynes's role, see Skidelsky, *Keynes: Fighting for Freedom.* The comparison, and the rivalry, between Keynes and White is a major theme of Benn Steil, *The Battle of Bretton Woods: John Maynard Keynes, Harry Dexter White, and the Making of a New World Order* (Princeton: Princeton University Press, 2013). Steil makes much of the fact that White worked for and was sympathetic to the Soviet Union, but it is not clear just how this connection materially affected his role in the process.

34. Steil, *Battle of Bretton Woods*, 143.

35. That is largely the perspective of Steil in *Battle of Bretton Woods.* An approach that focuses more on the collaboration of the US and UK is John Ikenberry, "A World Economy Restored: Expert Consensus and the Anglo-American Postwar Settlement," *International Organization* 46, no. 1 (1992): 289-321.

36. See Cass Sunstein, *The Second Bill of Rights: FDR's Unfinished Revolution and Why We Need It More Than Ever* (New York: Basic Books, 2004).

37. Cited in Borgwardt, *New Deal for the World*, 49.

38. Morgenthau quote from May 1942, cited in Eric Helleiner, *Forgotten Foundations of Bretton Woods: International Development and the Making of the Postwar Order* (Ithaca: Cornell University Press, 2014).

39. White, cited in Helleiner, *Forgotten Foundations*, 117.

40. See Jessica Reinisch, "Internationalism in Relief: The Birth (and Death) of UNRRA," *Past and Present* 210, no. 6 (2011): 258-89; and also Borgwardt, *New Deal for the World*, 118-21.

41. See Robert Hilderbrand, *Dumbarton Oaks: The Origins of the United Nations and the Search for Postwar Security* (Chapel Hill: University of North Carolina Press, 1990).

42. A thorough early account is Ruth Russell, *A History of the United Nations Charter: The Role of the United States, 1940-1945* (Washington, DC: Brookings Institution, 1958).

43. Hoopes and Brinkley, *FDR and the Creation of the U.N.*, 145–56. The text of the UN Charter is reprinted in the appendix.

44. Schlesinger, *Act of Creation*, 193–222.

45. Arthur H. Vandenberg, "American Foreign Policy," January 10, 1945, U.S. Congress, Senate, *Congressional Record*, 79th Cong., 1st sess., 1–7.

46. Gallup Organization, Gallup Poll #1945-0343: Aftermath of War/Employment, Gallup Organization (Cornell University, Ithaca, NY: Roper Center for Public Opinion Research, 1945), Dataset, DOI: doi=10.25940/ROPER-31087326, at https://ropercenter.cornell.edu/?gclid=EAIaIQobChMItpO4ipyP9QIVlPbjBx09VwcoEAAYASAAEgIbZfD_BwE. Interestingly, when the same poll asked respondents whether the US should use poison gas against Japanese soldiers, they answered no by a margin of 63-31 percent.

47. On "embedded liberalism," see John Ruggie, "International Regimes, Transactions, and Change: Embedded Liberalism in the Postwar Economic Order," *International Organization* 36, no. 2 (1982).

THREE Toward a Cold War World Order

1. Stalin, quoted in Odd Arne Westad, *The Cold War: A World History* (New York: Basic Books, 2017), 63–64. For the original, see Georgi Dimitrov, *The Diary of Georgi Dimitrov, 1933–1949*, ed. Ivo Banac (New Haven: Yale University Press, 2008), 358.

2. Tony Judt, *Postwar: A History of Europe since 1945* (New York: Penguin, 2005), chapter 4.

3. See Norman Naimark, *Stalin and the Fate of Europe: The Postwar Struggle for Sovereignty* (Cambridge, MA: Harvard University Press, 2019).

4. Speech delivered by Stalin at a meeting of voters of the Stalin Electoral District, Moscow, February 9, 1946, *Wilson Center Digital Archive*. On the US response, see Louis Menand, *The Free World: Art and Thought in the Cold War* (New York: Farrar, Strauss & Giroux, 2021), 21–23.

5. Douglas, cited in James Forrestal, *The Forrestal Diaries*, ed. Walter Millis (New York: Viking, 1951), 134.

6. Michael Hunt, *The World Transformed: 1945 to the Present* (New York: Oxford University Press, 2014), 41–42.

7. On Kennan's background and evolution, see Anders Stephanson, *Kennan and the Art of Foreign Policy* (Cambridge, MA: Harvard University Press, 1989); and John Lewis Gaddis, *George F. Kennan: An American Life* (New York: Penguin, 2012).

8. George Kennan, "Telegram," February 22, 1946, *National Security Archive* website. Quotations from Kennan in subsequent paragraphs are from this source.

9. Anne Applebaum, *Iron Curtain: The Crushing of Eastern Europe, 1944–1956* (New York: Random House, 2012), xxix. For other accounts, see Norman Naimark, "The Sovietization of Eastern Europe, 1945–1953," in Melvin Leffler and Odd Arne Westad, eds., *The Cambridge History of the Cold War* (Cambridge: Cambridge University Press, 2010); and Mark Kramer, "Stalin, Soviet Policy and the Establishment of a Soviet Bloc in Eastern Europe," in Timothy Snyder and Ray Brandon, eds., *Stalin and Europe: Imitation and Domination, 1928–1953* (New York: Oxford University Press, 2014).

10. Bernard Wasserstein, *Barbarism and Civilization: A History of Europe in Our Time* (Oxford: Oxford University Press, 2007), 437.

11. On Bulgaria and Romania, see Westad, *Cold War*, 80–82.

12. Applebaum, *Iron Curtain*, 71.

13. Dean Acheson, *Present at the Creation* (New York: Norton, 1969), 217.

14. Cited in Elizabeth Edwards Spalding, *The First Cold Warrior: Harry Truman, Containment, and the Remaking of Liberal Internationalism* (Lexington: University Press of Kentucky, 2006), 33. For background on Truman's beliefs and policies, see David McCullough, *Truman* (New York: Simon & Schuster, 1992); and Alonzo Hamby, *Man of the People: A Life of Harry S. Truman* (New York: Oxford University Press, 1995).

15. The note to Byrnes was dated January 5, 1946, and apparently discussed with him two days later. See Spalding, *First Cold Warrior*, 30.

16. The Clifford memorandum appears as an appendix in Arthur Krock, *Memoirs: Sixty Years on the Firing Line* (New York: Funk & Wagnalls, 1968), cited in Spalding, *First Cold Warrior*, 53–60.

17. Harry S. Truman, "Special Message to the Congress on Greece and Turkey," March 12, 1947, *The American Presidency Project*, https://presidency.ucsb.edu. For more detail, see McCullough, *Truman*, 547–49.

18. Isser Woloch, *The Postwar Moment: Progressive Forces in Britain, France, and the United States After World War II* (New Haven: Yale University Press, 2019), 332–36.

19. See George C. Herring, *The American Century and Beyond: U.S. Foreign Relations, 1893–2014* (New York: Oxford University Press, 2017), 314; James Carroll, *House of War: The Pentagon and the Disastrous Rise of American Power* (Boston: Houghton Mifflin, 2006), 106–11.

20. James T. Patterson, *Mr. Republican: A Biography of Robert A. Taft* (Boston: Houghton Mifflin, 1972), 369–72.

21. On the Marshall Plan, see Michael Hogan, *The Marshall Plan: America, Britain and the Reconstruction of Western Europe* (Cambridge: Cambridge University Press, 1987); and, more recently, Benn Steil, *The Marshall Plan: Dawn of the Cold War* (New York: Simon & Schuster, 2018).

22. Andrei Gromyko, *Memoirs*, trans. Harold Shukman (London: Hutchinson, 1989), 109.

23. "Memorandum of Conversation," April 15, 1947, in *Foreign Relations of the United States* (hereafter *FRUS*), 1947, 2:340.

24. "Memorandum by the Undersecretary of State for Economic Affairs: The European Crisis," May 27, 1947, George C. Marshall Foundation, https://www.marshall foundation.org.

25. "Text of Marshall's Speech at Harvard, June 4, 1947" (for delivery June 5), also available at the Marshall Foundation website.

26. After saying yes, Bidault qualified his answer by adding that France could be relied upon if given time *and* if it could avoid civil war. See Judt, *Postwar*, 113–17.

27. Steil claims that Stalin was stimulated to toughen the Soviet stance by reports originating from Soviet spies Guy Burgess and Donald Maclean. Perhaps, but the Soviets

had sufficient reason, and sufficient information, for making the decision they did without its spies. See Steil, *Marshall Plan*, 127–28.

28. Masaryk, cited in Naimark, *Stalin and the Fate of Europe*, 19–20.

29. Steil, *Marshall Plan*, 240.

30. Herrick Chapman, *France's Long Reconstruction: In Search of the Modern Republic* (Cambridge, MA: Harvard University Press, 2018), 179–81; Woloch, *Postwar Moment*, 335–42; Jean-Pierre Rioux, *The Fourth Republic, 1944–1958* (Cambridge: Cambridge University Press, 1987), 112–32.

31. The Hungarian Communist's comment came at the founding meeting of the Cominform and is cited in Naimark, *Stalin and the Fate of Europe*, 134. Togliatti, cited in Naimark, *Stalin and the Fate of Europe*, 132.

32. Paul Ginsborg, *A History of Contemporary Italy: Society and Politics, 1943–1988* (London: Penguin, 1990), 115–18.

33. Clay, cited in Naimark, *Stalin and the Fate of Europe,* 186. Naimark's chapter on the blockade, 157–95, is the most recent account.

34. Reuter, cited in Peter Auer, *Ihr Völker der Welt: Ernst Reuter und die Blockade von Berlin* (Berlin: Jaron, 1998), 6–7.

35. A. J. Nicholls, *The Bonn Republic: West German Democracy, 1945–1990* (London: Longman, 1997), 70.

36. Lovett to Harriman, December 3, 1948, *FRUS*, 1948, 3:303, 305, cited in Steil, *Marshall Plan*, 318.

37. See David Armitage, *The Declaration of Independence: A Global History* (Cambridge, MA: Harvard University Press, 2007).

38. Hence titles like Acheson's *Present at the Creation.*

39. There has been some debate on the precise economic effects of Marshall Plan aid. Alan Milward argued somewhat counterintuitively that Europe was already set to recover from the depths of the postwar crisis in 1947. See Milward, *The Reconstruction of West Europe, 1945–51* (Berkeley: University of California Press, 1984). Most other scholars tend to see its effects more positively.

40. On the vexed question of Soviet and Chinese involvement, see Westad, *Cold War*, 166–69.

41. These events would lead to the creation in the United States of what has been labeled the "national security state." See, among others, Michael Hogan, *A Cross of Iron: Harry S. Truman and the Origins of the National Security State, 1945–1954* (Cambridge: Cambridge University Press, 1998); and Aaron Friedberg, *In the Shadow of the Garrison State* (Princeton: Princeton University Press, 2000).

42. See Odd Arne Westad, *The Global Cold War* (Cambridge: Cambridge University Press, 2005).

43. Westad, *Cold War*, 180–82.

44. Graham Allison, "The Myth of the Liberal Order," *Foreign Affairs,* July/August 2018, argues persuasively that the "liberal order" that is now supposedly threatened was actually a "Cold War Order." The truly intriguing question is how and in what ways a Cold War order advanced or, on occasion, inhibited the development of a liberal international order.

FOUR In Search of Stability and Prosperity

1. Anne Applebaum, *Iron Curtain: The Crushing of Eastern Europe, 1944–1956* (New York: Random House, 2012), chapter 12; Tony Judt, *Postwar: A History of Europe since 1945* (New York: Penguin, 1945), 177–87; and Bernard Wasserstein, *Barbarism and Civilization: A History of Europe in Our Time* (Oxford: Oxford University Press, 2007), 489–93.

2. Louis Menand, *The Free World: Art and Thought in the Cold War* (New York: Farrar, Straus & Giroux, 2021), 28, 342.

3. Gomułka was an early leader of the Polish Communists, but his rival for the leadership was more slavishly devoted to Moscow. As a result, Gomulka was sacked in 1948, but he avoided the fate of so many others and so was around to ascend to the leadership in 1956.

4. The estimate comes from Judt, *Postwar*, 318.

5. See Odd Arne Westad, *Restless Empire: China and the World since 1750* (New York: Basic Books, 2012).

6. Odd Arne Westad, *The Cold War: A World History* (New York: Basic Books, 2017), 237.

7. For the quote from Mao and the estimate of deaths from the Great Leap Forward, see Westad, *Cold War*, 243–44. Given the sheer chaos of the moment and the lack of transparency of the regime, all such estimates are debatable, but most scholars put the number at 35 million or more.

8. Geir Lundestad, "Empire by Invitation: The United States and Western Europe, 1945–1952," *Journal of Peace Research* 23, no. 3 (September 1986): 263–77.

9. For useful comparisons, see Peter Hall, *Governing the Economy: The Politics of State Intervention in Britain and France* (New York: Oxford University Press, 1986); and Claire Andrieu, "La France à gauche de l'Europe," *Le mouvement social* 134 (1986): 131–54.

10. Jean-Pierre Rioux, *The Fourth Republic, 1944–1958* (Cambridge: Cambridge University Press, 1987), 170–87, 336–43. See also Herrick Chapman, *France's Long Reconstruction: In Search of the Modern Republic* (Cambridge, MA: Harvard University Press, 2018).

11. See Paul Ginsborg, *A History of Contemporary Italy: Society and Politics, 1943–1988* (London: Penguin, 1990), 150–57.

12. Robert Collins, *More: The Politics of Economic Growth in Postwar America* (Oxford: Oxford University Press, 2000).

13. Isser Woloch, *The Postwar Moment: Progressive Forces in Britain, France and the United States After World War II* (New Haven: Yale University Press, 2019). There has been much recent scholarship documenting the inequities of social provision in the United States during and since the New Deal. See, among others, Ira Katznelson, *When Affirmative Action Was White: An Untold History of Racial Inequality in Twentieth-Century America* (New York: Norton, 2005).

14. On the essential role of unions in the postwar era, and of the efforts to develop new trade unions with more extensive rights in Germany, see Leon Fink, *Undoing the Liberal World Order: Progressive Ideals and Political Realities since World War II* (New

York: Columbia University Press, 2022), chapter 2: "The Good Postwar: German Worker Rights, 1945–1950."

15. On employers' strategies, see Howell Harris, *The Right to Manage: Industrial Relations Policies of American Business in the 1940s* (Madison: University of Wisconsin Press, 1982).

16. On the outcome of the postwar settlement as a belated triumph of social democracy, see Sheri Berman, *The Primacy of Politics: Social Democracy and the Making of Europe's Twentieth Century* (Cambridge: Cambridge University Press, 2006).

17. See Charles Kindleberger, *Europe's Postwar Growth: The Role of Labor Supply* (Cambridge, MA: Harvard University Press, 1967); Barry Eichengreen, *The European Economy since 1945: Coordinated Capitalism and Beyond* (Princeton: Princeton University Press, 2007); and Judt, *Postwar*, 330–37.

18. The key work here is Thomas Piketty, *Capital in the Twenty-First Century*, trans. Arthur Goldhammer (Cambridge, MA: Harvard University Press, 2014). Piketty built on empirical work that he and colleagues such as Anthony Atkinson and Emmanuel Saez carried out over a number of years.

19. The French term was introduced by Jean Fourastié, *Les Trente glorieuses* (Paris: Fayard, 1979).

20. See Wolfram Kaiser, *Christian Democracy and the Origins of the European Union* (Cambridge: Cambridge University Press, 2007), chapter 5; and Martin Conway, "The Age of Christian Democracy: The Frontiers of Success and Failure," in Thomas Kselman and Joseph Buttigieg, eds., *European Christian Democracy: Historical Legacies and Comparative Perspectives* (Notre Dame: University of Notre Dame Press, 2003).

21. The record of Pope Pius XII continues to be the subject of dispute. The Vatican sought to resolve the debate by publishing eleven volumes of documents between 1965 and 1981—*Actes et documents du Saint Siège relatifs à la Seconde Guerre Mondiale*—on the pope's reign, but they have been seriously criticized. In March 2020 scholars finally got access to the actual documents in the Vatican's Secret Archive, but it was closed after a week because of the coronavirus pandemic. According to the *Washington Post* (April 29, 2020), initial reports were not favorable to defenders of the pope. On the more complicated story of the previous pope, see David Kertzer, *The Pope and Mussolini: The Secret History of Pius XI and the Rise of Fascism in Europe* (New York: Random House, 2014).

22. Kaiser, *Christian Democracy and the European Union*, 149–50. The classic statement is *Devant la crise mondiale: Manifeste de catholiques européens séjournant en Amérique*, ed. Jose Antonio de Aguirre y Lecube (New York: Éditions de la Maison française, 1942). See also Samuel Moyn, *Christian Human Rights* (Philadelphia: University of Pennsylvania Press, 2015).

23. Michael Schaller, *The American Occupation of Japan: The Origins of the Cold War in Asia* (New York: Oxford University Press, 1985).

24. Lawrence Beer, "Japan (1947): Forty Years of the Post-war Constitution," in Vernon Bogdanor, ed., *Constitutions in Democratic Politics* (Aldershot, UK: Gower, 1988), 173–205.

25. For a thoughtful analysis, see Karel van Wolferen, *The Enigma of Japanese Power* (New York: Knopf, 1989).

26. Committee on Parties, *Toward a More Responsible Two-Party System*, special supplement to the *American Political Science Review* 40 (September, 1950).

27. The recent polarization of American parties has led to a reexamination of the American Political Science Association report. See Mark Wickham-Jones, *Whatever Happened to Party Government?* (Ann Arbor: University of Michigan Press, 2018); Sam Rosenfeld, *The Polarizers: Postwar Architects of Our Partisan Era* (Chicago: University of Chicago Press, 2018); and Frances McCall Rosenbluth and Ian Shapiro, *Responsible Parties: Saving Democracy from Itself* (New Haven: Yale University Press, 2018). For an assessment, see James Cronin, "Responsible Parties, Responsible Government and the Present Crisis," *Commonwealth and Comparative Politics* 57, no. 4 (2019): 487–94.

28. See Steve Fraser and Gary Gerstle, eds., *The Rise and Fall of the New Deal Order, 1930–1980* (Princeton: Princeton University Press, 1989); and Jefferson Cowie, *The Great Exception: The New Deal and the Limits of American Politics* (Princeton: Princeton University Press, 2016).

29. Nelson Lichtenstein, "From Corporatism to Collective Bargaining: Organized Labour and the Eclipse of Social Democracy in the Postwar Era," in Fraser and Gerstle, *New Deal Order*, chapter 5.

30. Harry S. Truman, "Radio Address to the American People on the Veto of the Taft-Hartley Bill," June 20, 1947, *The American Presidency Project*, https://presidency. ucsb.edu.

31. James Patterson, *Mr. Republican: A Biography of Robert A. Taft* (Boston: Houghton Mifflin, 1972), chapters 32–35.

32. President Dwight Eisenhower to Edgar Eisenhower, November 8, 1954, in Dwight Eisenhower Diary, Dwight D. Eisenhower Papers as President of the United States, 1953–1961, Dwight D. Eisenhower Library, https://catalog.archives.gov/id/186596.

33. President's Committee on Civil Rights, *To Secure These Rights: The Report of the President's Committee on Civil Rights* (Washington, DC: GPO, 1947).

34. For a summary, see William Hitchcock, *The Age of Eisenhower: America and the World in the 1950s* (New York: Simon & Schuster, 2018).

35. See Mary Dudziak, *Cold War Civil Rights: Race and the Image of American Democracy* (Princeton: Princeton University Press, 2000); and Thomas Borstelmann, *The Cold War and the Color Line: American Race Relations in the Global Arena* (Cambridge, MA: Harvard University Press, 2001).

FIVE   Political Stability

1. Scholars of Eastern Europe have, of course, described changes that occurred there and shown that society and politics were not completely frozen with the imposition of Communist rule. There was some flexibility and de facto bargaining, but repression remained the central technique of rule.

2. Maurice Larkin, *France since the Popular Front* (Oxford: Clarendon, 1997), 263–69.

3. Two nineteenth-century examples are instructive: the repeal of the Corn Laws in 1846 and the "marriage of iron and rye" in the German tariff of 1879. See Cheryl Schonhardt-Bailey, "Parties and Interests in the 'Marriage of Iron and Rye,' " *British Journal of Political Science* 28, no. 2 (1998): 291–322; and Schonhardt-Bailey, *From the Corn Laws to Free Trade: Interests, Ideas, and Institutions in Historical Perspective* (Cambridge, MA: MIT Press, 2006).

4. On the Reciprocal Trade Agreements Act, see Craig VanGrasstek, *Trade and American Leadership: The Paradoxes of Wealth and Power from Alexander Hamilton to Donald Trump* (Cambridge: Cambridge University Press, 2019), 100–104.

5. Carl Strikwerda, "The European Origins of the New International Order" (paper presented at the online Conference of Europeanists, June 2021).

6. See Alan Milward, *The UK and the European Community*, vol. 1: *The Rise and Fall of a National Strategy, 1945–1963* (London: Frank Cass, 2002).

7. Tyler Anbinder, *Nativism and Slavery: The Northern Know-Nothing Party and the Politics of the 1850s* (New York: Oxford University Press, 1992).

8. Andrew Gyory, *Closing the Gate: Race, Politics and the Chinese Exclusion Act* (Chapel Hill: University of North Carolina Press, 1998).

9. Daniel Okrent, *The Guarded Gate: Bigotry, Eugenics and the Law That Kept Two Generations of Jews, Italians and Other European Immigrants out of America* (New York: Scribner, 2019).

10. See Tony Judt, *Postwar: A History of Europe since 1945* (New York: Penguin, 2005), 22–32; and Mark Mazower, *No Enchanted Palace: The End of Empire and the Ideological Origins of the United Nations* (Princeton: Princeton University Press, 2009).

11. Herrick Chapman, *France's Long Reconstruction: In Search of the Modern Republic* (Cambridge, MA: Harvard University Press, 2018), 58–74.

12. Judt, *Postwar*, 335. For more detail, see Stephen Castles and Godula Kosack, *Immigrant Workers and Class Structure in Western Europe*, 2nd ed. (New York: Oxford University Press, 1985).

13. This remained true even if the economy was more "national" and less international in the war and postwar years. See David Edgerton, *The Rise and Fall of the British Nation: A Twentieth-Century History* (London: Allen Lane, 2018).

14. The contradictory policies of encouraging emigration and also recruiting foreign workers are described in Kathleen Paul's *Whitewashing Britain: Race and Citizenship in the Postwar Era* (Ithaca: Cornell University Press, 1997).

15. The act would become gradually less liberal over time and would finally be replaced by the British Nationality Act of 1981. See Randall Hansen, *Citizenship and Immigration in Postwar Britain: The Institutional Origins of a Multicultural Nation* (Oxford: Oxford University Press, 2000).

16. Jia Lynn Wong, *One Mighty and Irresistible Tide: The Epic Struggle over American Immigration, 1924–1965* (New York: Norton, 2020).

17. Nicholas Lemann, *The Promised Land: The Great Black Migration and How It Changed America* (New York: Knopf, 1991).

18. "Platform of the States Rights Democratic Party," August 14, 1948, *The American Presidency Project,* https://presidency.ucsb.edu.

19. Ezra Klein, *Why We're Polarized* (New York: Avid Reader, 2021).

20. Steven Livingston, "John F. Kennedy, Martin Luther King Jr., and the Phone Call That Changed History," *Time,* June 20, 2017.

21. Cited in Wallace's obituary, *New York Times,* September 14, 1998.

22. For an overview, see John Springhall, *Decolonization since 1945: The Collapse of European Overseas Empires* (New York: Palgrave, 2001). As the world's largest empire, the British story is particularly relevant and told well in John Darwin, *Britain and Decolonisation: The Retreat from Empire in the Post-war World* (London: Macmillan, 1988).

23. See Carolyn Elkins, *Imperial Reckoning: The Untold Story of Britain's Gulag in Kenya* (New York: Henry Holt, 2005); and David Anderson, *Histories of the Hanged: The Dirty War in Kenya and the End of Empire* (London: Weidenfeld & Nicolson, 2005).

24. See Todd Shepard, *The Invention of Decolonization: The Algerian War and the Remaking of France* (Ithaca: Cornell University Press, 2008).

25. The classic study is Alistair Horne, *A Savage War of Peace: Algeria, 1954–1962* (London: Macmillan, 1977), but recent research has added many further details. See, more generally, Anthony Clayton, *The Wars of French Decolonization* (London: Routledge, 2014).

26. The resolution was justified by misleading reports of an encounter in the Gulf of Tonkin. See Odd Arne Westad, *The Cold War: A World History* (New York: Basic, 2017), 321. There is a vast literature on the US involvement in Vietnam. George Herring, *America's Longest War: The United States and Vietnam* (New York: McGraw-Hill, 2002), is a useful place to start.

27. Cited in Doris Kearns Goodwin, *Lyndon Johnson and the American Dream* (New York: Harper & Row, 1976), 202.

28. See "Black Opposition to Vietnam," section 13, *Amistad Digital Resource* on SNCC and King.

29. For an overview, see Richard Vinen, *The Long '68* (London: Penguin, 2018).

30. Colin Crouch and Alessandro Pizzorno, *The Resurgence of Class Conflict in Western Europe since 1968* (London: Macmillan, 1978).

SIX Liberalism and Liberal Order, Modified

1. See Francis Gavin, *Gold, Dollars, and Power: The Politics of International Monetary Relations, 1958–1971* (Chapel Hill: University of North Carolina Press, 2006).

2. Meg Jacobs, *Panic at the Pump: The Energy Crisis and the Transformation of American Politics in the 1970s* (New York: Hill & Wang, 2016), 4.

3. The most comprehensive study is Daniel Yergin, *The Prize: The Epic Quest for Oil, Money and Power* (New York: Free Press, 2008).

4. Germany was a major exception, where a policy referred to as ordoliberalism dominated.

5. The new model has been labeled neoliberalism by some, market fundamentalism by others. In the realm of international economic relations the new orthodoxy has been termed the "Washington Consensus."

6. Pairing the two as "liberal market economies" is common in the so-called varieties of capitalism literature. The classic statement is Peter Hall and David Soskice, eds., *Varieties of Capitalism: The Institutional Foundations of Comparative Advantage* (Oxford: Oxford University Press, 2001). On the different trajectories of Britain and the United States, see James Cronin, "Convergence by Conviction: Politics and Economics in the Emergence of the 'Anglo-American Model,' " *Journal of Social History* 33, no. 4 (Summer 2000): 781–804.

7. On whether the loan was really necessary, see Kathleen Burk and Alec Cairncross, *Goodbye, Great Britain: The 1976 IMF Crisis* (New Haven: Yale University Press, 1992); and Edmund Dell, *A Hard Pounding: Politics and Economic Crisis* (Oxford: Oxford University Press, 1991).

8. James Cronin, *New Labour's Pasts: The Labour Party and Its Discontents* (London: Longman, 2004), 191, and more generally, chapter 5.

9. Judith Stein, *Pivotal Decade: How the United States Traded Factories for Finance in the Seventies* (New Haven: Yale University Press, 2010).

10. President Carter, February 2, 1977, *The American Presidency Project*, https://presidency.ucsb.edu.

11. President Carter, February 8, 1977, *The American Presidency Project*.

12. President Carter, April 18, 1977, *The American Presidency Project*.

13. Daniel Sargent, *A Superpower Transformed: The Remaking of American Foreign Relations in the 1970s* (Oxford: Oxford University Press, 2015), 240–42, 247–50.

14. President Carter, October 24, 1978, *The American Presidency Project*.

15. President Carter, July 15, 1979, *The American Presidency Project*.

16. Sargent, *A Superpower Transformed*, 282–85; Stein, *Pivotal Decade*, 227–37.

17. James Watt, Testimony to the House Interior Committee, February 5, 1981.

18. Stockman's admission was reported in William Greider's article "The Education of David Stockman," *Atlantic*, December 1981.

19. David M. O'Brien, "Meese's Agenda for Ensuring the Reagan Legacy," *Los Angeles Times*, September 28, 1986, https://www.latimes.com/archives/la-xpm-1986-09-28-op-9537-story.html.

20. On the transformation of international economic policy, see James Cronin, *Global Rules: America, Britain and a Disordered World* (New Haven: Yale University Press, 2014), chapter 5.

21. Rawi Abdelal, "Of Learning and Forgetting: Centrism, Populism, and the Legitimacy Crisis of Globalization," in Peter Katzenstein and Jonathan Kirschner, eds., *The Downfall of the American Order?* (Ithaca: Cornell University Press, 2022), chapter 6.

22. John Williamson, "What Washington Means by Policy Reform," in Williamson, ed., *Latin American Adjustment: How Much Has Happened?* (Washington, DC: Institute for International Economics, 1990), 7–38. For a recent study of the process, see Alexander Kentikelenis and Sarah Babb, "The Making of Neoliberal Globalization: Norm Substitution and the Politics of Clandestine Institutional Change," *American Journal of Sociology* 124, no. 6 (May 2019): 1720–62.

23. See Peter Hall, "Policy Paradigms, Social Learning and the State: The Case of Economic Policy-making in Britain," *Comparative Politics* 25, no. 3 (April 1993): 275–96.

24. There is a substantial literature on the development of neoliberal economic thinking. Among others, see Richard Cockett, *Thinking the Unthinkable: Think-tanks and the Economic Counter-revolution* (London: HarperCollins, 1994); Angus Burgin, *The Great Persuasion: Reinventing Free Markets since the Depression* (Cambridge, MA: Harvard University Press, 2012); and Daniel Stedman Jones, *Masters of the Universe: Hayek, Friedman and the Birth of Neoliberal Politics* (Princeton: Princeton University Press, 2012). Most of these focus on the United States and Britain. For the story more broadly, see Quinn Slobodian, *Globalists: The End of Empire and the Birth of Neoliberalism* (Cambridge, MA: Harvard University Press, 2018); and also Monica Prasad, *The Politics of Free Markets: The Rise of Neoliberal Policies in Britain, France, Germany and the United States* (Chicago: University of Chicago Press, 2006); and, with a change in terminology from neoliberal to market fundamentalism, Fred Block and Margaret Somers, *The Power of Market Fundamentalism: Karl Polanyi's Critique* (Cambridge, MA: Harvard University Press, 2014).

25. Friedrich Hayek, *The Road to Serfdom* (London: Routledge & Sons, 1944).

26. There is considerable debate about the usefulness of the term neoliberalism. It has often been deployed by those on the left as a term of abuse rather than analysis. It also does not resonate with most Americans or with scholars and commentators focused on the United States. The term's boundaries are also poorly delineated. It is used here to denote the market-oriented framework for economic policy that came to dominate the thinking of conservatives and other policy makers in the 1970s and 1980s and has remained powerful since. There is no effort here to distinguish neoliberal or neoliberalism from terms like market-oriented, pro-market, market fundamentalism or fundamentalist, or free-market. On the controversy and possible uses in a British context, see the essays in Aled Davies, Ben Jackson, and Florence Sutcliffe-Braithewaite, eds., *The Neoliberal Age? Britain since the 1970s* (London: UCL Press, 2021). The term has begun to be used more routinely by scholars of the US. See, for example, Gary Gerstle, *The Rise and Fall of the Neoliberal Order: America and the World in the Free Market Era* (New York: Oxford University Press, 2022); and Leon Fink, *Undoing the Liberal World Order* (New York: Columbia University Press, 2022).

SEVEN The End of the Cold War and the Expansion of Liberal Order

1. This was the assumption of those who made up "Team B," created to second-guess CIA estimates that supposedly underestimated Soviet strength. See George Herring, *The American Century and Beyond: U.S. Foreign Relations, 1893–2014* (New York: Oxford University Press, 2017), 520–21.

2. Fred Halliday, *The Coming of the Second Cold War* (London: Verso, 1983).

3. On US policy in the 1980s, see Hal Brands, *Making the Unipolar Moment: U.S. Foreign Policy and the Rise of the Post–Cold War Order* (Ithaca: Cornell University Press, 2016).

4. Jeane Kirkpatrick, "Dictatorships and Double Standards," *Commentary*, November 1979.

5. Herring, *The American Century and Beyond*, 562, 597.

6. Thatcher, BBC interview with John Cole, December 17, 1984, Margaret Thatcher Foundation website. More broadly, see Archie Brown, *The Human Factor: Gorbachev, Reagan, and Thatcher, and the End of the Cold War* (Oxford: Oxford University Press, 2020).

7. George Shultz, *Turmoil and Triumph: My Years as Secretary of State* (New York: Scribner's, 1993), 760.

8. For a useful overview, see Philipp Ther, *Europe since 1989: A History* (Princeton: Princeton University Press, 2016), esp. chapters 2 and 3.

9. On East Germany, see Charles Maier, *Dissolution: The Crisis of Communism and the End of East Germany* (Princeton: Princeton University Press, 1997); and Mary Elise Sarotte, *The Collapse: The Accidental Opening of the Berlin Wall* (New York: Basic, 2014), and *1989: The Struggle to Create Post–Cold War Europe*, rev. ed. (Princeton: Princeton University Press, 2014).

10. There is a vast literature on the collapse of the Soviet Union. For a useful introduction, see Stephen Kotkin, *Armageddon Averted: The Soviet Collapse, 1970–2000* (Oxford: Oxford University Press, 2001, 2008); for a more recent account, see Vladislav Zubok, *Collapse: The Fall of the Soviet Union* (New Haven: Yale University Press, 2021).

11. See Thomas Carothers, *In the Name of Democracy: U.S. Policy toward Latin America in the Reagan Years* (Berkeley: University of California Press, 1991); Hal Brands, *Latin America's Cold Wars* (Cambridge, MA: Harvard University Press, 2010); and James Cronin, *Global Rules: America, Britain and a Disordered World* (New Haven: Yale University Press, 2014), 162–65.

12. See Ariel Colonomos, *Moralizing International Relations: Called to Account* (New York: Palgrave Macmillan, 2008); and Samuel Moyn, *The Last Utopia: Human Rights in History* (Cambridge, MA: Harvard University Press, 2010).

13. European Union and Government of South Africa, "Agreement on Trade, Development and Cooperation," *Official Journal of the European Communities*, December 4, 1944.

14. Independent Commission on Kosovo, *The Kosovo Report* (2000), cited in Cronin, *Global Rules*, 287. The International Commission on Intervention and State Sovereignty issued its report *The Responsibility to Protect* in December 2001. It was formally approved by the UN in 2005.

15. On the inadequacy of diplomacy attending the expansion of NATO, see M. E. Sarotte, *Not One Inch: America, Russia, and the Making of Post–Cold War Stalemate* (New Haven: Yale University Press, 2021).

16. See Cronin, *Global Rules*, 229–30, for further background.

17. Lake, "From Containment to Enlargement" (speech at Johns Hopkins University, September 21, 1993).

18. President William Clinton, *A National Security Strategy of Engagement and Enlargement*, July 21, 1994, *The American Presidency Project*, https://presidency.ucsb.edu.

19. Andrew Bacevich, *American Empire: The Realities and Consequences of U.S. Diplomacy* (Cambridge, MA: Harvard University Press, 2002). Bacevich was trying to explain why the United States continued to spend so much on the military after the end of the Cold War. Defense spending would in fact drop significantly. In the US, it was 6.4 percent of GDP in 1985 but dropped to 3.1 percent by 2000; in the UK, it constituted 5.1 percent of GDP in 1985 but only 2.5 percent in 2000. Not the "peace dividend" some had argued for, but more than trivial. See Cronin, *Global Rules*, 251–56.

20. On the critical role of neoliberalism in the creation of the post–Cold War order, see Ther, *Europe since 1989*.

EIGHT The Center Ceases to Hold

1. The extensive literature on polarization is extremely useful. See, for example, Ezra Klein, *Why We're Polarized* (New York: Avid Reader, 2021); Sam Rosenfeld, *The Polarizers: Postwar Architects of Our Partisan Era* (Chicago: University of Chicago Press, 2018); Thomas Mann and Norman Ornstein, *It's Even Worse Than It Looks* (New York: Basic Books, 2013); Matt Grossman and David Hopkins, *Asymmetrical Politics: Ideological Republicans and Group Interest Democrats* (New York: Oxford University Press, 2016); and Jacob Hacker and Paul Pierson, "Confronting Asymmetric Polarization," in Nathaniel Persily, ed., *Solutions to Political Polarization in America* (New York: Cambridge University Press, 2015), 59–72.

2. A large literature exists on the rise of identity politics and its implications for the center-left. For a recent critique, see Mark Lilla, *The Once and Future Liberal: After Identity Politics* (New York: HarperCollins, 2017). For an older and less critical view, see Ronald Inglehart, *The Silent Revolution: Changing Values and Political Styles among Western Publics* (Princeton: Princeton University Press, 1977).

3. Rosenfeld, *Polarizers*, 108–13, 121–22.

4. Senator Birch Bayh, 1969, cited in Byron Shafer, *Quiet Revolution: The Struggle for the Democratic Party and the Shaping of Post-reform Politics* (New York: Russell Sage, 1983), 167.

5. Phillips, testimony at the McGovern-Fraser Commission, April 25, 1969, and Dutton, correspondence with Leroy Collins, April 22, 1969, cited in Rosenfeld, *Polarizers*, 137.

6. *Milwaukee Sentinel*, September 4, 1972.

7. See Stanley Greenberg, *Middle Class Dreams: Politics and Power of the New American Majority,* rev. ed. (New Haven: Yale University Press, 1996).

8. See "Current Employment Statistics: 100 Years of Employment, Hours and Earnings," *Monthly Labor Review,* August 2016. Accessed online from the Bureau of Labour Statistics.

9. For her comments, see the *Washington Post*, May 13, 1992. On the meeting at which Clinton spoke, see Anthony Lewis, "Black and White," *New York Times*, June 18, 1992.

10. John Judis and Ruy Teixeira, *The Emerging Democratic Majority* (New York: Scribner, 2002).

11. Bernard Wasserstein, *Barbarism and Civilization: A History of Europe in Our Time* (Oxford: Oxford University Press, 2007), 642–43.

12. Tony Judt, *Postwar: A History of Europe since 1945* (New York: Penguin, 2005), 473–77.

13. Arthur Goldhammer and George Ross, "Reluctantly Center Left? The French Case," in James Cronin, George Ross, and James Shoch, eds., *What's Left of the Left: Democrats and Social Democrats in Changing Times* (Durham: Duke University Press, 2011), 141–61; Judt, *Postwar*, 549–54.

14. These concerns produced a large literature on "the affluent worker" during the 1960s. See especially John Goldthorpe, David Lockwood, Frank Bechofer, and Jennifer Platt, "The Affluent Worker and the Thesis of Embourgeoisement: Some Preliminary Findings," *Sociology* 1, no. 1 (January 1967): 11–31; and subsequent books from the study: Goldthorpe et al., *The Affluent Worker in the Class Structure* (Cambridge: Cambridge University Press, 1968); and *The Affluent Worker: Political Attitudes and Behavior* (Cambridge: Cambridge University Press, 1969).

15. James Cronin, *New Labour's Pasts: The Labour Party and Its Discontents* (London: Longman, 2004), 39–43.

16. "How Britain Voted since October 1974," *Ipsos Mori* online, May 11, 2010.

17. Jacob Hacker and Paul Pierson, *Let Them Eat Tweets: How the Right Rules in an Age of Extreme Inequality* (New York: Liveright, 2020), 79–90.

18. Cited in Philipp Ther, *Europe since 1989: A History* (Princeton: Princeton University Press, 2016), 40.

19. Hacker and Pierson, in *Let Them Eat Tweets*, make roughly this argument, though while we talk here about market fundamentalism or neoliberalism, they speak about the promotion and defense of plutocracy and the "plutocratic populism" that allows it to succeed politically. See also Jan-Werner Muller, *Democracy Rules* (New York: Allen Lane, 2021).

20. "How the TUC Learned to Love the EU and How the Affair Turned Out," History and Policy Trade Union Forum, November 27, 2010, *History and Policy* website. For the full text of Thatcher's speech, see Thatcher, "Speech to the College of Europe," September 20, 1988, on the Margaret Thatcher Foundation website.

21. Eisenhower, cited in Daniel Galvin, *Presidential Party Building: Dwight D. Eisenhower to George W. Bush* (Princeton: Princeton University Press, 2010), 57.

22. William Buckley and Brent Bozell, *McCarthy and His Enemies: The Record and Its Meaning* (Chicago: Regnery, 1954), cited in Heather Richardson, *To Make Men Free: A History of the Republican Party* (New York: Basic, 2014), 248.

23. See James Jackson Kilpatrick, "Right and Power in Arkansas," *National Review*, September 28, 1957, 273–75.

24. Rosenfeld, *Polarizers*, 80. The term was apparently coined by Frank Meyer.

25. See Rick Perlstein, *Before the Storm: Barry Goldwater and the Unmaking of the American Consensus* (New York: Hill & Wang, 2001).

26. Mary Brennan, *Turning Right in the 1960s: The Conservative Capture of the GOP* (Chapel Hill: University of North Carolina Press, 1995), 23.

27. Barry Goldwater, *The Conscience of a Conservative* (New York: Hillman Books, 1960).

28. Brennan, *Turning Right*, 88–99; and Perlstein, *Before the Storm*, chapter 20.

29. Schlafly's book was self-published. Thousands of copies were distributed in California by the John Birch Society. Reagan's "A Time for Choosing" was broadcast on October 27, 1964.

30. Rosenfeld, *Polarizers*, 127. This coalition made up what Kevin Phillips labeled the "emerging Republican majority." See Phillips, *The Emerging Republican Majority* (New Rochelle, NY: Arlington House, 1969).

31. Richardson, *To Make Men Free*, 291.

32. Gingrich, cited in Rosenfeld, *Polarizers*, 208, citing as the source Steven Gillon, *The Pact: Bill Clinton, Newt Gingrich, and the Rivalry That Defined a Generation* (New York: Oxford University Press, 2008), 38.

33. See Frances FitzGerald, *The Evangelicals: The Struggle to Shape America* (New York: Simon & Schuster, 2017); Daniel Williams, *God's Own Party: The Making of the Christian Right* (Oxford: Oxford University Press, 2010); and Daniel Schlozman, *When Movements Anchor Parties: Electoral Alignments in American History* (Princeton: Princeton University Press, 2015), 77–107.

34. Jimmy Carter, *White House Diary* (New York: Farrar, Strauss & Giroux, 2010), 469.

35. Donald Critchlow, *Phyllis Schlafly and Grassroots Conservatism* (Princeton: Princeton University Press, 2005); Jane Mansbridge, *Why We Lost the ERA* (Chicago: University of Chicago Press, 1986).

36. On gun rights and the NRA, see Hacker and Pierson, *Let Them Eat Tweets*, 90–97; and Scott Melzer, *Gun Crusaders: The NRA's Culture War* (New York: New York University Press, 2009).

37. Kevin Kruse and Julian Zelizer, *Fault Lines: A History of the United States since 1974* (New York: Norton, 2019), 181–85.

38. Rosenfeld, *Polarizers*, 270.

39. See Timothy Stanley, *The Crusader: The Life and Tumultuous Times of Pat Buchanan* (New York: St. Martin's, 2012), on Buchanan's background.

40. Patrick Joseph Buchanan, "Culture War Speech: Address to the Republican National Convention," August 17, 1992, *Voices of Democracy: US Oratory Project* website. Subsequent quotations from Buchanan are taken from this source.

41. Julian Zelizer, *Burning Down the House: Newt Gingrich, the Fall of a Speaker, and the Rise of the New Republican Party* (New York: Penguin, 2020).

42. "Republican Contract with America," 1994, *Wayback Machine Internet Archive.*

43. Rosenfeld, *Polarizers*, 270–71.

NINE   Challenges to Liberal Order, at Home and Abroad

1. See James Cronin, *Global Rules: America, Britain and a Disordered World* (New Haven: Yale University Press, 2014), 286–87. Blair gave his speech on the "Doctrine of International Community" on April 22, 1999, at the Chicago Economic Club.

2. On the neo-conservatives, see Justin Vaisse, *Neo-Conservatism: The Biography of a Movement* (Cambridge, MA: Belknap Press of Harvard University Press, 2010); and James Mann, *Rise of the Vulcans: The History of Bush's War Cabinet* (New York: Viking, 2004).

3. Frédéric Bozo, *A History of the Iraq Crisis: France, the United States and Iraq, 1991–2003* (Washington, DC: Woodrow Wilson Center Press and New York: Columbia University Press, 2016).

4. On the impact of Deng Xiaoping, see Ezra Vogel's *Deng Xiaoping and the Transformation of China* (Cambridge, MA: Belknap Press of Harvard University Press, 2011).

5. David Autor, David Dorn, and Gordon Hanson, "The China Shock: Learning from Labor Market Adjustment to Large Changes in Trade," *Annual Review of Economics* 8 (August 2016): 205–40.

6. Brad DeLong estimated the losses at just three hundred thousand jobs; and other studies stressed that employment losses in vulnerable industries would be made up by growth elsewhere, with a suitable delay. See J. Bradford DeLong, "NAFTA and Other Trade Deals Have Not Gutted American Manufacturing. Period," *VOX*, January 24, 2017; and also Gillian Tett, "The 'China Shock' Has Not Been as Bad as Donald Trump Thinks," *Financial Times,* January 10, 2019. For a review of what has become a substantial literature, see Scott Lincicome, "Testing the 'China Shock': Was Normalizing Trade with China a Mistake?" Policy analysis #895, Cato Institute, Washington, DC, July 8, 2020, https://doi.org/10.36009/PA.891. The Cato Institute, an echt neoliberal organization, predictably supports virtually all efforts to promote free trade, but the literature reviewed covers a wide range.

7. See Masha Gessen, *The Man without a Face: The Unlikely Rise of Vladimir Putin* (New York: Riverhead, 2012), 23–42; and Gessen, *The Future Is History: How Totalitarianism Reclaimed Russia* (New York: Riverhead, 2017); see also Peter Pomerantsev, *Nothing Is True and Everything Is Possible: The Surreal Heart of the New Russia* (New York: Public Affairs, 2014).

8. "Polish Head Rejects Putin Attack," *BBC News*, December 24, 2004, http://news.bbc.co.uk/2/hi/europe/4122721.stm.

9. Michael McFaul, *From Cold War to Hot Peace* (Boston: Houghton Mifflin, 2018), 72, 240.

10. Quotations from Vladimir Putin, "Speech and the Following Discussion at the Munich Conference on Security Policy," February 10, 2007, available on the website of the President of Russia.

11. David Galbreath, "Putting the Colour in Revolutions: The OSCE and Civil Society in the Post-Soviet Region," *Journal of Communist Studies and Transition Politics* 25, nos. 2–3 (2010): 161–80.

12. "Syria Crisis: Cameron Loses Commons Vote on Syria Action," *BBC News*, August 30, 2013, https://www.bbc.com/news/uk-politics-23892783.

13. Much has been written on the Great Recession, though debate remains on its precise cause or causes. A useful overview of its progress and development is Adam

Tooze, *Crashed: How a Decade of Financial Crises Changed the World* (New York: Viking, 2018).

14. TARP was part of the Emergency Economic Stabilization Act, passed in September 2008. The other major legislation to cope with the crisis was the American Recovery and Reinvestment Act of February 2009.

15. See "Current Employment Statistics: 100 Years of Employment, Hours and Earnings," *Monthly Labor Review,* August 2016. Accessed online from the Bureau of Labour Statistics.

16. The G-20 is a group of nineteen states and the European Union founded in 1999 in the aftermath of the Asian financial crisis. In September 2008, it officially replaced the G7/G8.

17. Martin Wolf, "Seeds of Its Own Destruction," *Financial Times*, March 8, 2009; Martin Jacques, "The Death of Neoliberalism and the Crisis in Western Politics," *Guardian*, August 21, 2016.

18. For an overview of the difficulties and defeats experienced by center-left parties, see Donald Sassoon, *Morbid Symptoms: An Anatomy of a World in Crisis* (London: Verso, 2021), chapter 4.

19. Arthur Goldhammer and George Ross, "Reluctantly Center-Left? The French Case," in James Cronin, George Ross, and James Shoch, eds., *What's Left of the Left: Democrats and Social Democrats in Changing Times* (Durham: Duke University Press, 2011), 150–51.

20. Data presented here on migration to both the UK and the US rely on official statistics. For reviews and summaries, see "Migrants in the UK: An Overview," November 6, 2020, *Migration Observatory*, https://migrationobservatory.ox.ac.uk/resources/briefings/migrants-in-the-uk-an-overview/; "Births by Parents' Country of Birth, England and Wales, 2015," Office of National Statistics, https://www.ons.gov.uk/peoplepopulationandcommunity/birthsdeathsandmarriages/livebirths/bulletins/parentscountryofbirthenglandandwales/2015 for the UK. For the US, see Elaine Kamarck and Christine Stenglein, "How Many Undocumented Immigrants Are There in the United States and Who Are They?" Brookings Institution, November 12, 2019, (https://www.brookings.edu). The piece relies on data from the US Department of Homeland Security and from the Pew Research Center, https://www.pewresearch.org; and also Jeanne Batalova et al., "Frequently Requested Statistics on Immigrants and Immigration in the United States," February 11, 2021, *Migration Policy Institute*, https://www.migrationpolicy.org/article/frequently-requested-statistics-immigrants-and-immigration-united-states-2020#children-immigrants.

21. See Brian Stelter, *Hoax: Donald Trump, Fox News and the Dangerous Distortion of Truth* (New York: Simon & Schuster, 2020); and Jane Mayer, "The Making of the Fox News White House," *New Yorker,* March 4, 2019.

22. Truth was the main casualty. See Sophia Rosenfeld, *Democracy and Truth: A Short History* (Philadelphia: University of Pennsylvania Press, 2019), chapter 4.

23. As a political phenomenon, populism has had a long history and generated an extensive literature. For a summary of early work, see Ghita Ionescu and Ernest Gellner,

eds., *Populism: Its Meanings and National Characteristics* (London: Weidenfeld & Nicolson, 1969). For more recent discussions, see Pippa Norris and Ronald Inglehart, *Cultural Backlash: Trump, Brexit, and Authoritarian Populism* (Cambridge: Cambridge University Press, 2019); Cas Mudde, *Populism: A Very Short Introduction*, 2nd ed. (New York: Oxford University Press, 2017); and Jan-Werner Muller, *What Is Populism?* (Philadelphia: University of Pennsylvania Press, 2016). Not everyone is content to describe recent developments as populism. See, for example, Jonathan Hopkin, *Anti-system Politics: The Crisis of Market Liberalism in Rich Democracies* (Oxford: Oxford University Press, 2020); Thomas Frank, *The People, No: A Brief History of Anti-populism* (New York: Metropolitan, 2020); and Wolfgang Streeck, "The Return of the Repressed," *New Left Review*, no. 104 (March–April 2017).

24. "How Tucker Carlson and the Far Right Embraced Hungary's Authoritarian Leader," *Guardian*, August 8, 2021.

25. Kenneth Vogel and Benjamin Novak, "Hungary's Leader Fights Criticism in US via Vast Influence Campaign," *New York Times*, October 4, 2021.

26. Phillip Connor, "Number of Refugees to Europe Surges to 1.3 Million in 2015," Pew Research Center, August 2016, https://www.pewresearch.org.

27. Rob Ford and Matthew Goodwin, *Revolt on the Right: Explaining Public Support for the Radical Right in Britain* (London: Routledge, 2014); Matthew Goodwin and Caitlin Milazzo, *UKIP: Inside the Campaign to Redraw the Map of British Politics* (Oxford: Oxford University Press, 2015).

28. Norris and Inglehart, *Cultural Backlash*, 374. A substantial literature has emerged on Brexit. Useful titles include Harold Clarke, Matthew Goodwin, and Paul Whiteley, *Brexit! Why Britain Voted to Leave the European Union* (Cambridge: Cambridge University Press, 2017); and Tim Shipman, *All Out War: The Full Story of Brexit* (London: William Collins, 2016).

29. Phil Wilson, "Corbyn Sabotaged Labour's Remain Campaign. He Must Resign," *Guardian*, June 26, 2016.

30. For the long view, see Vernon Bogdanor, *Britain and Europe in a Troubled World* (New Haven: Yale University Press, 2020); and, for a still longer view, Beatrice Heuser, *Brexit in History: Sovereignty or a European Union?* (London: C. Hurst, 2019).

31. In winning the 2019 election, the Tories managed to break through the "red wall" of Labour seats in the north and in the process handed Labour a huge loss and forced the resignation of Jeremy Corbyn. For a view of the election from the Labour side, see Gabriel Pogrund and Patrick Maguire, *Left Out: The Inside Story of Labour under Corbyn* (London: Bodley Head, 2020).

32. "Jared Kushner Bragged in April That Trump Was Taking the Country Back from the Doctors," *CNN*, October 28, 2020.

33. Hastert is remembered for two things: the Hastert Rule, which says the Republican House leadership will not bring legislation to the floor unless a "majority of the majority" support it; and his fall from grace over child molestation.

34. Jane Mayer, *Dark Money: The Hidden History of the Billionaires behind the Rise of the Radical Right* (New York: Doubleday, 2016).

35. Cited in Stelter, *Hoax*, 41. Huddy later sued Fox for sexual harassment by Bill O'Reilly and reached a settlement in 2017.

36. Barack Obama, *A Promised Land* (New York: Crown, 2020), 672.

37. Americans for Prosperity was founded by the Koch brothers in 2004. FreedomWorks was originally linked to the Koch brothers, but subsequently led by Dick Armey, former House Republican majority leader. On their role in the Tea Party, see Vanessa Williamson, Theda Skocpol, and John Coggin, "The Tea Party and the Remaking of Republican Conservatism," *Perspectives on Politics* 9, no. 1 (March 2011); and Theda Skocpol and Vanessa Williamson, *The Tea Party and the Remaking of Republican Conservatism* (New York: Oxford University Press, 2012). On the lingering influence of the Tea Party, see Geoffrey Kabaservice, "The Tea Party Morphed into Trumpism," *Washington Post*, December 4, 2020.

38. Andy Barr, "The GOP's No-Compromise Pledge," *Politico*, October 28, 2010.

39. Karl Rove, "The GOP Targets State Legislatures," *Wall Street Journal*, March 4, 2010. For more detail, see David Daley, *Ratf**ked: Why Your Vote Doesn't Count* (New York: Liveright, 2016); and the extensive review and discussion by Elizabeth Kolbert, "Drawing the Line: How Redistricting Turned America from Blue to Red," *New Yorker*, June 27, 2016.

40. "How a Strategy of Targeting State Legislative Races in 2010 Led to a Republican U.S. House Majority in 2013," *REDMAP: The Redistricting Majority Project*, http://www.redistrictingmajorityproject.com.

41. The 1987 advertisement is reprinted in Charlie Laderman and Brendan Simms, *Donald Trump: The Making of a World View* (London: Endeavour, 2017), 30–31. In 1987 Japan was the prime example of a country taking advantage of the US; in 2011 it was China.

42. As Laderman and Simms note, Trump's earliest comments about Obama had been quite favorable. Laderman and Simms, *Donald Trump*, 55–57.

43. Stelter, *Hoax*, 44–47; Erik Wemple, " 'Fox and Friends': Donald Trump's Very Own Media Bubble," *Washington Post*, July 25, 2015.

44. Obama, who spent eight years dealing with Republican obstinacy, well understood the affinity between Trump and other Republicans. He thought "the difference . . . was Trump's lack of inhibition." See Obama, *Promised Land*, 675.

45. Thomas Piketty has labeled these cosmopolitan elites "Brahmins," perhaps not the most helpful metaphor. See Piketty, *Capital and Ideology*, trans. Arthur Goldhammer (Cambridge, MA: Belknap Press of Harvard University Press, 2020). More generally, some left-wing critics have argued that in embracing—or, more accurately, acquiescing—to neoliberalism, liberals and center-left parties effectively chose more or less consciously to abandon the working class. This is an oversimplification of a complex process.

46. The literature on the meaning of the 2016 election is vast and enlightening. On the question of race versus economics, analyses right after the election emphasized economics. This perspective was reinforced by the appearance of a number of journalistic and/or ethnographic accounts of working-class communities ravaged by opioids, of laid-off workers, hillbillies and others "left behind" by technological change and alleg-

edly condescended to by liberal, coastal elites. Subsequently, the consensus shifted toward an emphasis on race. See Norris and Inglehart, *Cultural Backlash;* Alan Abramowitz, *The Great Alignment: Race, Party Transformation and the Rise of Donald Trump* (New Haven: Yale University Press, 2018); and John Sides, Michael Tesler, and Lynn Vavreck, *Identity Crisis: The 2016 Presidential Campaign and the Battle for the Meaning of America* (Princeton: Princeton University Press, 2018).

Conclusion

1. See Sarah Churchwell, *Behold America: The Entangled History of "America First" and "the American Dream"* (New York: Basic, 2018). On the way Joe McCarthy prefigured Trump, see Beverly Gage, "McCarthyism Was Never Defeated. Trumpism Won't Be Either," *Washington Post,* December 4, 2020; and also Larry Tye, *Demagogue: The Life and Long Shadow of Senator Joe McCarthy* (New York: Houghton Mifflin Harcourt, 2020). The seemingly contradictory link between the sentiments animating isolationism and McCarthyism was noted by Arthur Schlesinger Jr. in "The New Isolationism," *Atlantic Monthly,* May 1952.

2. The phrase "liberal international order" came into wide use only in the 1990s. See Francis Fukuyama, "Liberalism and Its Discontents," *American Purpose,* October 5, 2020. Fukuyama writes, "This post–Cold War world would collectively come to be known as the liberal international order." Liberal order, internationally and domestically, had become at least a partial reality in the 1940s, but the phrase, or variations on it, were not commonly used until later.

3. For an early assessment of the impact of the Trump administration on US foreign relations and liberal order, see Jonathan Kirshner, "Trump's Long Shadow and the End of American Credibility," *Foreign Affairs,* March/April 2021. For his successor's efforts to reverse it, see Jessica Matthews, "Losing No Time," *New York Review of Books,* May 27, 2021.

4. The rethinking of support for free trade and globalization has been occurring on the center-left as well as on the right. See Robert Kuttner, *Can Democracy Survive Global Capitalism?* (New York: Norton, 2018); John Judis, *The Politics of Our Time: Populism, Nationalism, Socialism* (New York: Columbia Global Reports, 2021); and Dani Rodrik, *The Globalization Paradox: Democracy and the Future of the World Economy* (New York: Norton, 2011). For a parallel argument about the danger of ignoring nationalism and the nation-state, see Jill Lepore, *This America: The Case for the Nation* (New York: Liveright, 2019).

5. On Trump's environmental record, see Cayli Baker, "The Trump Administration's Major Environmental Deregulations," *Brookings Brief,* December 15, 2020, Brookings Institution website, https://connect.brookings.edu/trumps-major-environmental-deregu lations-syria-under-the-assads-and-more?ecid=ACsprvu7PnvoEMwGCavHSyZbJlKJuw oPCGrIJ_Es61WYPx8iT346Z8BWXzxfo8SwkefEKfTRWRdo&utm_campaign= Brookings%20Brief&utm_medium=email&utm_content=103152261&utm_source=hs_ email.

6. On Bannon's remarks, see Philip Rucker and Robert Costa, "Bannon Vows a Daily Fight for 'Deconstruction of the Administrative State,' " *Washington Post,* February 23, 2017.

7. A useful, if early, effort to go beyond a simple balance sheet and assess the qualitative aspects of Trump's impact is George Packer, "A Political Obituary for Donald Trump," *Atlantic*, January/February 2021.

8. The point has been made forcefully in Steven Levitsky and Daniel Ziblatt, *How Democracies Die* (New York: Crown, 2018).

9. The Mueller Report is worth reading in its entirety. On the politics around it, see Philip Rucker and Carol Leonnig, *A Very Stable Genius: Donald J. Trump's Testing of America* (New York: Penguin, 2020), part 5. Trump's repeated criticism of the "deep state" was clearly self-serving and animated by a conspiratorial vision. On this, see the authors' sequel, Leonnig and Rucker, *I Alone Can Fix It: Donald J. Trump's Catastrophic Final Year* (New York: Penguin, 2021). For a more academic discussion of what the term "deep state" gets at, and how it might relate to the actual workings of the state, see Stephen Skowronek, John Dearborn, and Desmond King, *Phantoms of a Beleaguered Republic: The Deep State and the Unitary Executive* (Oxford: Oxford University Press, 2021).

10. His efforts along these lines have been widely reported and chronicled in some detail by Bob Woodward in *Rage* (New York: Simon & Schuster, 2020); and by John Bolton in *The Room Where It Happened: A White House Memoir* (New York: Simon & Schuster, 2020).

11. On the pandemic and its repercussions, see Lawrence Wright, *The Plague Year: America in the Time of Covid* (New York: Knopf, 2021); Colin Kahl and Thomas Wright, *Aftershocks: Pandemic Politics and the End of the Old Institutional Order* (New York: St. Martin's, 2021); and Adam Tooze, *Shutdown: How Covid Shook the World's Economy* (New York: Viking, 2021).

12. See Woodward, *Rage*.

13. Jacob Hacker and Paul Pierson, *Let Them Eat Tweets: How the Right Rules in an Age of Extreme Inequality* (New York: Liveright, 2020). Hacker and Pierson regard the resort to plutocratic populism as a solution to what Daniel Ziblatt has labeled the "Conservative Dilemma," a recurring challenge for elites keen to defend privilege in a democratic age. See Ziblatt, *Conservative Parties and the Birth of Democracy* (New York: Cambridge University Press, 2017).

Acknowledgments

Books don't write themselves; authors write them. They nevertheless have histories of which their authors are not always fully aware. I am acutely cognizant of the unique conditions attending the writing of the bulk of this book: the pandemic, the lockdown, and the fraught election of 2020 and its frightening aftermath. These circumstances upset the normal rhythms of academic life and the process of writing. Libraries and archives were hard, sometimes impossible, to access; and the routine interactions that happen through teaching, seminars, and conferences largely ceased. The ubiquity of online sources and means of communication may or may not have compensated for what was missing. Readers will have to judge that.

To understand the longer history behind this book requires blocking out, at least momentarily, the immediacy and intensity of the past couple of years and recalling the more distant intellectual roots of the current project. My last book, *Global Rules* (2014), focused on the period leading up to the end of the Cold War and the effects of both the Cold War and its ending on the construction and then extension of a liberal international order and the enlargement of the sphere of democratic politics. Since then, I have pondered the nature and fate of liberal order and the deeper roots of its successes and setbacks. Much of that rethinking occurred during a sabbatical in the fall of 2015, when I was able to profit from talks with colleagues at Bellagio, where my wife was a fellow, and at Sciences Po in Paris, where Riva Kastoryano helped to arrange my affiliation.

The effort meant adopting a more long-term and wider perspective that, one hopes, is reflected in this book. Three specific tasks had to be undertaken. First, it was necessary to revisit the origins and early history of liberal order and democracy in the era before and after the Second World War. The second was to look more carefully at the ways in which a stable liberal order was maintained from the 1950s into the 1990s, with particular attention to domestic politics and parties in the United States, Britain, and Europe. The third was to develop a more thorough understanding of the politics of the United States, the dominant power in the postwar liberal order and its effective anchor.

Some of this I could do on my own, mainly by reading, rereading, or rethinking the rich historiography of the postwar period. I needed a good deal of help with the rest of the agenda, but had the good fortune of having friends and colleagues with whom I could and did collaborate on a number of projects that helped me overcome my own deficiencies. In 2007–8, Jim Shoch, George Ross, and I—inspired and egged on by Lou Ferleger—decided to put together a volume titled *What's Left of the Left* (2011). We determined to concentrate not on the far left but on the center-left, and that meant looking not only at socialist or social democratic parties in Europe but also at the Labour Party in Britain and the Democratic Party in the United States. That focus also necessitated at least a broad familiarity with the history of their main opponents on the center-right.

Three other collaborations took things much further. In 2012 Vlad Perju, director of the Clough Center for the Study of Constitutional Democracy at Boston College, asked me to organize a colloquium on the 2012 election. I agreed, but on the understanding that I'd need lots of help assembling the right group of scholars to make sense of the election. Help came from Jim Shoch, whose knowledge of the literature on contemporary American politics is unsurpassed, and from Heather Richardson, who is the best source on the checkered history of the Republican Party. The conference was a big success, and Vlad and I decided it would be useful to repeat it for the election of 2016. That time I had additional help from my colleague David Hopkins. The two meetings introduced me to an array of scholars from whom I have continued to learn about American politics.

Just before our colloquium on the 2016 election, I took part in a conference at NYU on referenda organized by Larry Wolff. Shortly after the surprising outcome of the Brexit referendum, Larry was asked to put together a meeting on referenda and their potential for good or ill. He asked me and George Ross for advice, and we worked together to arrange what turned out to be an excellent series of discussions. Larry did the heavy lifting, but I was happy to help and learned much. The event was the moment when I first began to confront the issue of populism in contemporary politics. We met in October 2016, and most of us dismissed the possibility of a Trump victory in the election soon to happen, but we were at least worried enough to be wary and tentative.

My education on American politics would continue when Mark Wickham-Jones asked me to participate in a session at the meeting of the American Political Science Association to discuss the question of responsible parties. There I began to engage with a literature on partisan cohesion, party responsibility, and policy outcomes that informed later efforts to make sense of recent transformations of American politics.

These collaborations and engagements meant that, when I began to write the present book, I had much prior work to rely upon. Whether I have done justice to this research is for others to decide, but the key point is that I owe anything useful I have written to many others and their extensive labors.

My debts to other scholars and to previous collaborations are important to recognize, but I must also acknowledge those who have helped me through the actual writing of this book. Three close friends and colleagues—Bob Moeller, George Ross, and Jim Shoch—read the entire manuscript and made invaluable contributions. I took most of their advice. When I did not, I was likely mistaken, and readers should blame me and not them. I also profited from support from my home institution, Boston College, and my colleagues in the history department. More specifically, I want to thank Bee Lehman of the BC Library. Even greater thanks are owed to Anna Piecuch, who served as my research assistant in 2020–21. Anna knew how to find sources and references that I had no idea how to locate and she had great instincts about what to include, what to skip, and how to argue my case. I benefited as well from my ongoing connection to the Minda de Gunzburg Center for European Studies at Harvard University.

This is my second book published by Yale. The first, *Global Order* (2014), was handled with grace and efficiency by Heather McCallum in London. Heather also gave early advice on the present study and introduced me to her colleagues in New Haven. My editor there was Jaya Chatterjee, who was unfailingly professional and helpful. I also had the good fortune to have Robin DuBlanc assigned as copyeditor.

Writing through COVID-19 and its weird effects was hard, and going through the process made me extremely grateful to those friends who accompanied me. That includes our regular Zoom group—Barbara Baran, Jim Shoch, Jane Jenson, George Ross, Joanne Barkan, and Jon Friedman—as well as friends I was able to see in person—Leonie Gordon and Don Fanger, Becky and Dan Okrent, and Kathryn Stearns and Bob Bruce. Old friends Jon Schneer, Richard Price, and Paul Breines were there throughout. The pandemic and lockdown meant that I saw less of my friends and colleagues at Boston College—Alan Rogers, Jim O'Toole, Julian Bourg, Devin Pendas, David Quigley, Penny Ismay, and Prasannan Parthasarathi—but I much appreciated the encouragement they offered from a distance. A much wider circle of friends and colleagues made useful suggestions and comments.

No list of acknowledgments would be complete, or reliable, without mention of the people closest to me who were steady companions throughout the writing of this book. That means my daughters, Rebecca Cronin and Johanna Shelby, who not only encouraged me but also, while I was consumed by this project, gave birth to the three wonderful grandchildren to whom this book is dedicated. Even closer, in a literal sense, has been my wife, Laura Frader. Laura did not abandon her scholarship or her art to focus on my efforts, but she was with me and supportive throughout. She did not read every word that I wrote, but she read through big chunks of the manuscript and helped me solve difficult issues. It would be silly to say that I could not have got through it without her, but if I had been forced to do so, I would have been much less happy and, I suspect, much less successful.

Index